ROPE TRICK STEP 1.

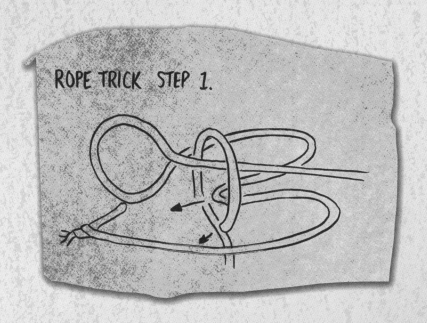

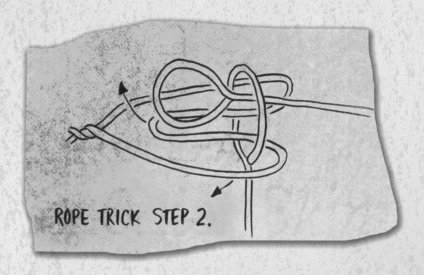

ROPE TRICK STEP 2.

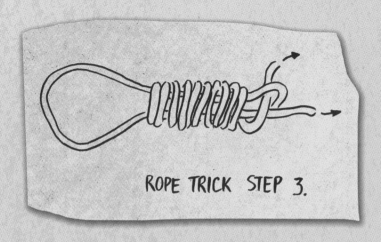

ROPE TRICK STEP 3.

MIND MGMT

MIND
MGMT

VOLUME FOUR: THE MAGICIAN

CREATED, WRITTEN,
AND ILLUSTRATED BY
MATT KINDT

"DREAM JOB" COLORS BY
SHARLENE KINDT

FOREWORD BY
TERRY MOORE

DARK HORSE BOOKS

PRESIDENT AND PUBLISHER
MIKE RICHARDSON

DIGITAL PRODUCTION
CLAY JANES

DESIGN
BRENNAN THOME
with **MATT KINDT**

ASSISTANT EDITOR
IAN TUCKER

EDITOR
BRENDAN WRIGHT

Special thanks to Sharlene Kindt.

MIND MGMT VOLUME 4: THE MAGICIAN

This volume collects issues #19–#24 of the Dark Horse comic-book series *MIND MGMT*, along with a story from *Dark Horse Presents* #31.

Published by Dark Horse Books
A division of Dark Horse Comics, Inc.
10956 SE Main Street
Milwaukie, OR 97222

DarkHorse.com

To find a comics shop in your area, call the Comic Shop Locator Service toll-free at (888) 266-4226.

International Licensing: (503) 905-2377

First edition: November 2014

ISBN 978-1-61655-391-3

Library of Congress Cataloging in Publication Control Number: 2014022134

10 9 8 7 6 5 4 3 2 1

Printed in China

Neil Hankerson, Executive Vice President | Tom Weddle, Chief Financial Officer | Randy Stradley, Vice President of Publishing | Michael Martens, Vice President of Book Trade Sales | Anita Nelson, Vice President of Business Affairs | Scott Allie, Editor in Chief | Matt Parkinson, Vice President of Marketing David Scroggy, Vice President of Product Development | Dale LaFountain, Vice President of Information Technology | Darlene Vogel, Senior Director of Print, Design, and Production | Ken Lizzi, General Counsel Davey Estrada, Editorial Director | Chris Warner, Senior Books Editor | Diana Schutz, Executive Editor Cary Grazzini, Director of Print and Development | Lia Ribacchi, Art Director | Cara Niece, Director of Scheduling | Mark Bernardi, Director of Digital Publishing

FOREWORD

I've been in comics for a long time, and I've never met Matt Kindt. I've never even met anybody who's met Matt Kindt. I've met Brian Bendis. He wrote the intro for the previous MIND MGMT collection, and he's never met this alleged Matt Kindt either. Recently, at a comic book convention, I walked by a guy sitting behind a sign that said, "Matt Kindt," but he looked normal, so I kept walking. Couldn't be him.

The irony is, this "Matt Kindt" creator has also been making comics for quite a while. Good comics. I mean, reeeeeally good comics. The kind of really good comics that make you famous and get your face splashed across the home pages of websites, magazines, podcasts, and convention programs. So where is all that? Was Matt Kindt in all those spots and I don't remember? Have I met him and can't recall? When I try to remember what the guy behind the "Matt Kindt" sign looked like, I can't. There's like a blank spot where a person was sitting.

Like his work, Matt Kindt is a mystery wrapped in an enigma. For some time now, this quiet creator has been crafting inspired stories and serving them to us in small bites served monthly on scraps of weathered pulp. If you tried to dissect the flavors involved, your head would explode—MIND MGMT is to the brain what Chris Ware's Acme Novelty Library books are to the eyes. Every chapter of this thought-provoking series utilizes deceptively simple imagery that conceals layers upon layers upon layers of seductive fiction.

Neil Gaiman once said, "It's the mystery that endures, not the answer." That's basically the $E = MC^2$ of fiction—easy to quote, hard to understand. MIND MGMT is like that. For example, Meru. She stays in my mind because I can't figure her out. Bill, the Magician, Lyme, Duncan . . . What the hell?! As characters, they are quarks I can't pin down. They're all over the map in time and space, and just when you think it's all one mad fustercluck, you notice the position pins on the map spell out a message. The Second Floor, the rundown of key safe houses, the snippets of prose and narrative in the margin, the 98 percent black drawings inside what appear to be 100 percent black panels . . . They're all strokes and splatters of a larger brush wielded by a master painter with a devious streak. Every answer reveals more questions, every flashback reveals questionable choices, every character is a novel, and every scene of recovered memory is like the flicker of a strobe light on approaching monsters.

MIND MGMT draws you in with all its postmodern charm posing as entertainment for the hip and slightly above average. But, when you catch yourself pouring over the latest issue with a magnifying glass and blue light, when your cheat sheets, charts, and notes on the story require a filing system, when you reach for a Perrier and think better of it . . . that's when you realize . . . this book is more than good; it's awesome. It's deep, it's complex, it works, and there's more to it than you can plumb. Like something found in nature, the mere existence of Matt Kindt's story leads philosophers to the building blocks of life and a showdown with the unified truth.

So, obviously I would love to meet whoever wrote and drew this masterpiece, because I have hours' worth of questions, but I doubt I ever will, because Matt Kindt is the Shakespeare of comics—a mysterious source of fiction too great for one writer. Future generations might even debate whether or not a man named Matt Kindt even existed, and I think Matt would love that. It's so MIND MGMT.

Terry Moore
Houston, TX, 2014

Terry Moore is the Eisner Award–winning creator of the beloved, long-running crime and romance series Strangers in Paradise and the acclaimed science-fiction epic Echo. Moore has written and drawn multiple characters for DC, Marvel, and Dark Horse, and his current self-published series, the horror ongoing Rachel Rising, is in development for television.

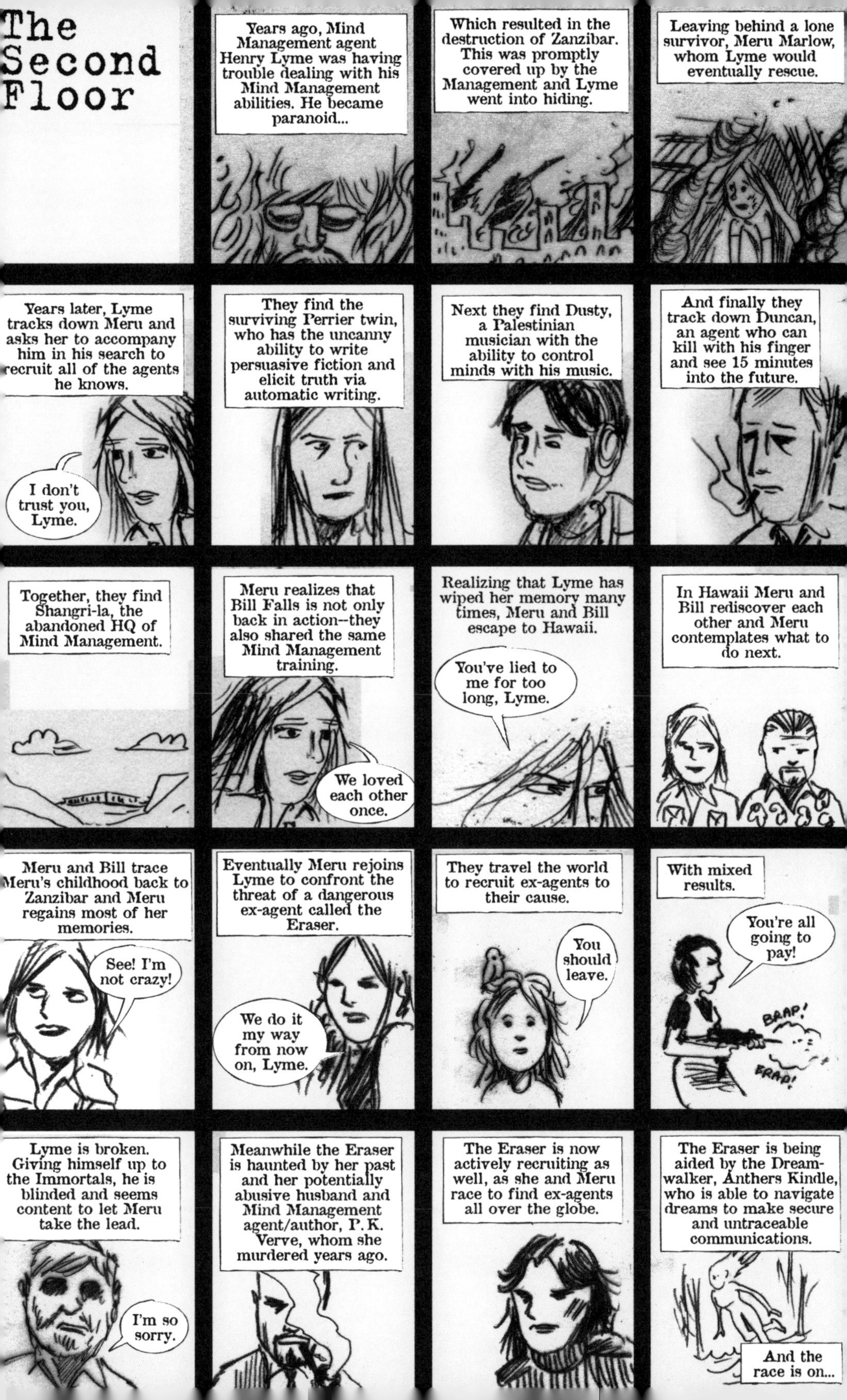
The Second Floor
Years ago, Mind Management agent Henry Lyme was having trouble dealing with his Mind Management abilities. He became paranoid...
Which resulted in the destruction of Zanzibar. This was promptly covered up by the Management and Lyme went into hiding.
Leaving behind a lone survivor, Meru Marlow, whom Lyme would eventually rescue.
Years later, Lyme tracks down Meru and asks her to accompany him in his search to recruit all of the agents he knows.
I don't trust you, Lyme.
They find the surviving Perrier twin, who has the uncanny ability to write persuasive fiction and elicit truth via automatic writing.
Next they find Dusty, a Palestinian musician with the ability to control minds with his music.
And finally they track down Duncan, an agent who can kill with his finger and see 15 minutes into the future.
Together, they find Shangri-la, the abandoned HQ of Mind Management.
Meru realizes that Bill Falls is not only back in action--they also shared the same Mind Management training.
We loved each other once.
Realizing that Lyme has wiped her memory many times, Meru and Bill escape to Hawaii.
You've lied to me for too long, Lyme.
In Hawaii Meru and Bill rediscover each other and Meru contemplates what to do next.
Meru and Bill trace Meru's childhood back to Zanzibar and Meru regains most of her memories.
See! I'm not crazy!
Eventually Meru rejoins Lyme to confront the threat of a dangerous ex-agent called the Eraser.
We do it my way from now on, Lyme.
They travel the world to recruit ex-agents to their cause.
You should leave.
With mixed results.
You're all going to pay!
BRAP!
BRAP!
Lyme is broken. Giving himself up to the Immortals, he is blinded and seems content to let Meru take the lead.
I'm so sorry.
Meanwhile the Eraser is haunted by her past and her potentially abusive husband and Mind Management agent/author, P.K. Verve, whom she murdered years ago.
The Eraser is now actively recruiting as well, as she and Meru race to find ex-agents all over the globe.
The Eraser is being aided by the Dream-walker, Anthers Kindle, who is able to navigate dreams to make secure and untraceable communications.
And the race is on...

PROLOGUE

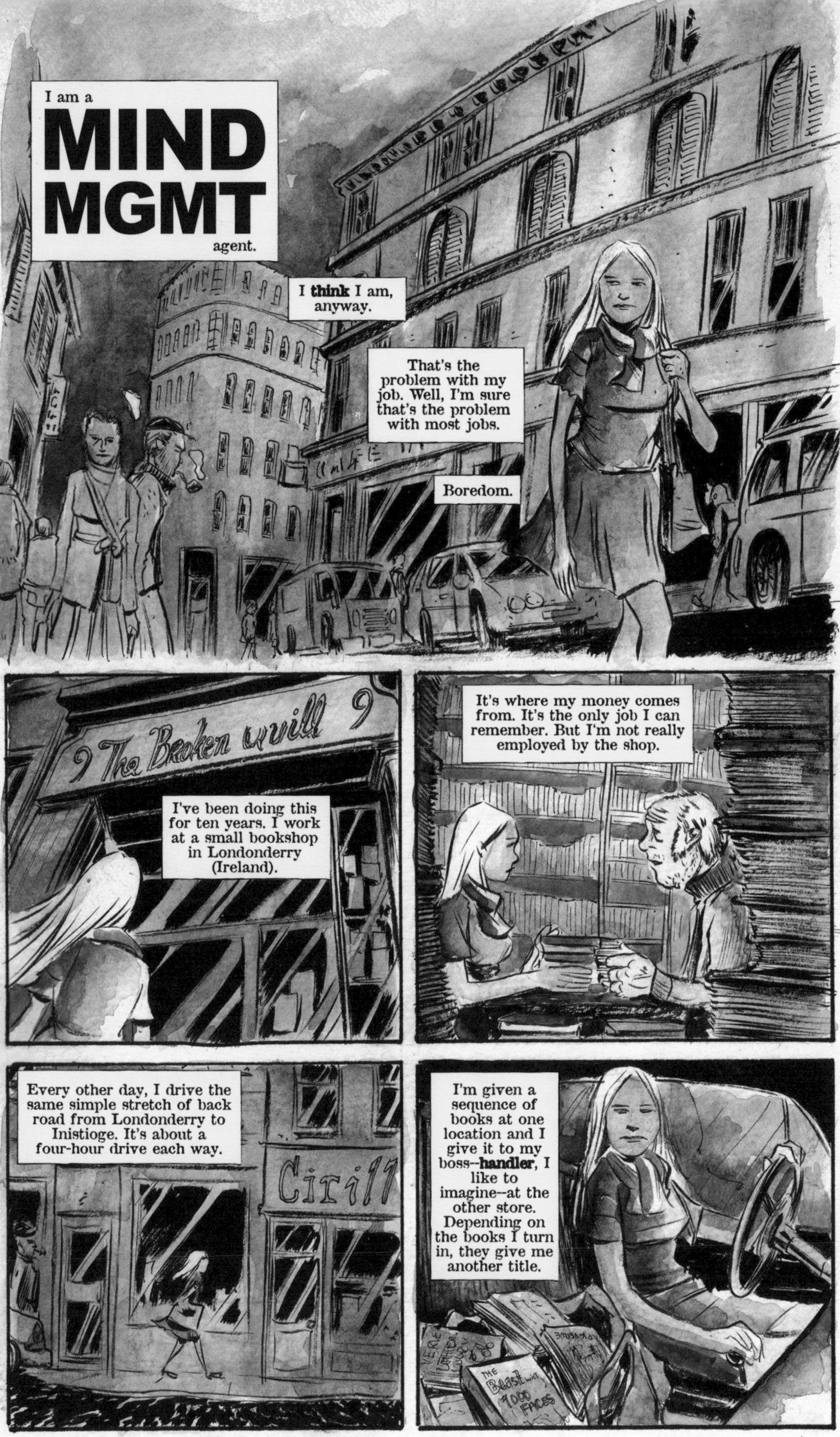
I am a
MIND
MGMT
agent.
I **think** I am, anyway.
That's the problem with my job. Well, I'm sure that's the problem with most jobs.
Boredom.
The Broken Quill
I've been doing this for ten years. I work at a small bookshop in Londonderry (Ireland).
It's where my money comes from. It's the only job I can remember. But I'm not really employed by the shop.
Every other day, I drive the same simple stretch of back road from Londonderry to Inistioge. It's about a four-hour drive each way.
I'm given a sequence of books at one location and I give it to my boss--**handler**, I like to imagine--at the other store. Depending on the books I turn in, they give me another title.
THE Beast with 1000 FACES

Therapy Session 017: Subject: Anthers Kindle. Initial diagnosis is that of Grandiose Delusions (GD).

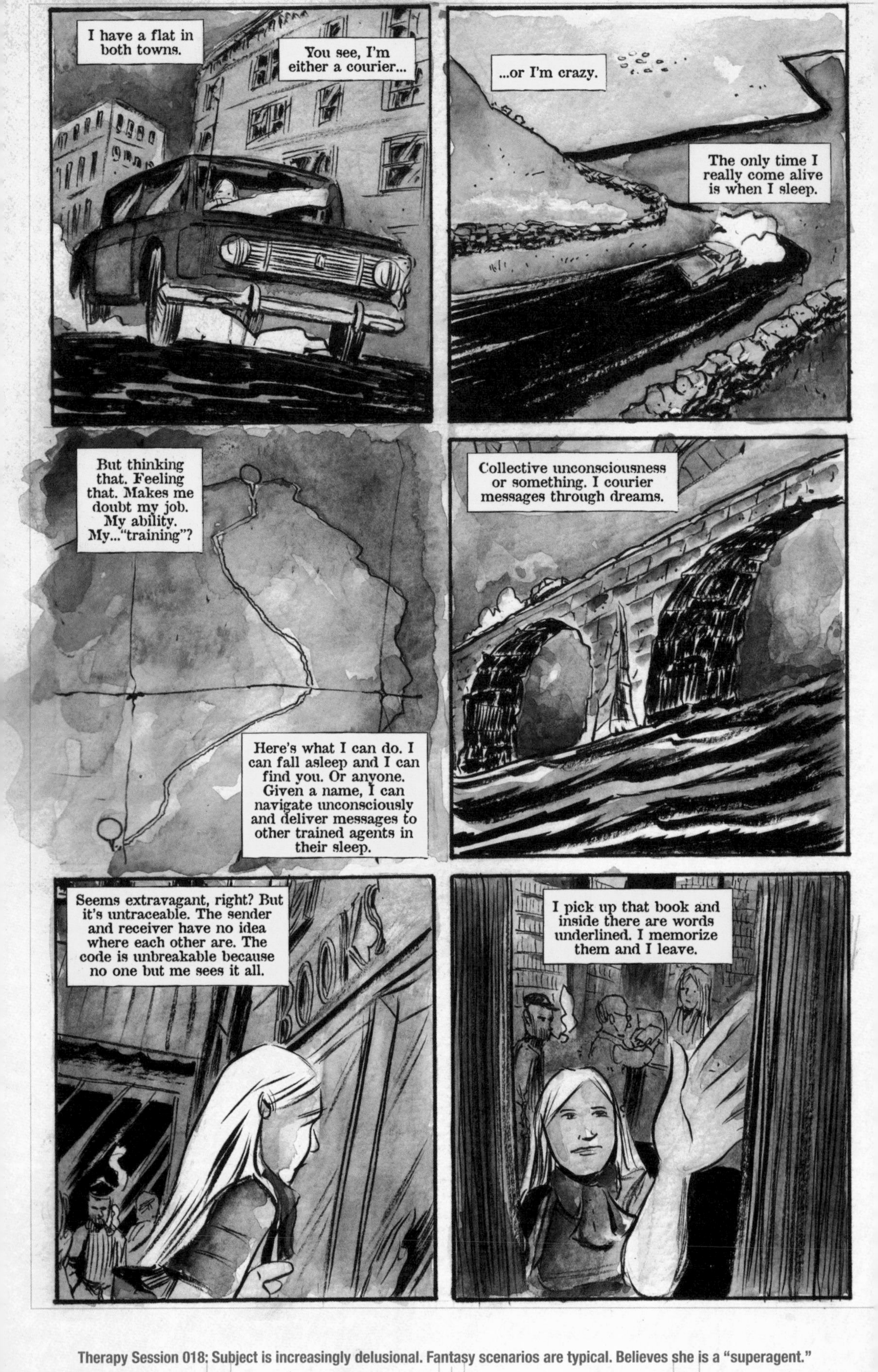
I have a flat in both towns.
You see, I'm either a courier...
...or I'm crazy.
The only time I really come alive is when I sleep.
But thinking that. Feeling that. Makes me doubt my job. My ability. My..."training"?
Here's what I can do. I can fall asleep and I can find you. Or anyone. Given a name, I can navigate unconsciously and deliver messages to other trained agents in their sleep.
Collective unconsciousness or something. I courier messages through dreams.
Seems extravagant, right? But it's untraceable. The sender and receiver have no idea where each other are. The code is unbreakable because no one but me sees it all.
BOOKS
I pick up that book and inside there are words underlined. I memorize them and I leave.

Therapy Session 018: Subject is increasingly delusional. Fantasy scenarios are typical. Believes she is a "superagent."

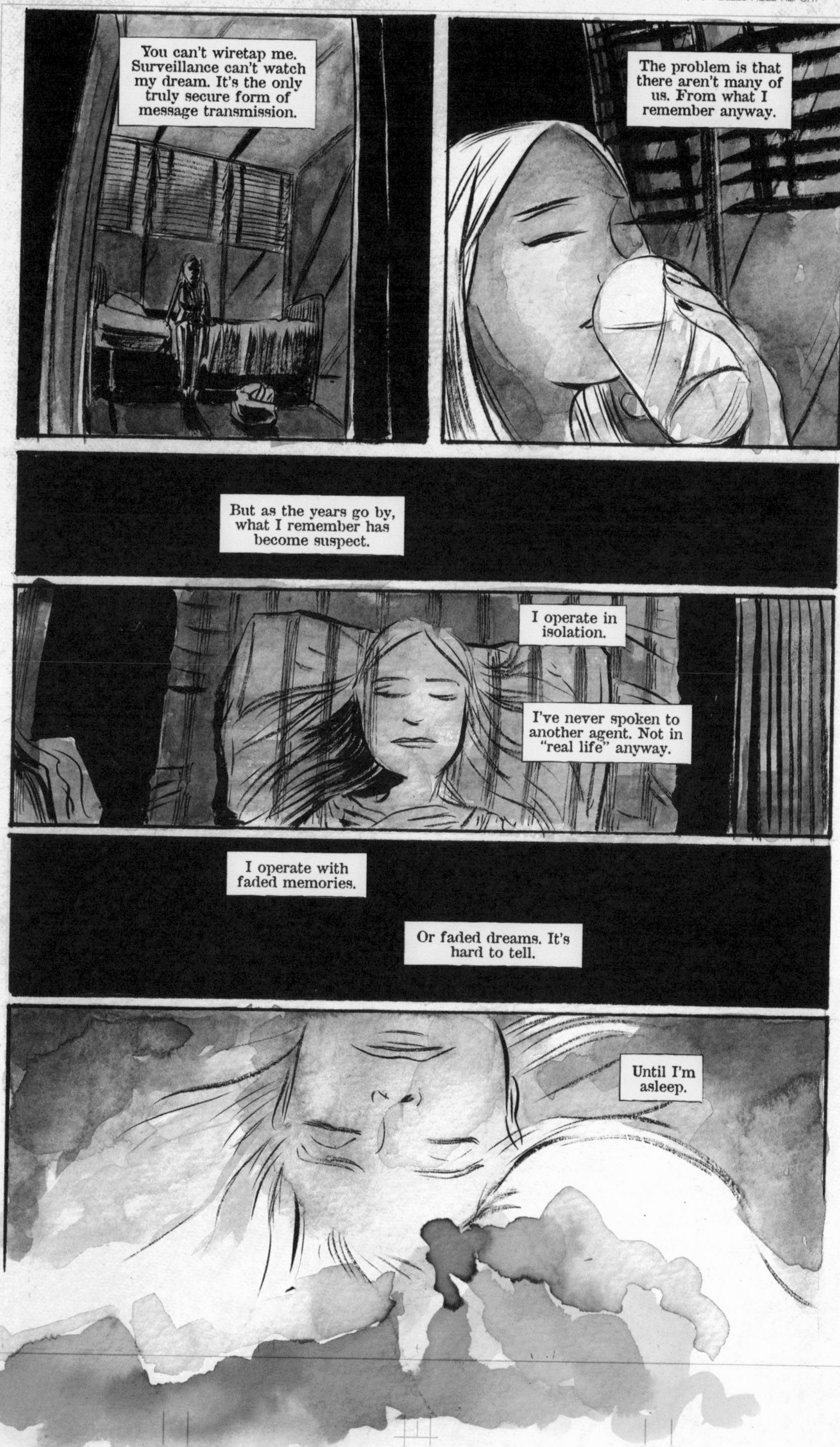
You can't wiretap me. Surveillance can't watch my dream. It's the only truly secure form of message transmission.
The problem is that there aren't many of us. From what I remember anyway.
But as the years go by, what I remember has become suspect.
I operate in isolation.
I've never spoken to another agent. Not in "real life" anyway.
I operate with faded memories.
Or faded dreams. It's hard to tell.
Until I'm asleep.

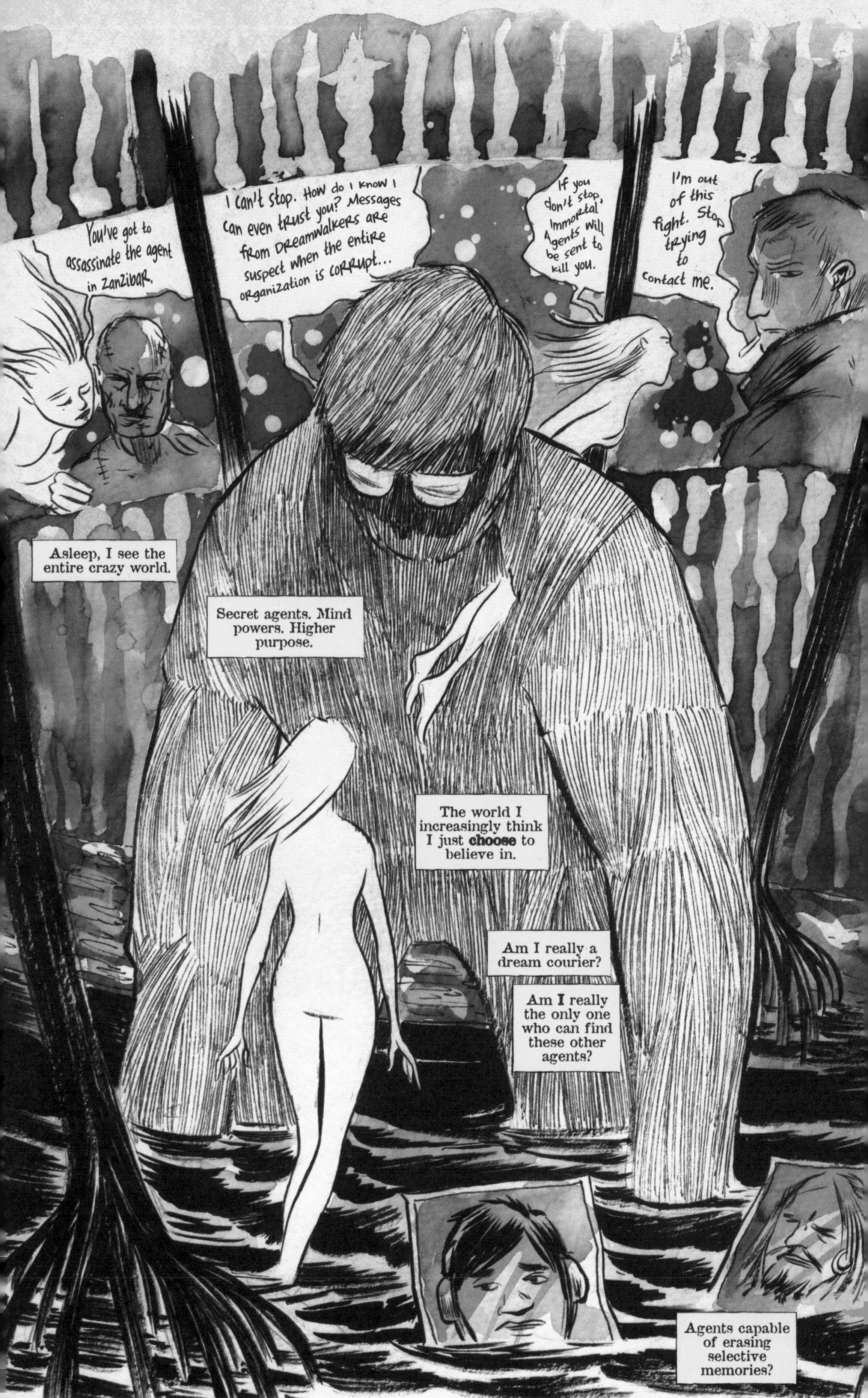
You've got to assassinate the agent in Zanzibar.
I can't stop. How do I know I can even trust you? Messages from Dreamwalkers are suspect when the entire organization is corrupt...
If you don't stop, Immortal Agents will be sent to kill you.
I'm out of this fight. Stop trying to contact me.
Asleep, I see the entire crazy world.
Secret agents. Mind powers. Higher purpose.
The world I increasingly think I just **choose** to believe in.
Am I really a dream courier?
Am **I** really the only one who can find these other agents?
Agents capable of erasing selective memories?

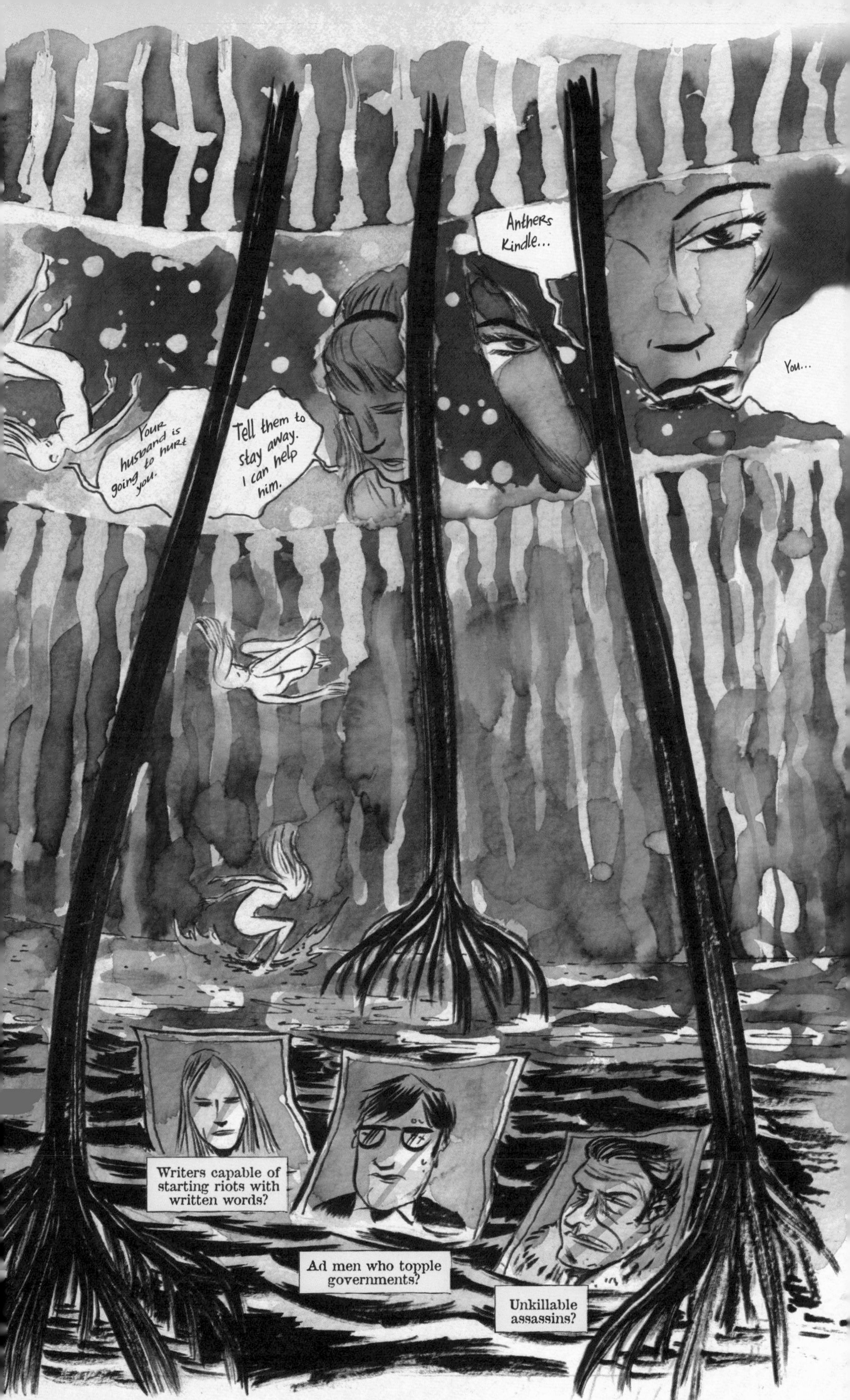

Your husband is going to hurt you.
Tell them to stay away. I can help him.
Anthers Kindle...
You...
Writers capable of starting riots with written words?
Ad men who topple governments?
Unkillable assassins?

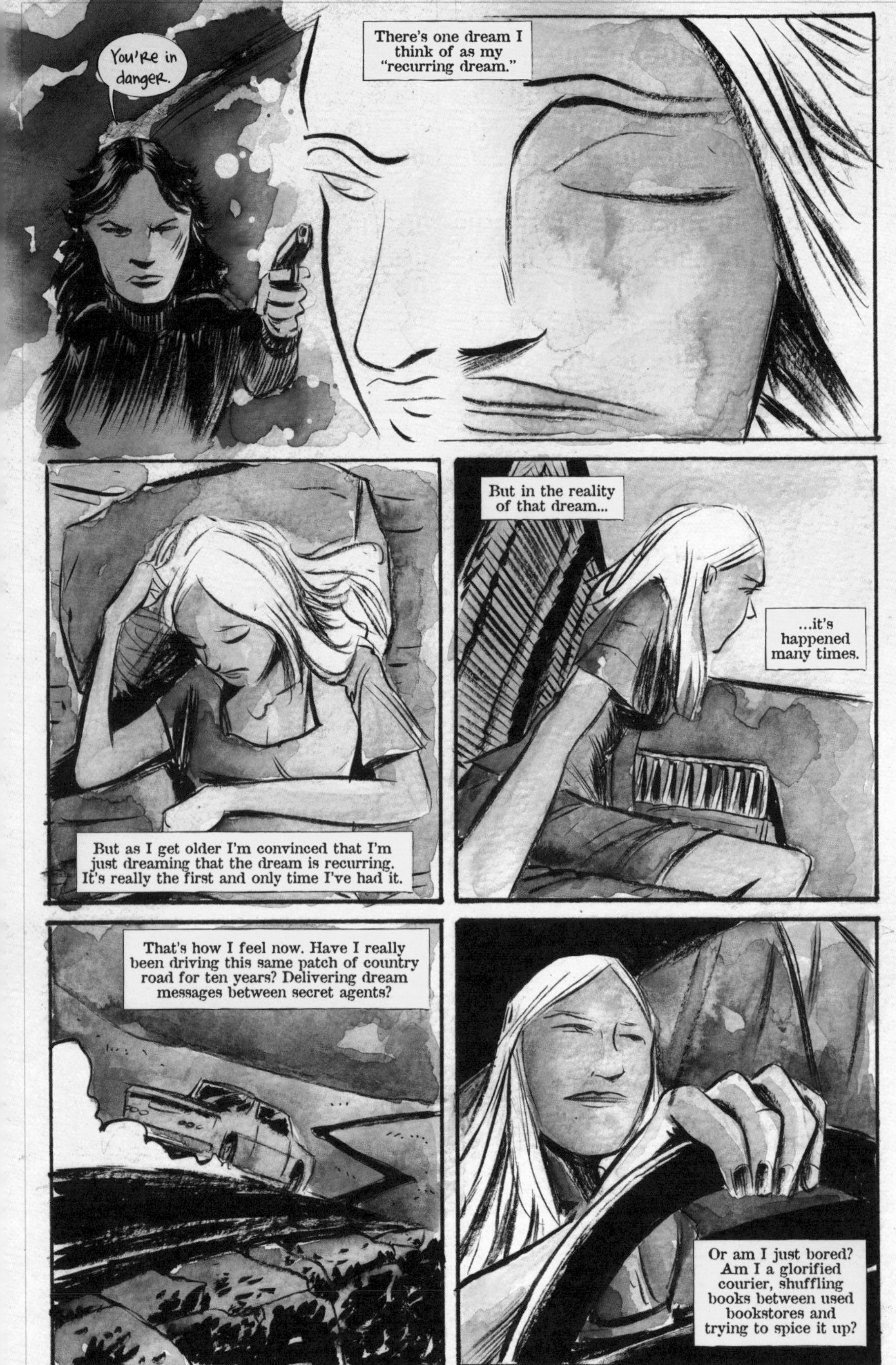
There's one dream I think of as my "recurring dream."
You're in danger.
But as I get older I'm convinced that I'm just dreaming that the dream is recurring. It's really the first and only time I've had it.
But in the reality of that dream...
...it's happened many times.
That's how I feel now. Have I really been driving this same patch of country road for ten years? Delivering dream messages between secret agents?
Or am I just bored? Am I a glorified courier, shuffling books between used bookstores and trying to spice it up?

Therapy Session 022: I believe the delusions are brought on to compensate for extreme lethargy and tedium in the workplace.

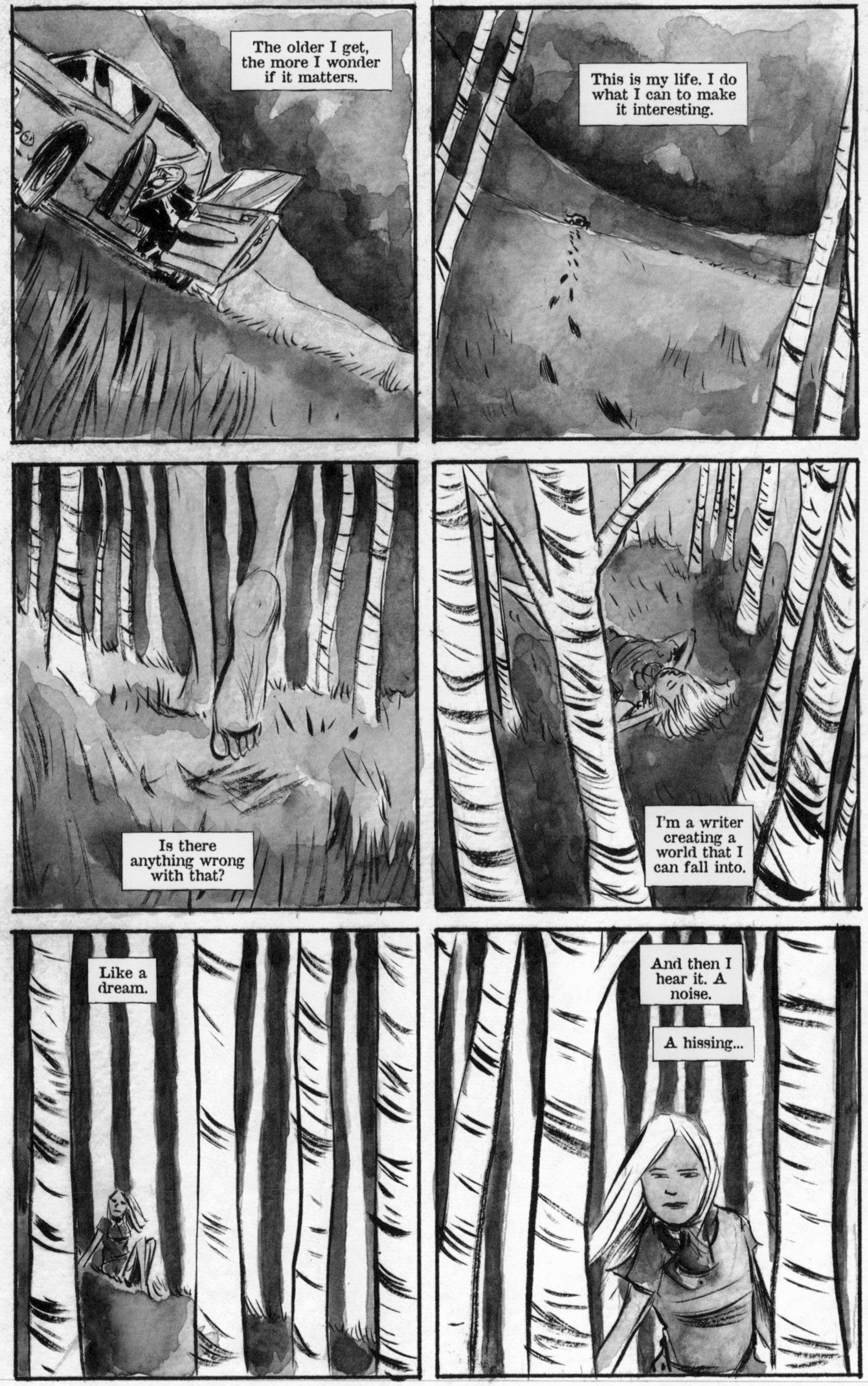
The older I get, the more I wonder if it matters.
This is my life. I do what I can to make it interesting.
Is there anything wrong with that?
I'm a writer creating a world that I can fall into.
Like a dream.
And then I hear it. A noise.
A hissing...

Therapy Session 023: Subject has stopped attending therapy sessions. Afraid she might have suffered a catastrophic schizophrenic event.

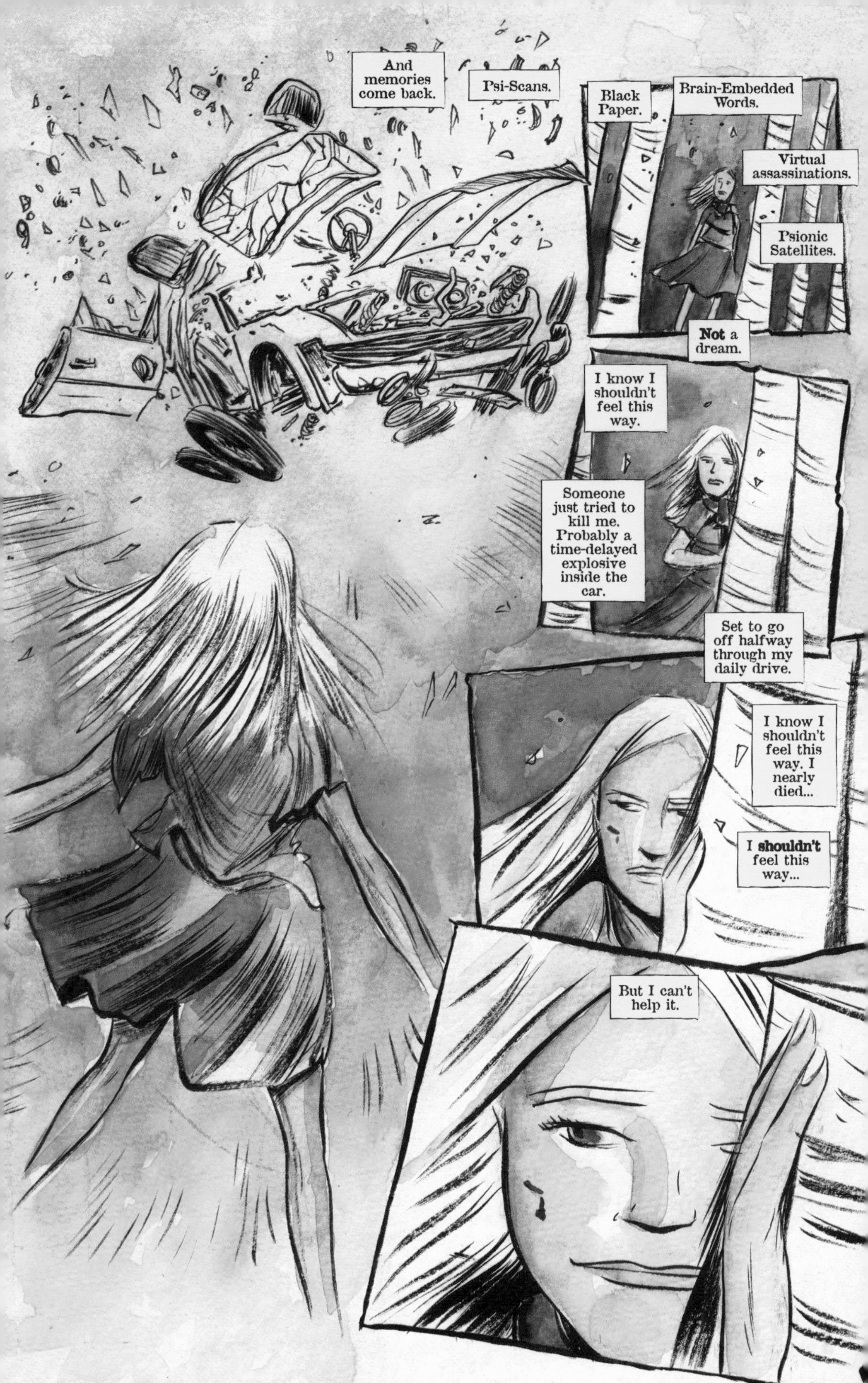
And memories come back.
Psi-Scans.
Black Paper.
Brain-Embedded Words.
Virtual assassinations.
Psionic Satellites.
Not a dream.
I know I shouldn't feel this way.
Someone just tried to kill me. Probably a time-delayed explosive inside the car.
Set to go off halfway through my daily drive.
I know I shouldn't feel this way. I nearly died...
I **shouldn't** feel this way...
But I can't help it.

End.

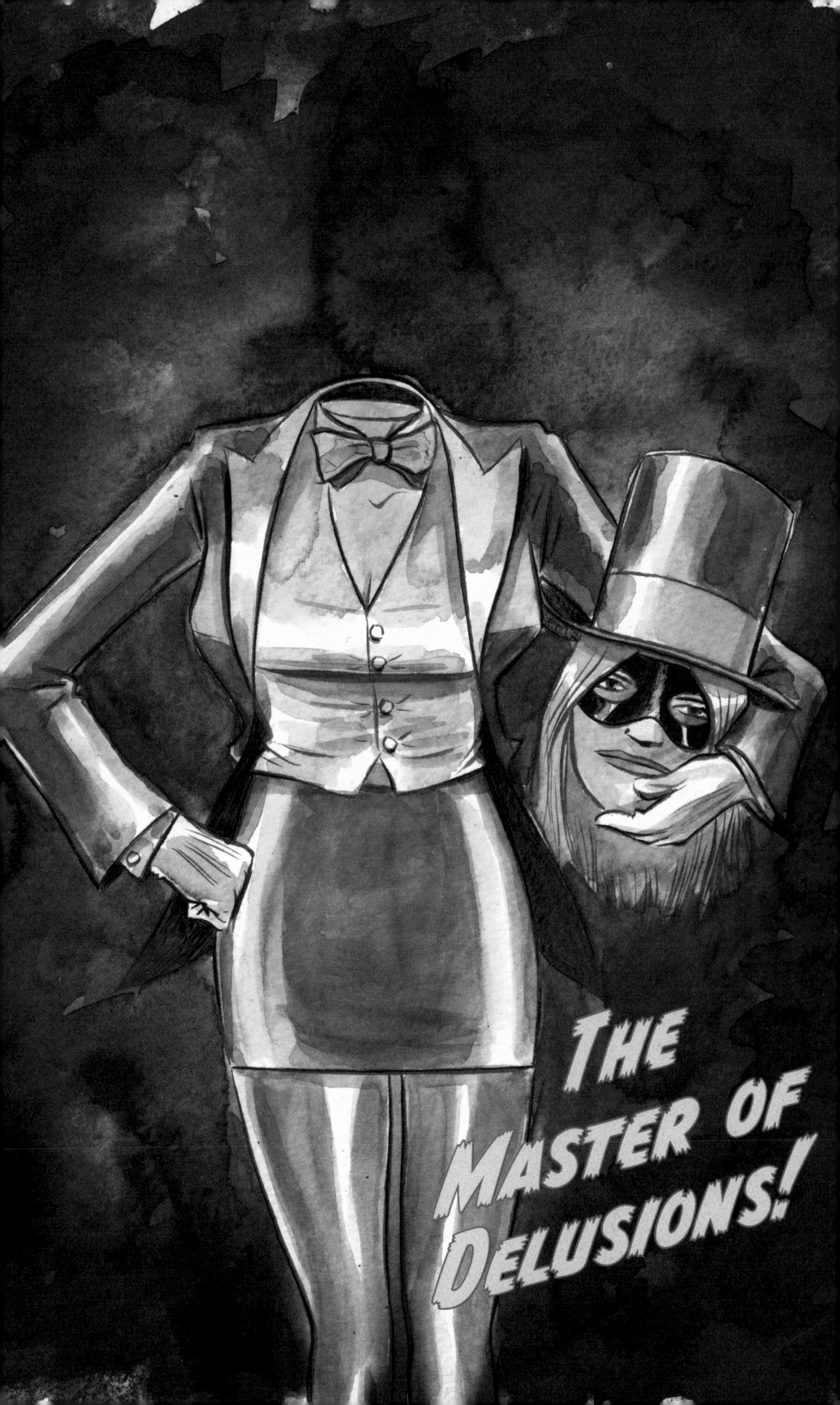
THE
MASTER OF
DELUSIONS!

19

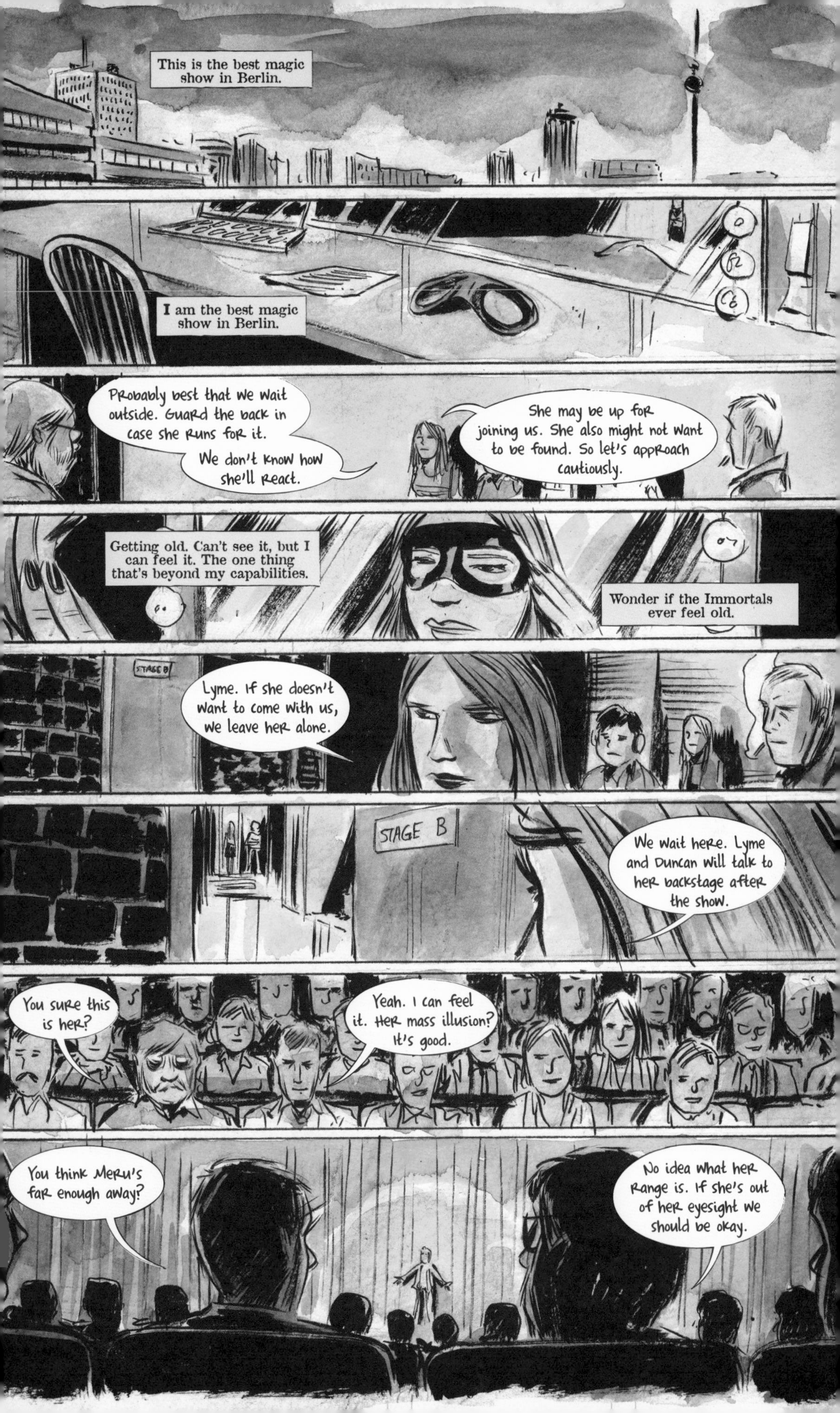
This is the best magic show in Berlin.
I am the best magic show in Berlin.
Probably best that we wait outside. Guard the back in case she runs for it.
We don't know how she'll react.
She may be up for joining us. She also might not want to be found. So let's approach cautiously.
Getting old. Can't see it, but I can feel it. The one thing that's beyond my capabilities.
Wonder if the Immortals ever feel old.
STAGE B
Lyme. If she doesn't want to come with us, we leave her alone.
STAGE B
We wait here. Lyme and Duncan will talk to her backstage after the show.
You sure this is her?
Yeah. I can feel it. Her mass illusion? It's good.
You think Meru's far enough away?
No idea what her range is. If she's out of her eyesight we should be okay.

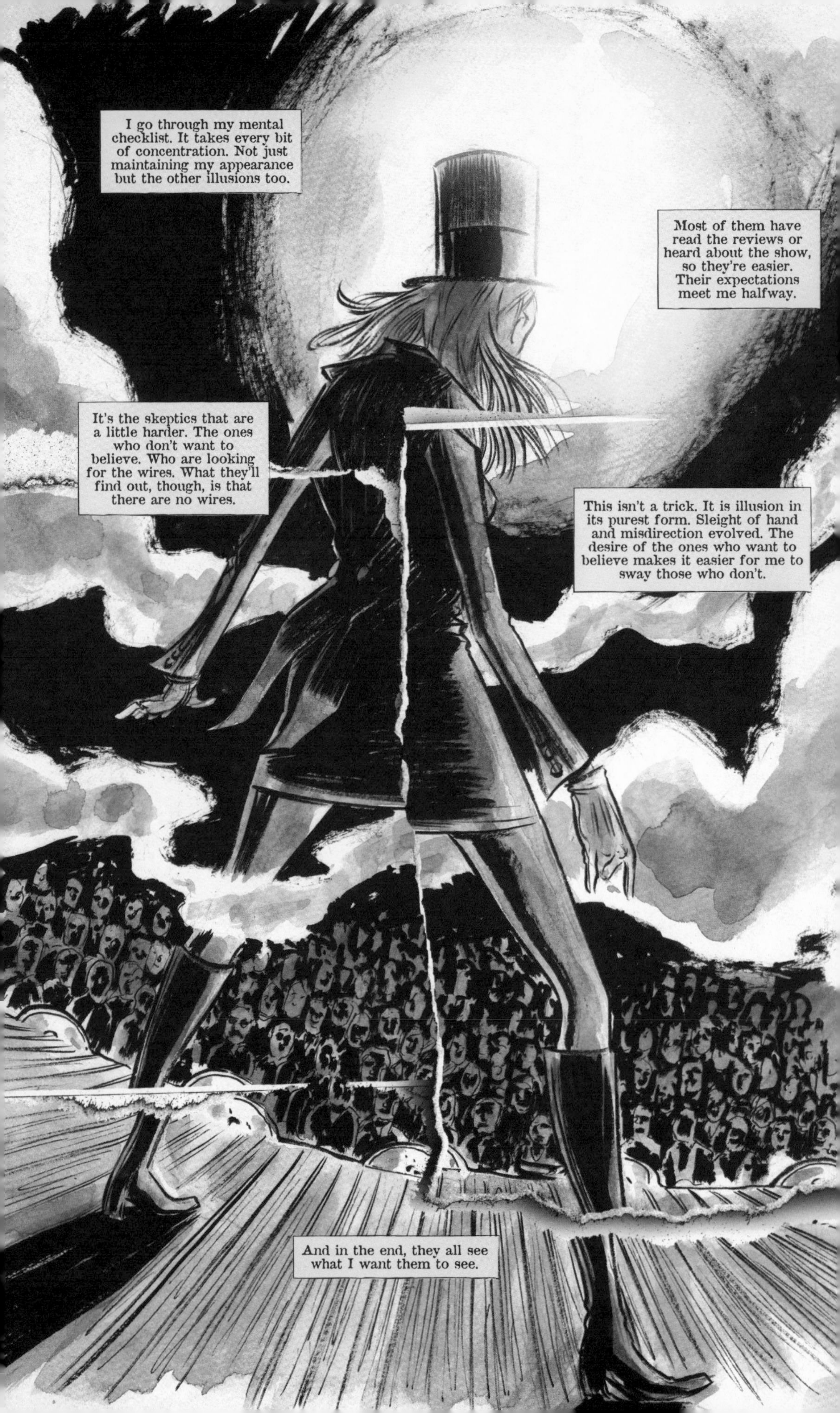
I go through my mental checklist. It takes every bit of concentration. Not just maintaining my appearance but the other illusions too.
Most of them have read the reviews or heard about the show, so they're easier. Their expectations meet me halfway.
It's the skeptics that are a little harder. The ones who don't want to believe. Who are looking for the wires. What they'll find out, though, is that there are no wires.
This isn't a trick. It is illusion in its purest form. Sleight of hand and misdirection evolved. The desire of the ones who want to believe makes it easier for me to sway those who don't.
And in the end, they all see what I want them to see.

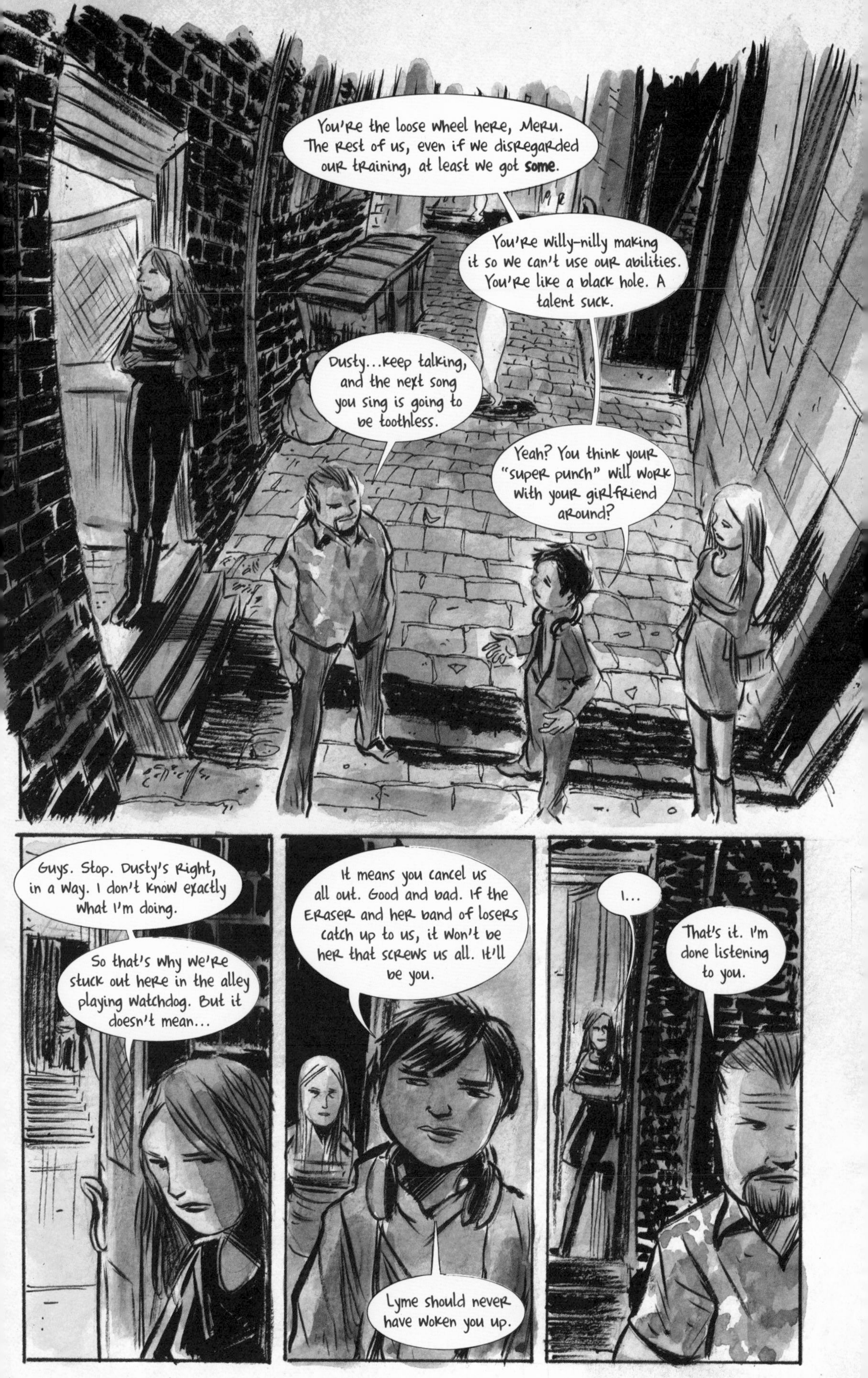
You're the loose wheel here, Meru. The rest of us, even if we disregarded our training, at least we got **some**.
You're willy-nilly making it so we can't use our abilities. You're like a black hole. A talent suck.
Dusty...keep talking, and the next song you sing is going to be toothless.
Yeah? You think your "super punch" will work with your girlfriend around?
Guys. Stop. Dusty's right, in a way. I don't know exactly what I'm doing.
So that's why we're stuck out here in the alley playing watchdog. But it doesn't mean...
It means you cancel us all out. Good and bad. If the Eraser and her band of losers catch up to us, it won't be her that screws us all. It'll be you.
Lyme should never have woken you up.
I...
That's it. I'm done listening to you.

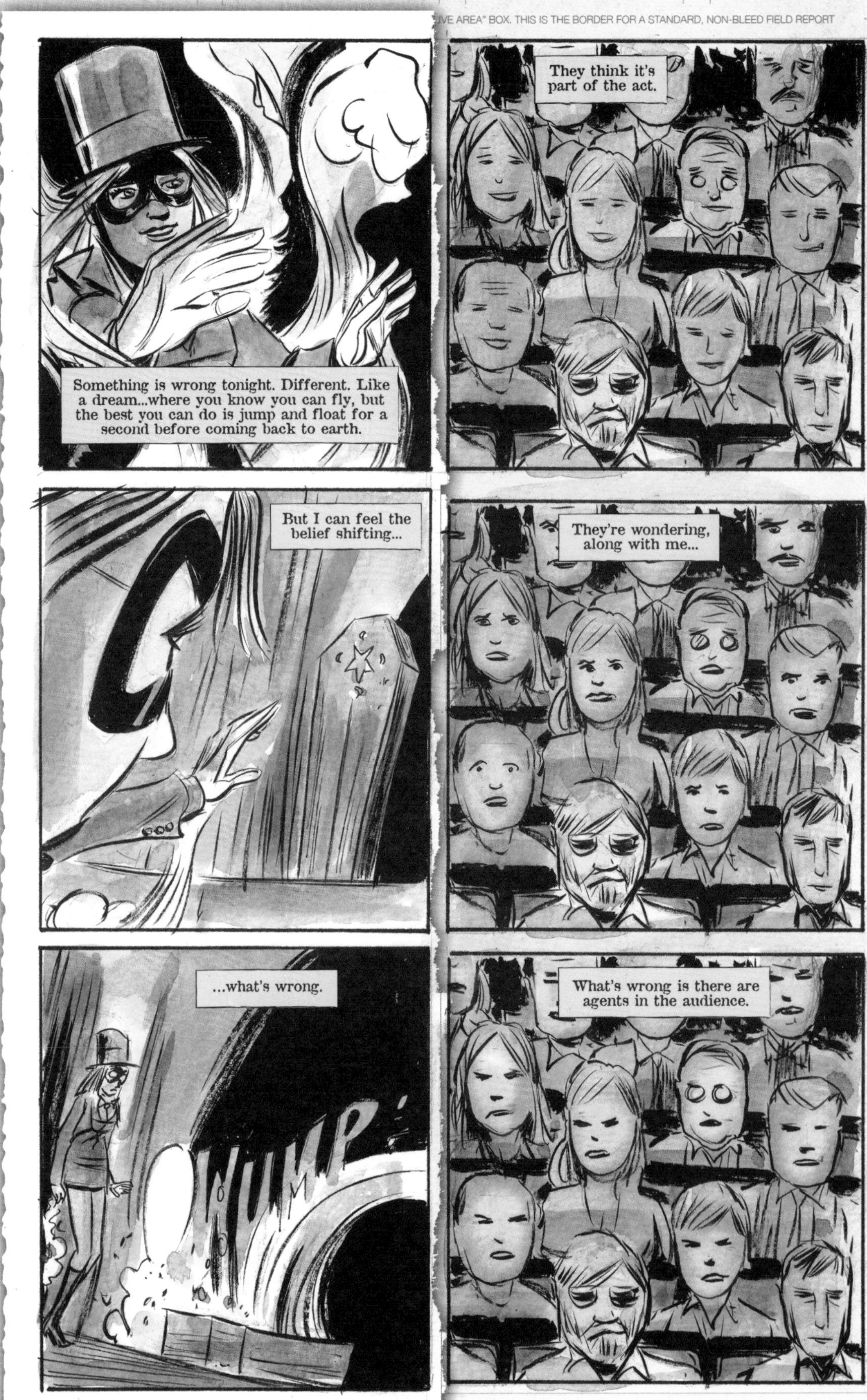

IVE AREA" BOX. THIS IS THE BORDER FOR A STANDARD, NON-BLEED FIELD REPORT
Something is wrong tonight. Different. Like a dream...where you know you can fly, but the best you can do is jump and float for a second before coming back to earth.
They think it's part of the act.
But I can feel the belief shifting...
They're wondering, along with me...
...what's wrong.
WUMP!
What's wrong is there are agents in the audience.

AREA" BOX. THIS IS THE BORDER FOR A STANDARD, NON-BLEED FIELD REPORT

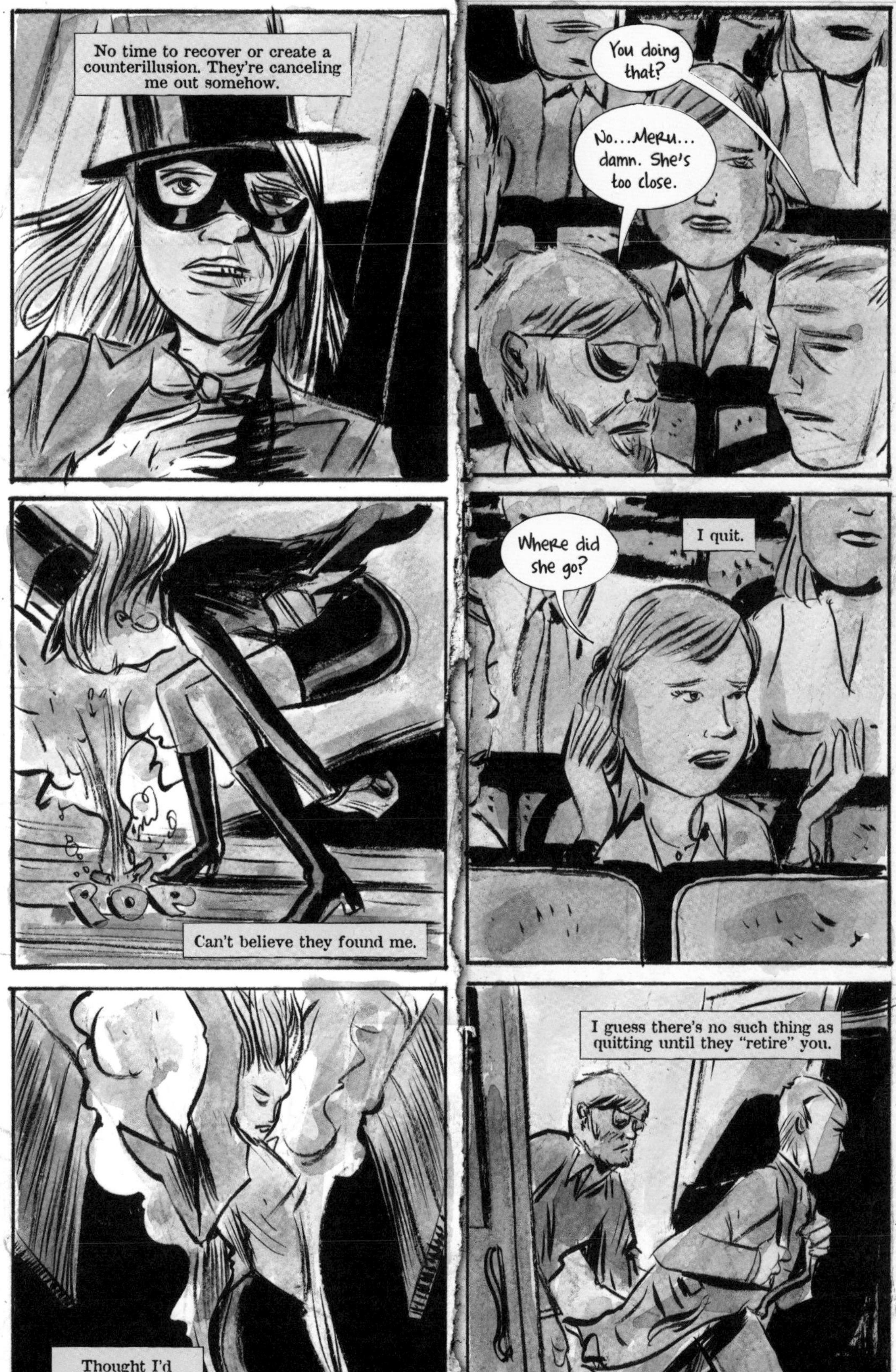

No time to recover or create a counterillusion. They're canceling me out somehow.
You doing that?
No... Meru... damn. She's too close.
Can't believe they found me.
Where did she go?
I quit.
Thought I'd covered my tracks and escaped the Management.
I guess there's no such thing as quitting until they "retire" you.

E AREA" BOX. THIS IS THE BORDER FOR A STANDARD, NON-BLEED FIELD REPORT

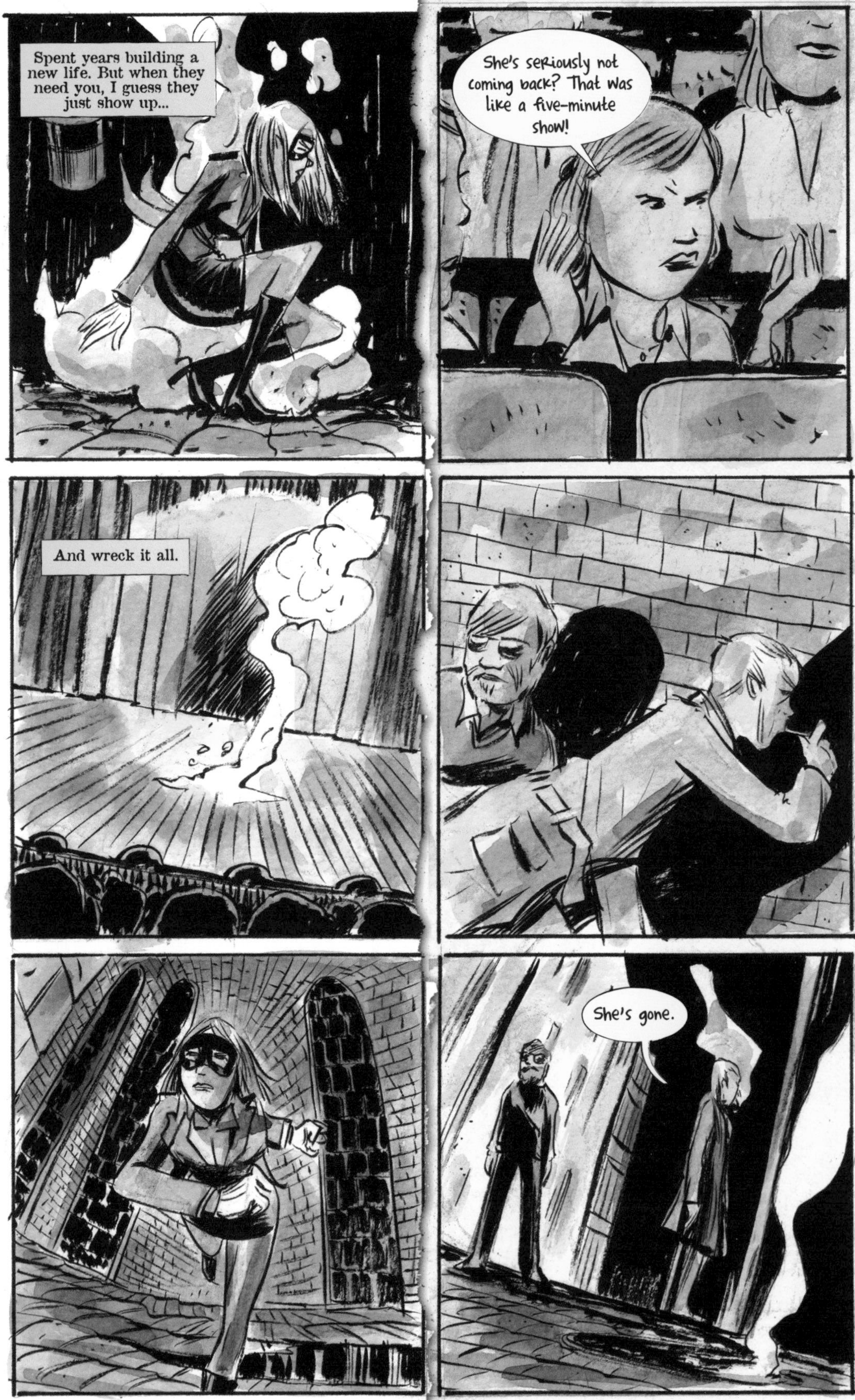

Spent years building a new life. But when they need you, I guess they just show up...
She's seriously not coming back? That was like a five-minute show!
And wreck it all.
She's gone.

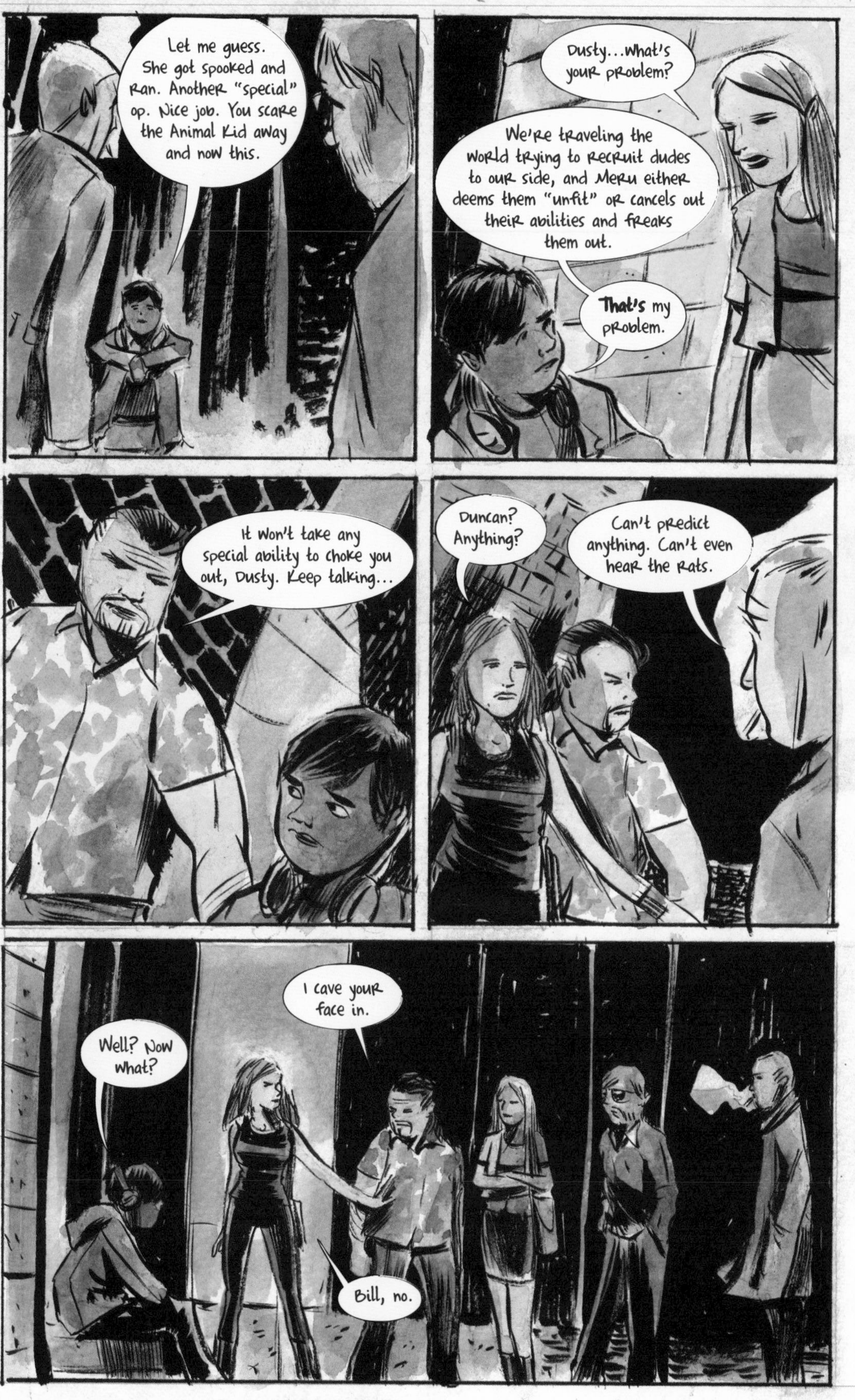
Let me guess. She got spooked and ran. Another "special" op. Nice job. You scare the Animal Kid away and now this.
Dusty...what's your problem?
We're traveling the world trying to recruit dudes to our side, and Meru either deems them "unfit" or cancels out their abilities and freaks them out.
That's my problem.
It won't take any special ability to choke you out, Dusty. Keep talking...
Duncan? Anything?
Can't predict anything. Can't even hear the rats.
Well? Now what?
I cave your face in.
Bill, no.

WHEN FILING REPORT ALL ESSENTIAL DETAILS MUST FALL WITHIN THIS SOLID "LIVE AREA" BOX. THIS IS THE BORDER FOR A STANDARD, NON-BLEED FIELD REPORT

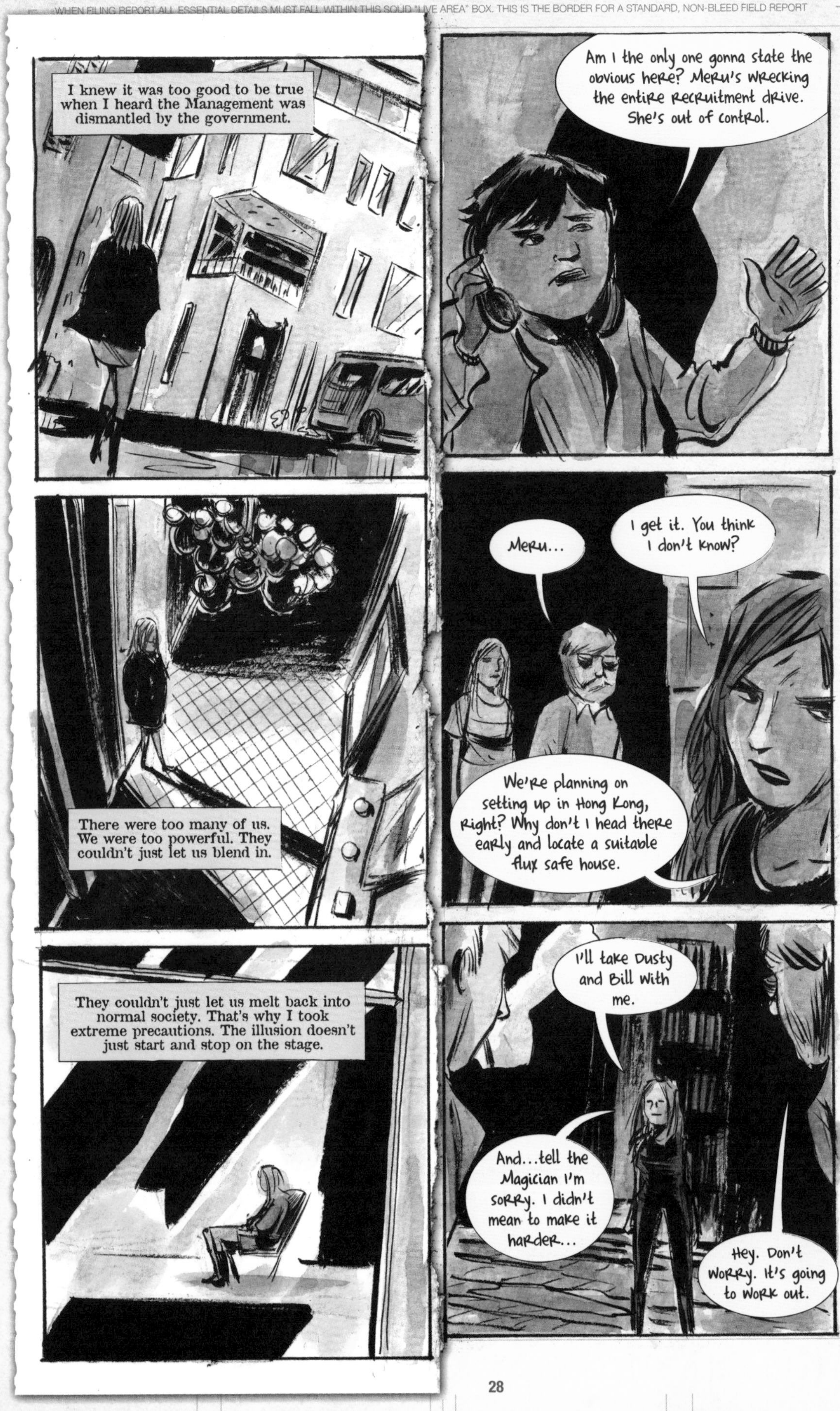

I knew it was too good to be true when I heard the Management was dismantled by the government.
There were too many of us. We were too powerful. They couldn't just let us blend in.
They couldn't just let us melt back into normal society. That's why I took extreme precautions. The illusion doesn't just start and stop on the stage.
Am I the only one gonna state the obvious here? Meru's wrecking the entire recruitment drive. She's out of control.
Meru...
I get it. You think I don't know?
We're planning on setting up in Hong Kong, right? Why don't I head there early and locate a suitable flux safe house.
I'll take Dusty and Bill with me.
And...tell the Magician I'm sorry. I didn't mean to make it harder...
Hey. Don't worry. It's going to work out.

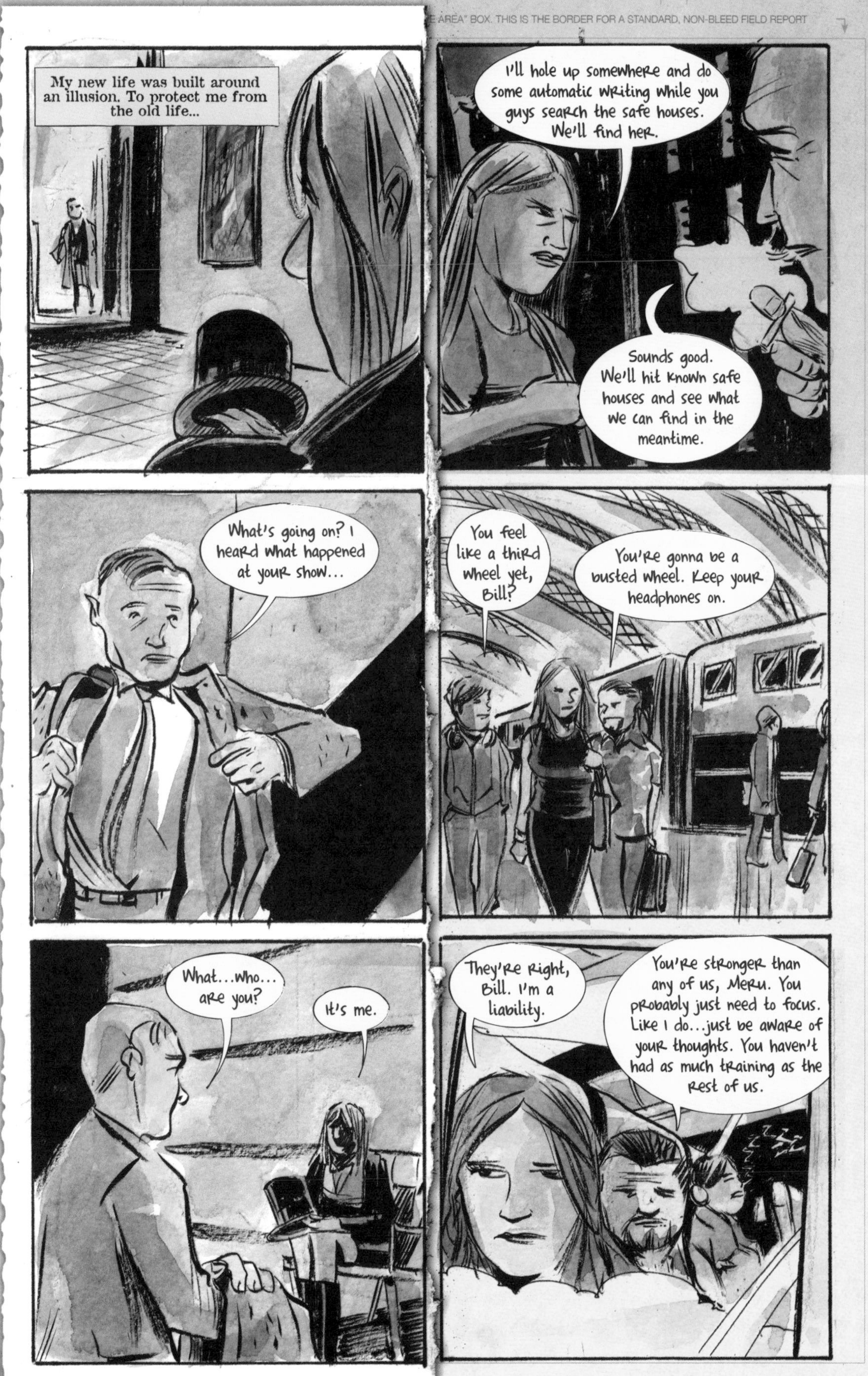

"AREA" BOX. THIS IS THE BORDER FOR A STANDARD, NON-BLEED FIELD REPORT
My new life was built around an illusion. To protect me from the old life...
I'll hole up somewhere and do some automatic writing while you guys search the safe houses. We'll find her.
Sounds good. We'll hit known safe houses and see what we can find in the meantime.
What's going on? I heard what happened at your show...
You feel like a third wheel yet, Bill?
You're gonna be a busted wheel. Keep your headphones on.
What...who... are you?
It's me.
They're right, Bill. I'm a liability.
You're stronger than any of us, Meru. You probably just need to focus. Like I do...just be aware of your thoughts. You haven't had as much training as the rest of us.

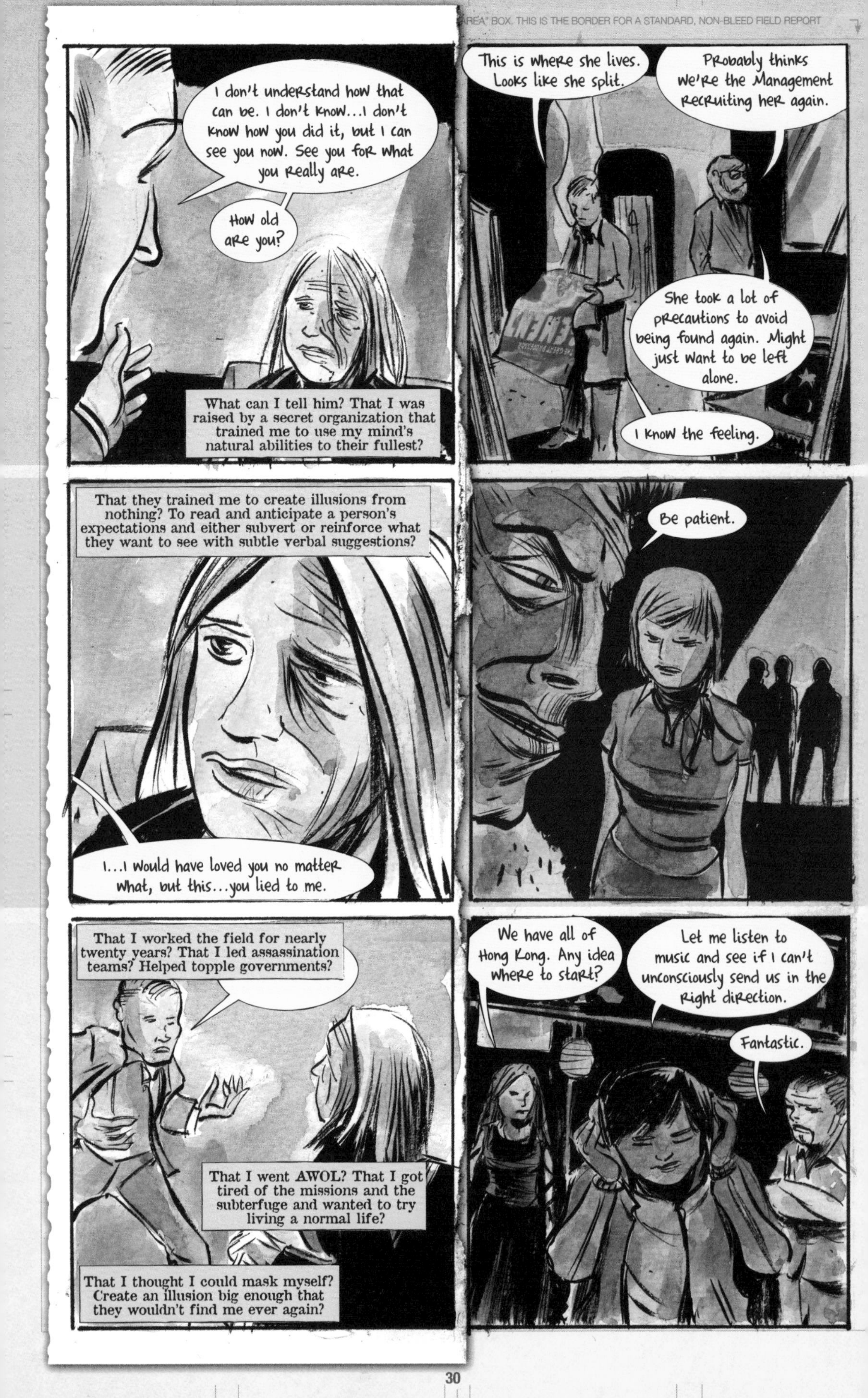
AREA" BOX. THIS IS THE BORDER FOR A STANDARD, NON-BLEED FIELD REPORT
I don't understand how that can be. I don't know...I don't know how you did it, but I can see you now. See you for what you really are.
How old are you?
What can I tell him? That I was raised by a secret organization that trained me to use my mind's natural abilities to their fullest?
That they trained me to create illusions from nothing? To read and anticipate a person's expectations and either subvert or reinforce what they want to see with subtle verbal suggestions?
I...I would have loved you no matter what, but this...you lied to me.
That I worked the field for nearly twenty years? That I led assassination teams? Helped topple governments?
That I went AWOL? That I got tired of the missions and the subterfuge and wanted to try living a normal life?
That I thought I could mask myself? Create an illusion big enough that they wouldn't find me ever again?
This is where she lives. Looks like she split.
Probably thinks we're the Management recruiting her again.
She took a lot of precautions to avoid being found again. Might just want to be left alone.
I know the feeling.
Be patient.
We have all of Hong Kong. Any idea where to start?
Let me listen to music and see if I can't unconsciously send us in the right direction.
Fantastic.

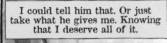

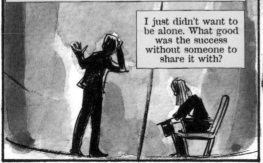

"AREA" BOX. THIS IS THE BORDER FOR A STANDARD, NON-BLEED FIELD REPORT
I could tell him that. Or just take what he gives me. Knowing that I deserve all of it.
I'm sure I loved him at some point. But I'm more sure that I loved using my abilities for fun. For profit. On easy targets. On people who just wanted to forget everything for a couple hours and enjoy themselves. No killing. No backstabbing. Just applause. Love. Laughter.
I just didn't want to be alone. What good was the success without someone to share it with?
My illusion is gone now. He sees me how I really am.
About thirty years older and beaten down.
I could tell him the whole truth. Instead I tell him that he's a fool. I know what these agents are capable of. If they want me they'll eventually get me. And he'll just end up as leverage.
He responds predictably.
Reminds me of old times, Lyme.
Yeah.
We did have some good ones. Before...
Yeah.
In place. Need orders.
You know we found plenty of safe houses on our own.
We don't just want to find a safe house. We want to find the right safe house.
Taxi!

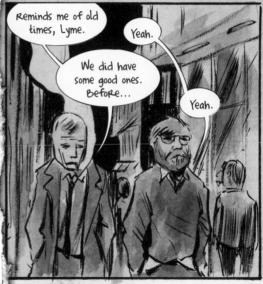

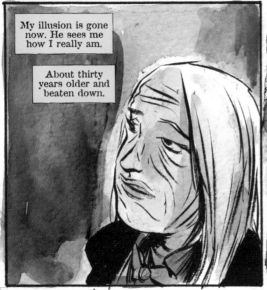

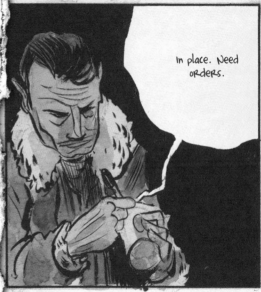

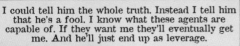

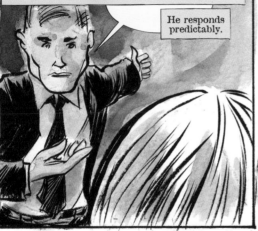

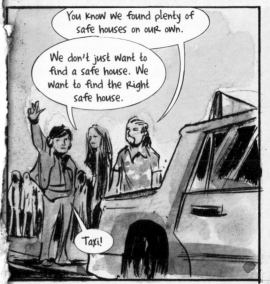

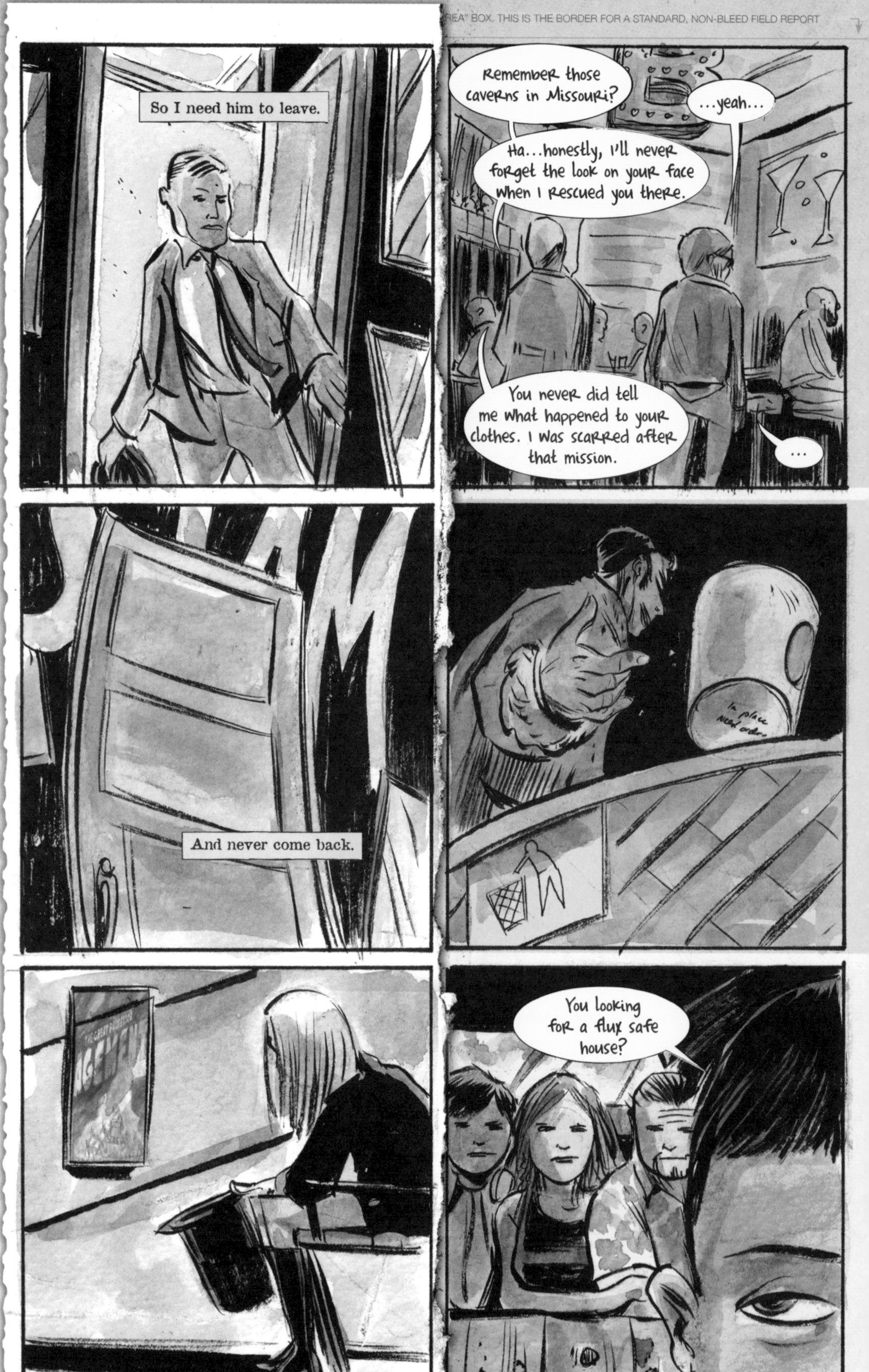
REA" BOX. THIS IS THE BORDER FOR A STANDARD, NON-BLEED FIELD REPORT
So I need him to leave.
Remember those caverns in Missouri?
...yeah...
Ha...honestly, I'll never forget the look on your face when I rescued you there.
You never did tell me what happened to your clothes. I was scarred after that mission.
...
And never come back.
You looking for a flux safe house?

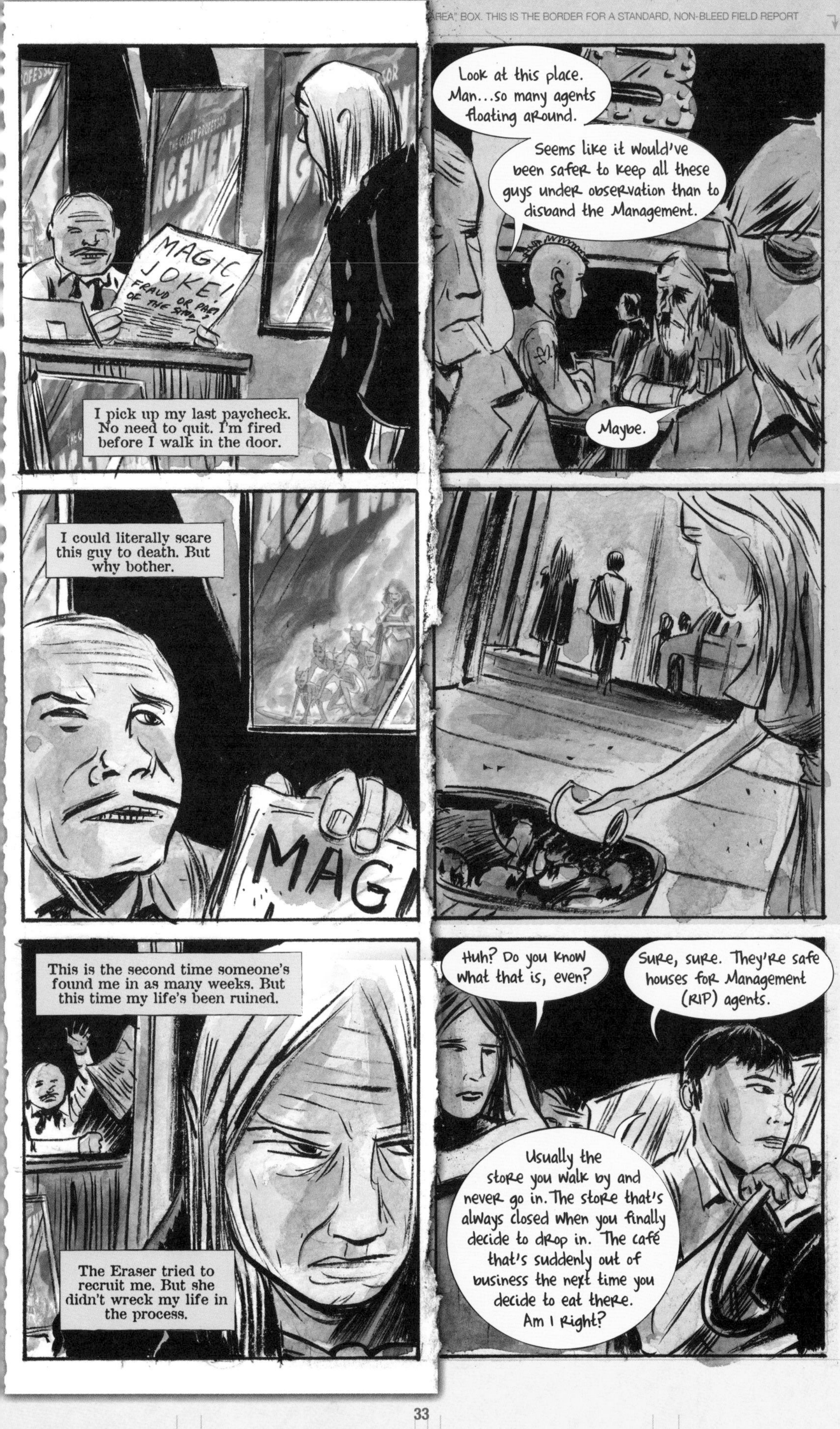
AREA," BOX. THIS IS THE BORDER FOR A STANDARD, NON-BLEED FIELD REPORT
MAGIC JOKE! FRAUD OR PART OF THE SHOW?
I pick up my last paycheck. No need to quit. I'm fired before I walk in the door.
I could literally scare this guy to death. But why bother.
MAGI
This is the second time someone's found me in as many weeks. But this time my life's been ruined.
The Eraser tried to recruit me. But she didn't wreck my life in the process.
Look at this place. Man...so many agents floating around.
Seems like it would've been safer to keep all these guys under observation than to disband the Management.
Maybe.
Huh? Do you know what that is, even?
Sure, sure. They're safe houses for Management (RIP) agents.
Usually the store you walk by and never go in. The store that's always closed when you finally decide to drop in. The café that's suddenly out of business the next time you decide to eat there. Am I right?

So apparently I won't be left alone. Time to choose sides.

You getting anything? What do you do exactly? Sense somebody's brain waves or something?

No.

Then how are you looking for this Magician?

I'm waiting for you to see her.

Oh.

There are still safe houses all over the place. I guess I shouldn't be surprised. No way you can just dissolve something as big as the Management.

I need a DREAMWALKER.

Write it on the flip side of your coaster.

You trust this guy?

Let's just see.

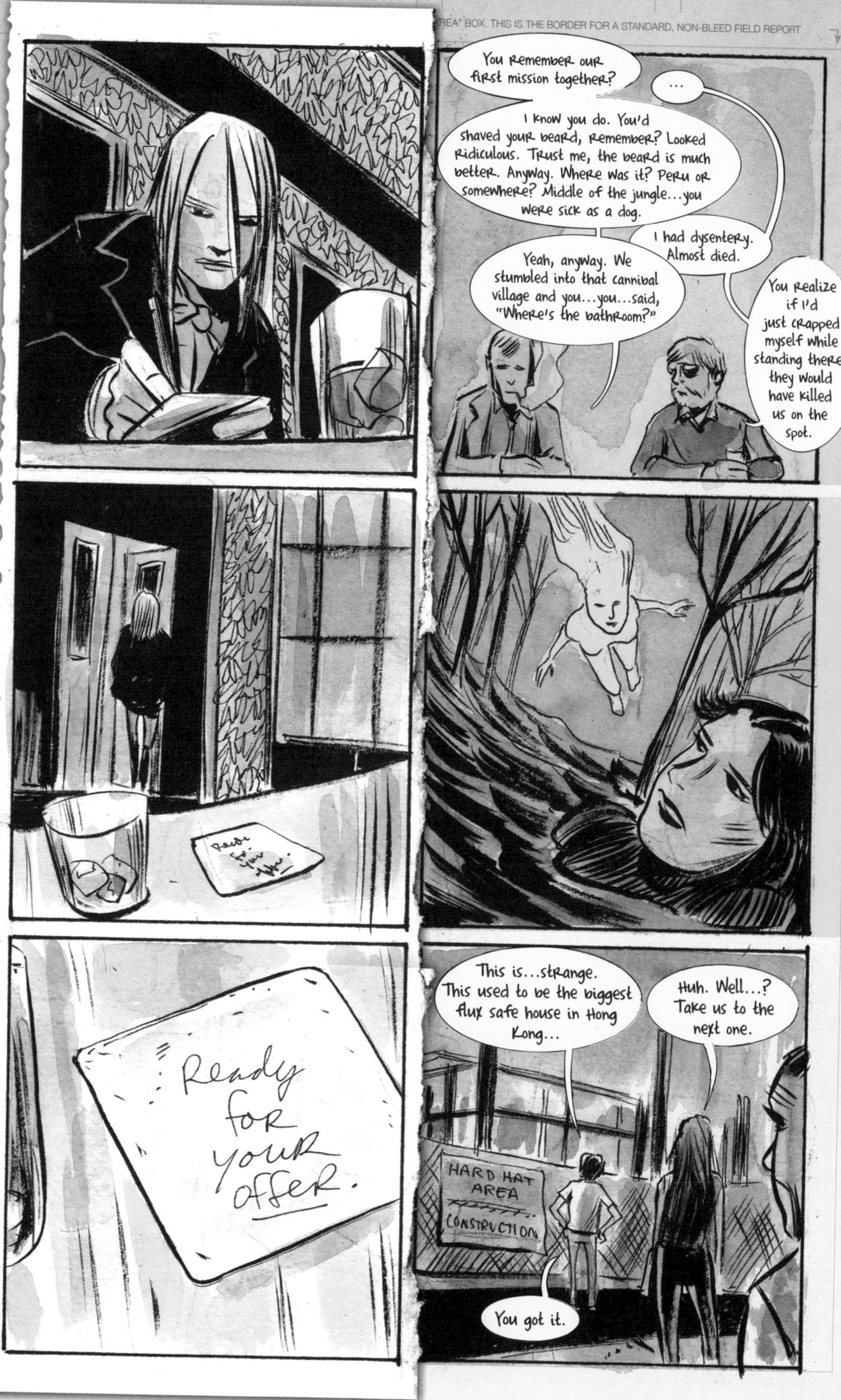
REA" BOX. THIS IS THE BORDER FOR A STANDARD, NON-BLEED FIELD REPORT
You remember our first mission together?
...
I know you do. You'd shaved your beard, remember? Looked ridiculous. Trust me, the beard is much better. Anyway. Where was it? Peru or somewhere? Middle of the jungle...you were sick as a dog.
I had dysentery. Almost died.
Yeah, anyway. We stumbled into that cannibal village and you...you...said, "Where's the bathroom?"
You realize if I'd just crapped myself while standing there, they would have killed us on the spot.
Ready for your offer.
This is...strange. This used to be the biggest flux safe house in Hong Kong...
Huh. Well...? Take us to the next one.
HARD HAT AREA
CONSTRUCTION
You got it.

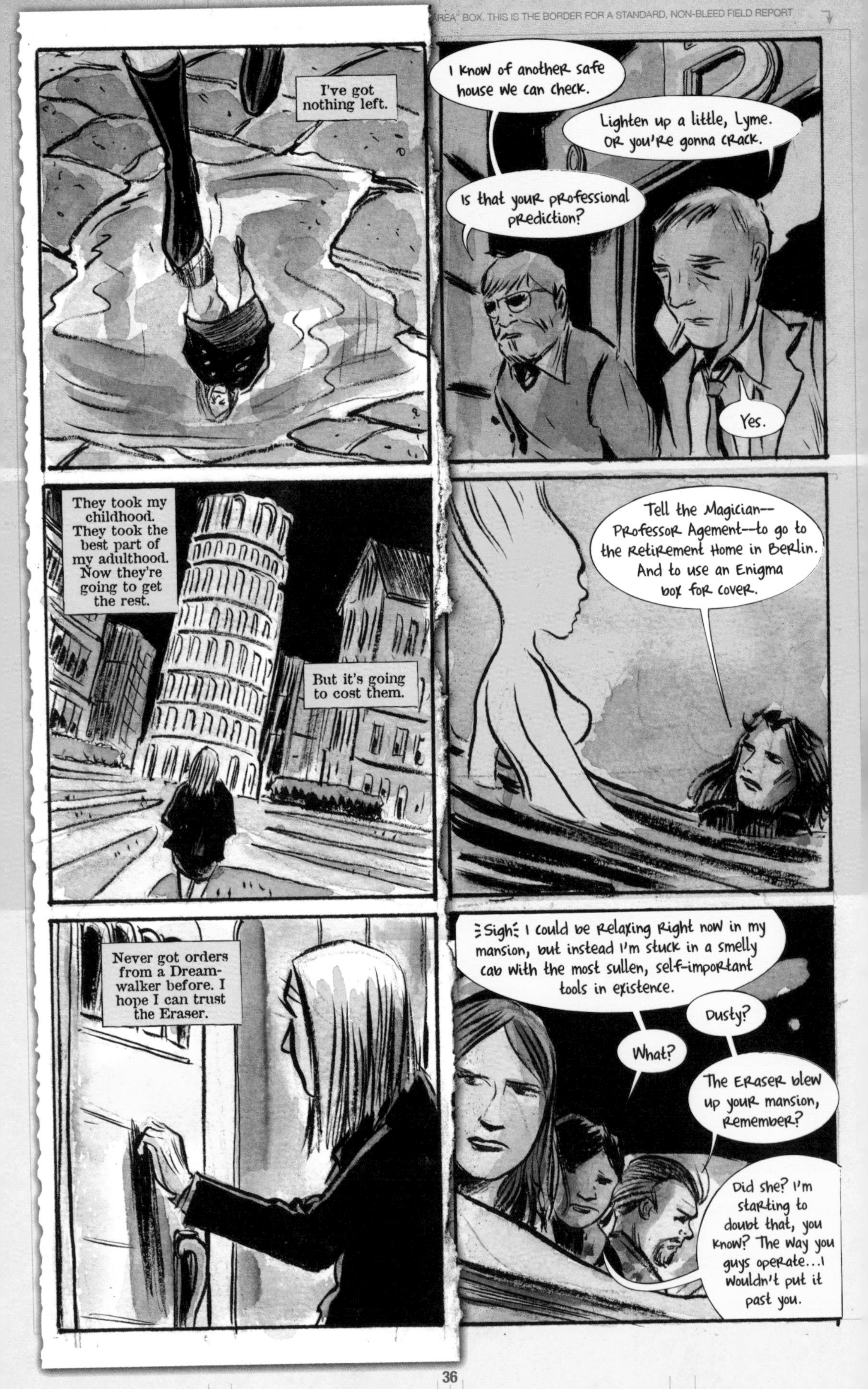
AREA" BOX. THIS IS THE BORDER FOR A STANDARD, NON-BLEED FIELD REPORT
I've got nothing left.
I know of another safe house we can check.
Lighten up a little, Lyme. Or you're gonna crack.
Is that your professional prediction?
Yes.
They took my childhood. They took the best part of my adulthood. Now they're going to get the rest.
But it's going to cost them.
Tell the Magician--Professor Agement--to go to the Retirement Home in Berlin. And to use an Enigma box for cover.
Never got orders from a Dream-walker before. I hope I can trust the Eraser.
Sigh I could be relaxing right now in my mansion, but instead I'm stuck in a smelly cab with the most sullen, self-important tools in existence.
Dusty?
What?
The Eraser blew up your mansion, remember?
Did she? I'm starting to doubt that, you know? The way you guys operate...I wouldn't put it past you.

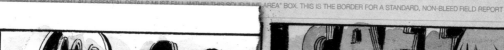

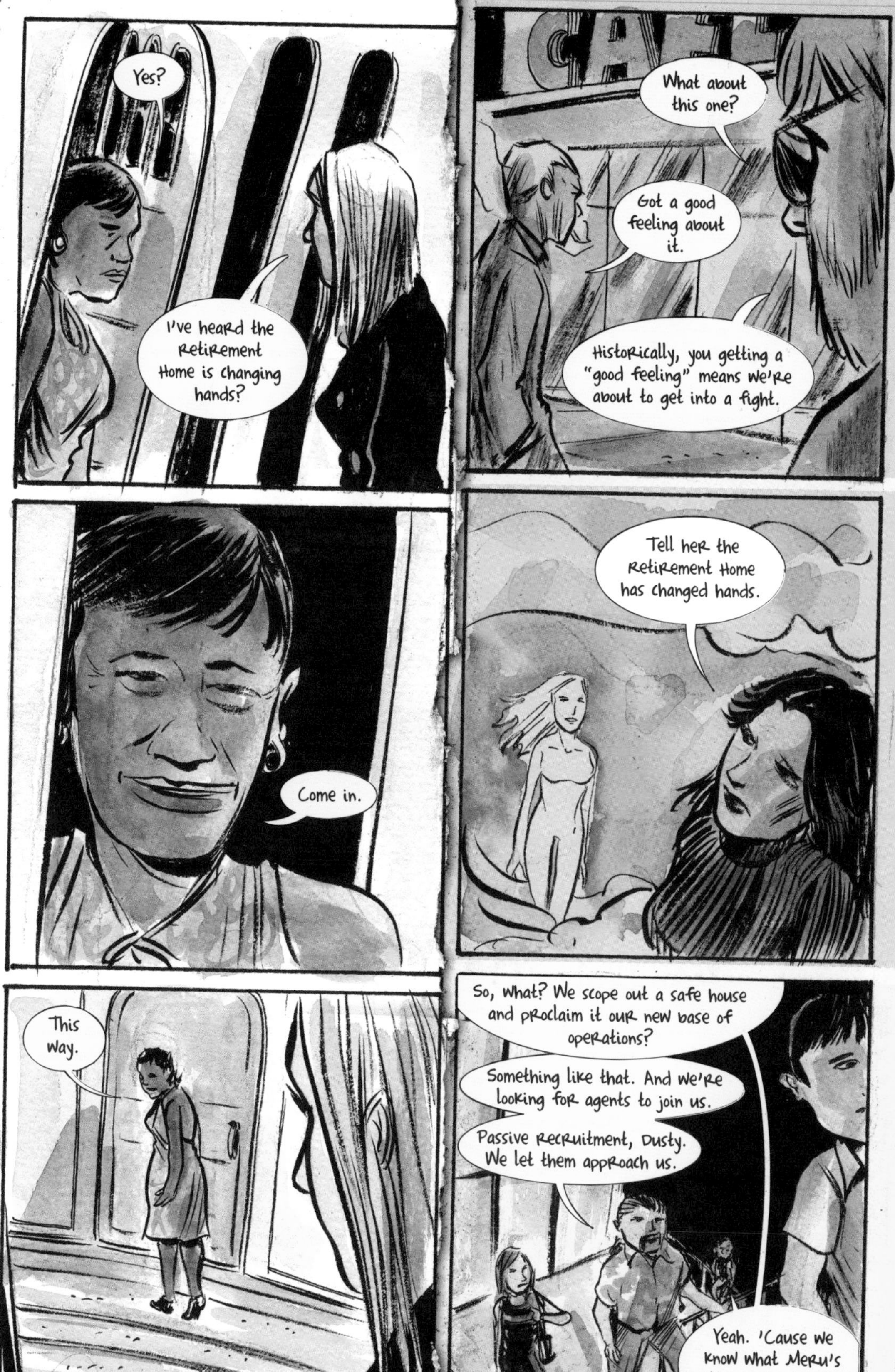
Yes?
I've heard the Retirement Home is changing hands?
Come in.
This way.
What about this one?
Got a good feeling about it.
Historically, you getting a "good feeling" means we're about to get into a fight.
Tell her the Retirement Home has changed hands.
So, what? We scope out a safe house and proclaim it our new base of operations?
Something like that. And we're looking for agents to join us.
Passive recruitment, Dusty. We let them approach us.
Yeah. 'Cause we know what Meru's active recruitment is like. Got it.

"AREA" BOX. THIS IS THE BORDER FOR A STANDARD, NON-BLEED FIELD REPORT

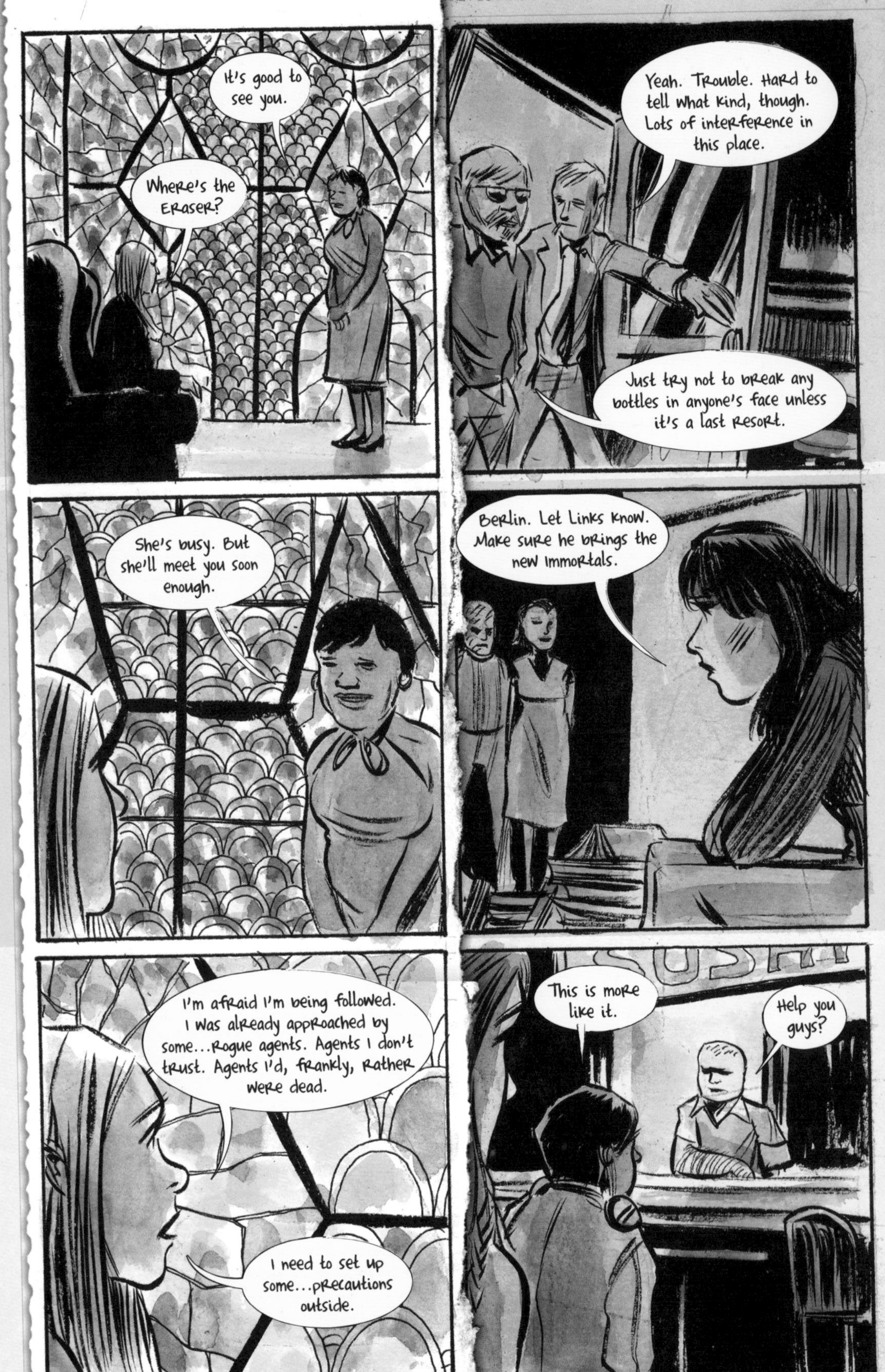
It's good to see you.
Where's the Eraser?
Yeah. Trouble. Hard to tell what kind, though. Lots of interference in this place.
Just try not to break any bottles in anyone's face unless it's a last resort.
She's busy. But she'll meet you soon enough.
Berlin. Let Links know. Make sure he brings the new Immortals.
I'm afraid I'm being followed. I was already approached by some...rogue agents. Agents I don't trust. Agents I'd, frankly, rather were dead.
I need to set up some...precautions outside.
This is more like it.
Help you guys?

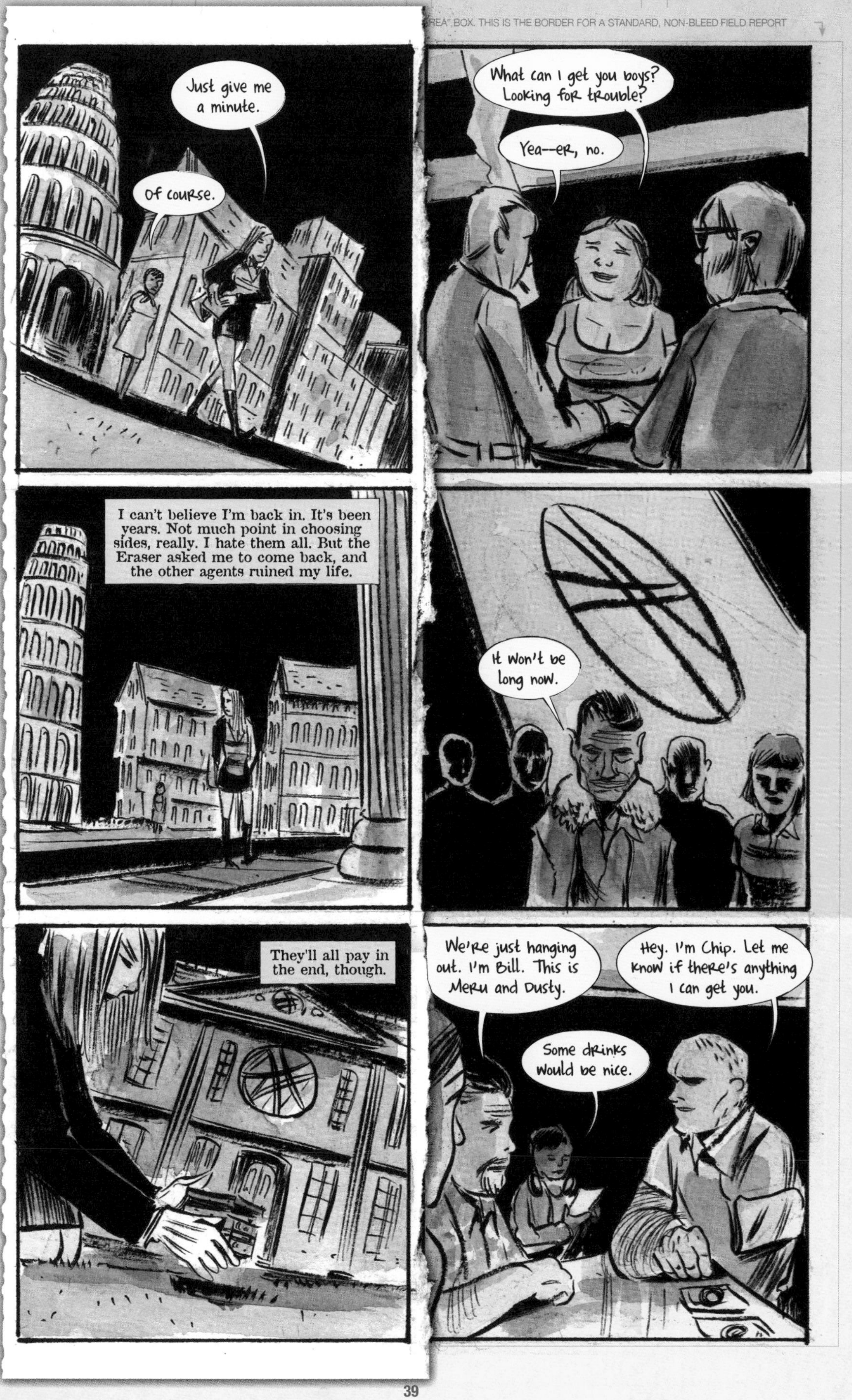
REA" BOX. THIS IS THE BORDER FOR A STANDARD, NON-BLEED FIELD REPORT
Just give me a minute.
Of course.
What can I get you boys? Looking for trouble?
Yea--er, no.
I can't believe I'm back in. It's been years. Not much point in choosing sides, really. I hate them all. But the Eraser asked me to come back, and the other agents ruined my life.
It won't be long now.
They'll all pay in the end, though.
We're just hanging out. I'm Bill. This is Meru and Dusty.
Hey. I'm Chip. Let me know if there's anything I can get you.
Some drinks would be nice.

"AREA" BOX. THIS IS THE BORDER FOR A STANDARD, NON-BLEED FIELD REPORT

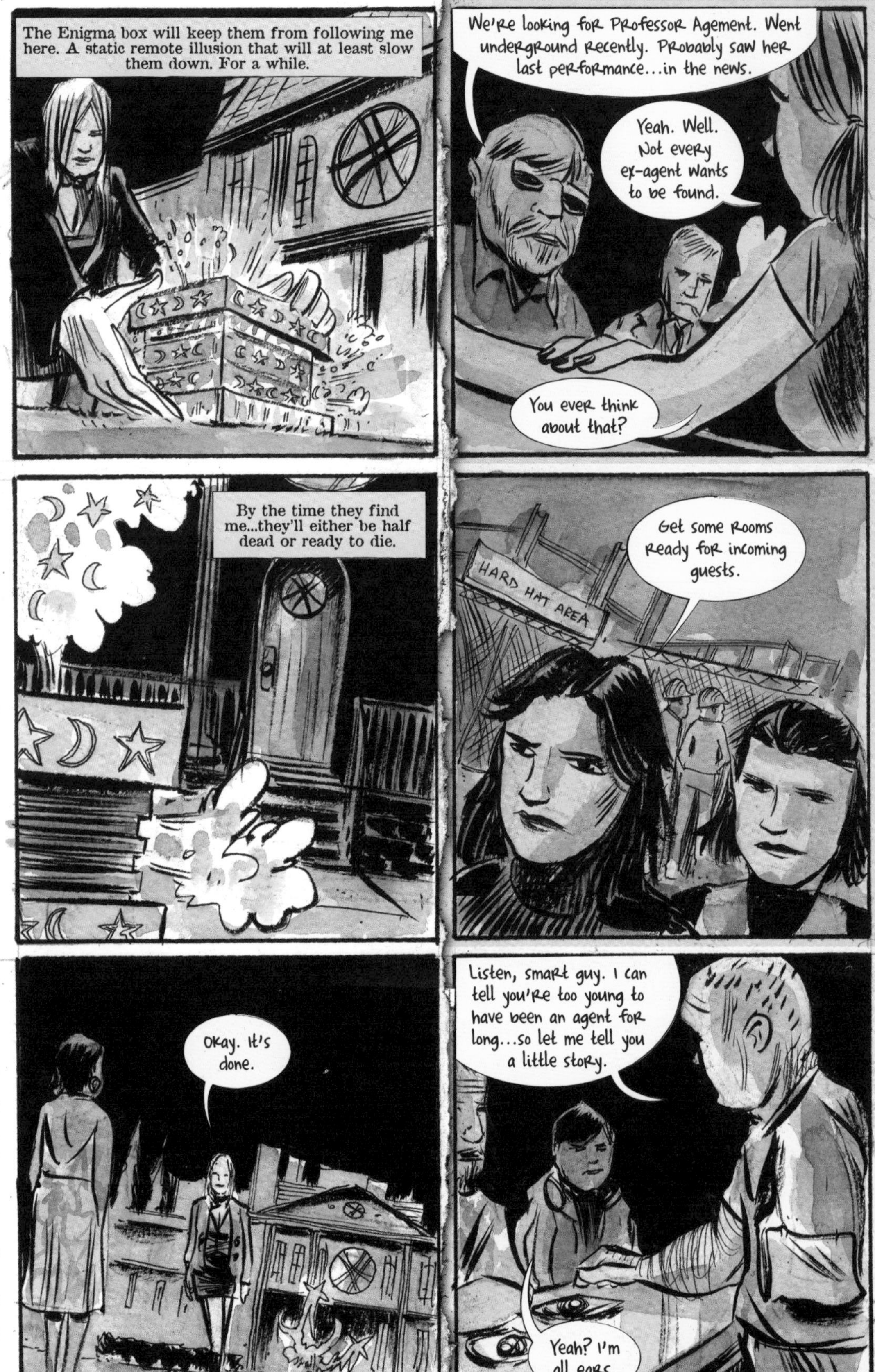
The Enigma box will keep them from following me here. A static remote illusion that will at least slow them down. For a while.
We're looking for Professor Agement. Went underground recently. Probably saw her last performance...in the news.
Yeah. Well. Not every ex-agent wants to be found.
You ever think about that?
By the time they find me...they'll either be half dead or ready to die.
HARD HAT AREA
Get some rooms ready for incoming guests.
Okay. It's done.
Listen, smart guy. I can tell you're too young to have been an agent for long...so let me tell you a little story.
Yeah? I'm all ears.

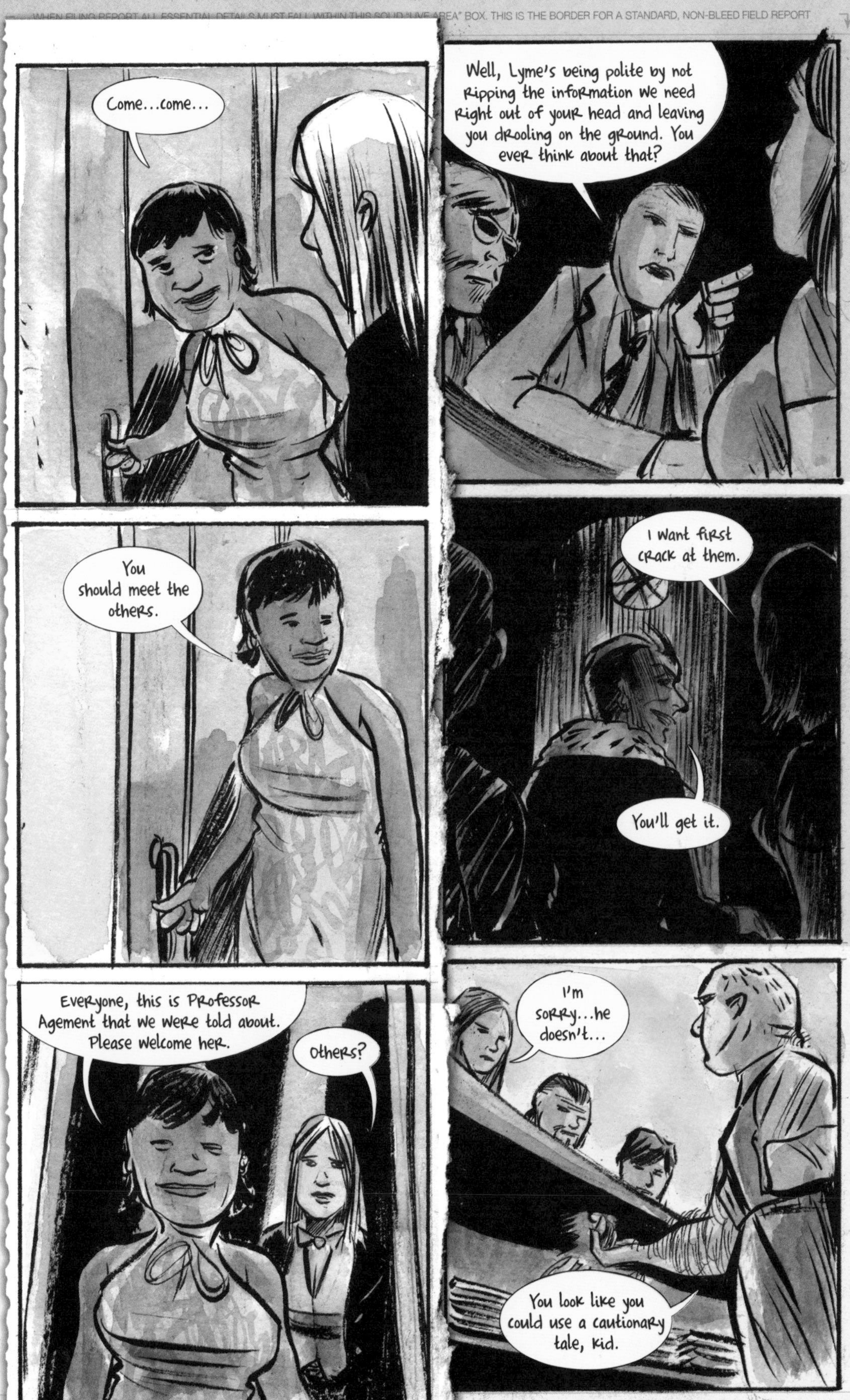
"LIVE AREA" BOX. THIS IS THE BORDER FOR A STANDARD, NON-BLEED FIELD REPORT
Come...come...
You should meet the others.
Everyone, this is Professor Agement that we were told about. Please welcome her.
Others?
Well, Lyme's being polite by not ripping the information we need right out of your head and leaving you drooling on the ground. You ever think about that?
I want first crack at them.
You'll get it.
I'm sorry...he doesn't...
You look like you could use a cautionary tale, kid.

WHEN FILING REPORT ALL ESSENTIAL DETAILS MUST FALL WITHIN THIS SOLID "LIVE AREA" BOX. THIS IS THE BORDER FOR A STANDARD, NON-BLEED FIELD REPORT

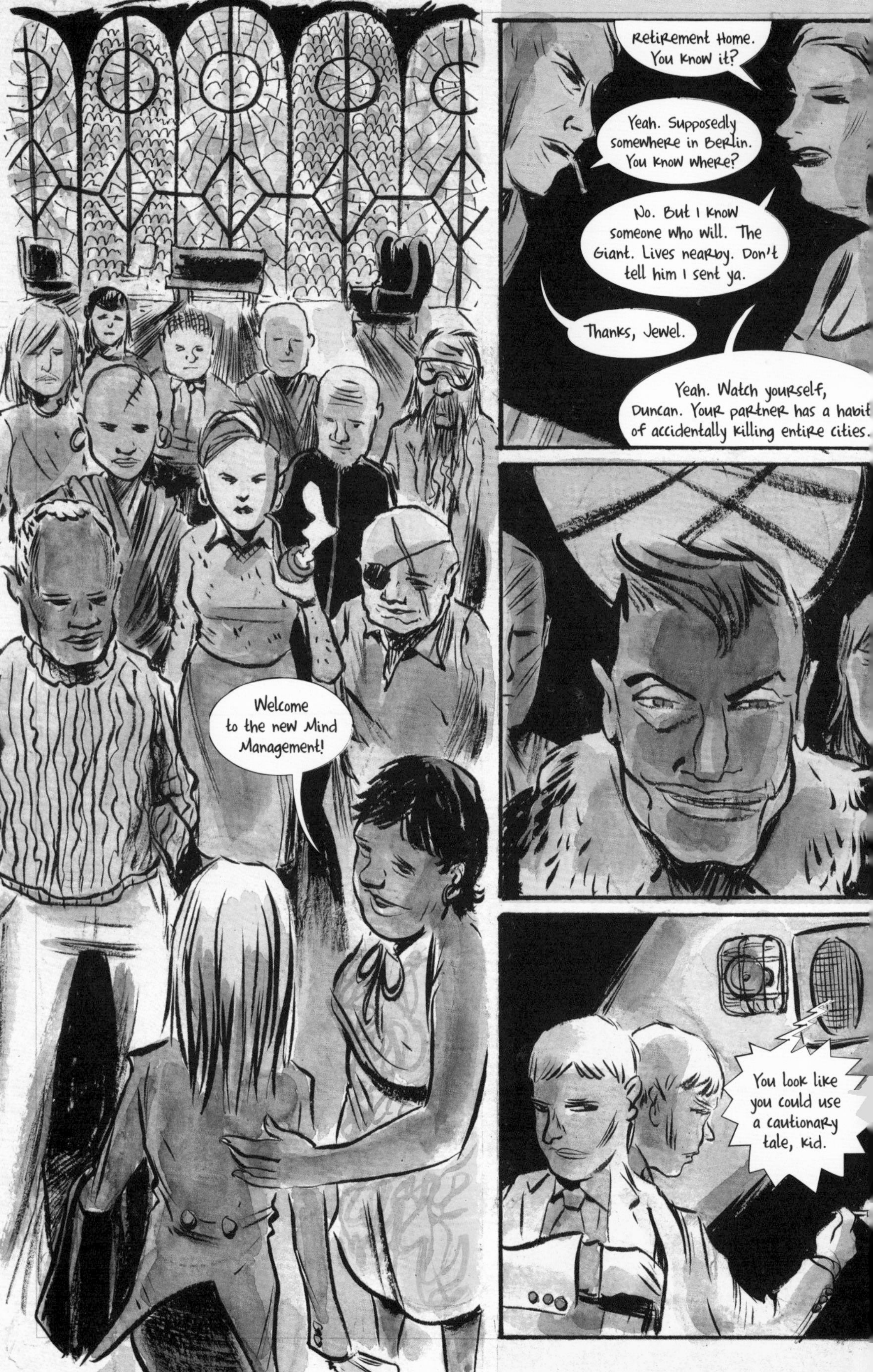

Welcome to the new Mind Management!
Retirement Home. You know it?
Yeah. Supposedly somewhere in Berlin. You know where?
No. But I know someone who will. The Giant. Lives nearby. Don't tell him I sent ya.
Thanks, Jewel.
Yeah. Watch yourself, Duncan. Your partner has a habit of accidentally killing entire cities.
You look like you could use a cautionary tale, kid.

MIND MGMT
Flux Safe Houses

Hawaii

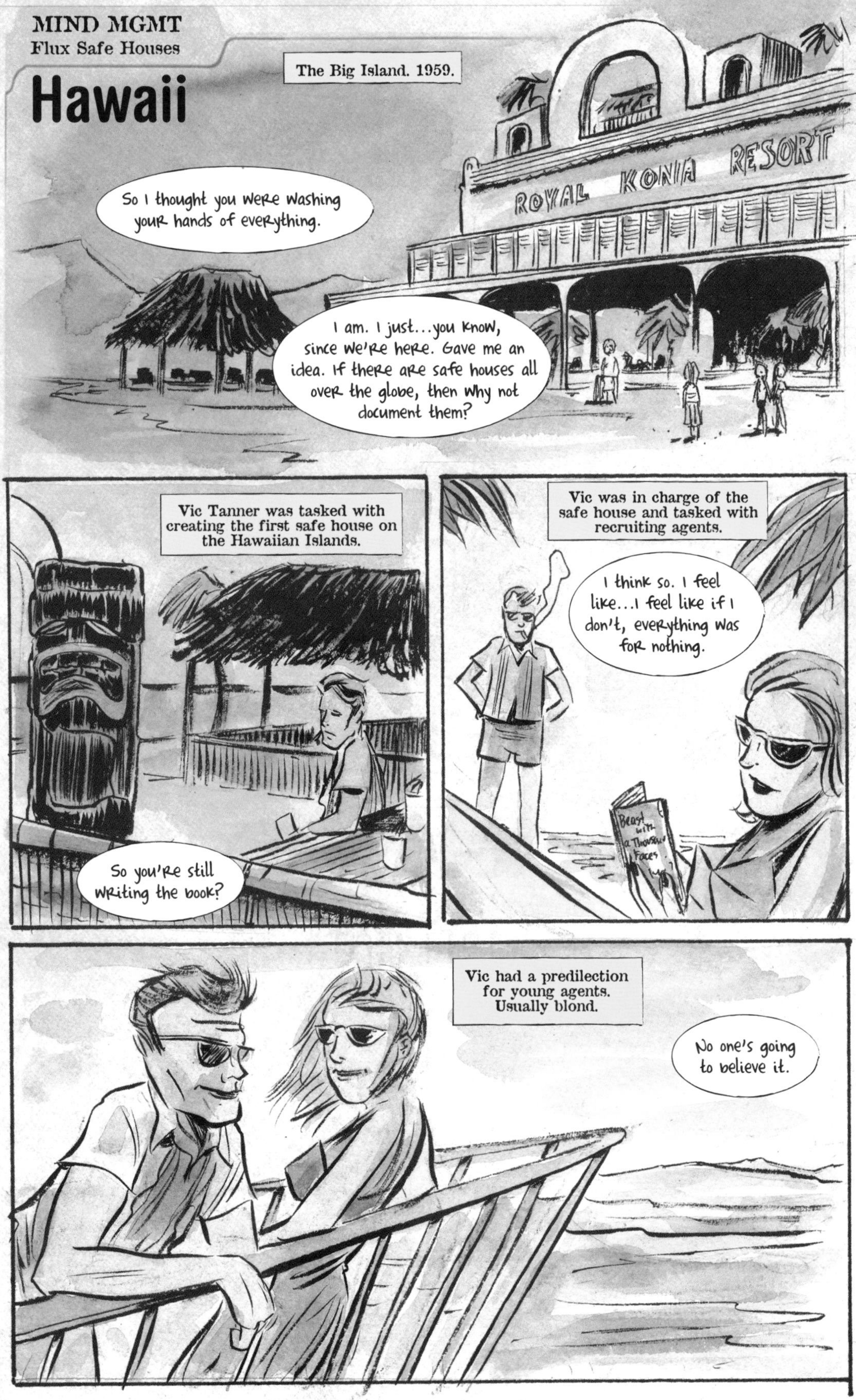
The Big Island. 1959.
ROYAL KONA RESORT
So I thought you were washing your hands of everything.
I am. I just...you know, since we're here. Gave me an idea. If there are safe houses all over the globe, then why not document them?
Vic Tanner was tasked with creating the first safe house on the Hawaiian Islands.
So you're still writing the book?
Vic was in charge of the safe house and tasked with recruiting agents.
I think so. I feel like...I feel like if I don't, everything was for nothing.
Beast with a Thousand Faces
Vic had a predilection for young agents. Usually blond.
No one's going to believe it.

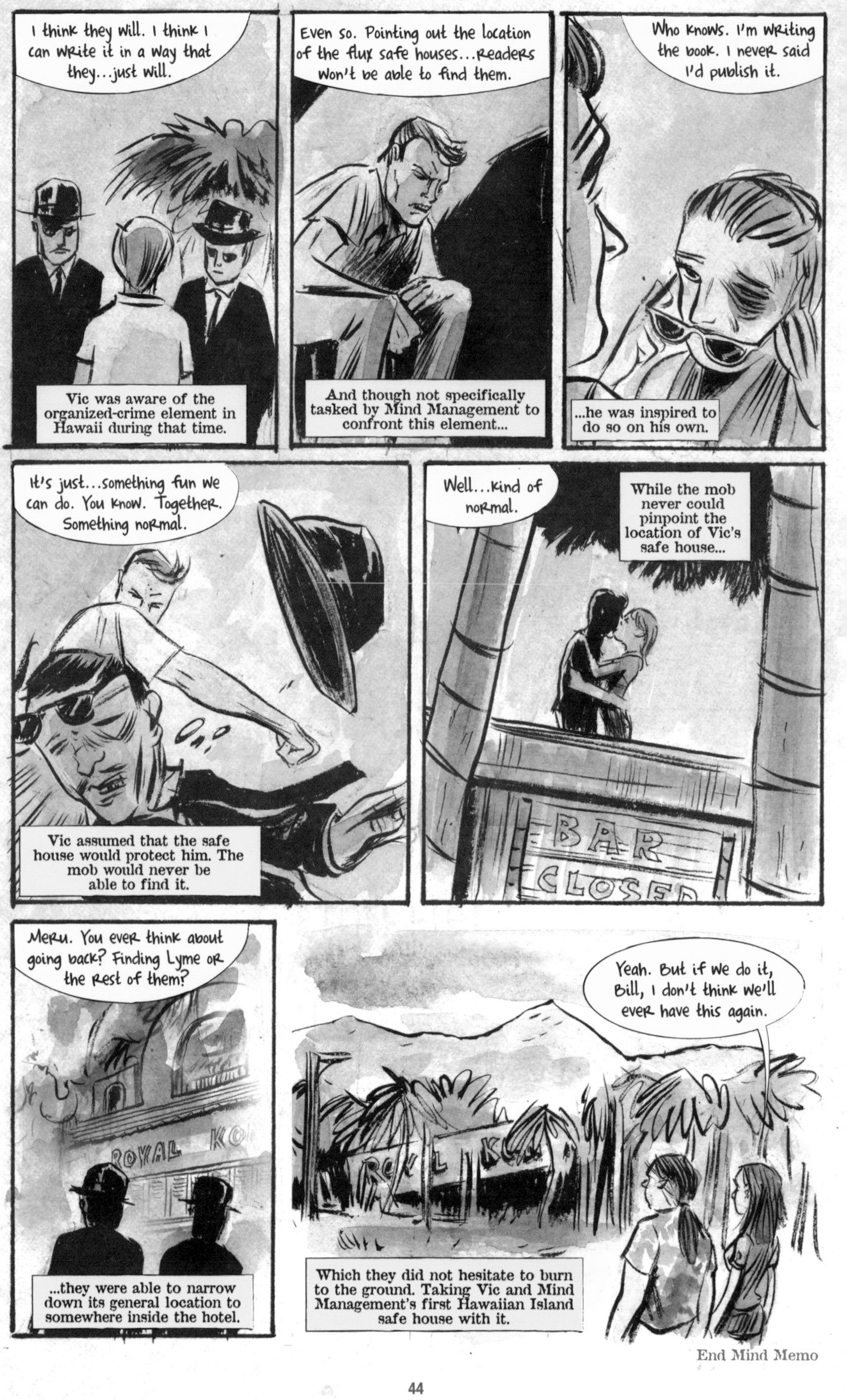
I think they will. I think I can write it in a way that they...just will.
Vic was aware of the organized-crime element in Hawaii during that time.
Even so. Pointing out the location of the flux safe houses...readers won't be able to find them.
And though not specifically tasked by Mind Management to confront this element...
Who knows. I'm writing the book. I never said I'd publish it.
...he was inspired to do so on his own.
It's just...something fun we can do. You know. Together. Something normal.
Vic assumed that the safe house would protect him. The mob would never be able to find it.
Well...kind of normal.
While the mob never could pinpoint the location of Vic's safe house...
BAR
CLOSED
Meru. You ever think about going back? Finding Lyme or the rest of them?
ROYAL KO
...they were able to narrow down its general location to somewhere inside the hotel.
Yeah. But if we do it, Bill, I don't think we'll ever have this again.
Which they did not hesitate to burn to the ground. Taking Vic and Mind Management's first Hawaiian Island safe house with it.

End Mind Memo

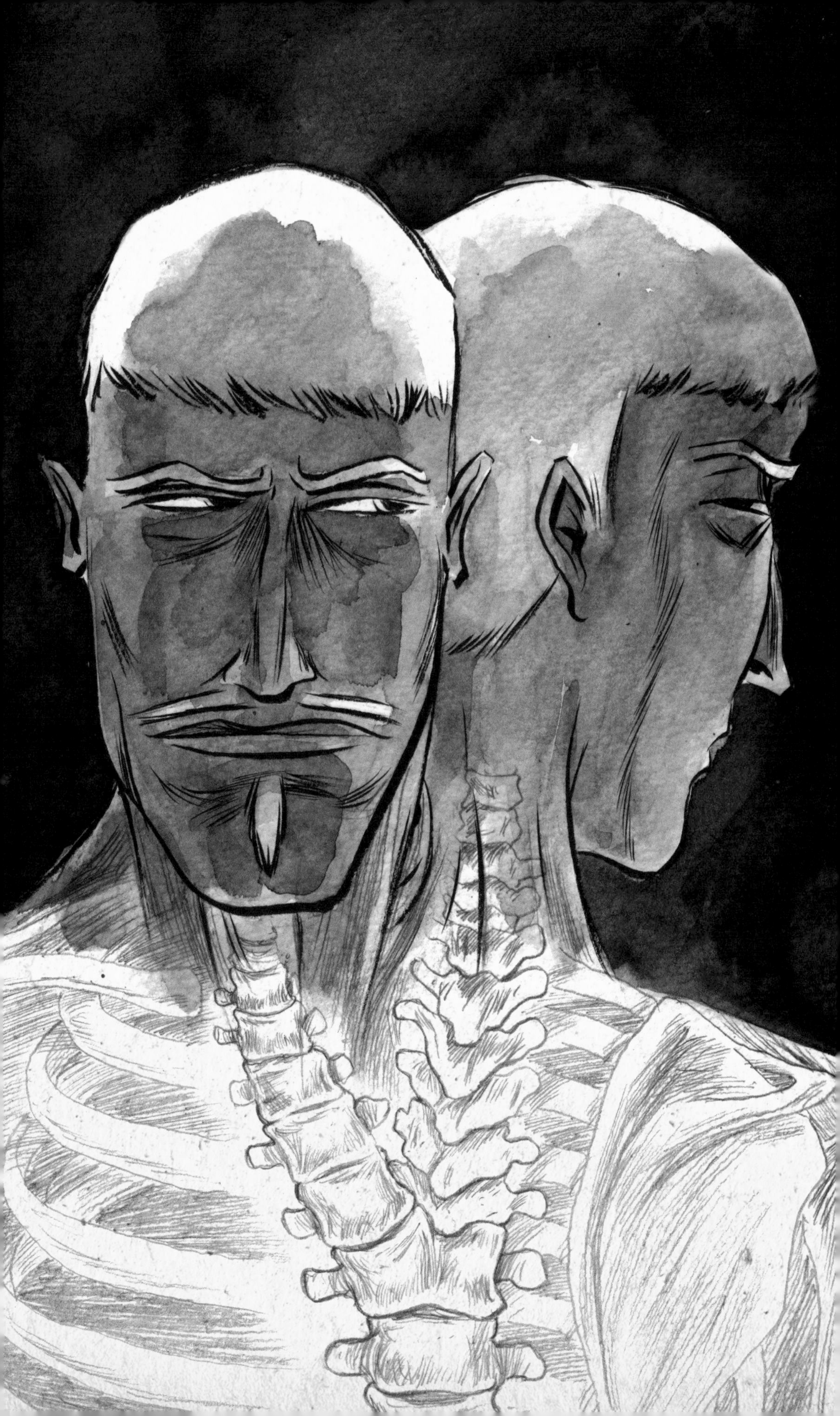

20

WHEN FILING REPORT ALL ESSENTIAL DETAILS MUST FALL WITHIN THIS SOLID "LIVE AREA" BOX. THIS IS THE BORDER FOR A STANDARD, NON-BLEED FIELD REPORT

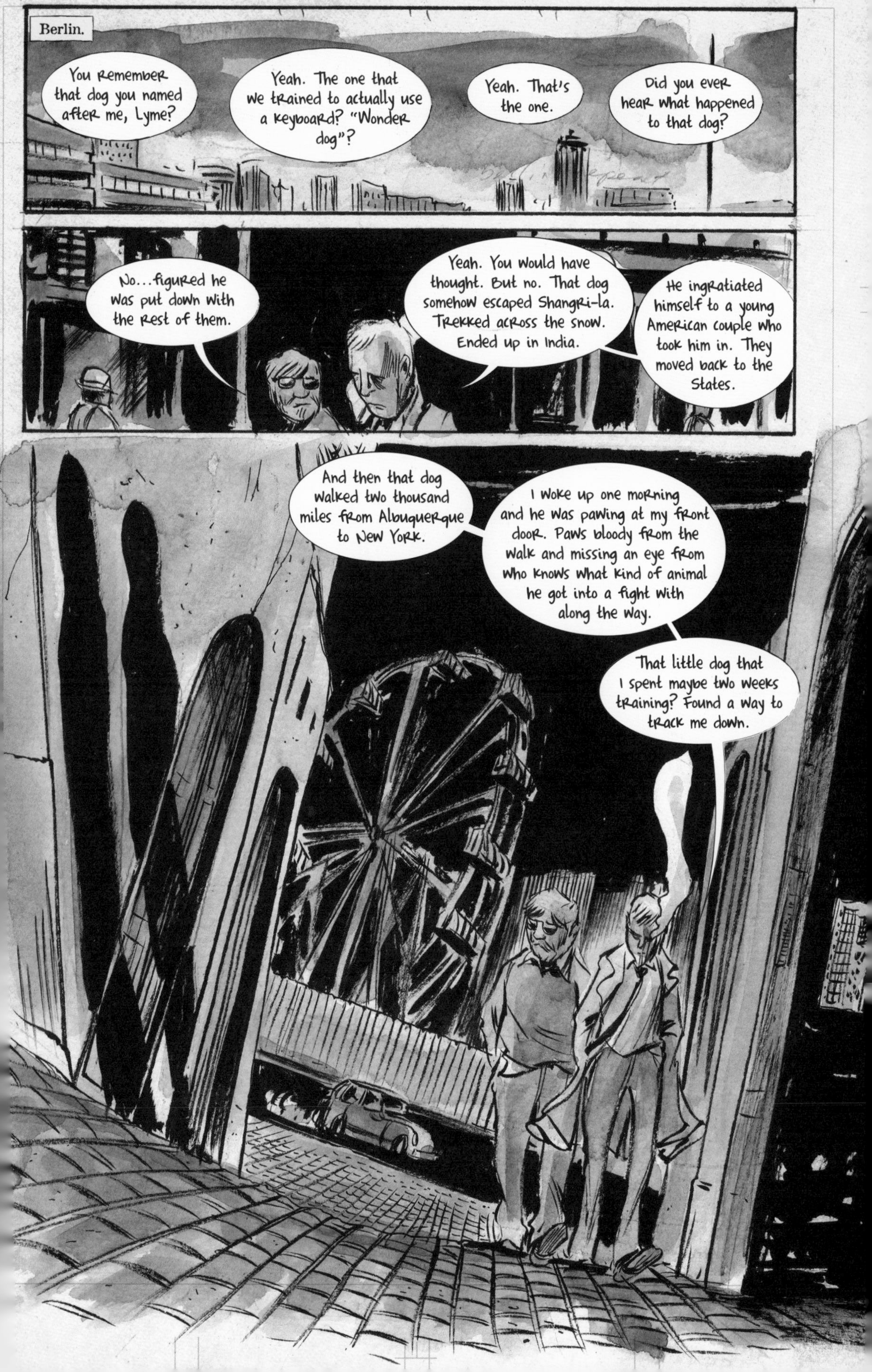
Berlin.
You remember that dog you named after me, Lyme?
Yeah. The one that we trained to actually use a keyboard? "Wonder dog"?
Yeah. That's the one.
Did you ever hear what happened to that dog?
No...figured he was put down with the rest of them.
Yeah. You would have thought. But no. That dog somehow escaped Shangri-La. Trekked across the snow. Ended up in India.
He ingratiated himself to a young American couple who took him in. They moved back to the States.
And then that dog walked two thousand miles from Albuquerque to New York.
I woke up one morning and he was pawing at my front door. Paws bloody from the walk and missing an eye from who knows what kind of animal he got into a fight with along the way.
That little dog that I spent maybe two weeks training? Found a way to track me down.

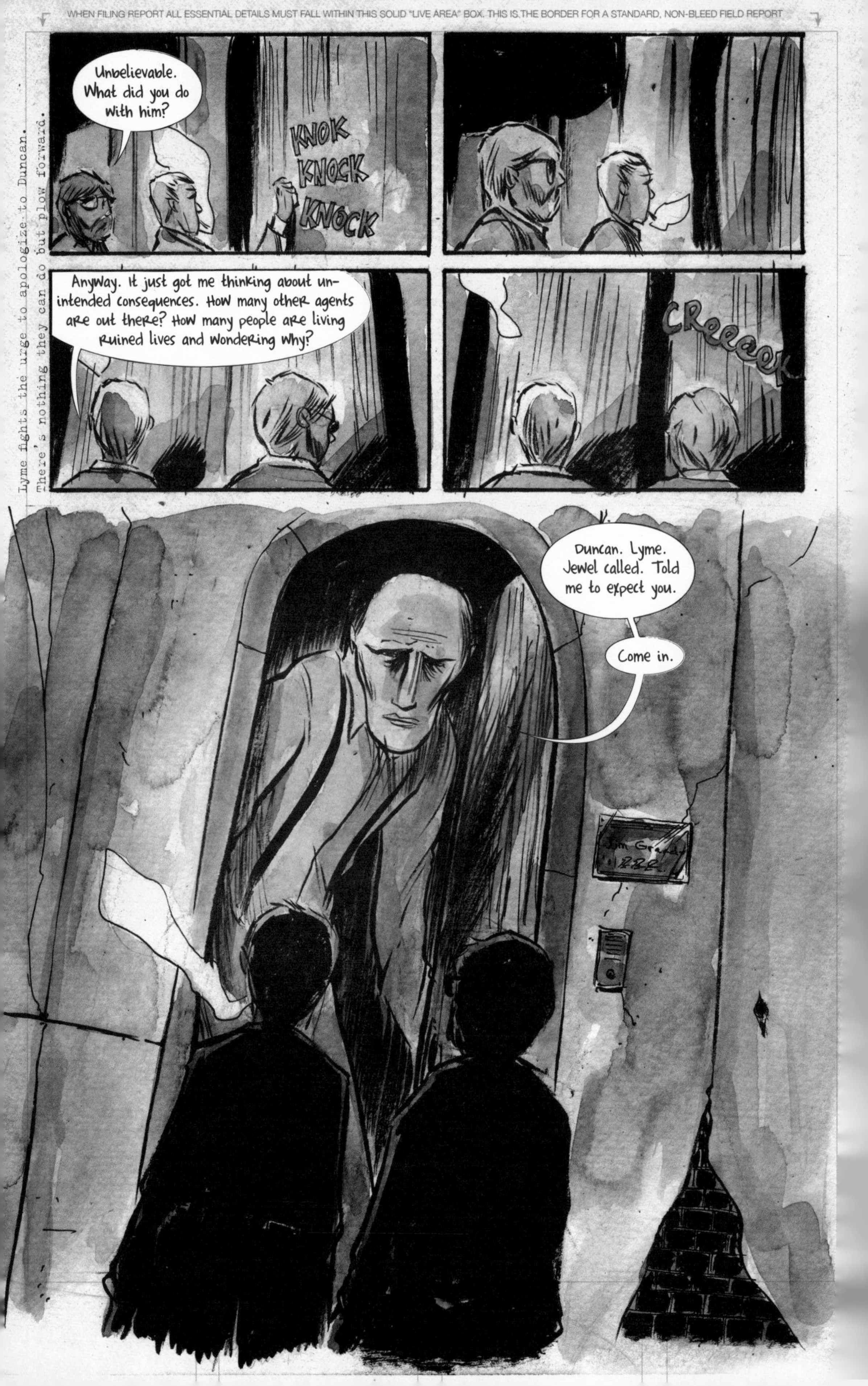
WHEN FILING REPORT ALL ESSENTIAL DETAILS MUST FALL WITHIN THIS SOLID "LIVE AREA" BOX. THIS IS THE BORDER FOR A STANDARD, NON-BLEED FIELD REPORT
Lyme fights the urge to apologize to Duncan.
There's nothing they can do but plow forward.
Unbelievable. What did you do with him?
KNOK KNOCK KNOCK
Anyway. It just got me thinking about unintended consequences. How many other agents are out there? How many people are living ruined lives and wondering why?
CReeeeeK
Duncan. Lyme. Jewel called. Told me to expect you.
Come in.

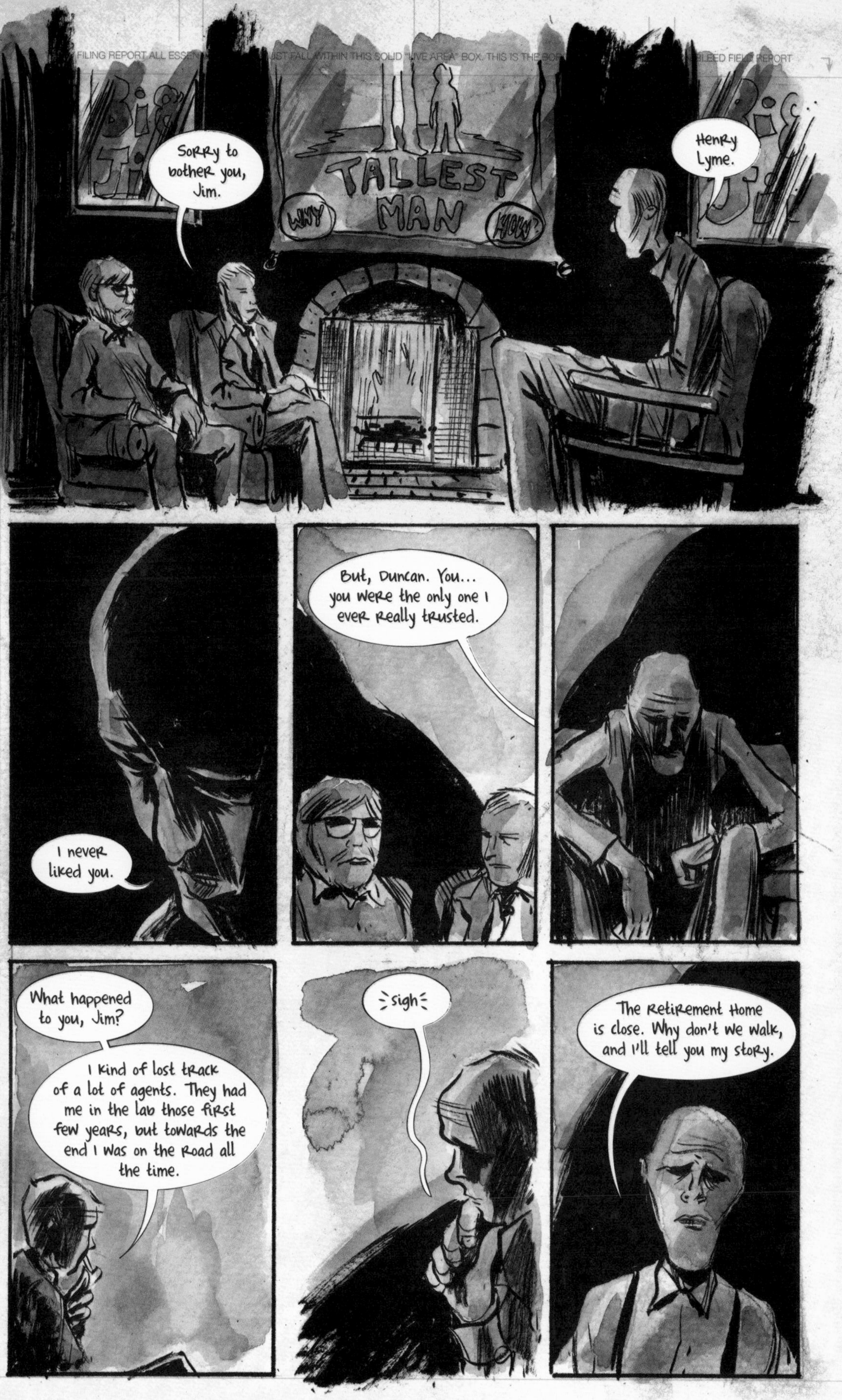
TALLEST MAN
WHY
HOW?
Sorry to bother you, Jim.
Henry Lyme.
I never liked you.
But, Duncan. You... you were the only one I ever really trusted.
What happened to you, Jim?
I kind of lost track of a lot of agents. They had me in the lab those first few years, but towards the end I was on the road all the time.
sigh
The Retirement Home is close. Why don't we walk, and I'll tell you my story.

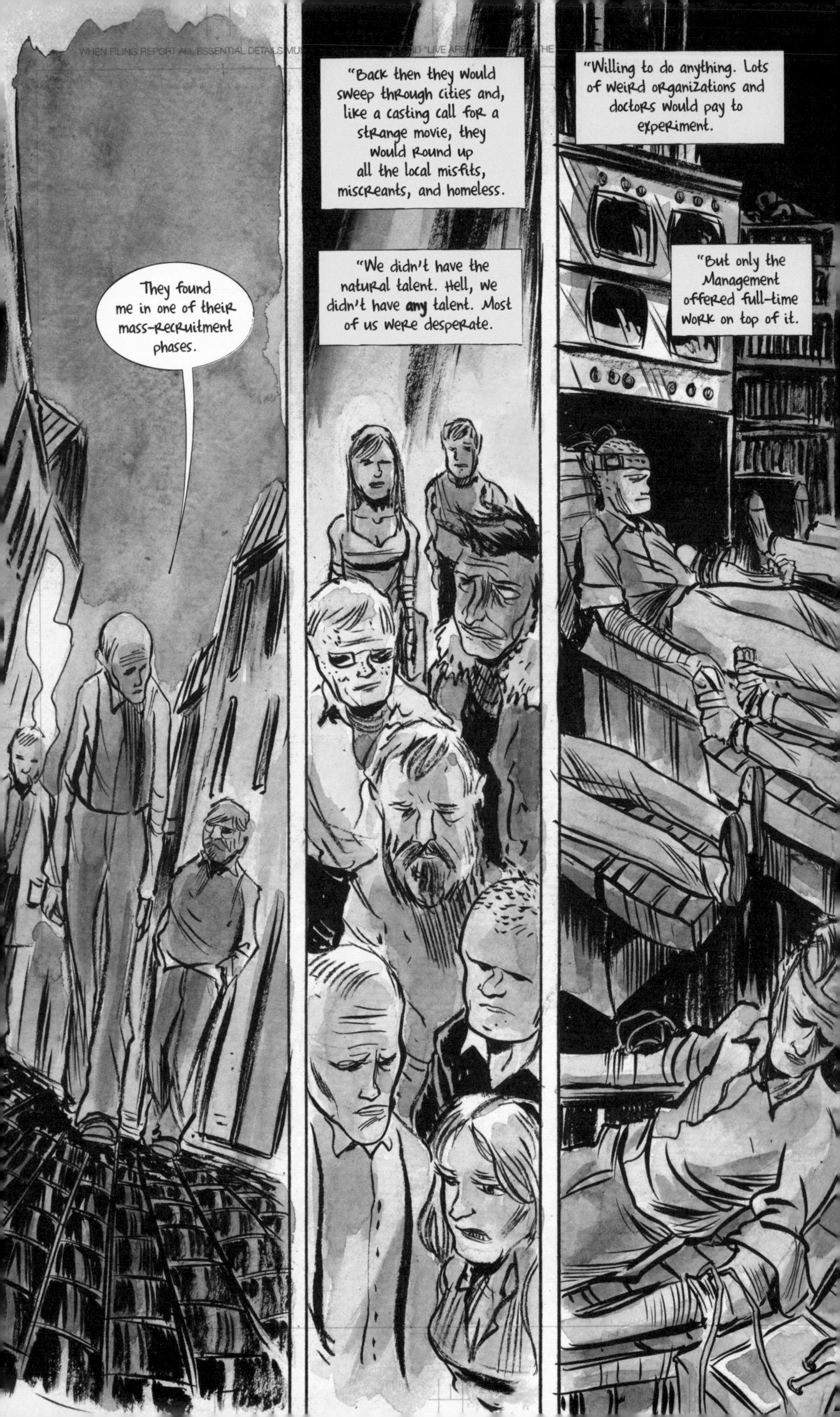

They found me in one of their mass-recruitment phases.
"Back then they would sweep through cities and, like a casting call for a strange movie, they would round up all the local misfits, miscreants, and homeless.
"We didn't have the natural talent. Hell, we didn't have **any** talent. Most of us were desperate.
"Willing to do anything. Lots of weird organizations and doctors would pay to experiment.
"But only the Management offered full-time work on top of it.

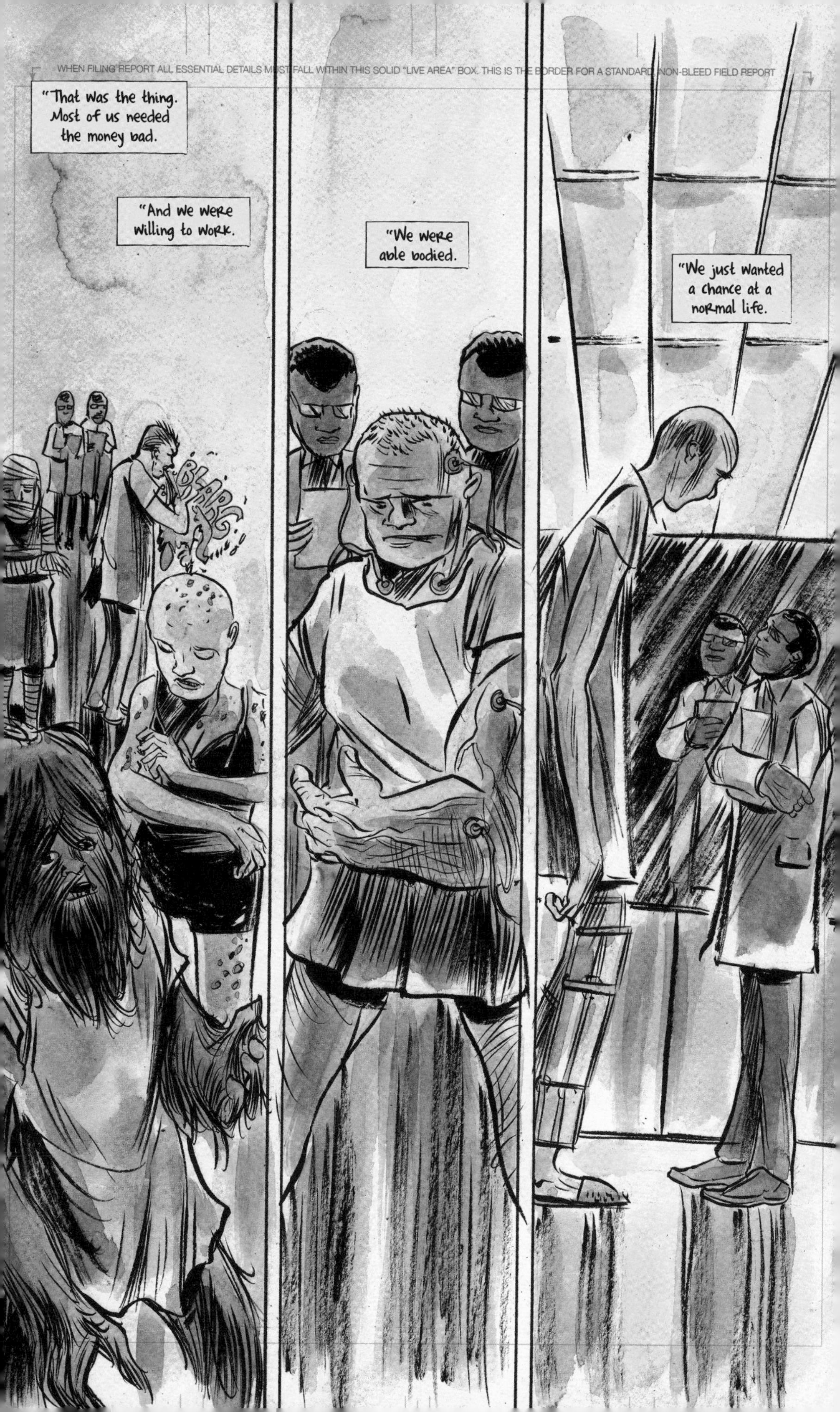
WHEN FILING REPORT ALL ESSENTIAL DETAILS MUST FALL WITHIN THIS SOLID "LIVE AREA" BOX. THIS IS THE BORDER FOR A STANDARD, NON-BLEED FIELD REPORT
"That was the thing. Most of us needed the money bad.
"And we were willing to work.
BLARG
"We were able bodied.
"We just wanted a chance at a normal life.

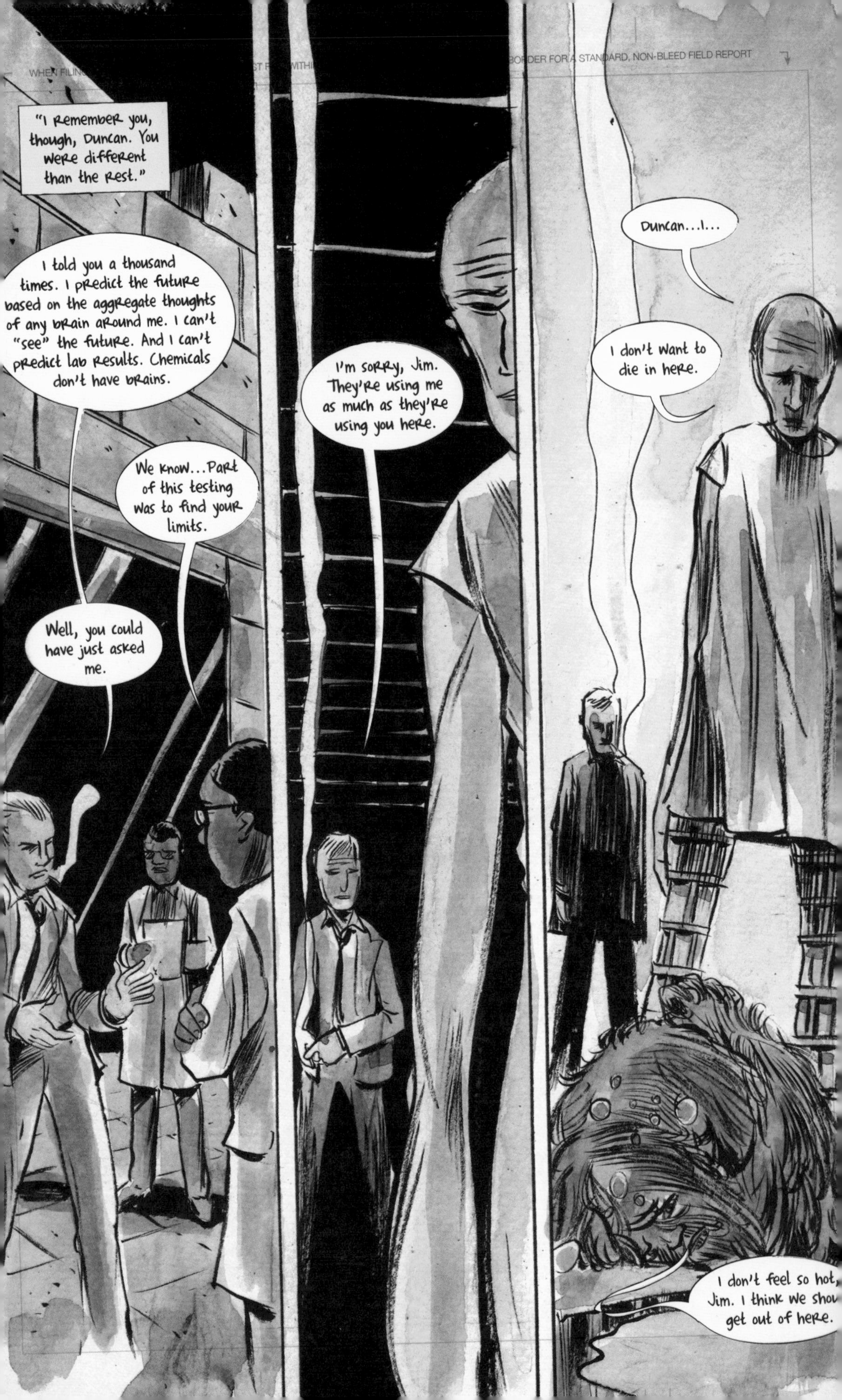
"I remember you, though, Duncan. You were different than the rest."
I told you a thousand times. I predict the future based on the aggregate thoughts of any brain around me. I can't "see" the future. And I can't predict lab results. Chemicals don't have brains.
We know... Part of this testing was to find your limits.
Well, you could have just asked me.
I'm sorry, Jim. They're using me as much as they're using you here.
Duncan... I...
I don't want to die in here.
I don't feel so hot, Jim. I think we shou get out of here.

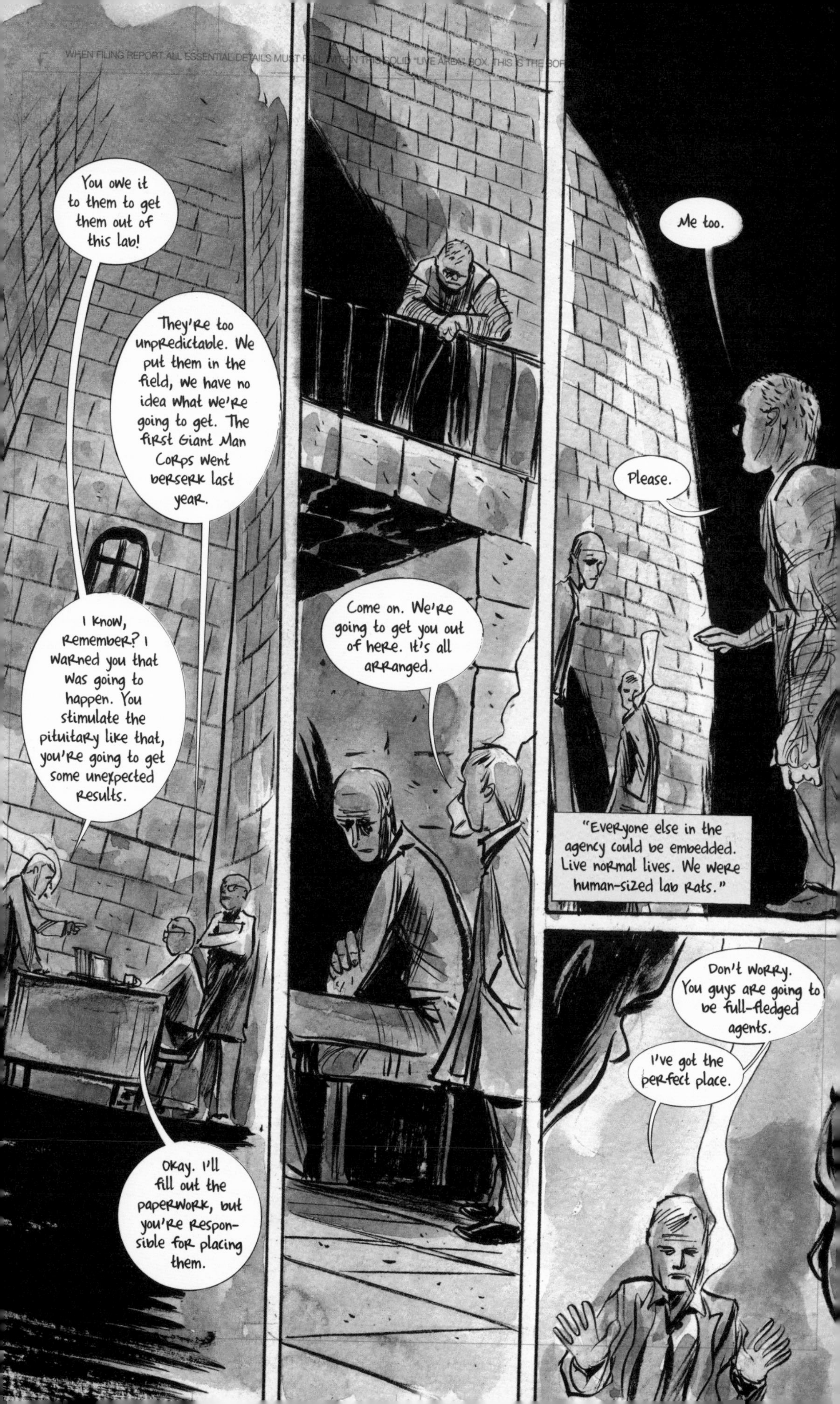

You owe it to them to get them out of this lab!
They're too unpredictable. We put them in the field, we have no idea what we're going to get. The first Giant Man Corps went berserk last year.
I know, remember? I warned you that was going to happen. You stimulate the pituitary like that, you're going to get some unexpected results.
Okay. I'll fill out the paperwork, but you're responsible for placing them.
Come on. We're going to get you out of here. It's all arranged.
Me too.
Please.
"Everyone else in the agency could be embedded. Live normal lives. We were human-sized lab rats."
Don't worry. You guys are going to be full-fledged agents.
I've got the perfect place.

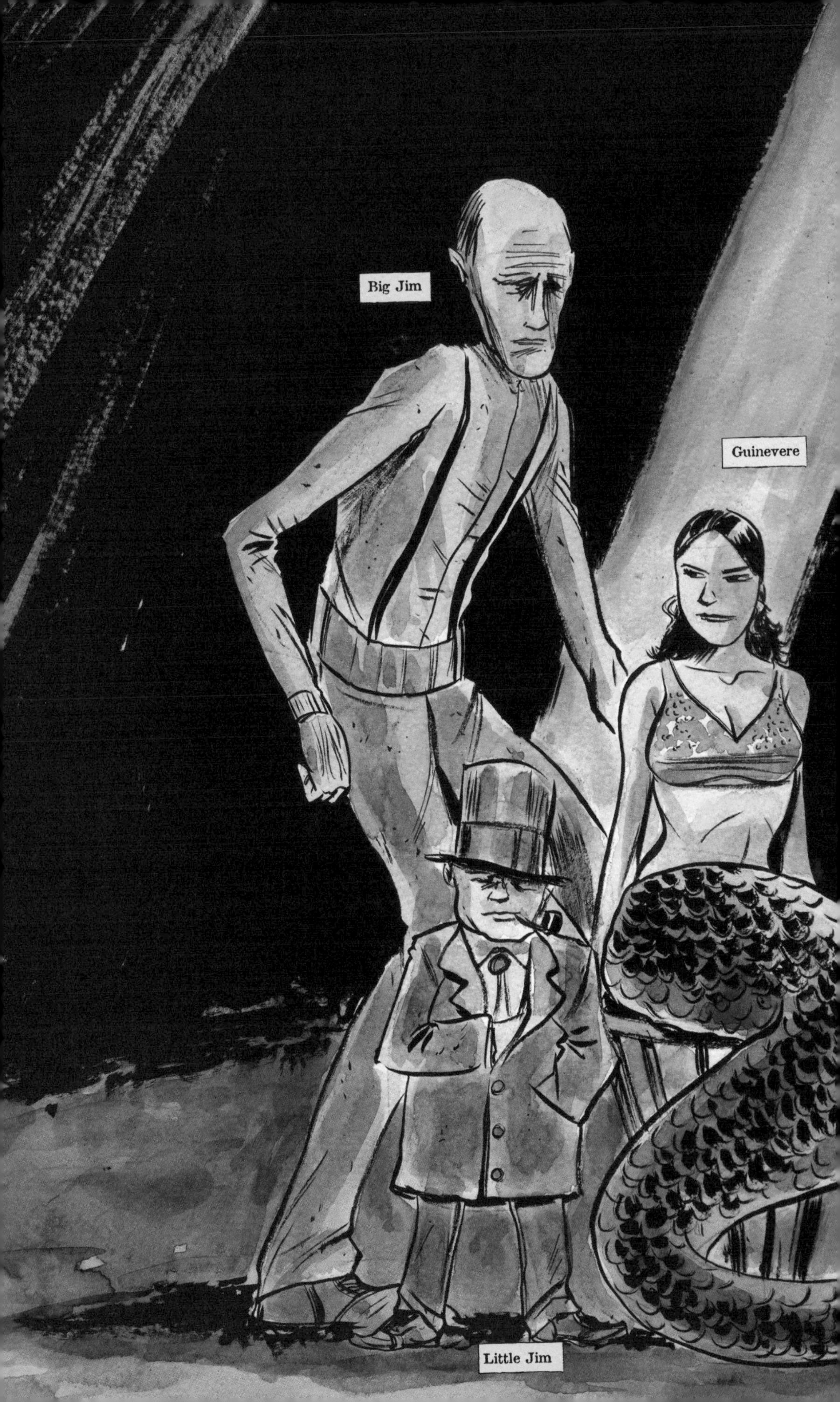
Big Jim
Guinevere
Little Jim

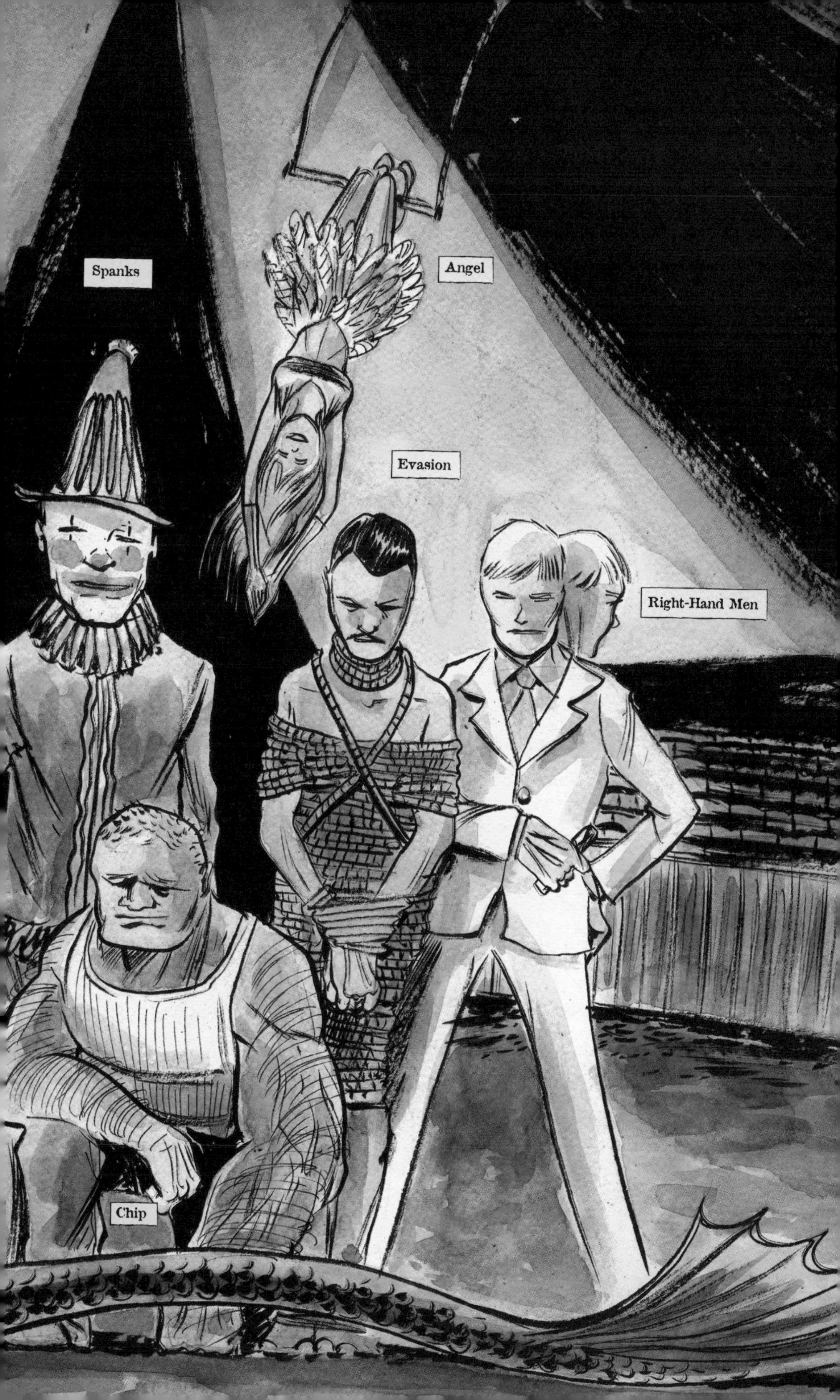
Spanks
Angel
Evasion
Right-Hand Men
Chip

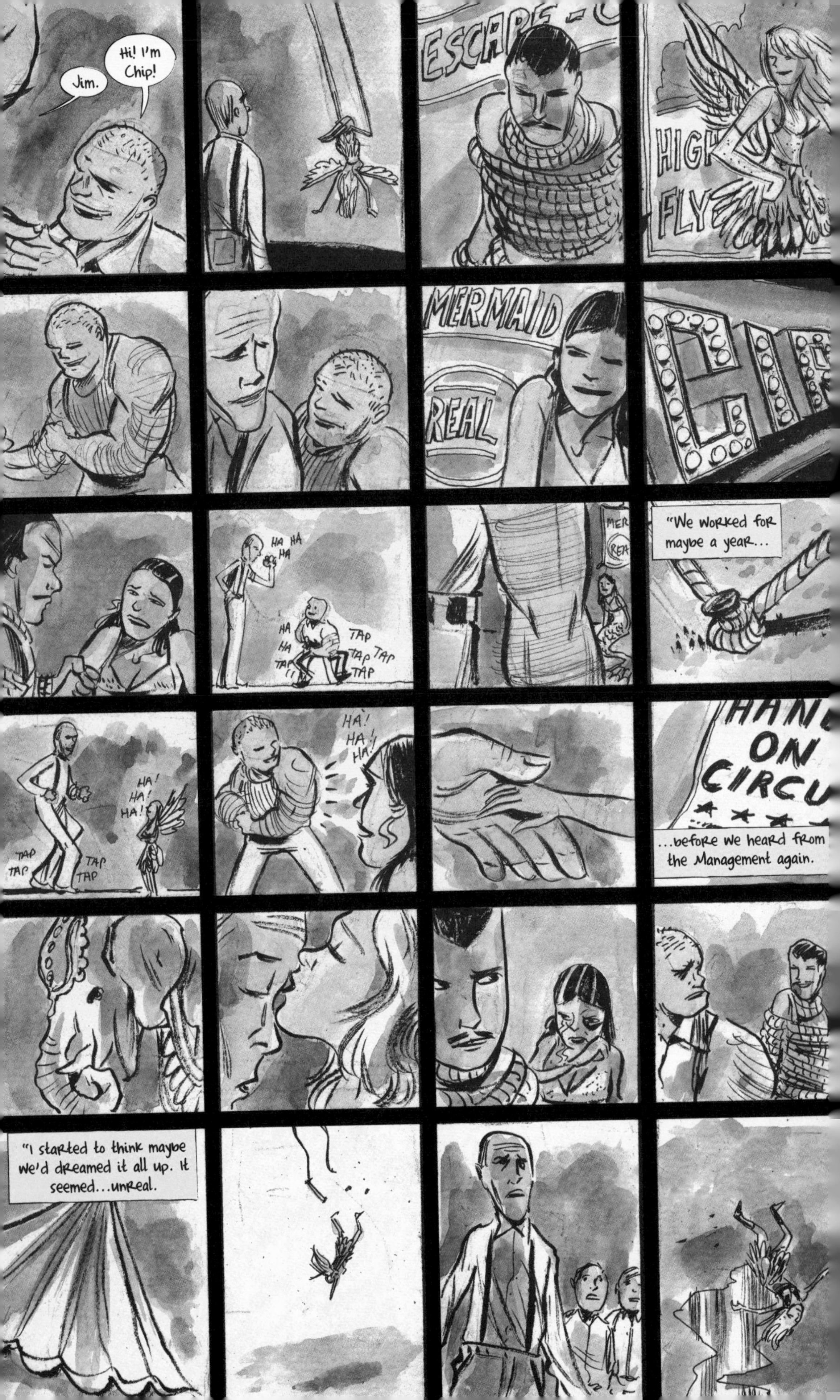

Hi! I'm Chip!
Jim.
ESCAPE
HIGH FLY
MERMAID
REAL
HA HA HA
HA HA TAP
TAP TAP TAP TAP
MER REA
"We worked for maybe a year...
TAP TAP
HA! HA! HA!
TAP TAP
HA! HA! HA!
ON CIRCU
...before we heard from the Management again.
"I started to think maybe we'd dreamed it all up. It seemed...unreal.

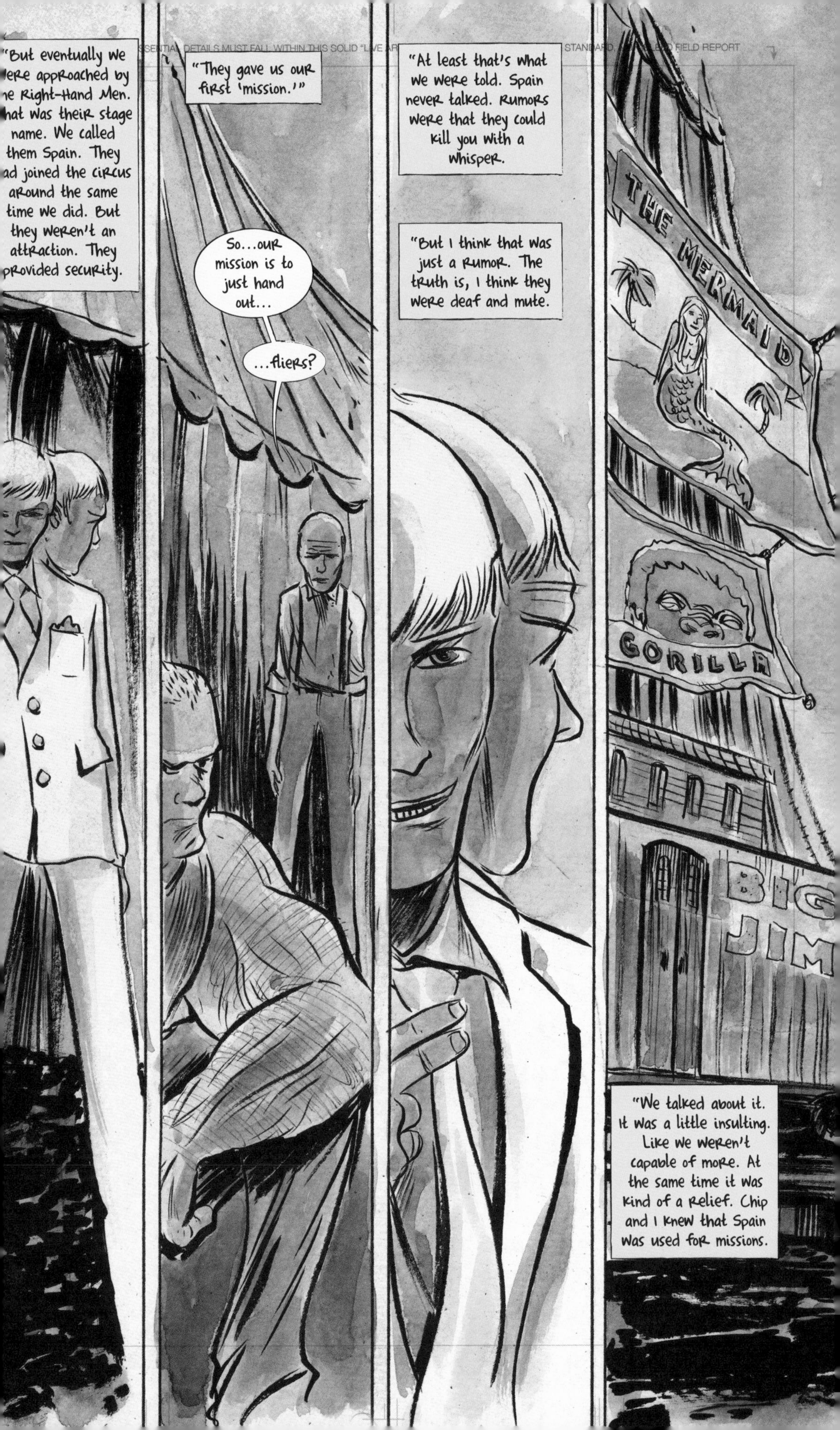
"But eventually we ere approached by ne Right-Hand Men. hat was their stage name. We called them Spain. They ad joined the circus around the same time we did. But they weren't an attraction. They provided security.
"They gave us our first 'mission.'"
So...our mission is to just hand out...
...fliers?
"At least that's what we were told. Spain never talked. Rumors were that they could kill you with a whisper.
"But I think that was just a rumor. The truth is, I think they were deaf and mute.
THE MERMAID
GORILLA
BIG JIM
"We talked about it. It was a little insulting. Like we weren't capable of more. At the same time it was kind of a relief. Chip and I knew that Spain was used for missions.

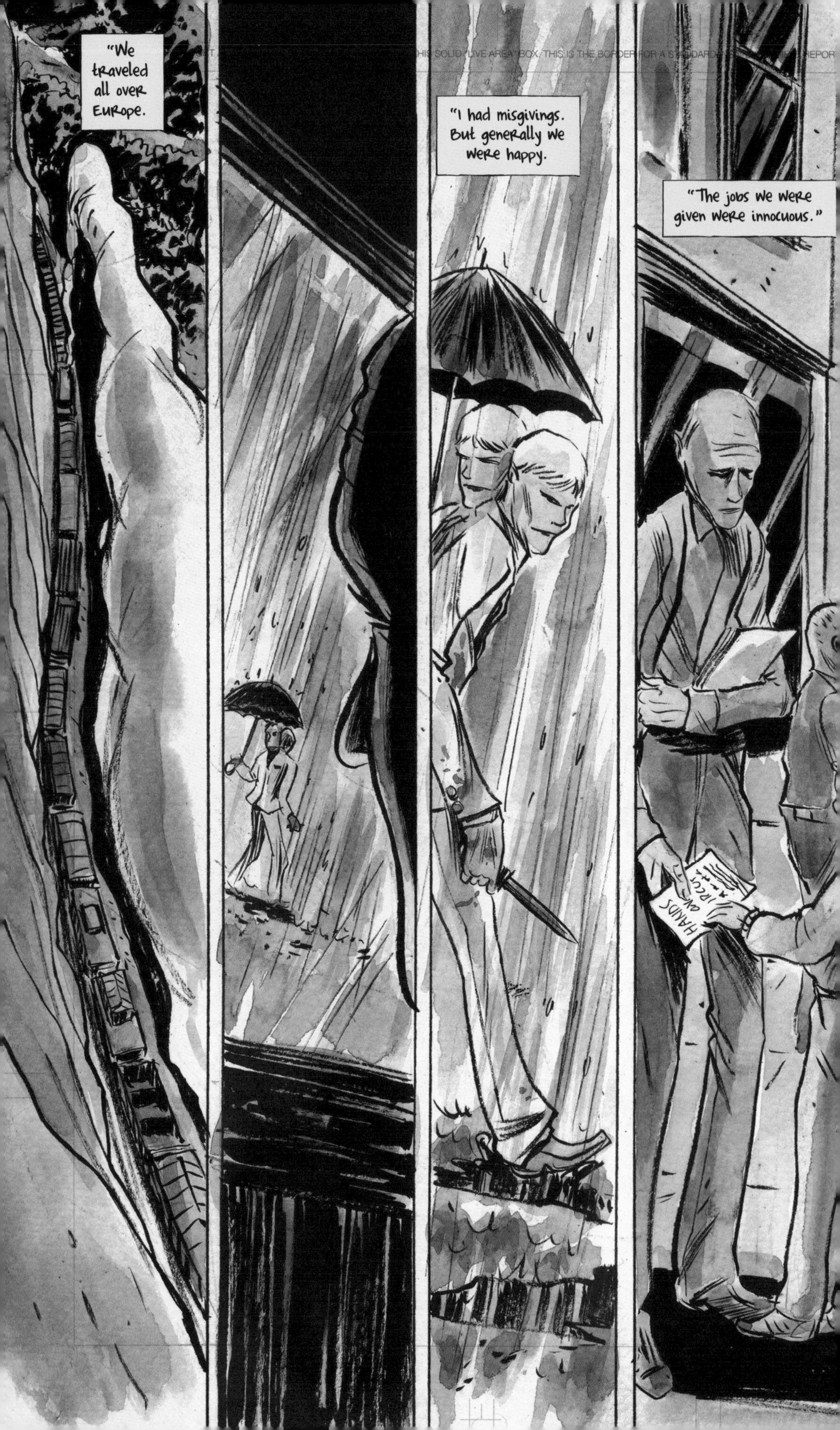
"We traveled all over Europe.
"I had misgivings. But generally we were happy.
"The jobs we were given were innocuous."

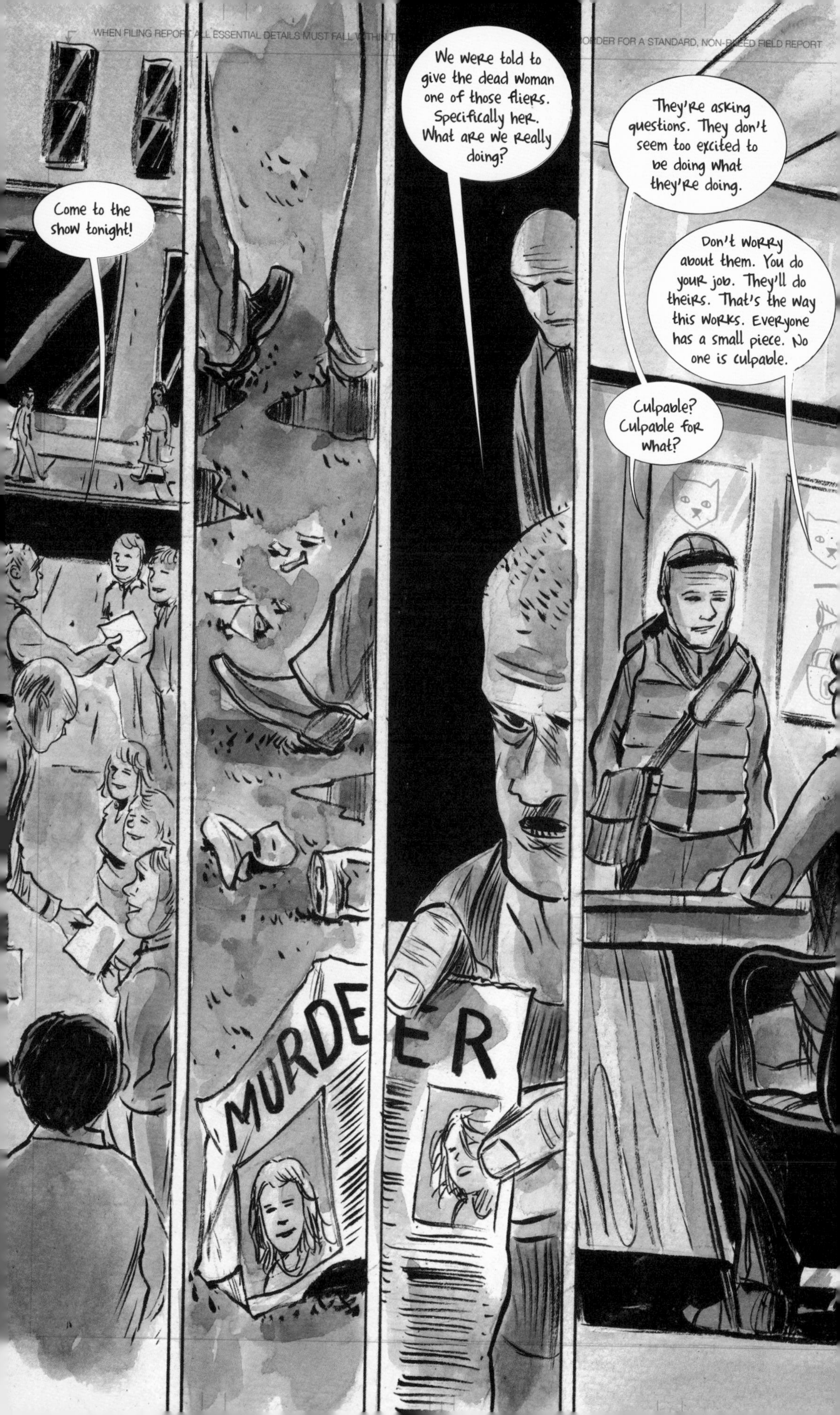
Come to the show tonight!
We were told to give the dead woman one of those fliers. Specifically her. What are we really doing?
MURDE
ER
They're asking questions. They don't seem too excited to be doing what they're doing.
Don't worry about them. You do your job. They'll do theirs. That's the way this works. Everyone has a small piece. No one is culpable.
Culpable? Culpable for what?

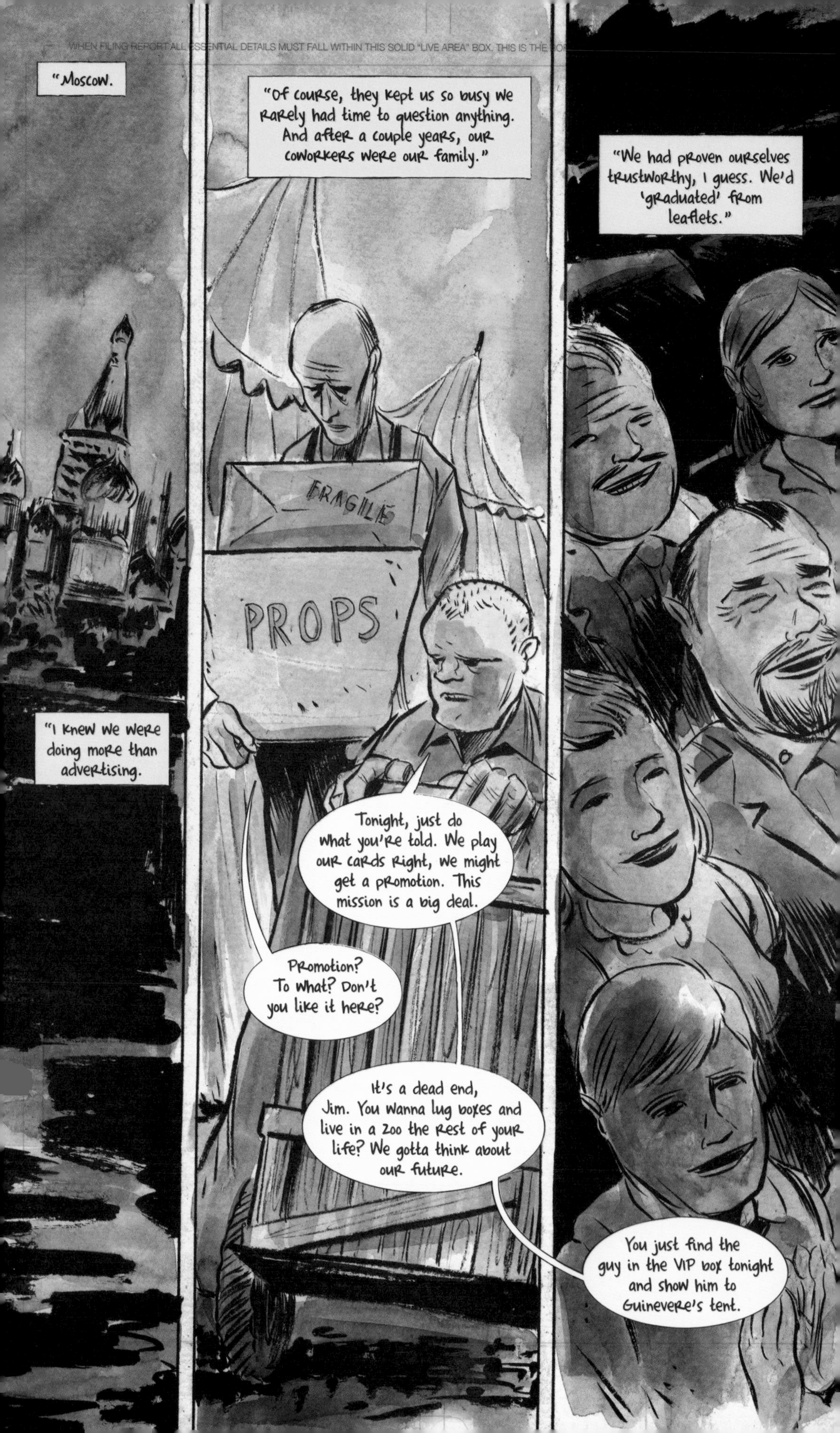
WHEN FILING REPORT ALL ESSENTIAL DETAILS MUST FALL WITHIN THIS SOLID "LIVE AREA" BOX. THIS IS THE
"Moscow.
"I knew we were doing more than advertising.
"Of course, they kept us so busy we rarely had time to question anything. And after a couple years, our coworkers were our family."
FRAGILE
PROPS
Tonight, just do what you're told. We play our cards right, we might get a promotion. This mission is a big deal.
Promotion? To what? Don't you like it here?
It's a dead end, Jim. You wanna lug boxes and live in a zoo the rest of your life? We gotta think about our future.
"We had proven ourselves trustworthy, I guess. We'd 'graduated' from leaflets."
You just find the guy in the VIP box tonight and show him to Guinevere's tent.

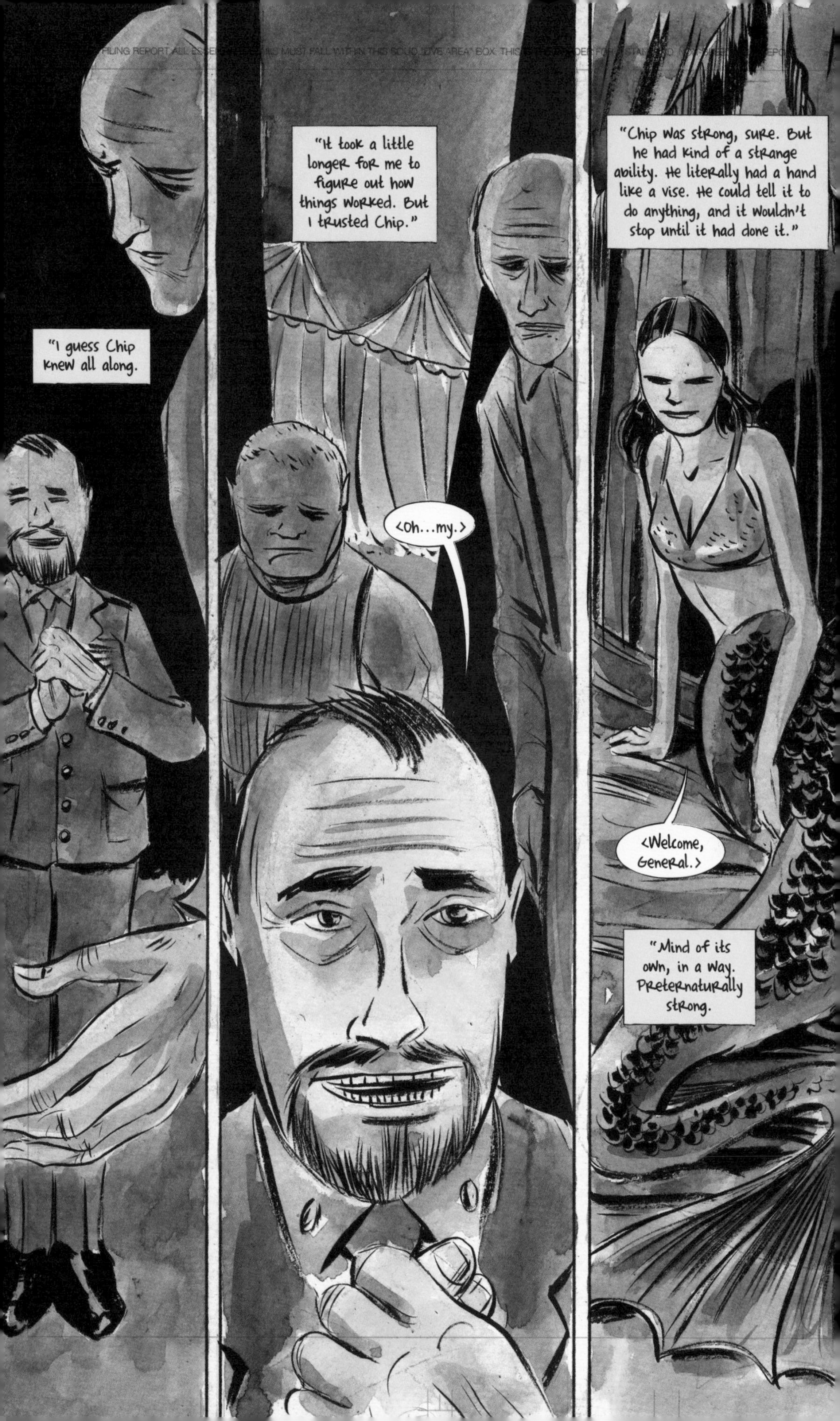
"I guess Chip knew all along.
"It took a little longer for me to figure out how things worked. But I trusted Chip."
<Oh...my.>
"Chip was strong, sure. But he had kind of a strange ability. He literally had a hand like a vise. He could tell it to do anything, and it wouldn't stop until it had done it."
<Welcome, General.>
"Mind of its own, in a way. Preternaturally strong.

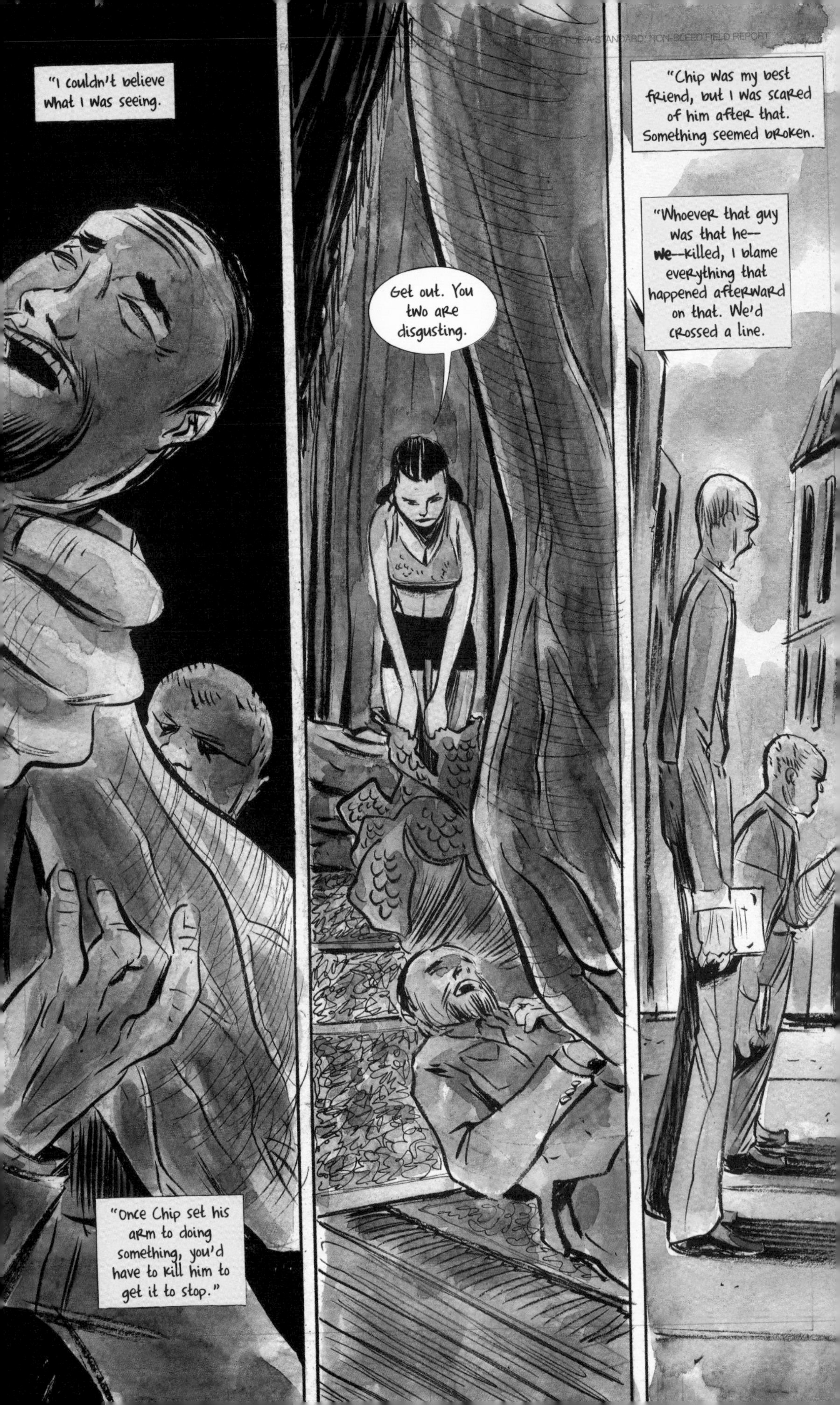
"I couldn't believe what I was seeing.
"Once Chip set his arm to doing something, you'd have to kill him to get it to stop."
Get out. You two are disgusting.
"Chip was my best friend, but I was scared of him after that. Something seemed broken.
"Whoever that guy was that he— ~~we~~—killed, I blame everything that happened afterward on that. We'd crossed a line.

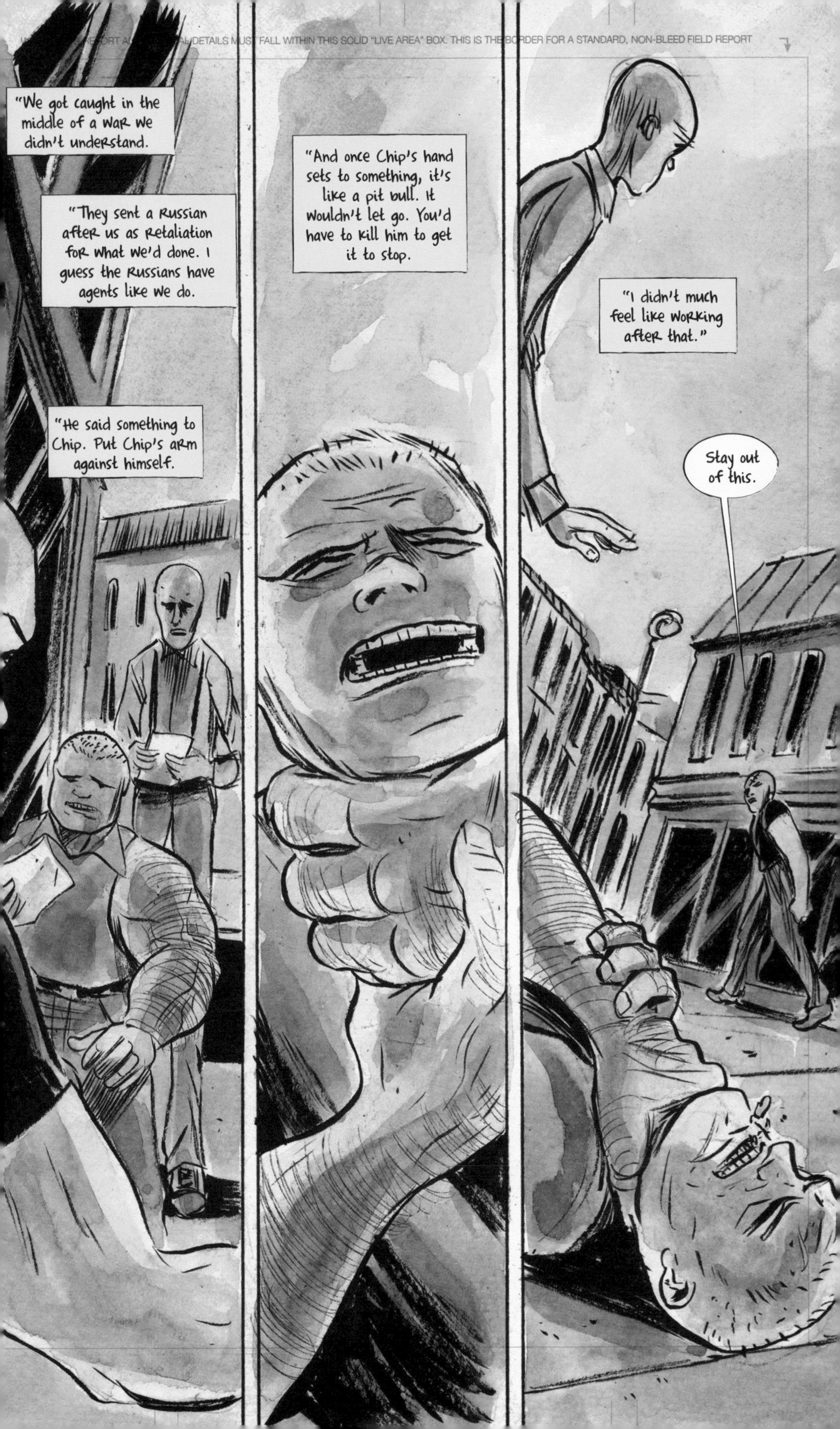
REPORT ALL ... DETAILS MUST FALL WITHIN THIS SOLID "LIVE AREA" BOX. THIS IS THE BORDER FOR A STANDARD, NON-BLEED FIELD REPORT
"We got caught in the middle of a war we didn't understand.
"They sent a Russian after us as retaliation for what we'd done. I guess the Russians have agents like we do.
"He said something to Chip. Put Chip's arm against himself.
"And once Chip's hand sets to something, it's like a pit bull. It wouldn't let go. You'd have to kill him to get it to stop.
"I didn't much feel like working after that."
Stay out of this.

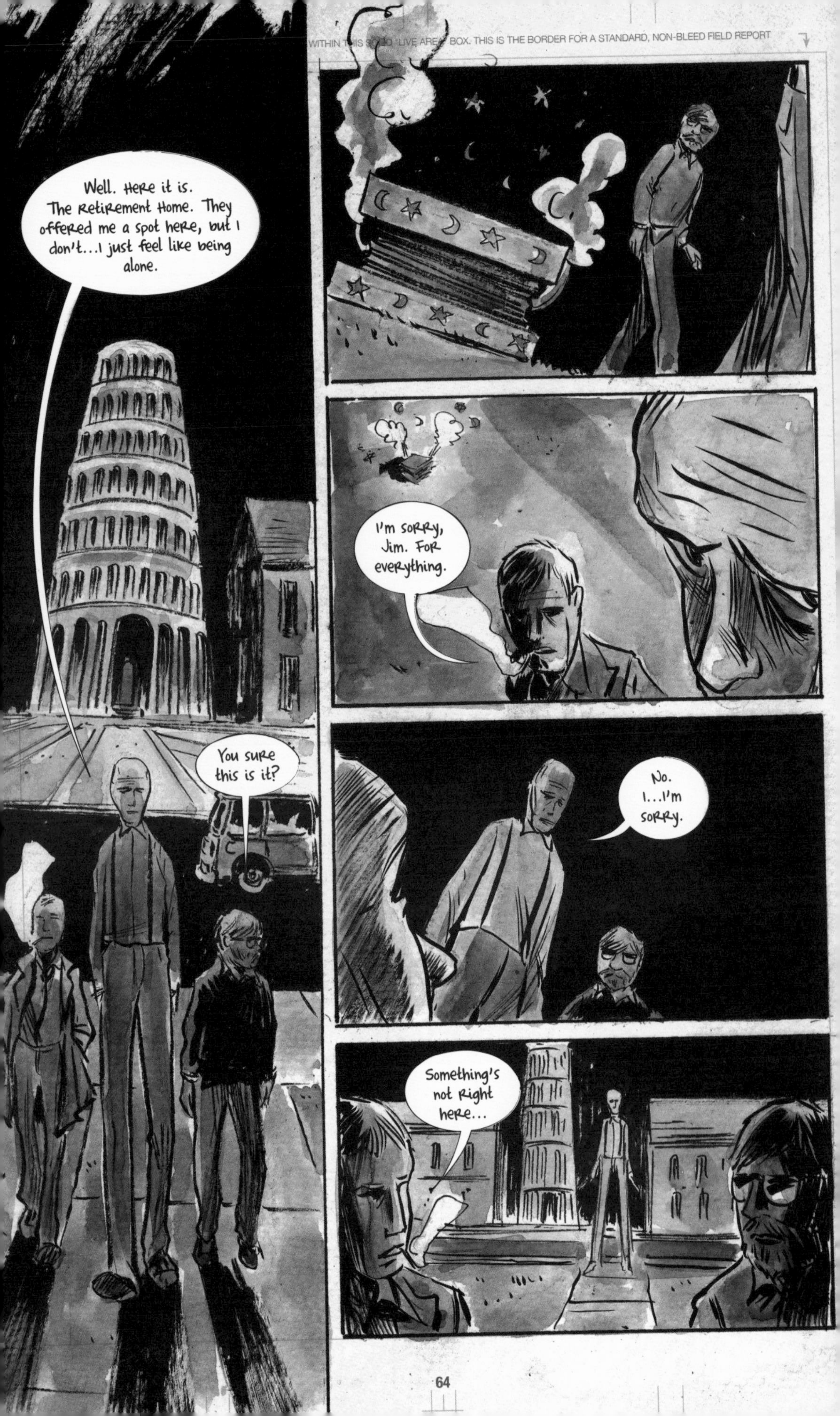

WITHIN THIS SOLID "LIVE AREA" BOX. THIS IS THE BORDER FOR A STANDARD, NON-BLEED FIELD REPORT
Well. Here it is. The Retirement Home. They offered me a spot here, but I don't...I just feel like being alone.
You sure this is it?
I'm sorry, Jim. For everything.
No. I...I'm sorry.
Something's not right here...

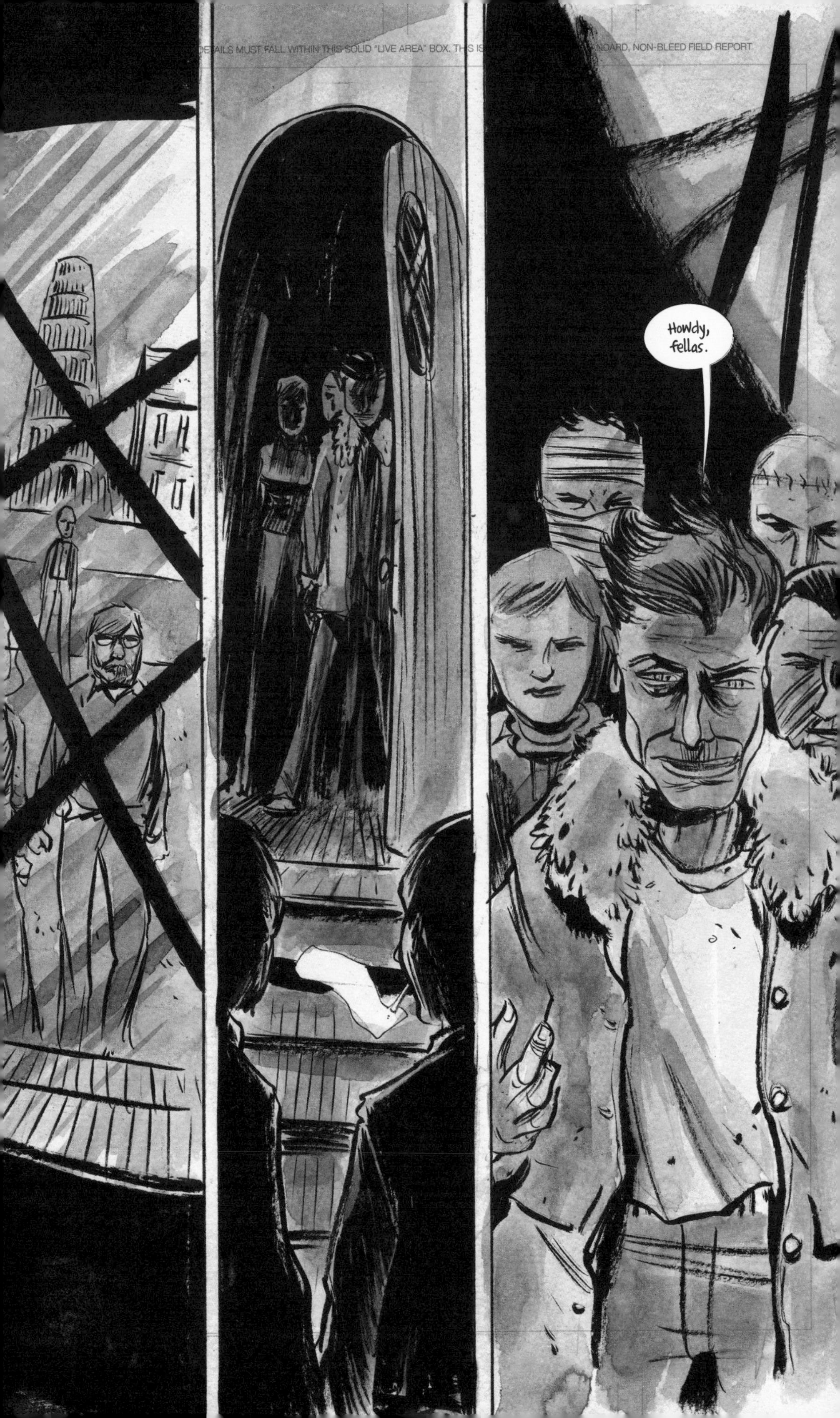
Howdy, fellas.

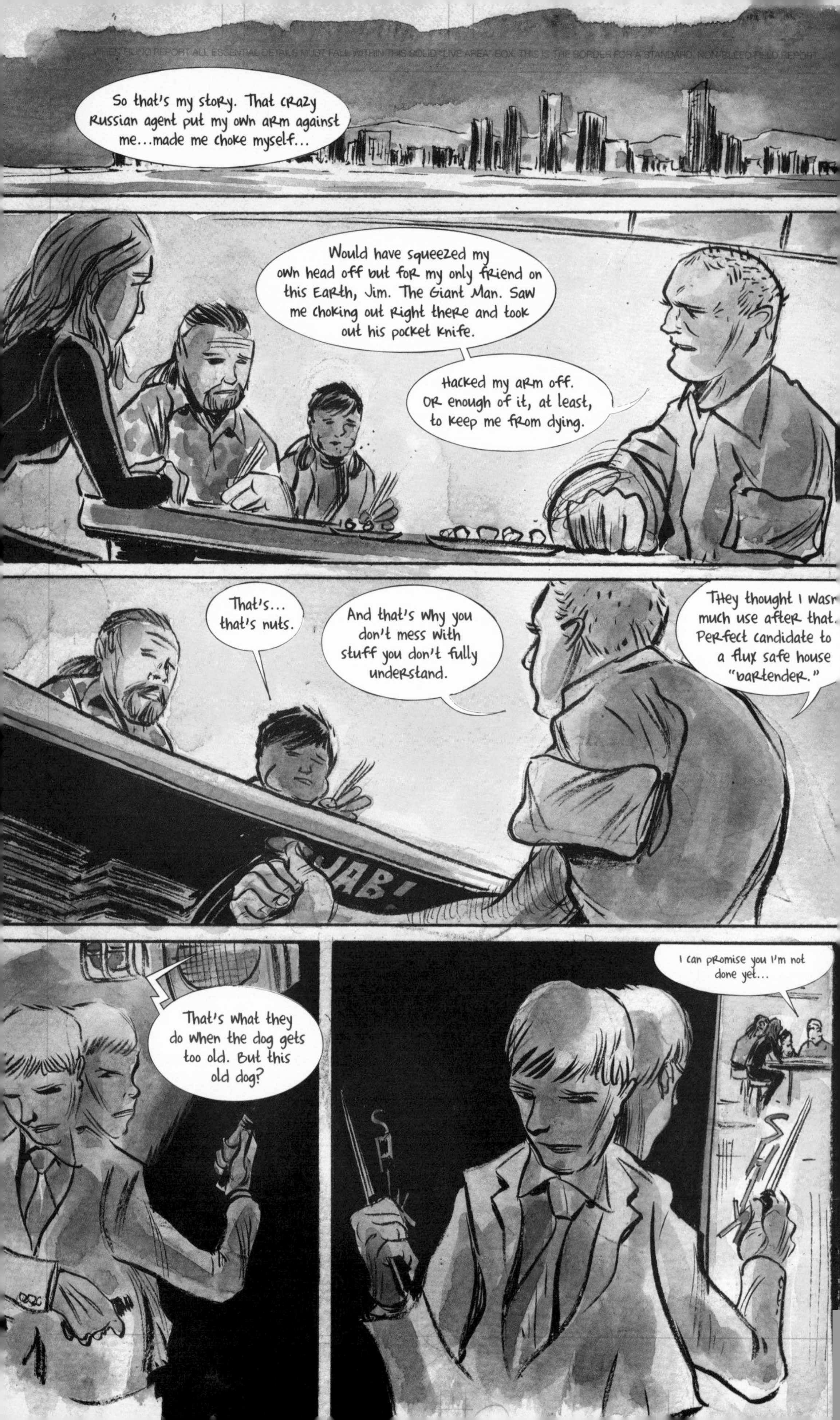
WHEN FILING REPORT ALL ESSENTIAL DETAILS MUST FALL WITHIN THIS SOLID "LIVE AREA" BOX. THIS IS THE BORDER FOR A STANDARD, NON-BLEED FIELD REPORT.
So that's my story. That crazy Russian agent put my own arm against me...made me choke myself...
Would have squeezed my own head off but for my only friend on this Earth, Jim. The Giant Man. Saw me choking out right there and took out his pocket knife.
Hacked my arm off. Or enough of it, at least, to keep me from dying.
That's... that's nuts.
And that's why you don't mess with stuff you don't fully understand.
They thought I wasn much use after that. Perfect candidate to a flux safe house "bartender."
JAB!
That's what they do when the dog gets too old. But this old dog?
I can promise you I'm not done yet...

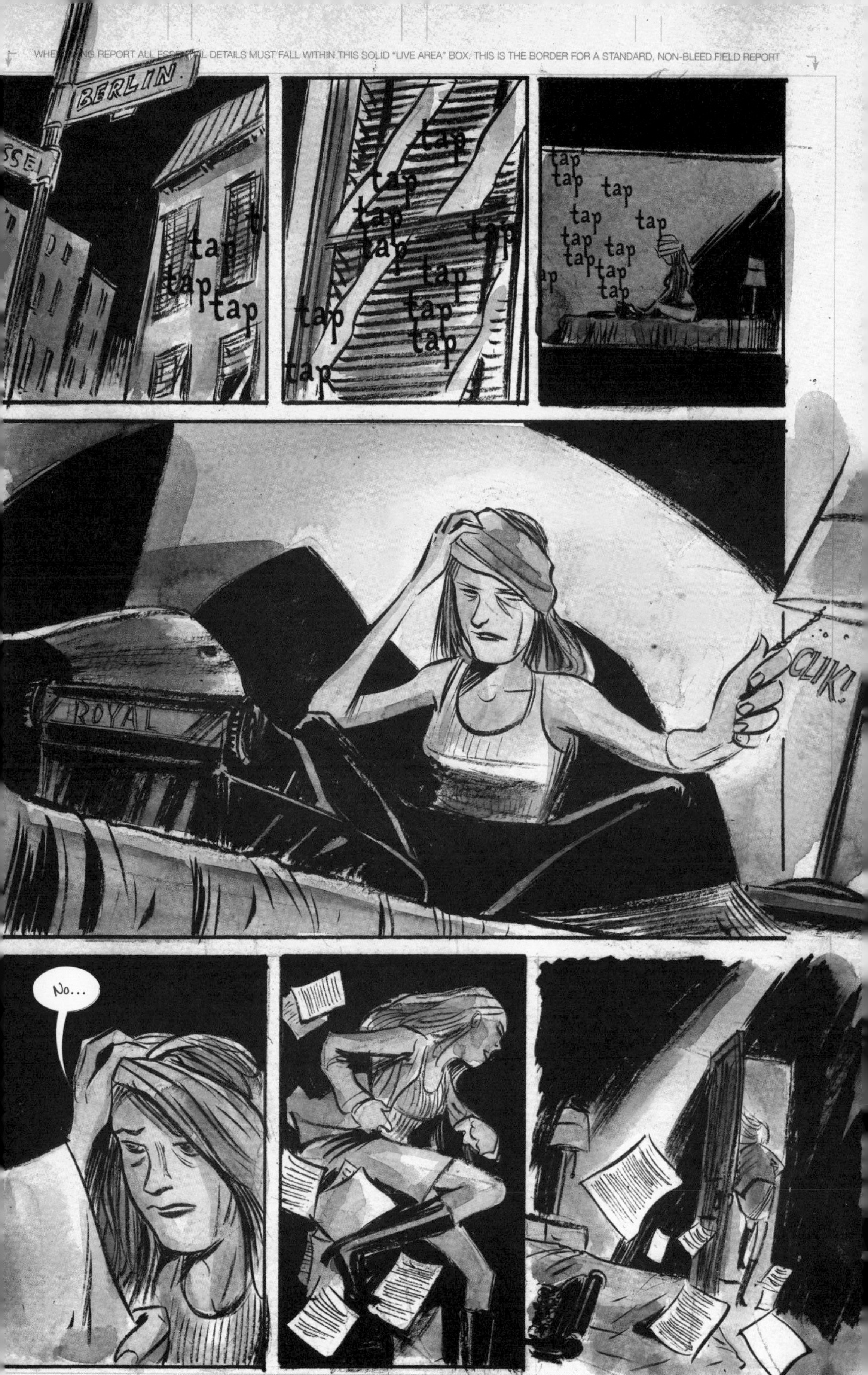
WHE NG REPORT ALL ESSE L DETAILS MUST FALL WITHIN THIS SOLID "LIVE AREA" BOX. THIS IS THE BORDER FOR A STANDARD, NON-BLEED FIELD REPORT
BERLIN
tap tap tap
tap tap tap tap tap tap tap tap tap tap
tap tap tap tap tap tap tap tap tap tap
ROYAL
CLIK!
No...

Meru, Dusty, Bill...talking to CHIP...we'll realize here that Chip is the big-armed guy from the Giant Man's story... Chip is recapping what JIM just told Duncan and Lyme...but we see that Chip has his hand on a button under the counter...

CHIP: Would have squeezed my own head off but for my only friend on this Earth, Jim. The Giant Man. Saw me choking out right there and took out his pocket knife. Hacked my arm off. Or enough of it, at least, to keep me from dying.

Chip continues to talk and Meru and the gang react to this crazy story...Chip presses the button under the counter.

DUSTY: That's...that's nuts.

CHIP: Yeah, well. Not really much use as an agent now. Perfect candidate to be a flux safe house "bartender."

Cut to a private room – a creepy looking back room in the bar – with curtains and candles. And the Siamese twins...! They're enjoying a coffee. We can see a red light by the door...it's off.

CHIP: That's what they do when the dog gets too old...too useless to do anything else. Better than being taken out back and shot, I guess.

The twins sip their coffee and they see the red light go on...

The twins stand up and put their jacket on...

Est. shot of Berlin. A small hotel room....we see a dark room and hear typing from the window...

Perrier as she sits with eyes closed typing...she's in the dark. Just SFX of typing.

Perrier's fingers typing...

Perrier stops typing...and turns on a lamp...

Perrier looks at the paper out of her typewriter.

PERRIER: No...

Perrier runs to the door and leaves...dropping the paper from her typewriter...

Two men carrying a body by hands and feet.

They swing the body up and into a trash bin.

CU of a dead Dusty in the trash bin.

Another man drags a body to a manhole in an alleyway.

The man drops the body into the manhole...

The body splashes into the sewer below.

CU of Lyme – dead.

LINKS: Let's go.

IMMORTAL: Where now?

LINKS: The Retirement Home.

T[...]
in [...]

DU[...]
from [...]
fight [...]

DUNCA[...]
me dow[...]

Lyme an[...]

LYME: Un[...]

Lyme and [...]

DUNCAN: ...[...]

Lyme and Du[...]

DUNCAN: Any[...]

DUNCAN: Uninte[...]ut me thinking. About...I don't know.
people are living ruined lives and wondering why? consequences. How many other agents are out there? How many

The door begins to open.

JIM standing in the doorway looming over Lyme and Duncan at the door.

JIM: Duncan. Lyme. Jewel called. Told me to expect you.

JIM: Come in.

L and D sitting in JIM's living room – in large furniture.

DUNCAN: Sorry to bother you, Jim.

WHEN FILING REPORT ALL ESSENTIAL DETAILS MUST FALL WITHIN THIS SOLID "LIVE AREA" BOX. THIS IS THE BORDER FOR A STANDARD, NON-BLEED FIELD REPORT

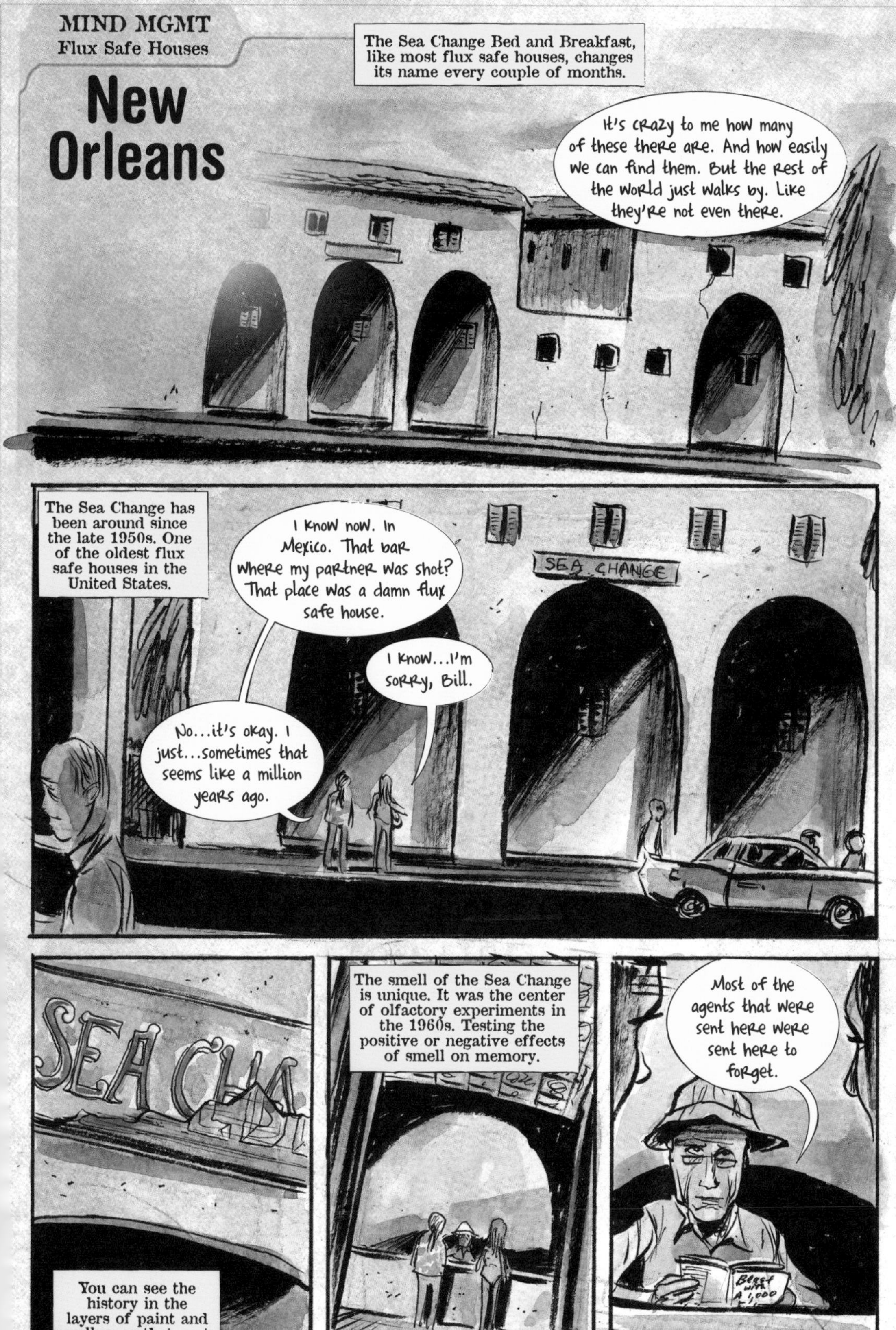
MIND MGMT
Flux Safe Houses
New Orleans
The Sea Change Bed and Breakfast, like most flux safe houses, changes its name every couple of months.
It's crazy to me how many of these there are. And how easily we can find them. But the rest of the world just walks by. Like they're not even there.
The Sea Change has been around since the late 1950s. One of the oldest flux safe houses in the United States.
SEA CHANGE
I know now. In Mexico. That bar where my partner was shot? That place was a damn flux safe house.
I know...I'm sorry, Bill.
No...it's okay. I just...sometimes that seems like a million years ago.
SEA CHA
You can see the history in the layers of paint and wallpaper that coat the place.
The smell of the Sea Change is unique. It was the center of olfactory experiments in the 1960s. Testing the positive or negative effects of smell on memory.
Most of the agents that were sent here were sent here to forget.

WHEN FILING REPORT ALL ESSENTIAL DETAILS MUST FALL WITHIN THIS SOLID "LIVE AREA" BOX. THIS IS THE BORDER FOR A STANDARD, NON-BLEED FIELD REPORT

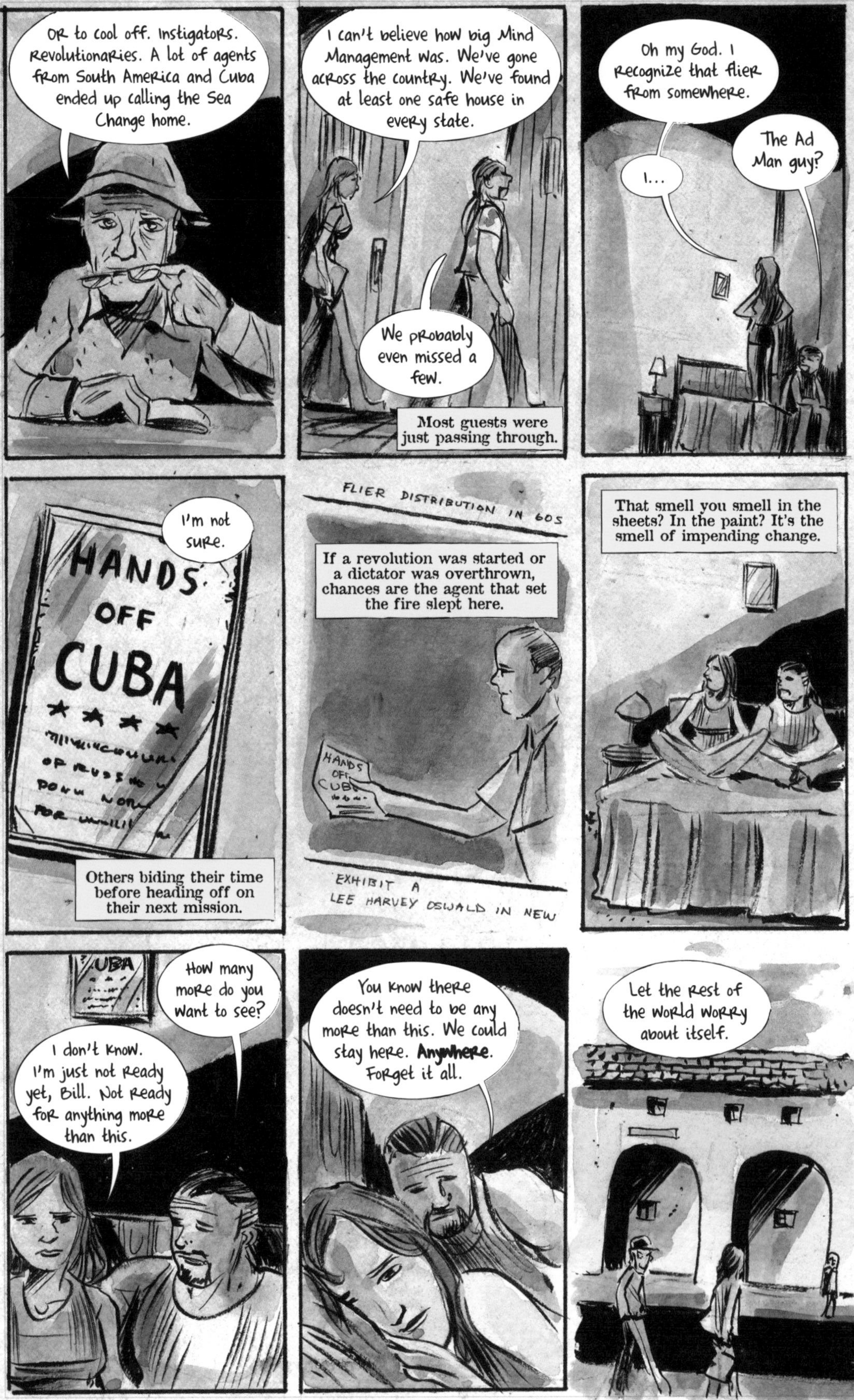

Or to cool off. Instigators. Revolutionaries. A lot of agents from South America and Cuba ended up calling the Sea Change home.
I can't believe how big Mind Management was. We've gone across the country. We've found at least one safe house in every state.
We probably even missed a few.
Most guests were just passing through.
Oh my God. I recognize that flier from somewhere.
I...
The Ad Man guy?
HANDS OFF CUBA
I'm not sure.
Others biding their time before heading off on their next mission.
FLIER DISTRIBUTION IN 60S
If a revolution was started or a dictator was overthrown, chances are the agent that set the fire slept here.
EXHIBIT A
LEE HARVEY OSWALD IN NEW
That smell you smell in the sheets? In the paint? It's the smell of impending change.
How many more do you want to see?
I don't know. I'm just not ready yet, Bill. Not ready for anything more than this.
You know there doesn't need to be any more than this. We could stay here. **Anywhere**. Forget it all.
Let the rest of the world worry about itself.

End Mind Mem

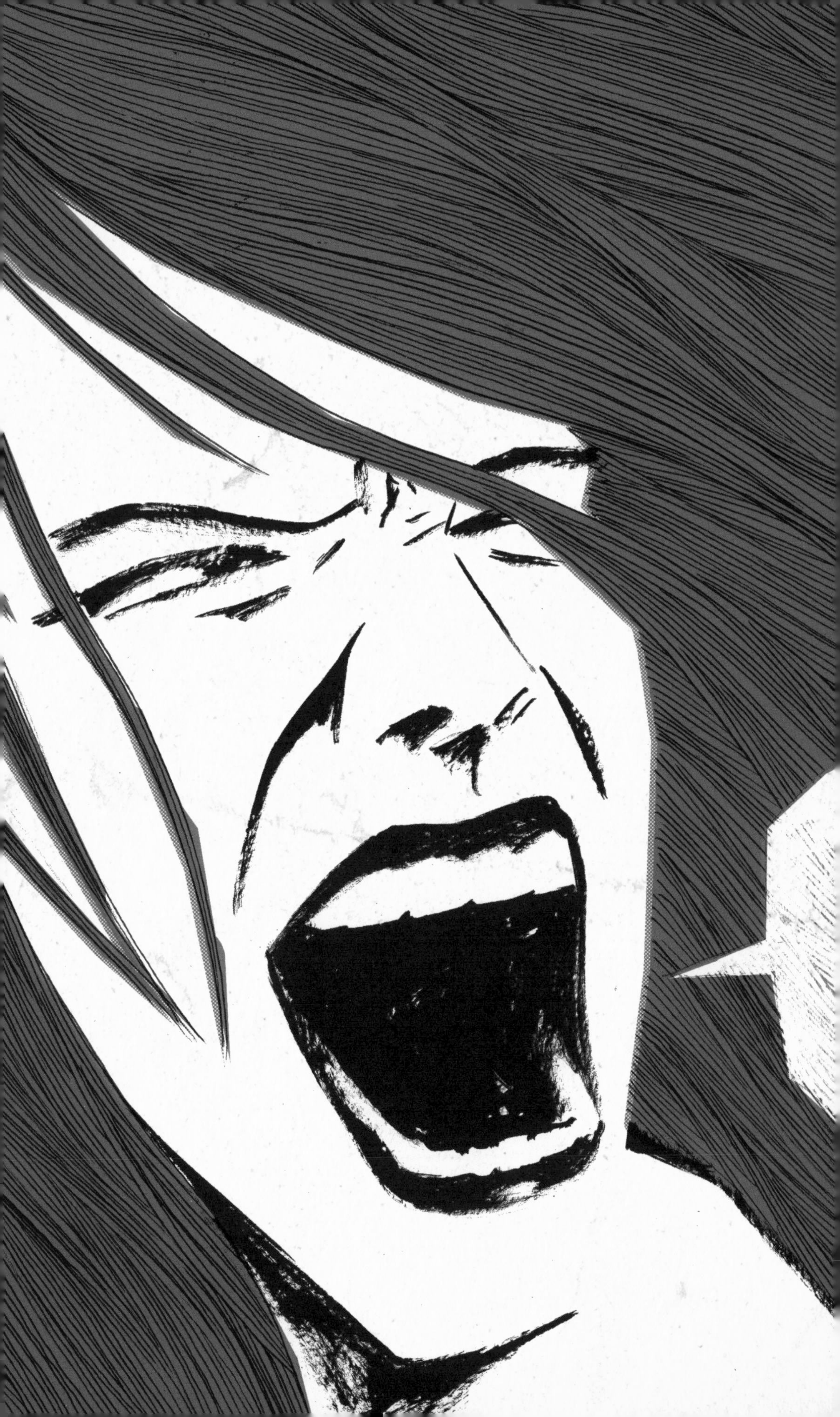

21

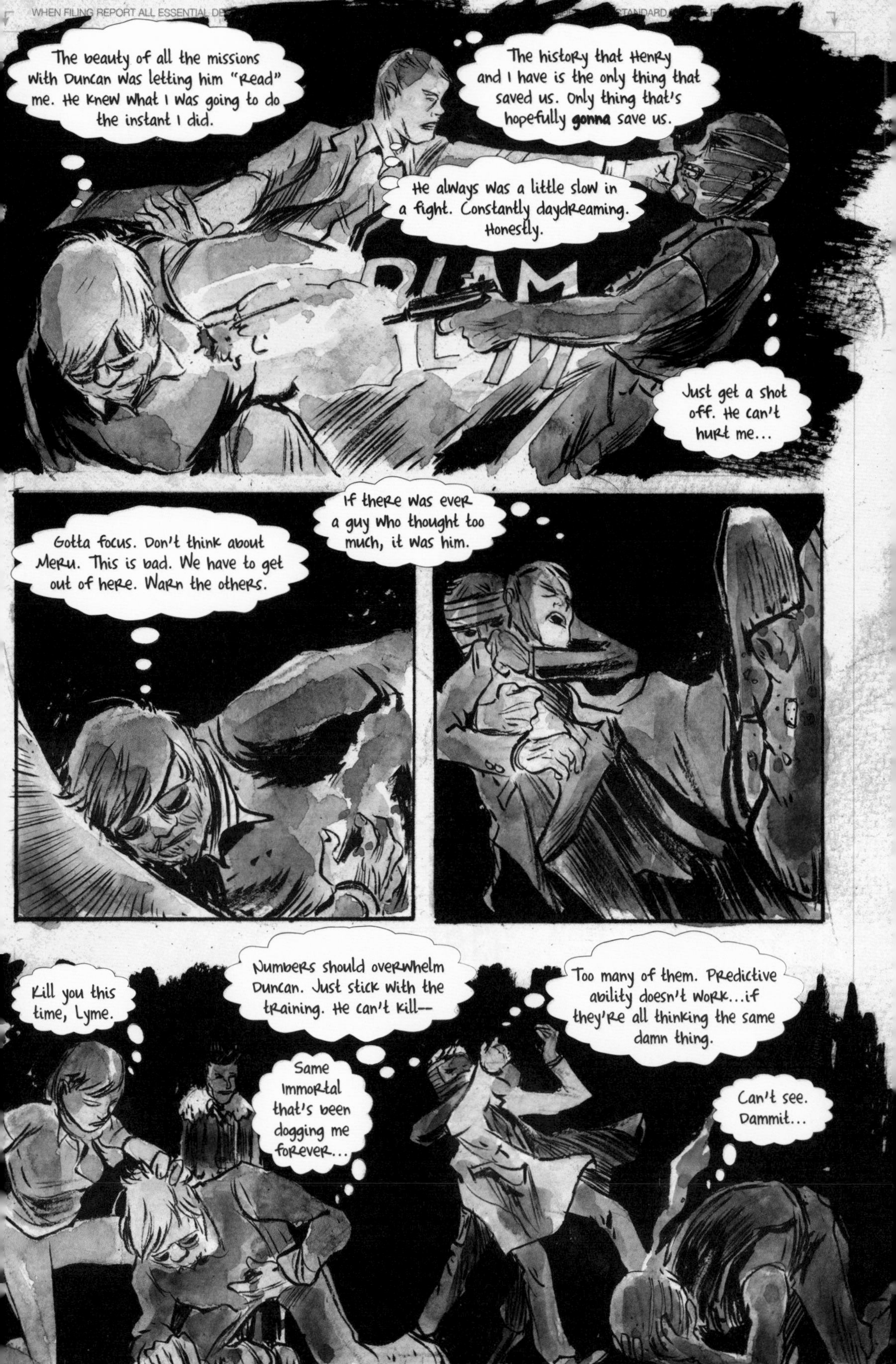

The beauty of all the missions with Duncan was letting him "read" me. He knew what I was going to do the instant I did.
The history that Henry and I have is the only thing that saved us. Only thing that's hopefully gonna save us.
He always was a little slow in a fight. Constantly daydreaming. Honestly.
Just get a shot off. He can't hurt me...
Gotta focus. Don't think about Meru. This is bad. We have to get out of here. Warn the others.
If there was ever a guy who thought too much, it was him.
Kill you this time, Lyme.
Numbers should overwhelm Duncan. Just stick with the training. He can't kill—
Same Immortal that's been dogging me forever...
Too many of them. Predictive ability doesn't work...if they're all thinking the same damn thing.
Can't see. Dammit...

Perrier Automatic Writing Session 211131 Lyme is becoming self-destructive. More of a hindrance to missions than an addition to them. Duncan is ignoring it.

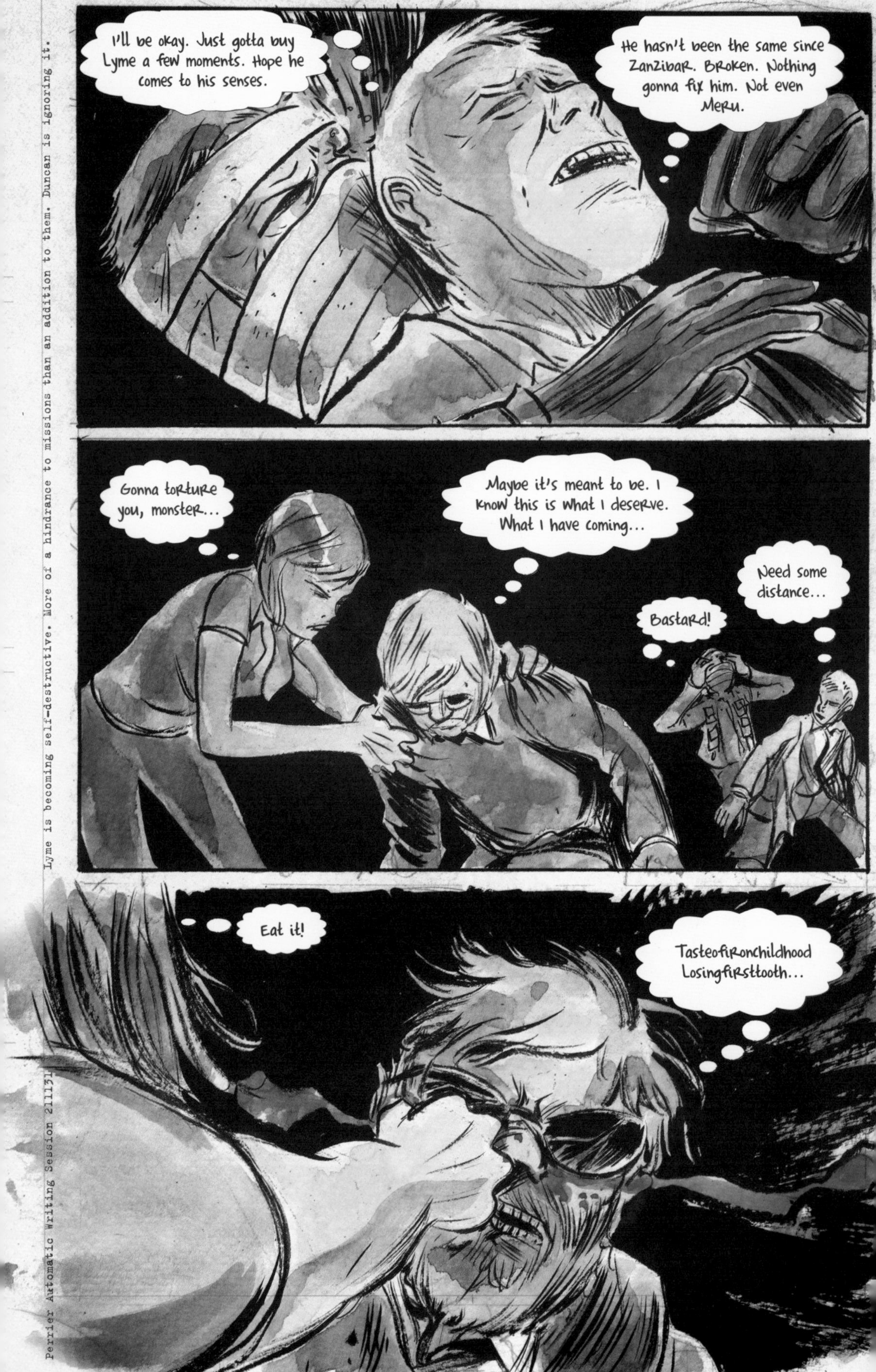
I'll be okay. Just gotta buy Lyme a few moments. Hope he comes to his senses.
He hasn't been the same since Zanzibar. Broken. Nothing gonna fix him. Not even Meru.
Gonna torture you, monster...
Maybe it's meant to be. I know this is what I deserve. What I have coming...
Need some distance...
Bastard!
Eat it!
Tasteofironchildhood Losingfirsttooth...

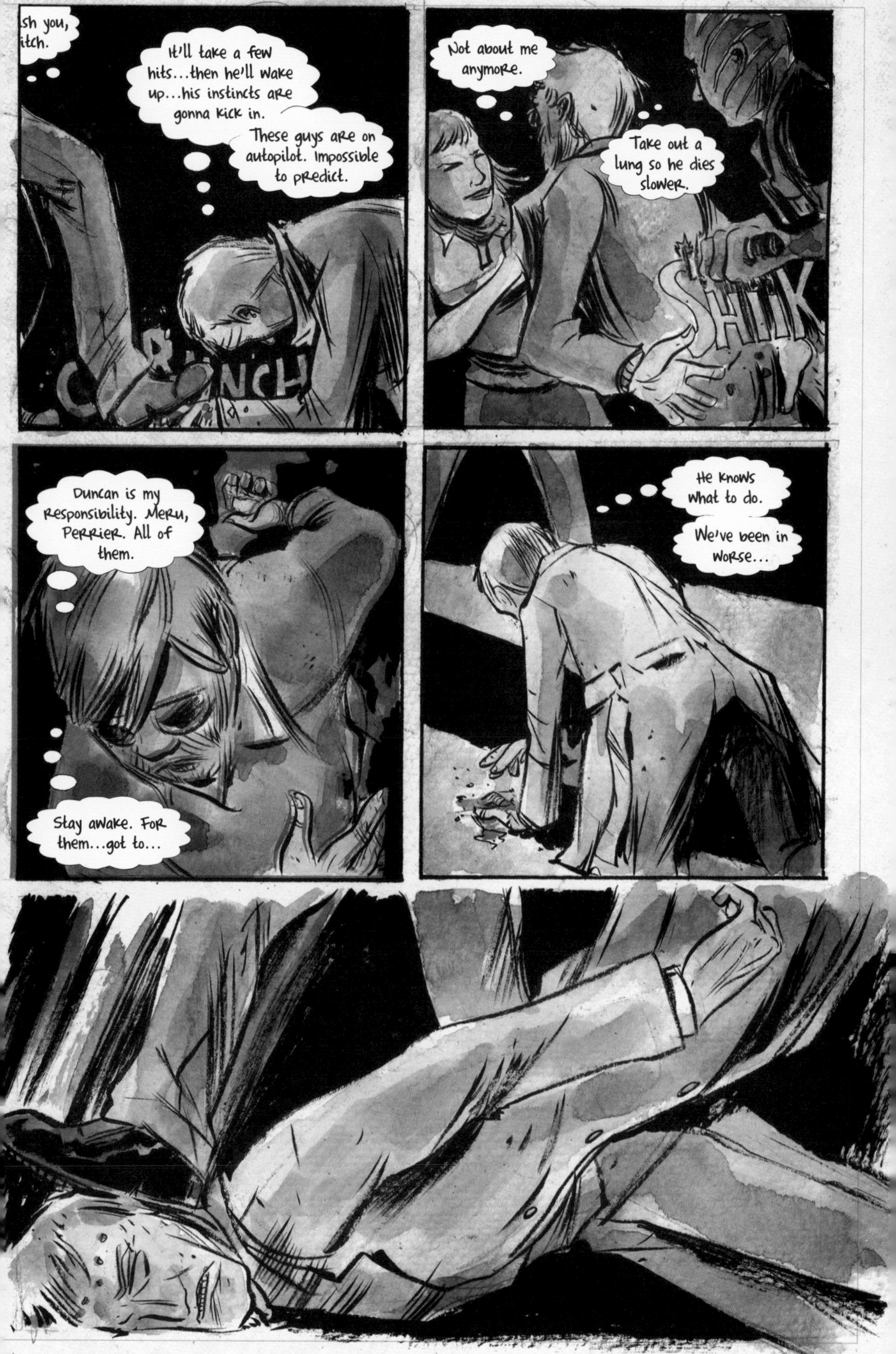
sh you,
itch.
It'll take a few hits...then he'll wake up...his instincts are gonna kick in.
These guys are on autopilot. Impossible to predict.
CRUNCH
Not about me anymore.
Take out a lung so he dies slower.
SHiiK
Duncan is my responsibility. Meru, Perrier. All of them.
Stay awake. For them...got to...
He knows what to do.
We've been in worse...

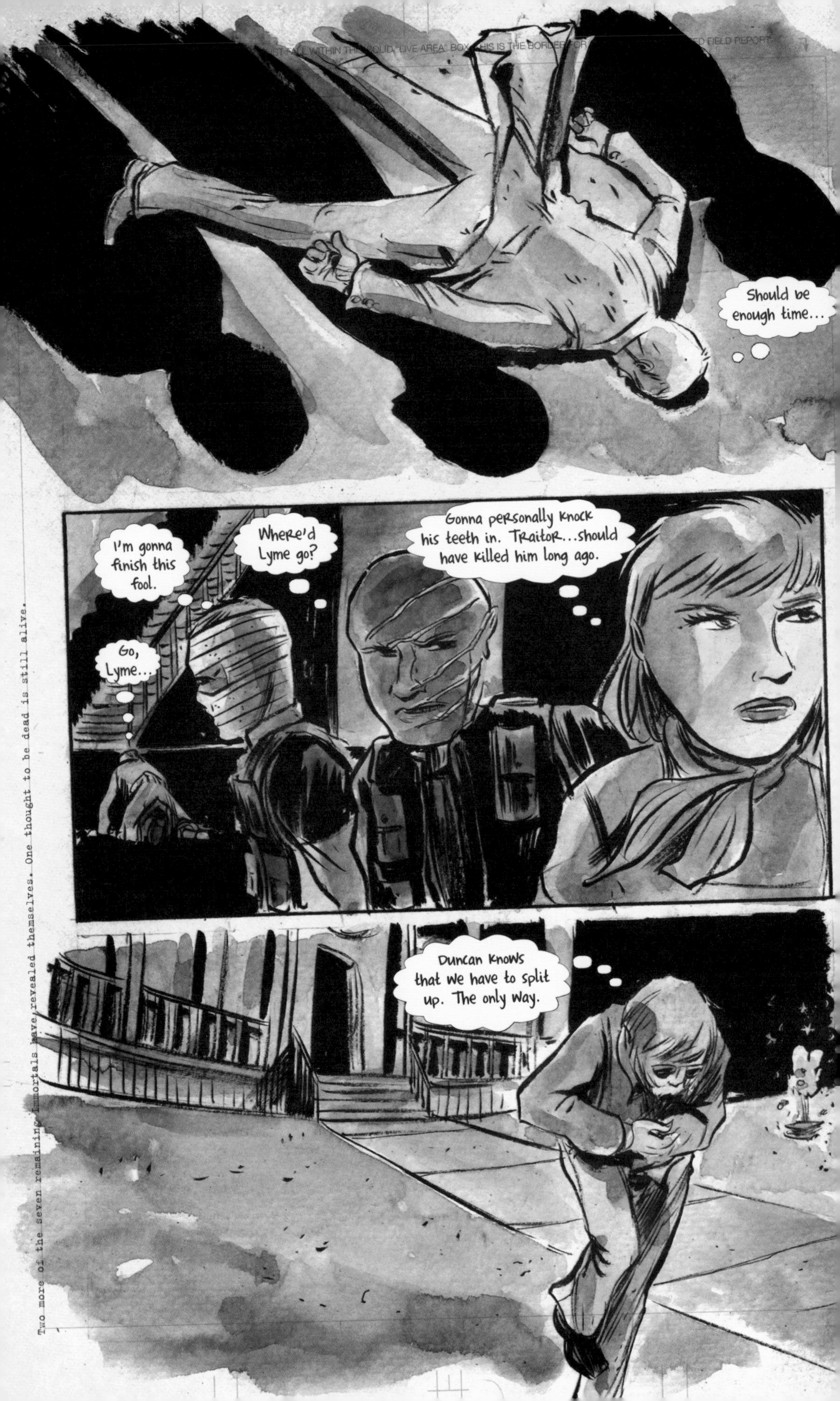
Should be enough time...
I'm gonna finish this fool.
Where'd Lyme go?
Gonna personally knock his teeth in. Traitor...should have killed him long ago.
Go, Lyme...
Duncan knows that we have to split up. The only way.

Two more of the seven remaining immortals have revealed themselves. One thought to be dead is still alive.

...he's not focused. He's heading into an even more dangerous trap.

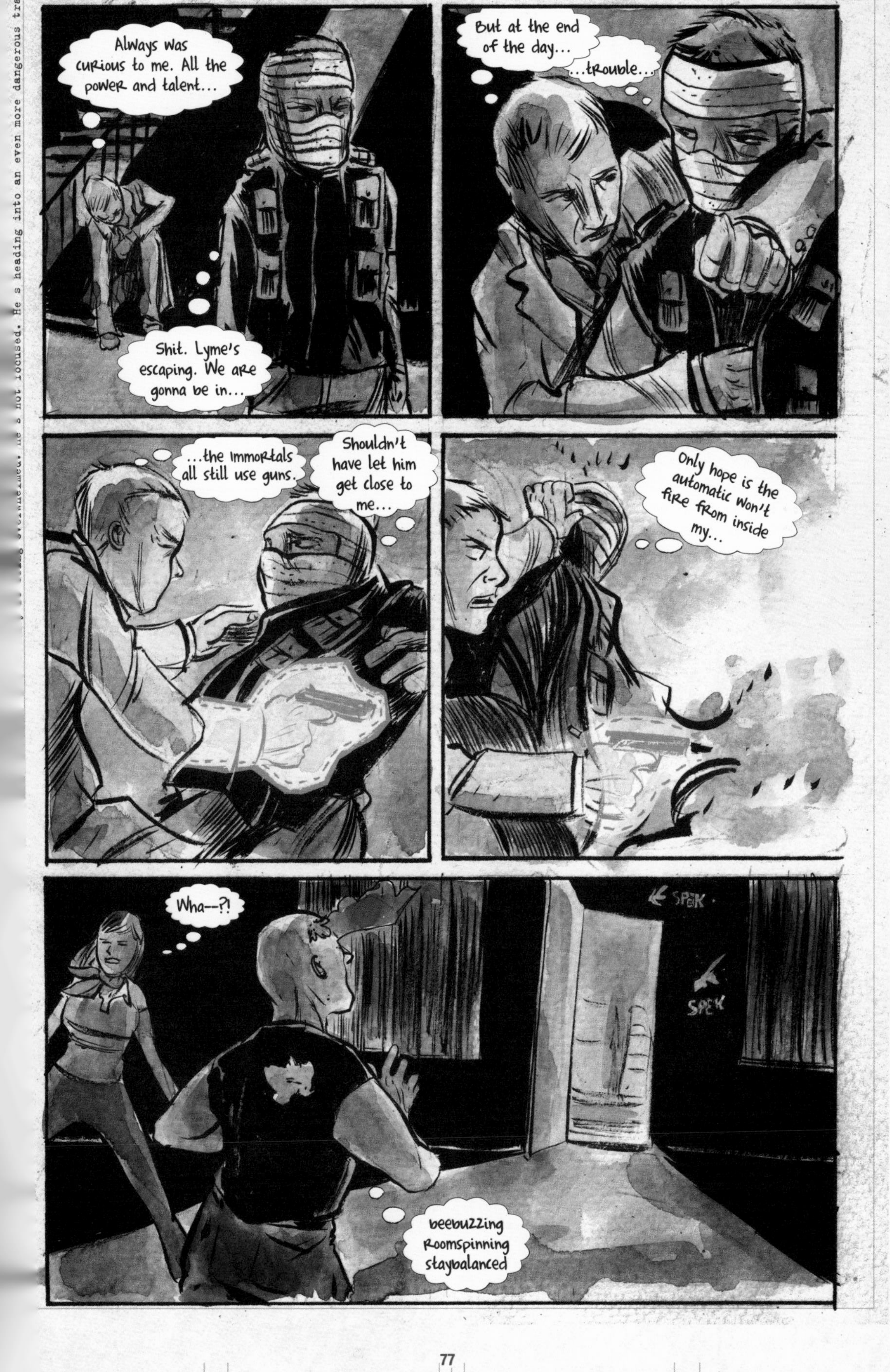
Always was curious to me. All the power and talent...
Shit. Lyme's escaping. We are gonna be in...
But at the end of the day...
...trouble...
...the Immortals all still use guns.
Shouldn't have let him get close to me...
Only hope is the automatic won't fire from inside my...
Wha--?!
SPEK
SPEK
beebuzzing
Roomspinning
staybalanced

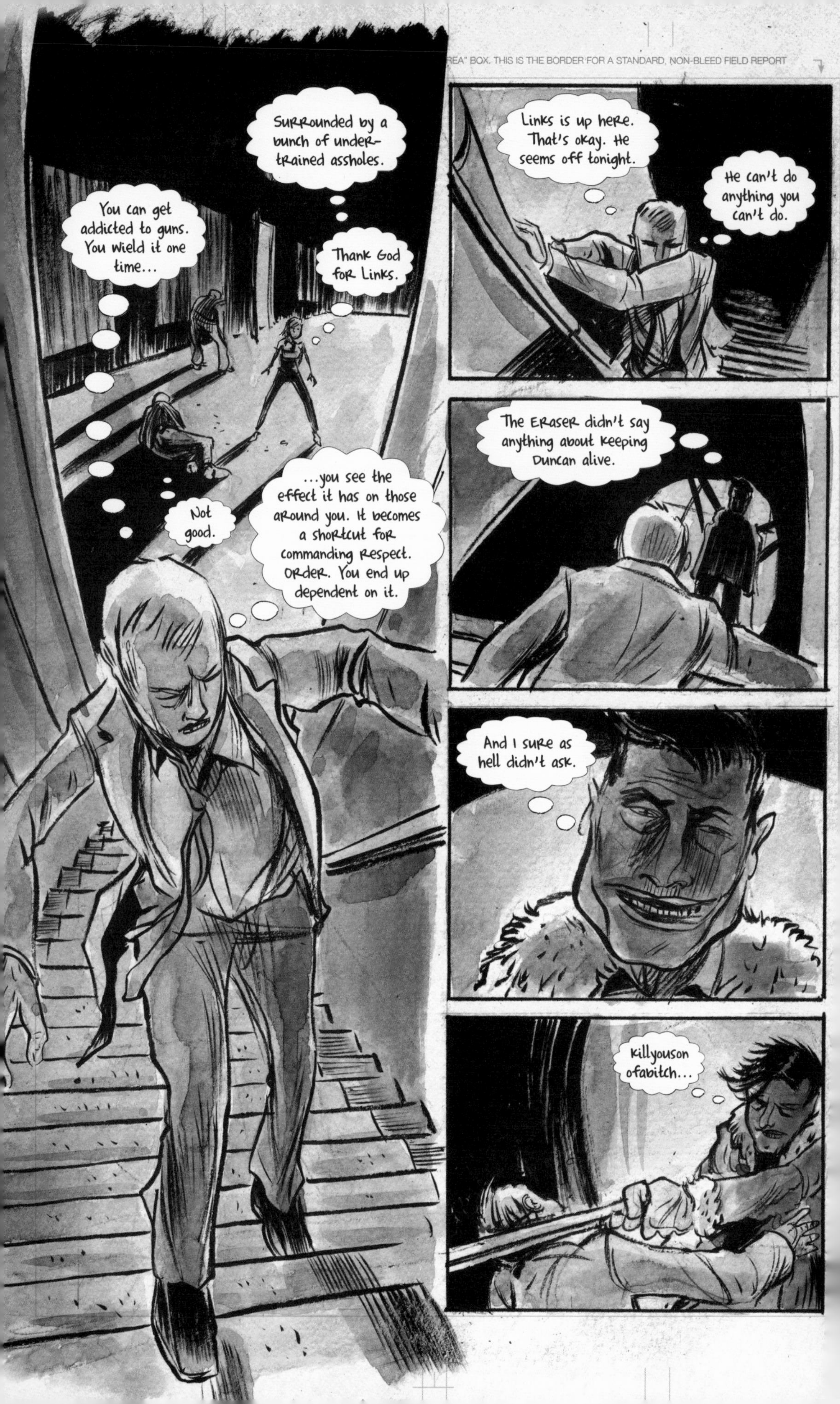
REA" BOX. THIS IS THE BORDER FOR A STANDARD, NON-BLEED FIELD REPORT
Surrounded by a bunch of under-trained assholes.
Thank God for Links.
You can get addicted to guns. You wield it one time...
...you see the effect it has on those around you. It becomes a shortcut for commanding respect. Order. You end up dependent on it.
Not good.
Links is up here. That's okay. He seems off tonight.
He can't do anything you can't do.
The Eraser didn't say anything about keeping Duncan alive.
And I sure as hell didn't ask.
Killyouson ofabitch...

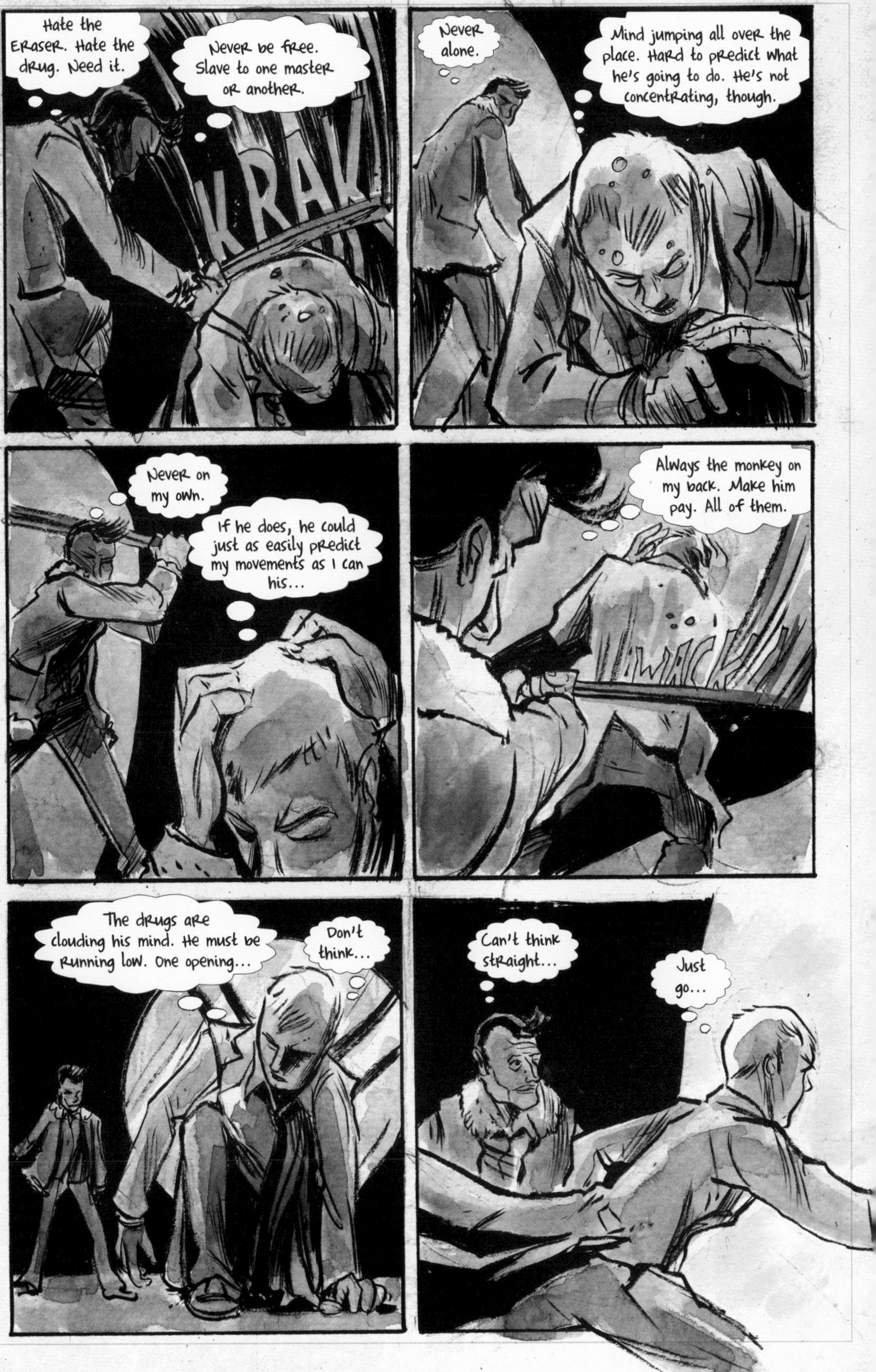
Hate the Eraser. Hate the drug. Need it.
Never be free. Slave to one master or another.
KRAK
Never alone.
Mind jumping all over the place. Hard to predict what he's going to do. He's not concentrating, though.
Never on my own.
If he does, he could just as easily predict my movements as I can his...
Always the monkey on my back. Make him pay. All of them.
WACK
The drugs are clouding his mind. He must be running low. One opening...
Don't think...
Can't think straight...
Just go...

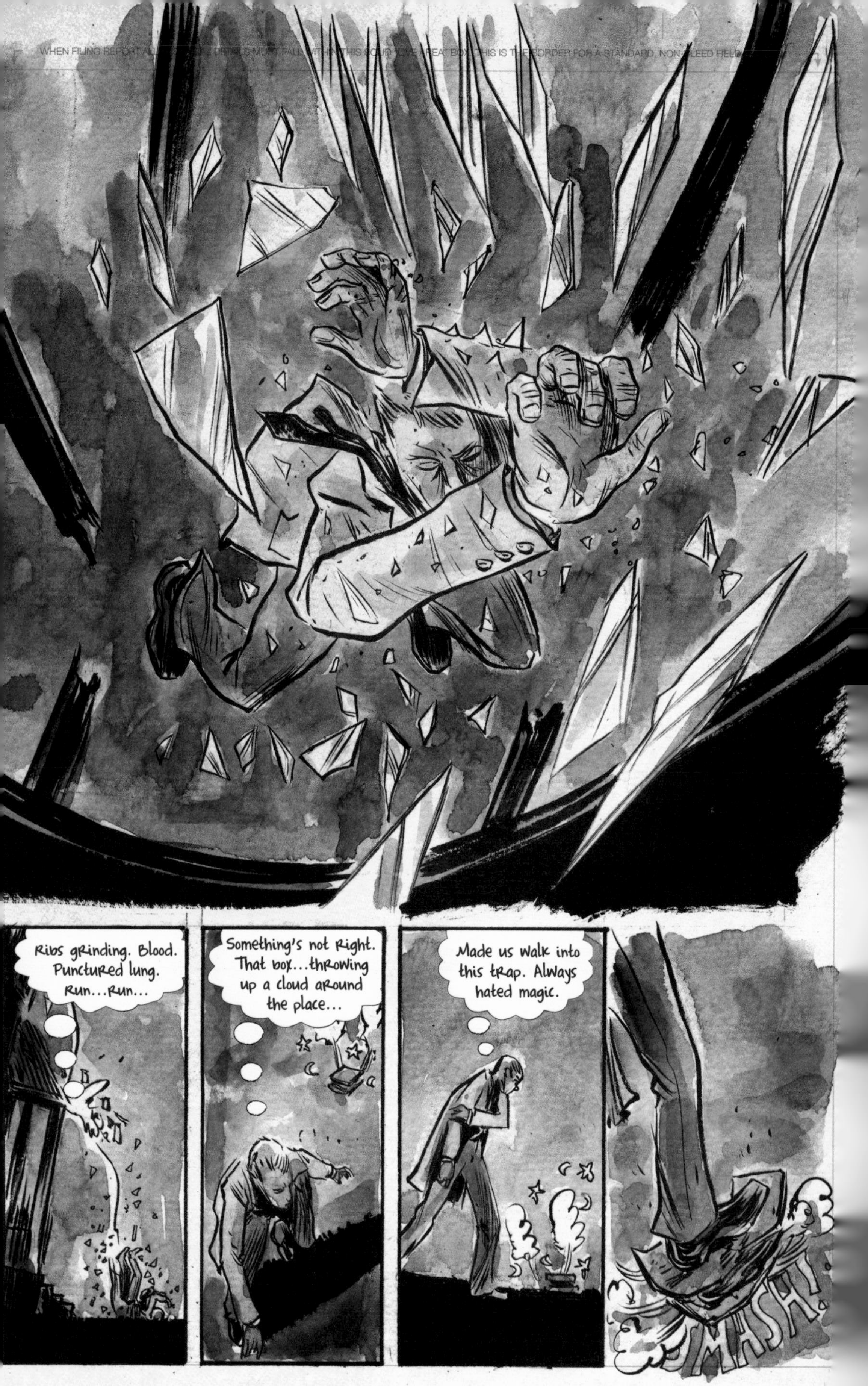
Ribs grinding. Blood. Punctured lung. Run...Run...
Something's not right. That box...throwing up a cloud around the place...
Made us walk into this trap. Always hated magic.
SMASH!

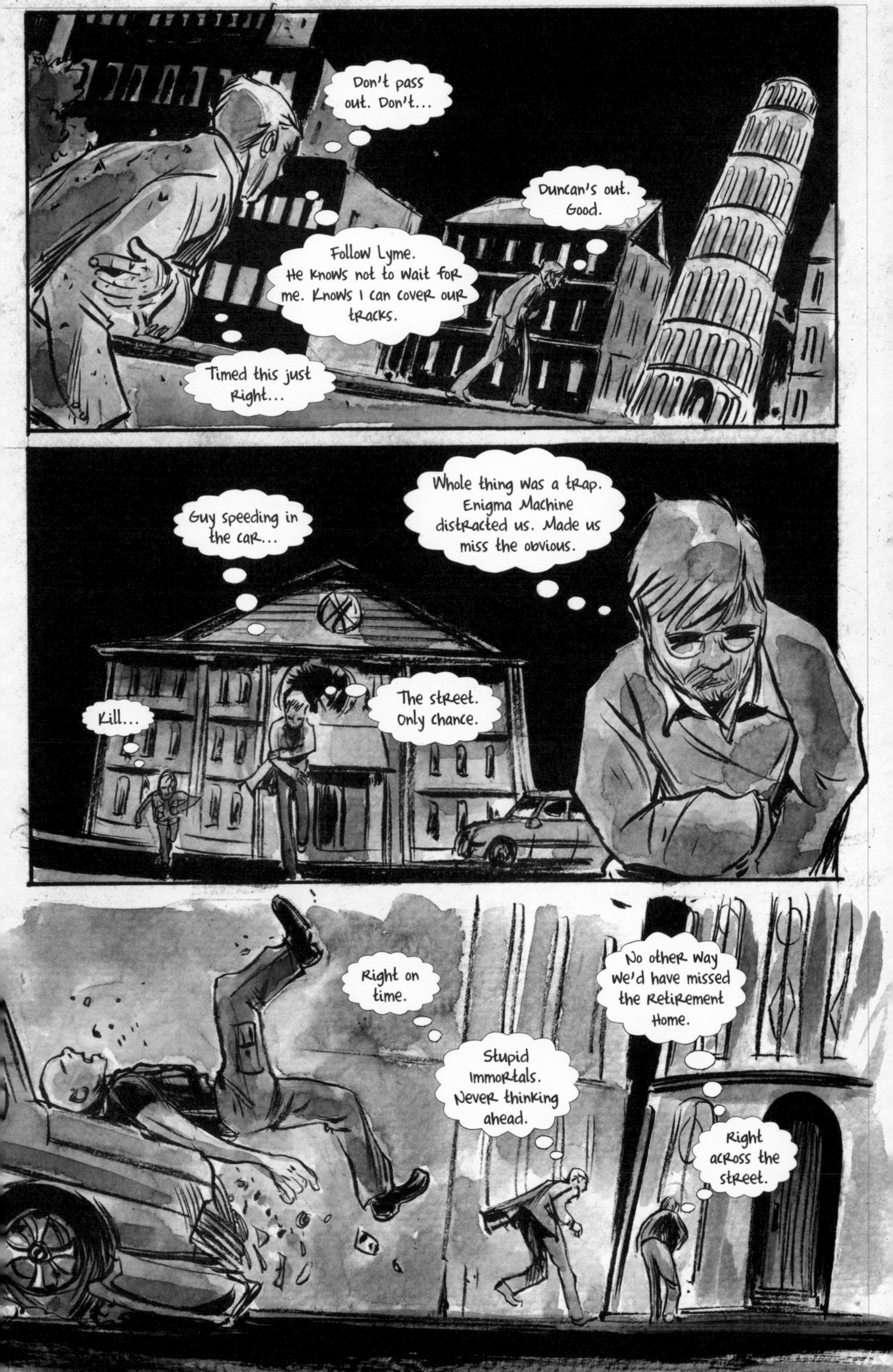
Don't pass out. Don't...
Duncan's out. Good.
Follow Lyme. He knows not to wait for me. Knows I can cover our tracks.
Timed this just right...
Guy speeding in the car...
Whole thing was a trap. Enigma Machine distracted us. Made us miss the obvious.
The street. Only chance.
Kill...
Right on time.
No other way we'd have missed the Retirement Home.
Stupid Immortals. Never thinking ahead.
Right across the street.

WHEN FILING REPORT ALL ESSENTIAL DETAILS MUST FALL WITHIN THIS SOLID "LIVE AREA" BOX. THIS IS THE BORDER FOR A STANDARD, NON-BLEED FIELD REPORT

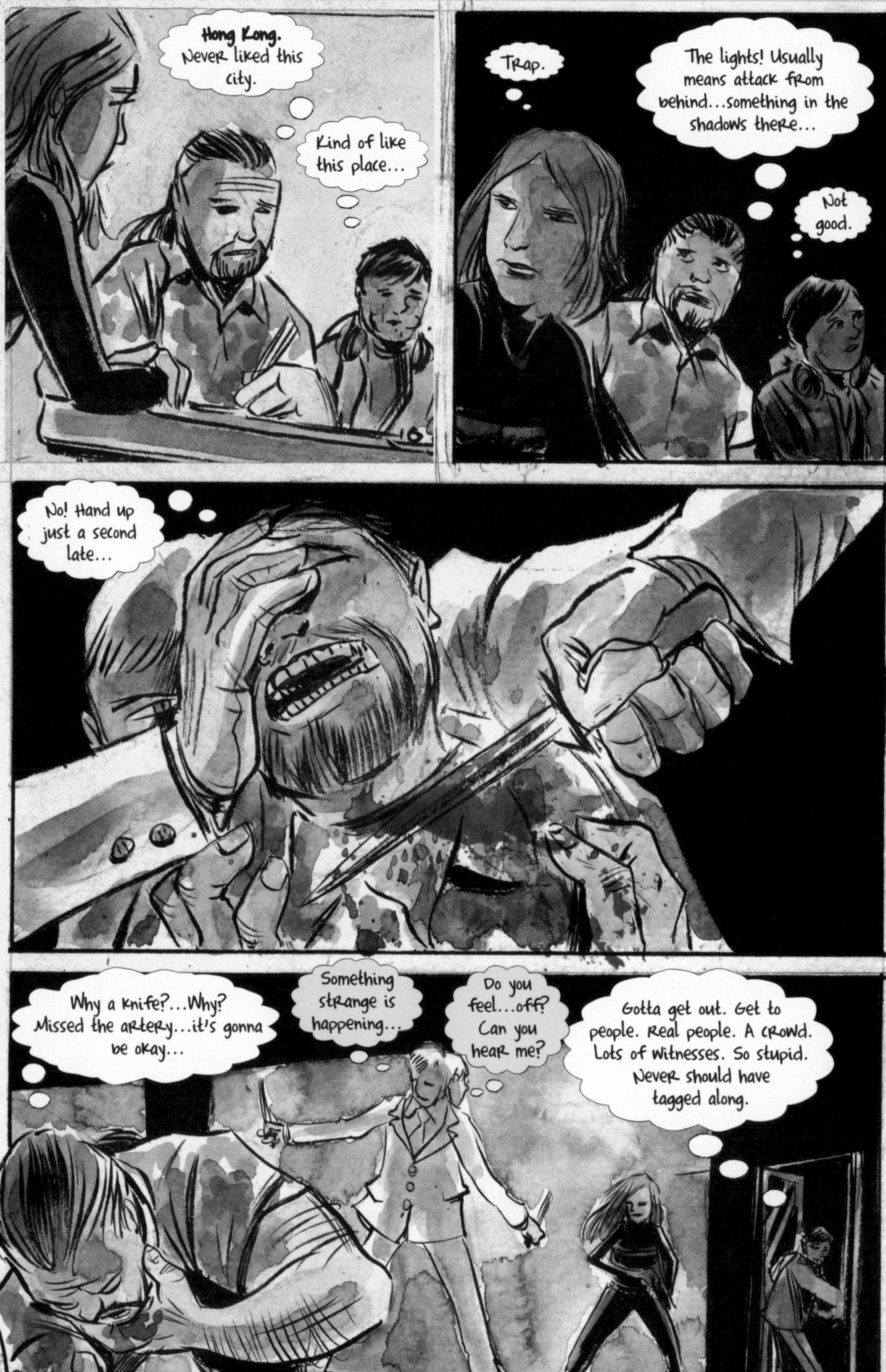
Hong Kong. Never liked this city.
Kind of like this place...
Trap.
The lights! Usually means attack from behind...something in the shadows there...
Not good.
No! Hand up just a second late...
Why a knife?...Why? Missed the artery...it's gonna be okay...
Something strange is happening...
Do you feel...off? Can you hear me?
Gotta get out. Get to people. Real people. A crowd. Lots of witnesses. So stupid. Never should have tagged along.

Hong Kong is much the same. A twin monstrosity is going to destroy them one by one. Showing just enough restraint however...under orders from someone else.

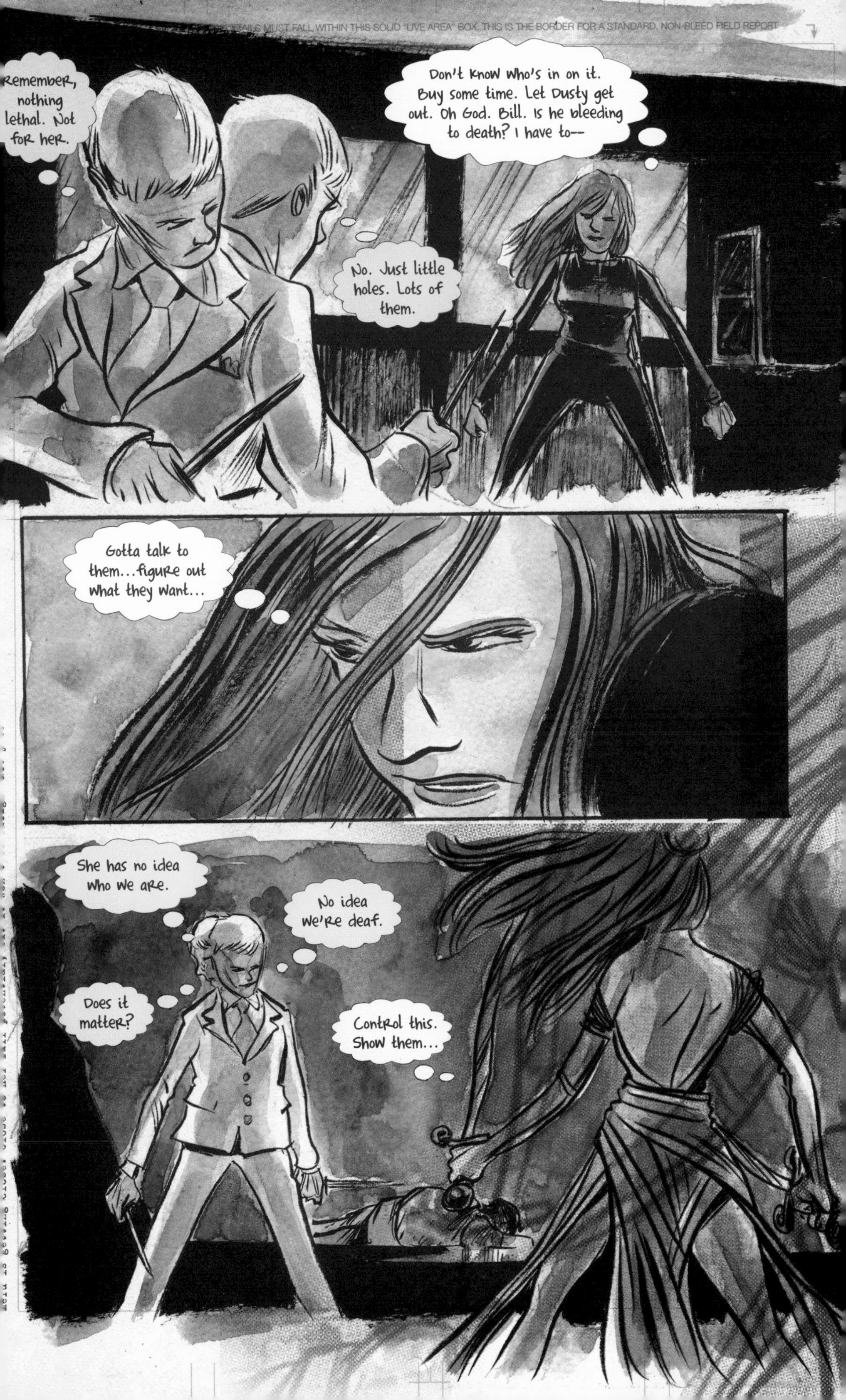
Remember, nothing lethal. Not for her.
Don't know who's in on it. Buy some time. Let Dusty get out. Oh God. Bill. Is he bleeding to death? I have to--
No. Just little holes. Lots of them.
Gotta talk to them...figure out what they want...
She has no idea who we are.
No idea we're deaf.
Does it matter?
Control this. Show them...

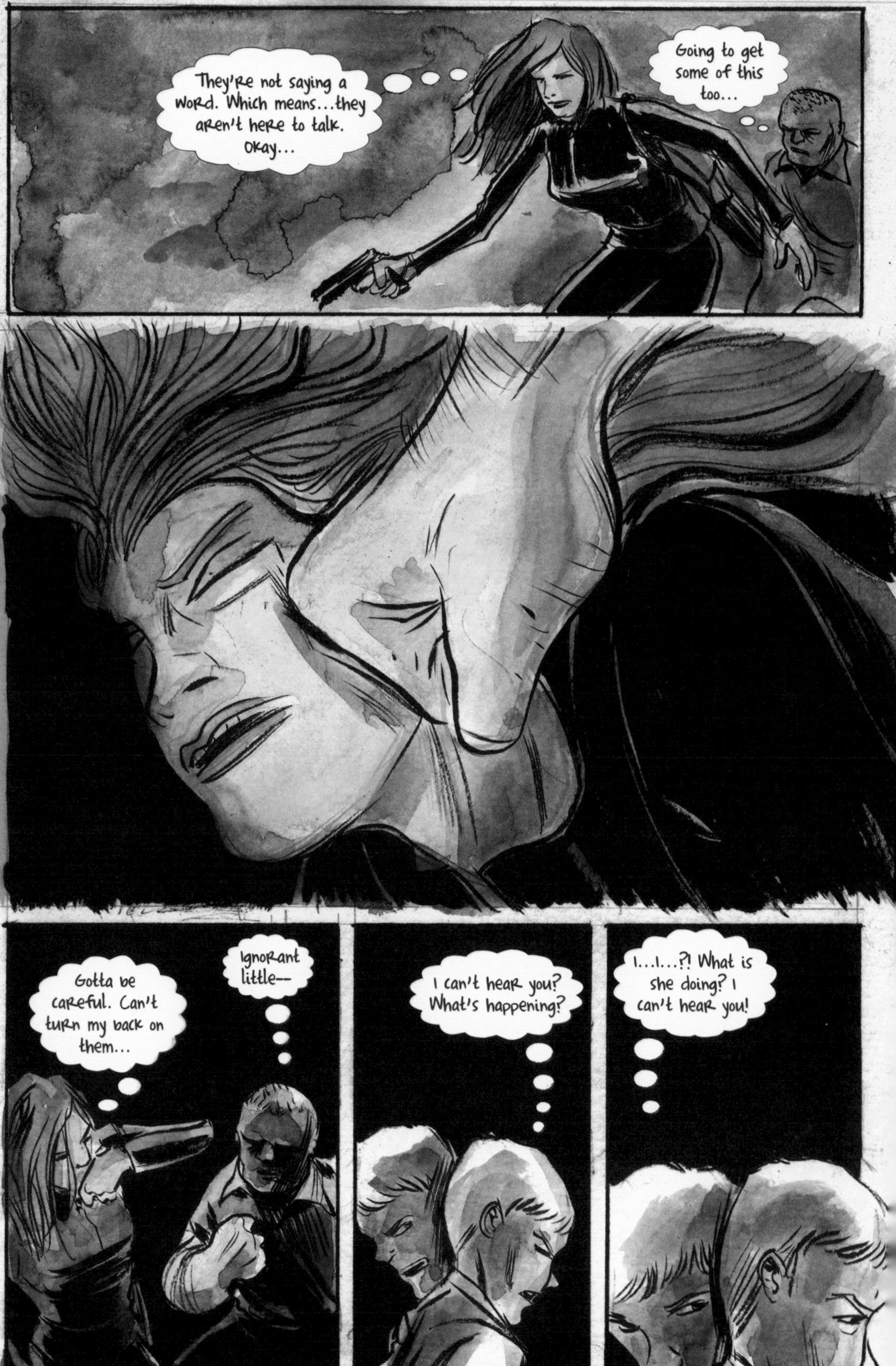
They're not saying a word. Which means...they aren't here to talk. Okay...
Going to get some of this too...
Gotta be careful. Can't turn my back on them...
Ignorant little--
I can't hear you? What's happening?
I...I...?! What is she doing? I can't hear you!

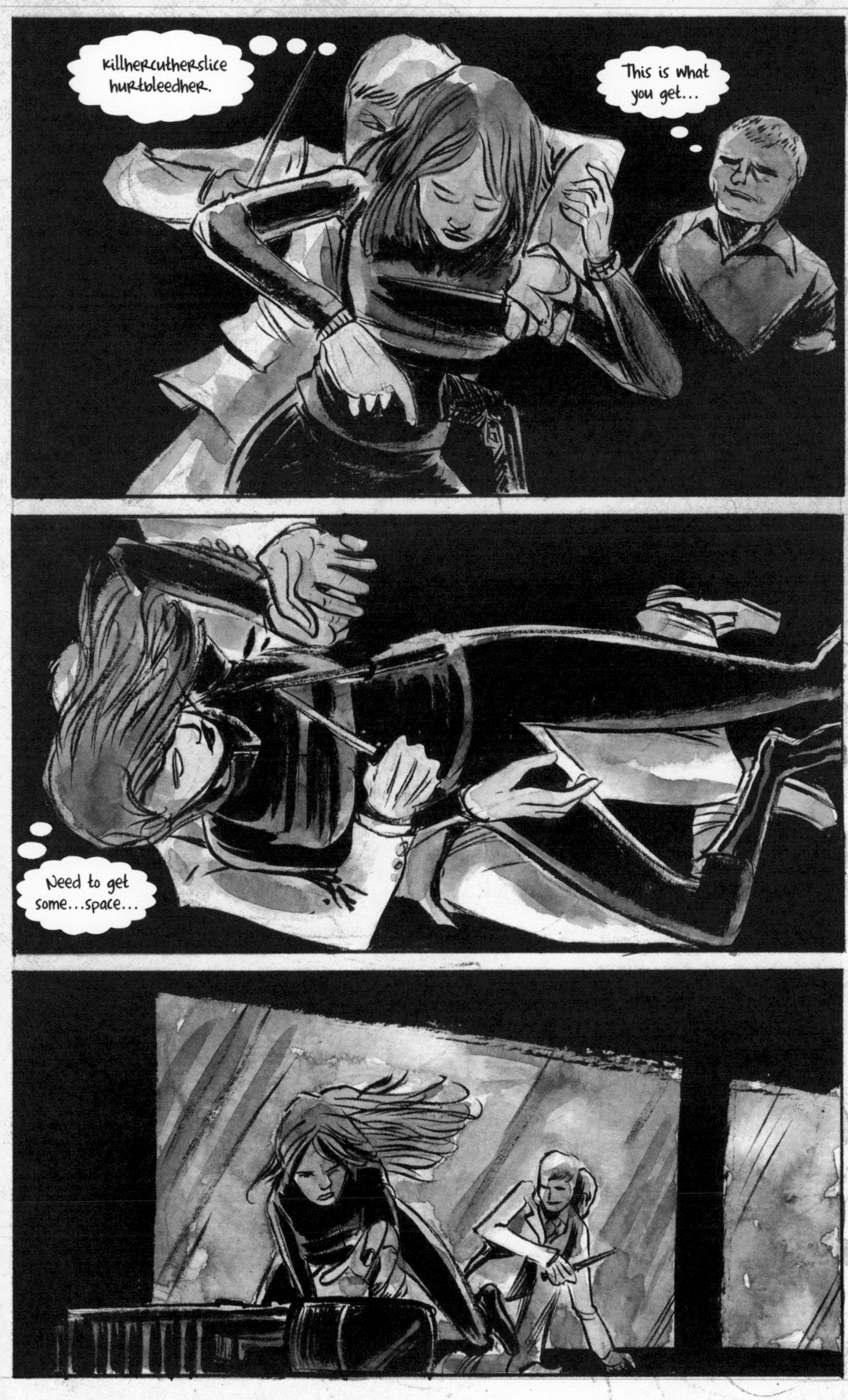
killhercutherslice hurtbleedher.
This is what you get...
Need to get some...space...

WHEN FILING REPORT ALL ESSENTIAL DETAILS MUST FALL WITHIN THIS SOLID "LIVE AREA" BOX. THIS IS THE BORDER FOR A STANDARD, NON-BLEED FIELD REPORT

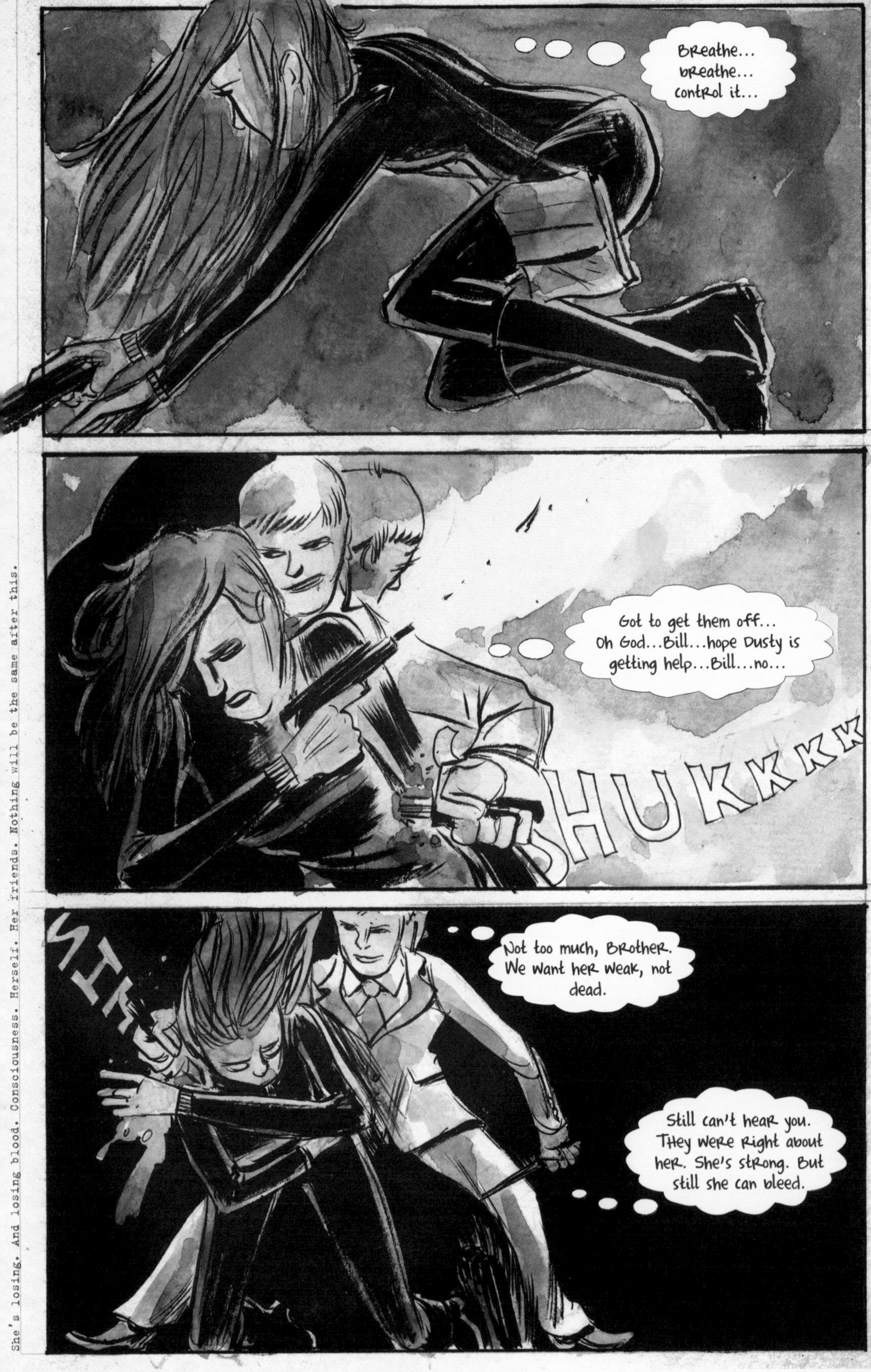

Breathe... breathe... control it...
Got to get them off... Oh God...Bill...hope Dusty is getting help...Bill...no...
SHUKKKK
Not too much, Brother. We want her weak, not dead.
Still can't hear you. They were right about her. She's strong. But still she can bleed.

She's losing. And losing blood. Consciousness. Herself. Her friends. Nothing will be the same after this.

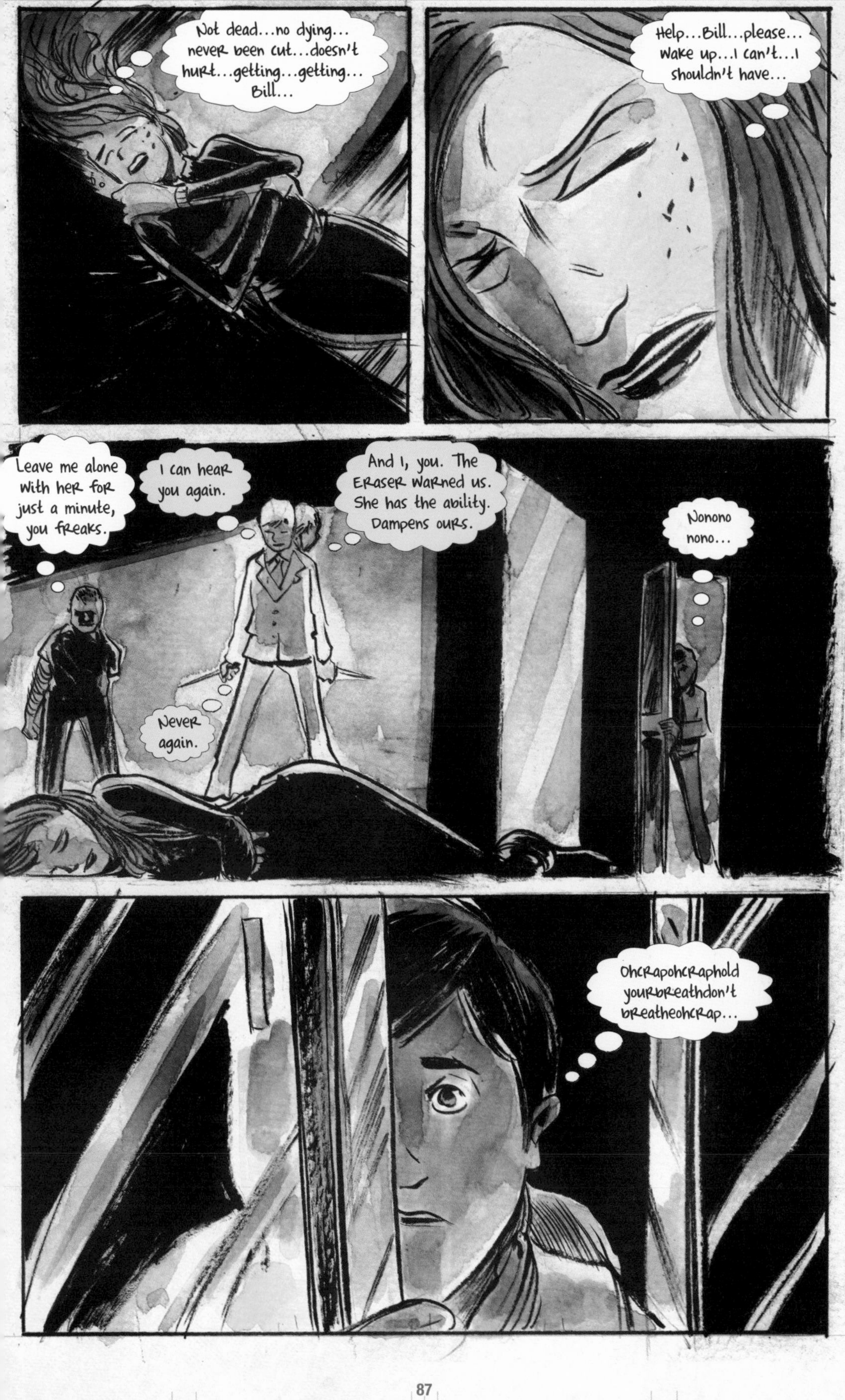
Not dead...no dying... never been cut...doesn't hurt...getting...getting... Bill...
Help...Bill...please... Wake up...I can't...I shouldn't have...
Leave me alone with her for just a minute, you freaks.
I can hear you again.
And I, you. The Eraser warned us. She has the ability. Dampens ours.
Nonono nono...
Never again.
Ohcrapohcraphold yourbreathdon't breatheohcrap...

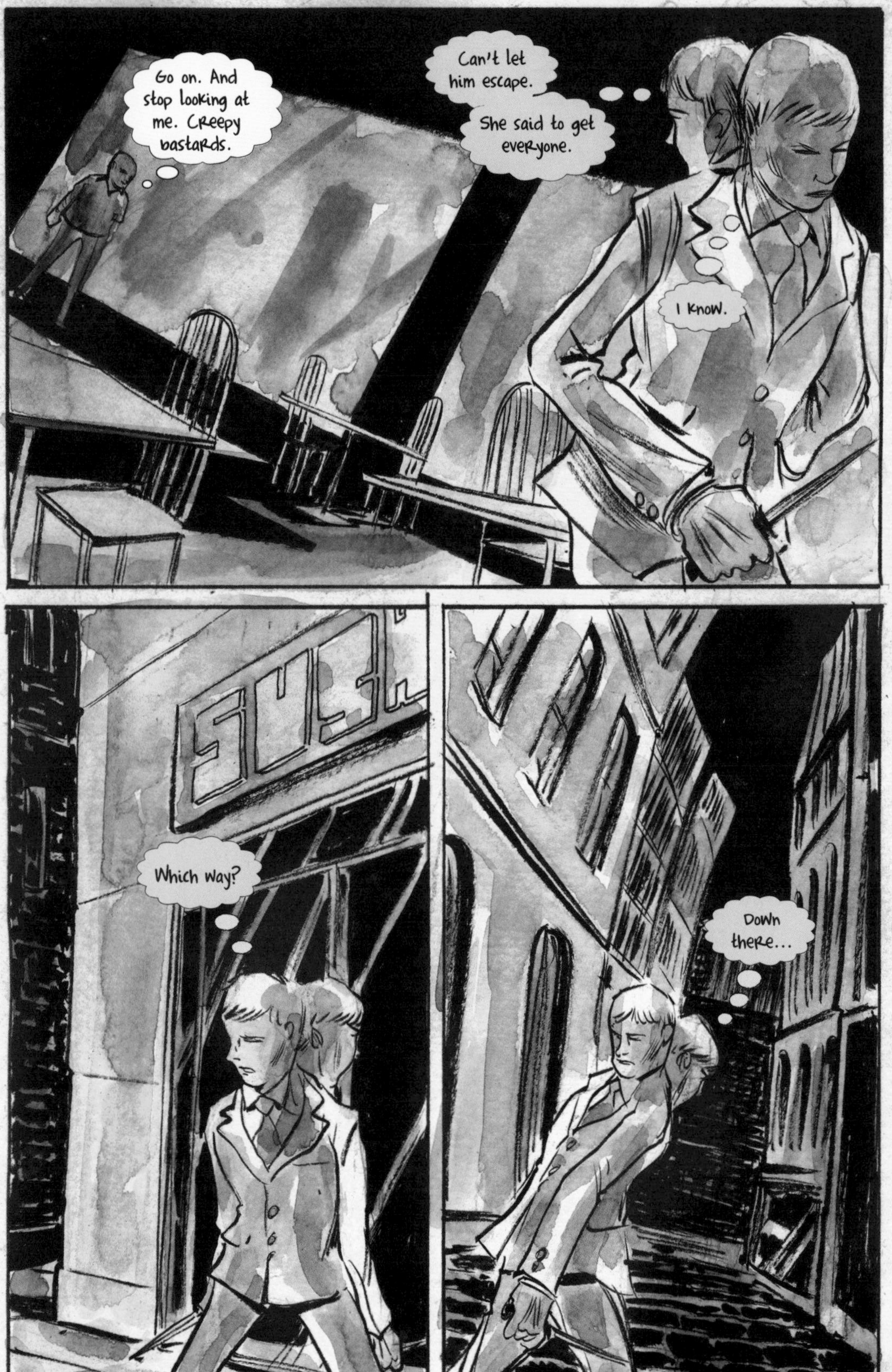
Go on. And stop looking at me. Creepy bastards.
Can't let him escape.
She said to get everyone.
I know.
Which way?
Down there...

Dusty running forever. Always. But about to stop. The two-headed monstrosity is going unchecked. Following orders...but not all of them.

WHEN FILING REPORT ALL ESSENTIAL DETAILS MUST FALL WITHIN THIS SOLID "LIVE AREA" BOX. THIS IS THE BORDER FOR A STANDARD, NON-BLEED FIELD REPORT

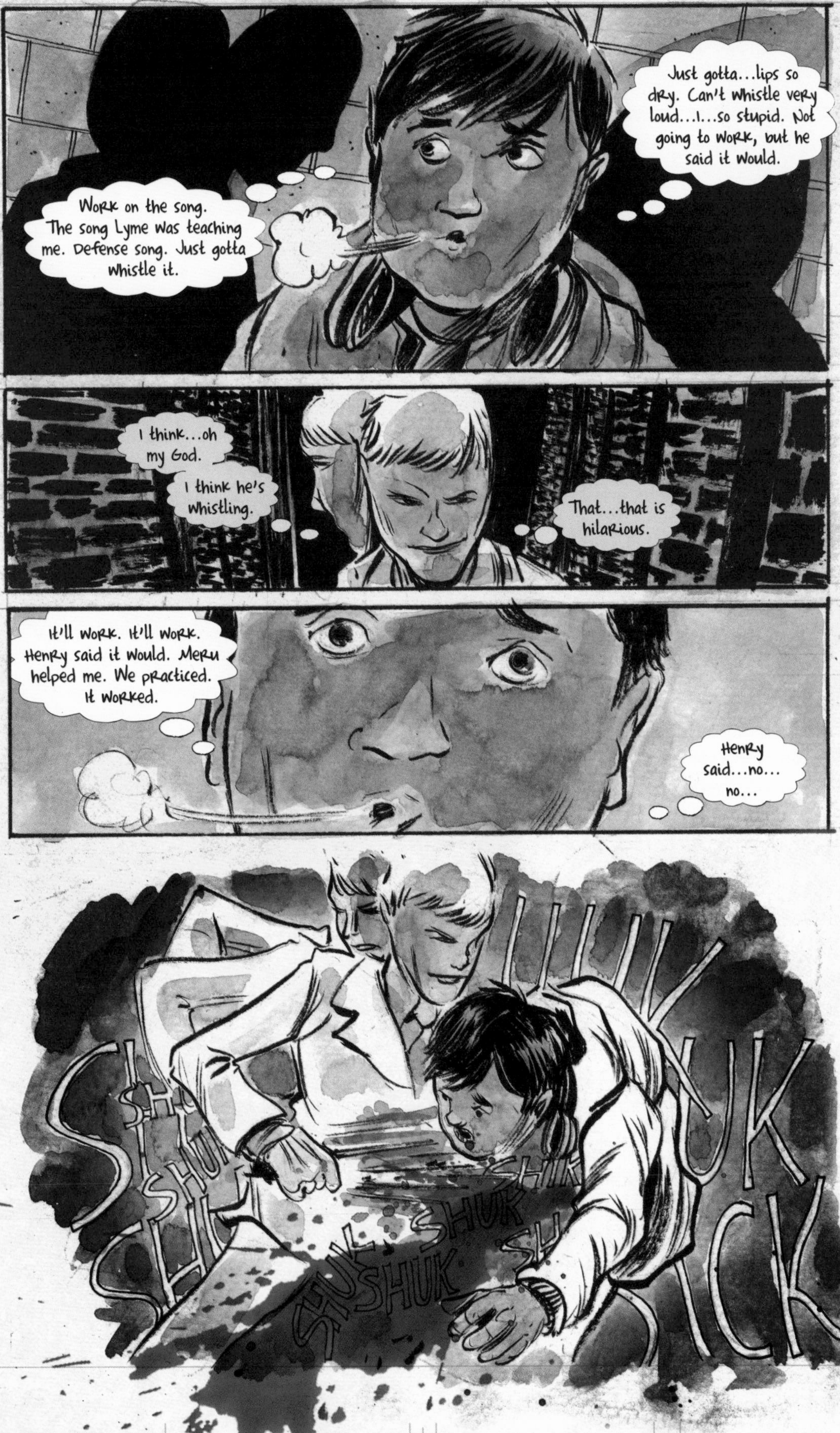
Work on the song. The song Lyme was teaching me. Defense song. Just gotta whistle it.
Just gotta...lips so dry. Can't whistle very loud...I...so stupid. Not going to work, but he said it would.
I think...oh my God.
I think he's whistling.
That...that is hilarious.
It'll work. It'll work. Henry said it would. Meru helped me. We practiced. It worked.
Henry said...no... no...
SHUK
SHUK SHUK

You're going to chase them. But you're going to be too late. You'll want to take the taxicab, but you shouldn't. And you won't.

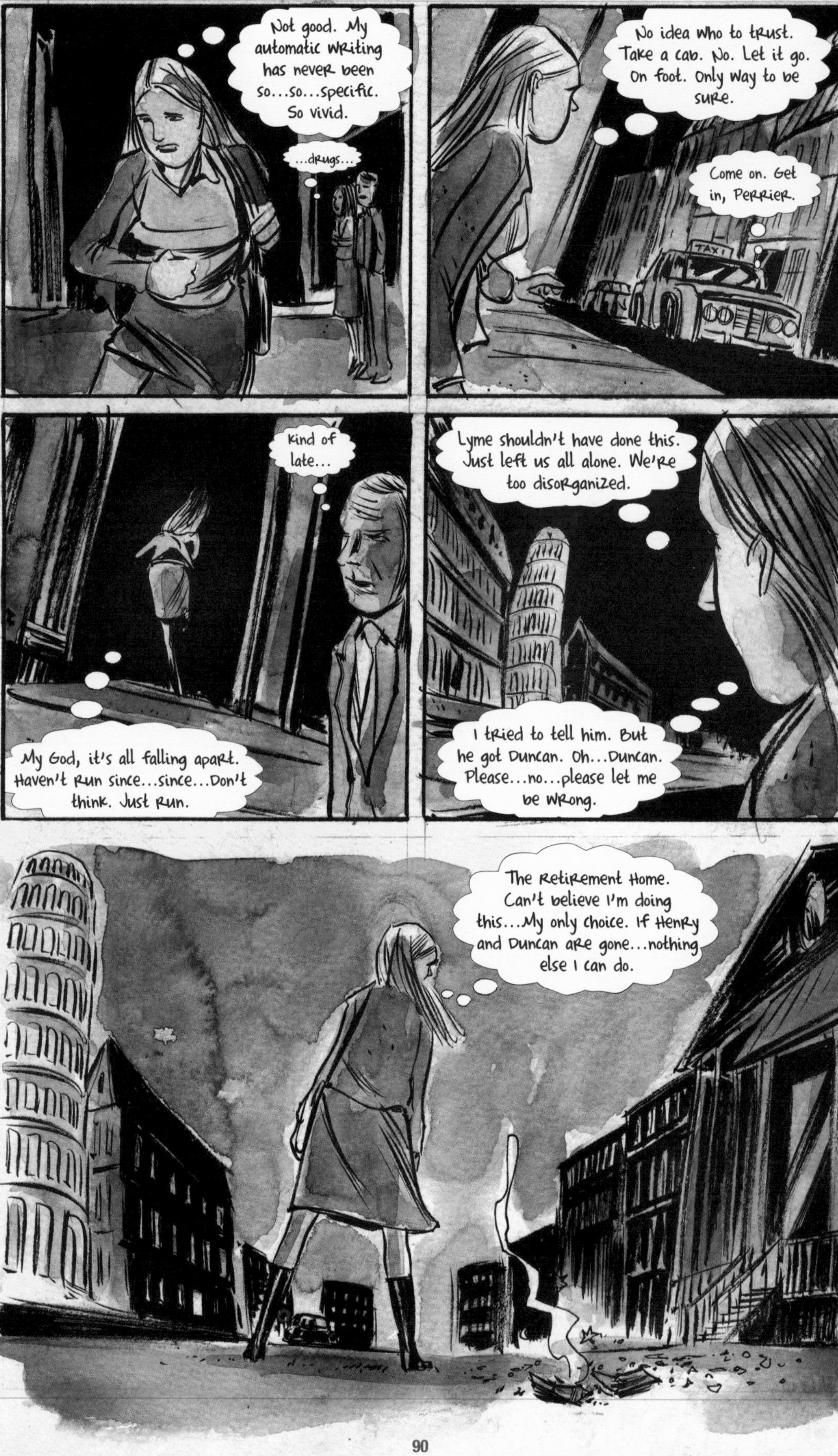
Not good. My automatic writing has never been so...so...specific. So vivid.
...drugs...
No idea who to trust. Take a cab. No. Let it go. On foot. Only way to be sure.
Come on. Get in, Perrier.
TAXI
Kind of late...
My God, it's all falling apart. Haven't run since...since...Don't think. Just run.
Lyme shouldn't have done this. Just left us all alone. We're too disorganized.
I tried to tell him. But he got Duncan. Oh...Duncan. Please...no...please let me be wrong.
The Retirement Home. Can't believe I'm doing this...My only choice. If Henry and Duncan are gone...nothing else I can do.

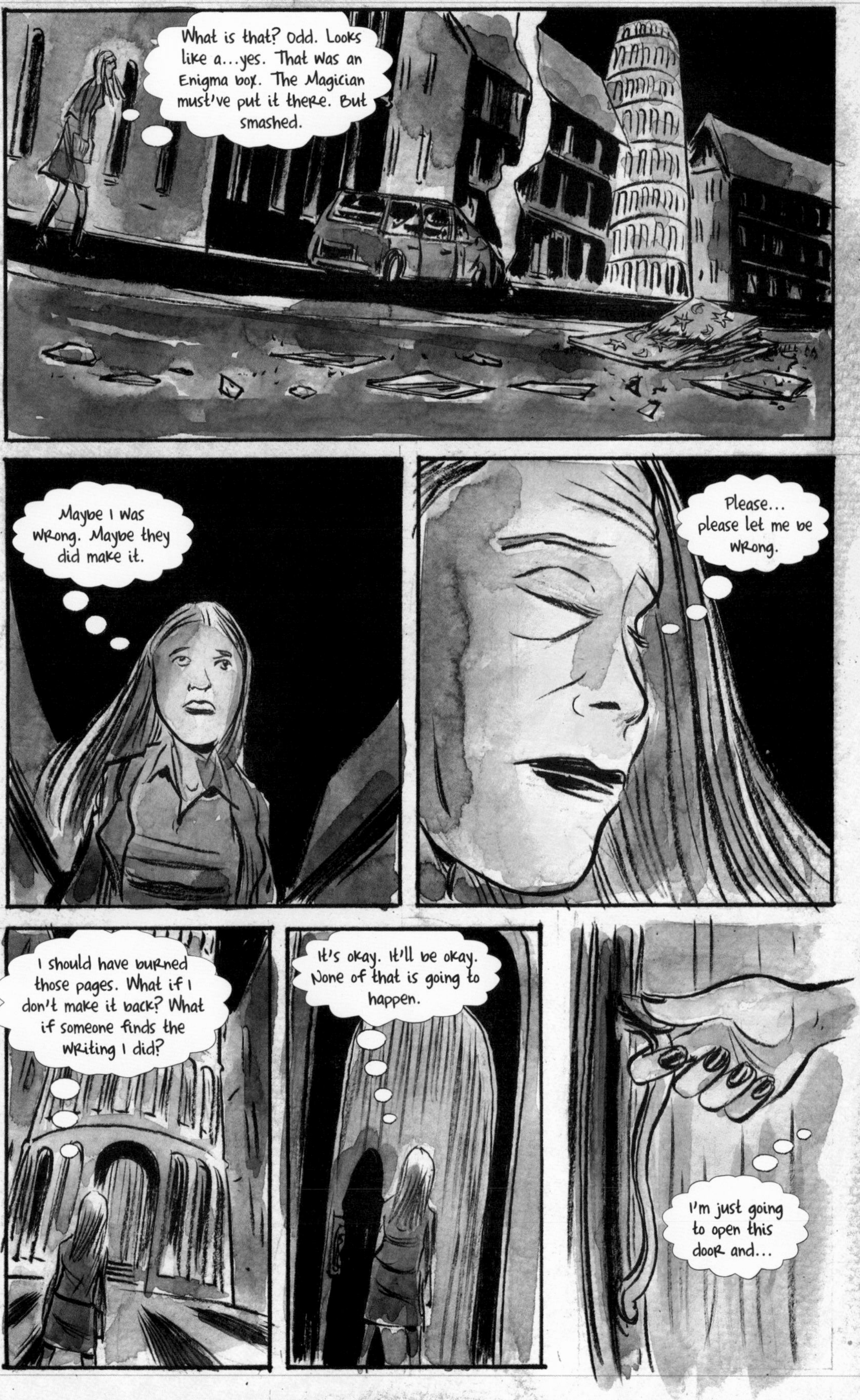
What is that? Odd. Looks like a...yes. That was an Enigma box. The Magician must've put it there. But smashed.
Maybe I was wrong. Maybe they did make it.
Please... please let me be wrong.
I should have burned those pages. What if I don't make it back? What if someone finds the writing I did?
It's okay. It'll be okay. None of that is going to happen.
I'm just going to open this door and...

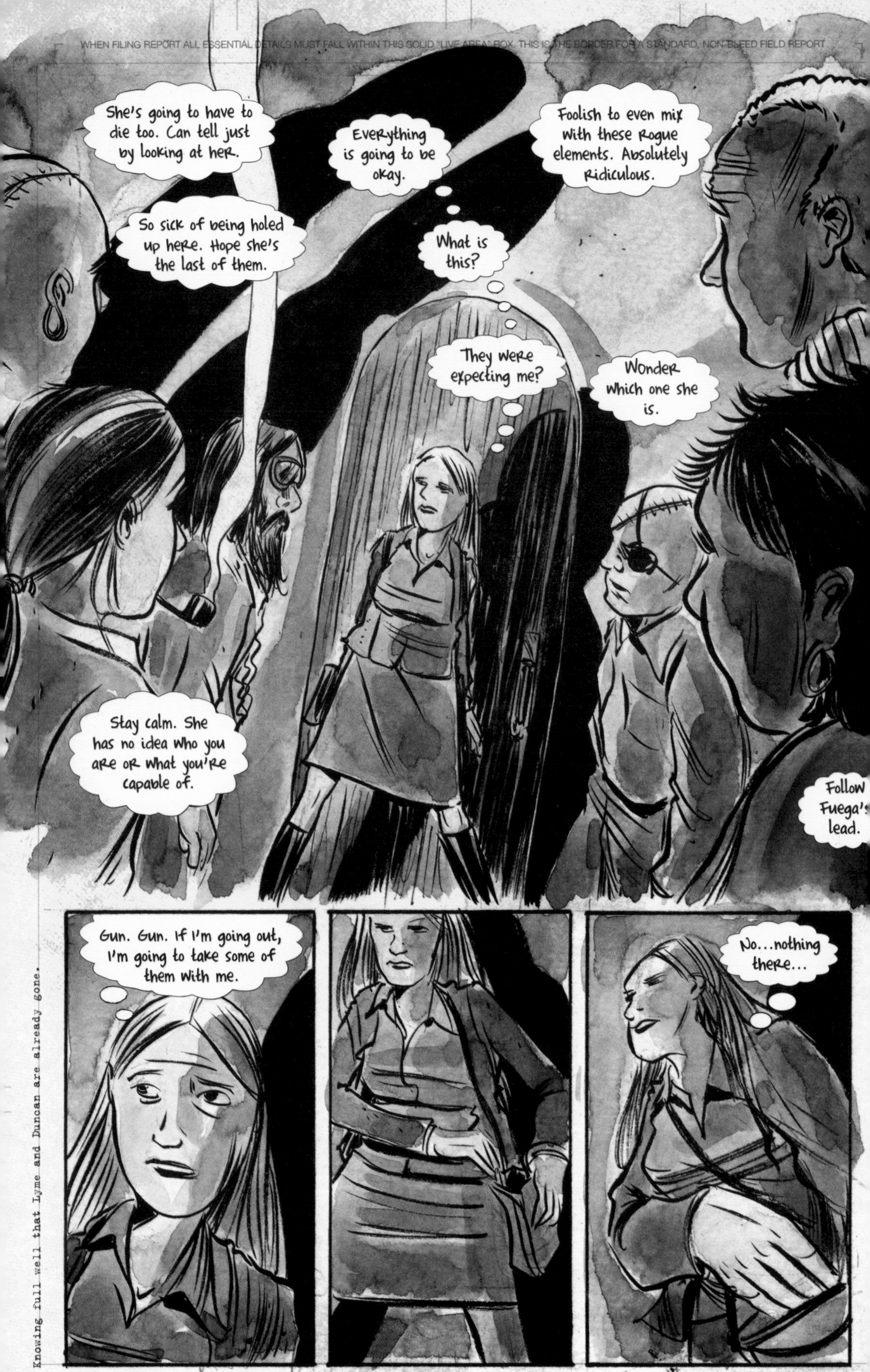
She's going to have to die too. Can tell just by looking at her.
Everything is going to be okay.
Foolish to even mix with these Rogue elements. Absolutely ridiculous.
So sick of being holed up here. Hope she's the last of them.
What is this?
They were expecting me?
Wonder which one she is.
Stay calm. She has no idea who you are or what you're capable of.
Follow Fuega's lead.
Gun. Gun. If I'm going out, I'm going to take some of them with me.
No...nothing there...

Knowing full well that Lyme and Duncan are already gone.

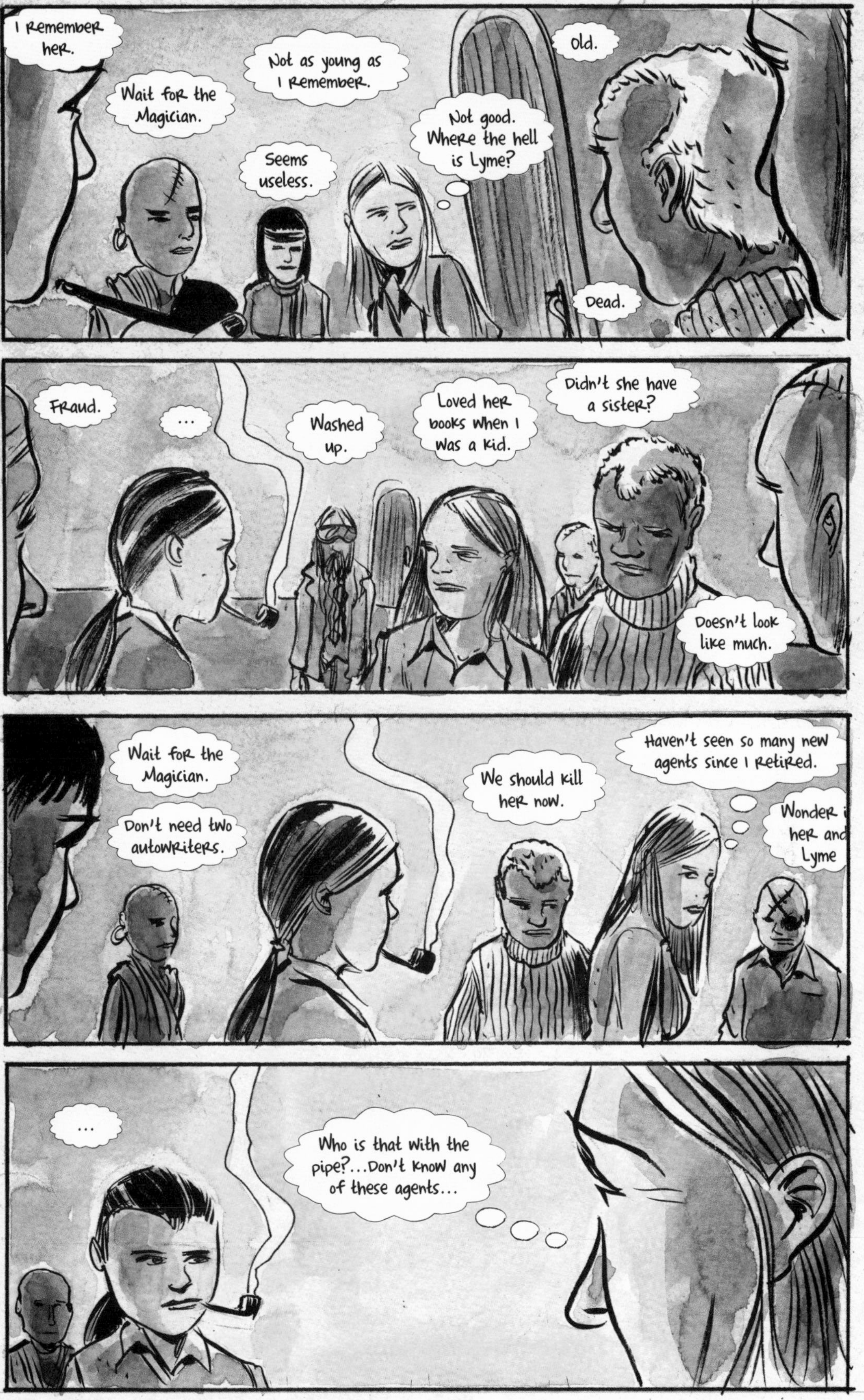
I remember her.
Wait for the Magician.
Not as young as I remember.
Seems useless.
Not good. Where the hell is Lyme?
Old.
Dead.
Fraud.
...
Washed up.
Loved her books when I was a kid.
Didn't she have a sister?
Doesn't look like much.
Wait for the Magician.
Don't need two autowriters.
We should kill her now.
Haven't seen so many new agents since I retired.
Wonder i her and Lyme
...
Who is that with the pipe?...Don't know any of these agents...

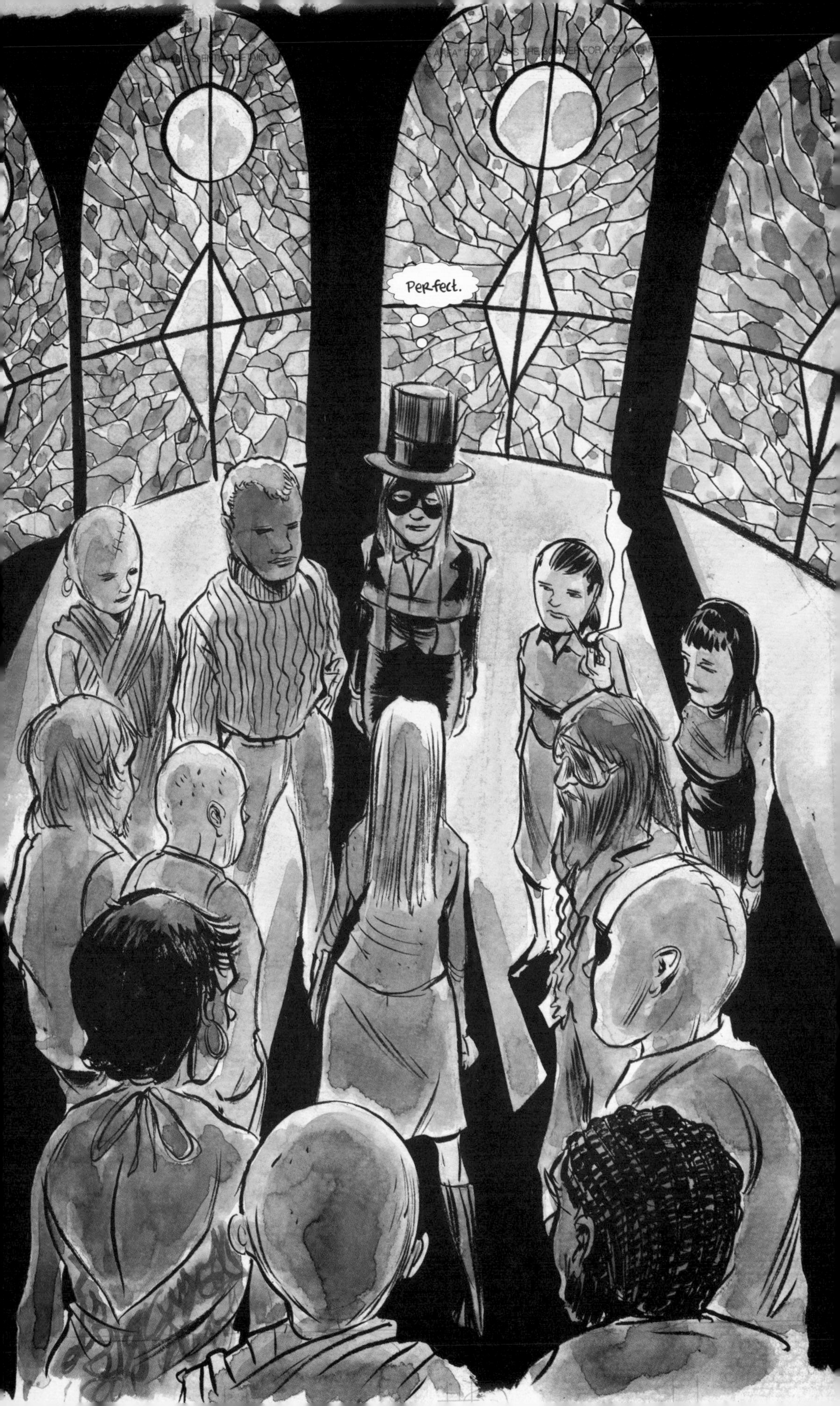
Perfect.

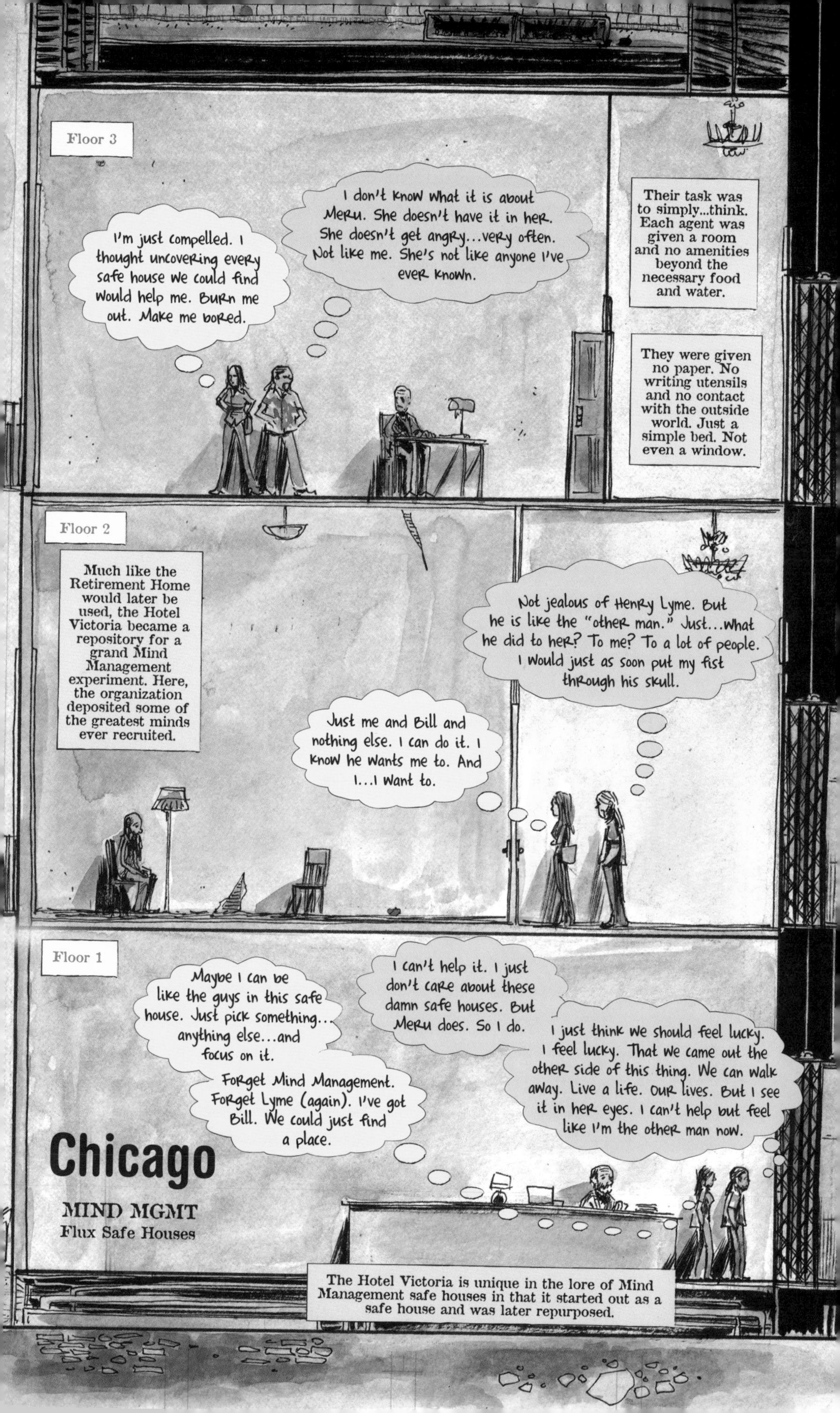

Floor 3
I'm just compelled. I thought uncovering every safe house we could find would help me. Burn me out. Make me bored.
I don't know what it is about Meru. She doesn't have it in her. She doesn't get angry...very often. Not like me. She's not like anyone I've ever known.
Their task was to simply...think. Each agent was given a room and no amenities beyond the necessary food and water.
They were given no paper. No writing utensils and no contact with the outside world. Just a simple bed. Not even a window.
Floor 2
Much like the Retirement Home would later be used, the Hotel Victoria became a repository for a grand Mind Management experiment. Here, the organization deposited some of the greatest minds ever recruited.
Not jealous of Henry Lyme. But he is like the "other man." Just...what he did to her? To me? To a lot of people. I would just as soon put my fist through his skull.
Just me and Bill and nothing else. I can do it. I know he wants me to. And I...I want to.
Floor 1
Maybe I can be like the guys in this safe house. Just pick something... anything else...and focus on it.
I can't help it. I just don't care about these damn safe houses. But Meru does. So I do.
Forget Mind Management. Forget Lyme (again). I've got Bill. We could just find a place.
I just think we should feel lucky. I feel lucky. That we came out the other side of this thing. We can walk away. Live a life. Our lives. But I see it in her eyes. I can't help but feel like I'm the other man now.
Chicago
MIND MGMT
Flux Safe Houses
The Hotel Victoria is unique in the lore of Mind Management safe houses in that it started out as a safe house and was later repurposed.

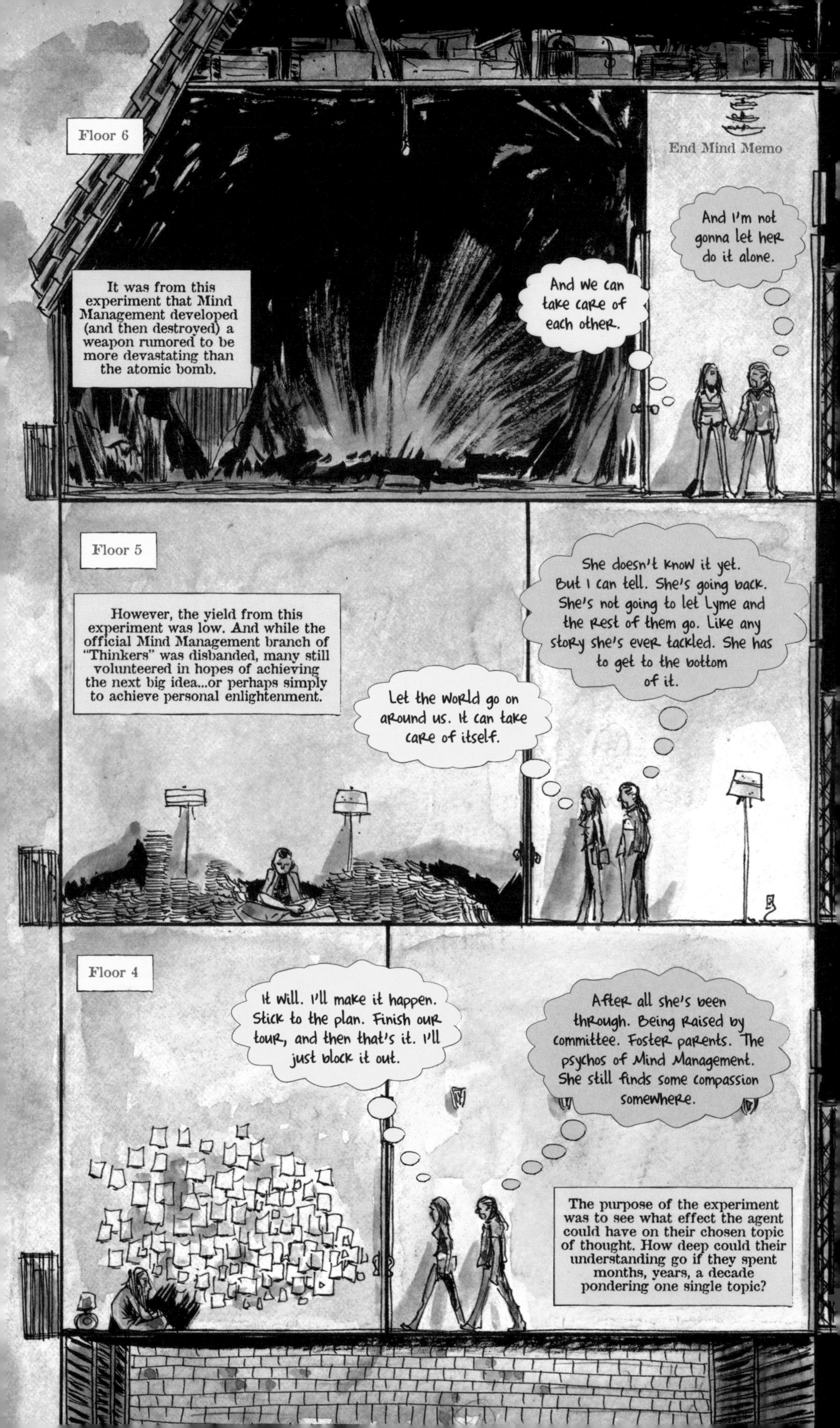
Floor 6
It was from this experiment that Mind Management developed (and then destroyed) a weapon rumored to be more devastating than the atomic bomb.
End Mind Memo
And we can take care of each other.
And I'm not gonna let her do it alone.
Floor 5
However, the yield from this experiment was low. And while the official Mind Management branch of "Thinkers" was disbanded, many still volunteered in hopes of achieving the next big idea...or perhaps simply to achieve personal enlightenment.
Let the world go on around us. It can take care of itself.
She doesn't know it yet. But I can tell. She's going back. She's not going to let Lyme and the rest of them go. Like any story she's ever tackled. She has to get to the bottom of it.
Floor 4
It will. I'll make it happen. Stick to the plan. Finish our tour, and then that's it. I'll just block it out.
After all she's been through. Being raised by committee. Foster parents. The psychos of Mind Management. She still finds some compassion somewhere.
The purpose of the experiment was to see what effect the agent could have on their chosen topic of thought. How deep could their understanding go if they spent months, years, a decade pondering one single topic?

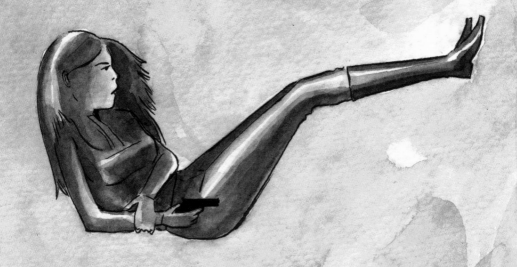

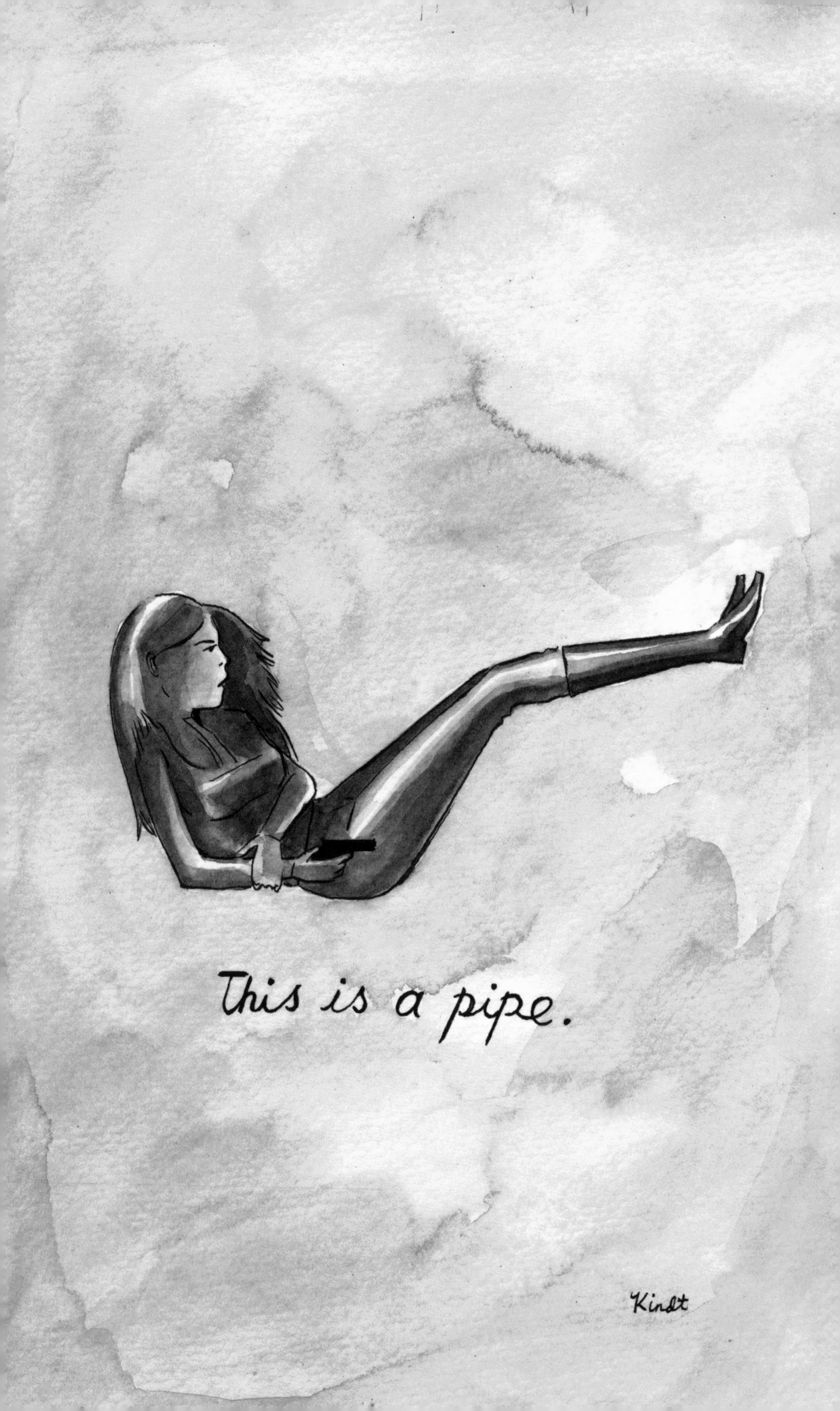

This is a pipe.

Kindt

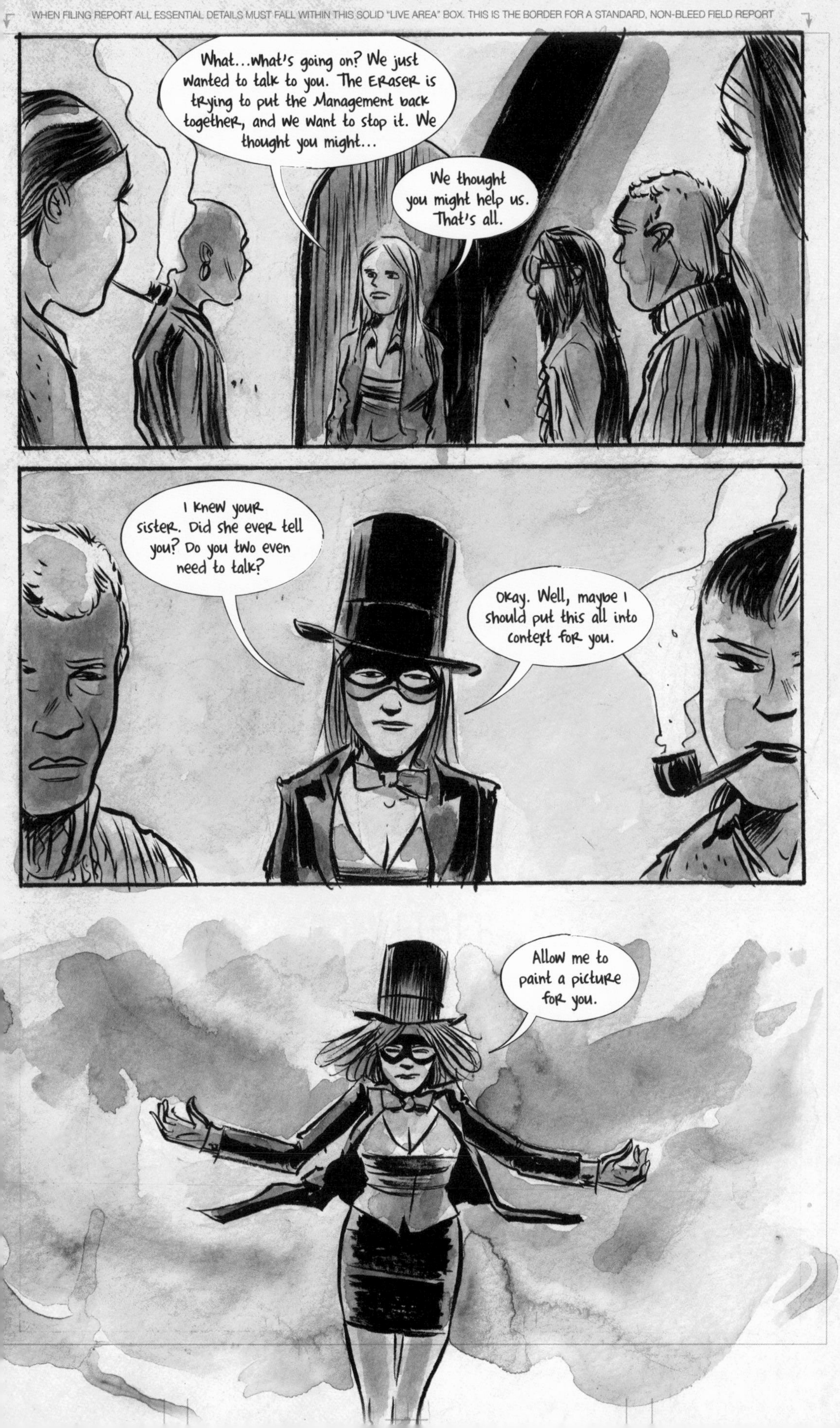
WHEN FILING REPORT ALL ESSENTIAL DETAILS MUST FALL WITHIN THIS SOLID "LIVE AREA" BOX. THIS IS THE BORDER FOR A STANDARD, NON-BLEED FIELD REPORT
What...what's going on? We just wanted to talk to you. The ERASER is trying to put the Management back together, and we want to stop it. We thought you might...
We thought you might help us. That's all.
I knew your sister. Did she ever tell you? Do you two even need to talk?
Okay. Well, maybe I should put this all into context for you.
Allow me to paint a picture for you.

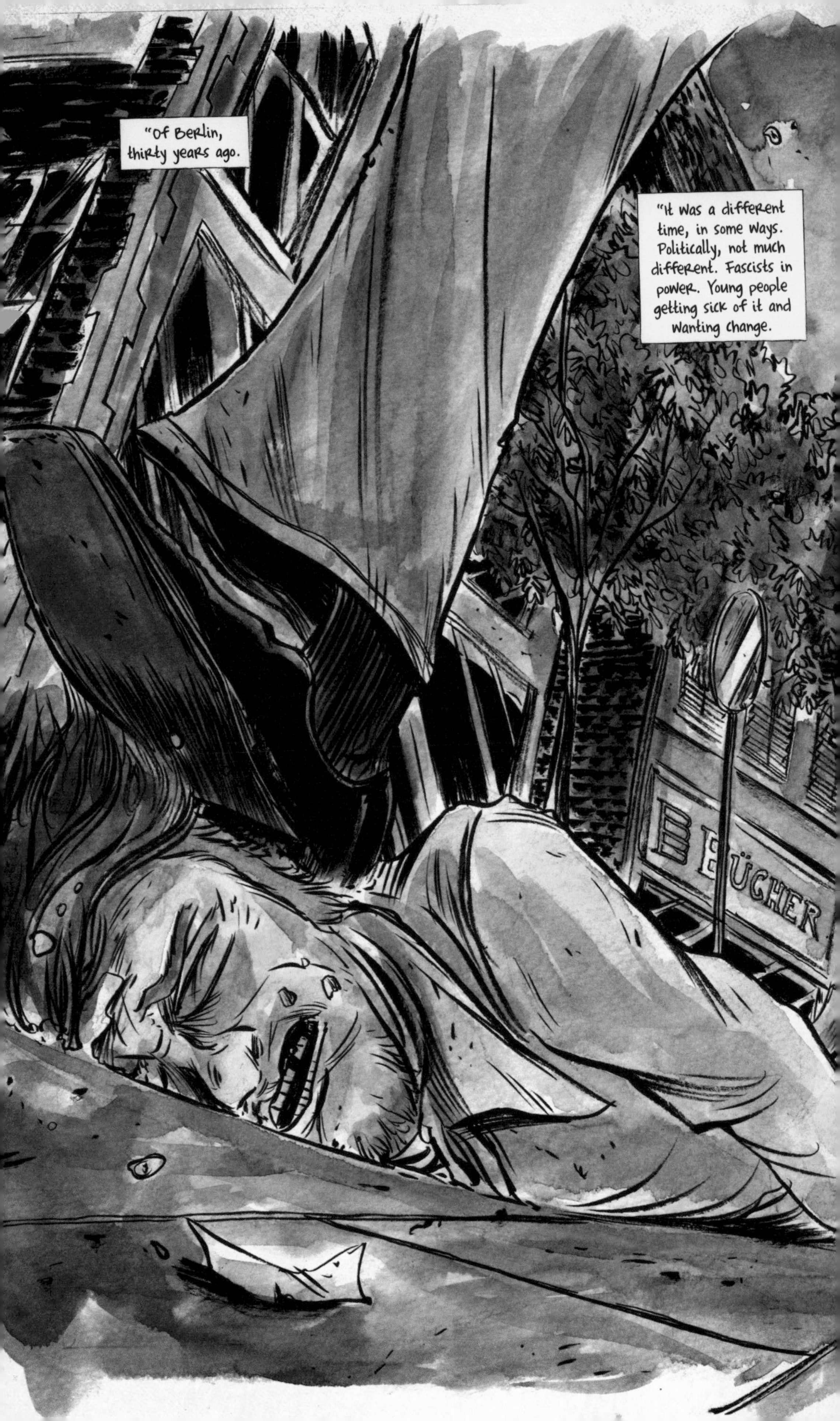
"Of Berlin, thirty years ago.
"It was a different time, in some ways. Politically, not much different. Fascists in power. Young people getting sick of it and wanting change.
BÜCHER

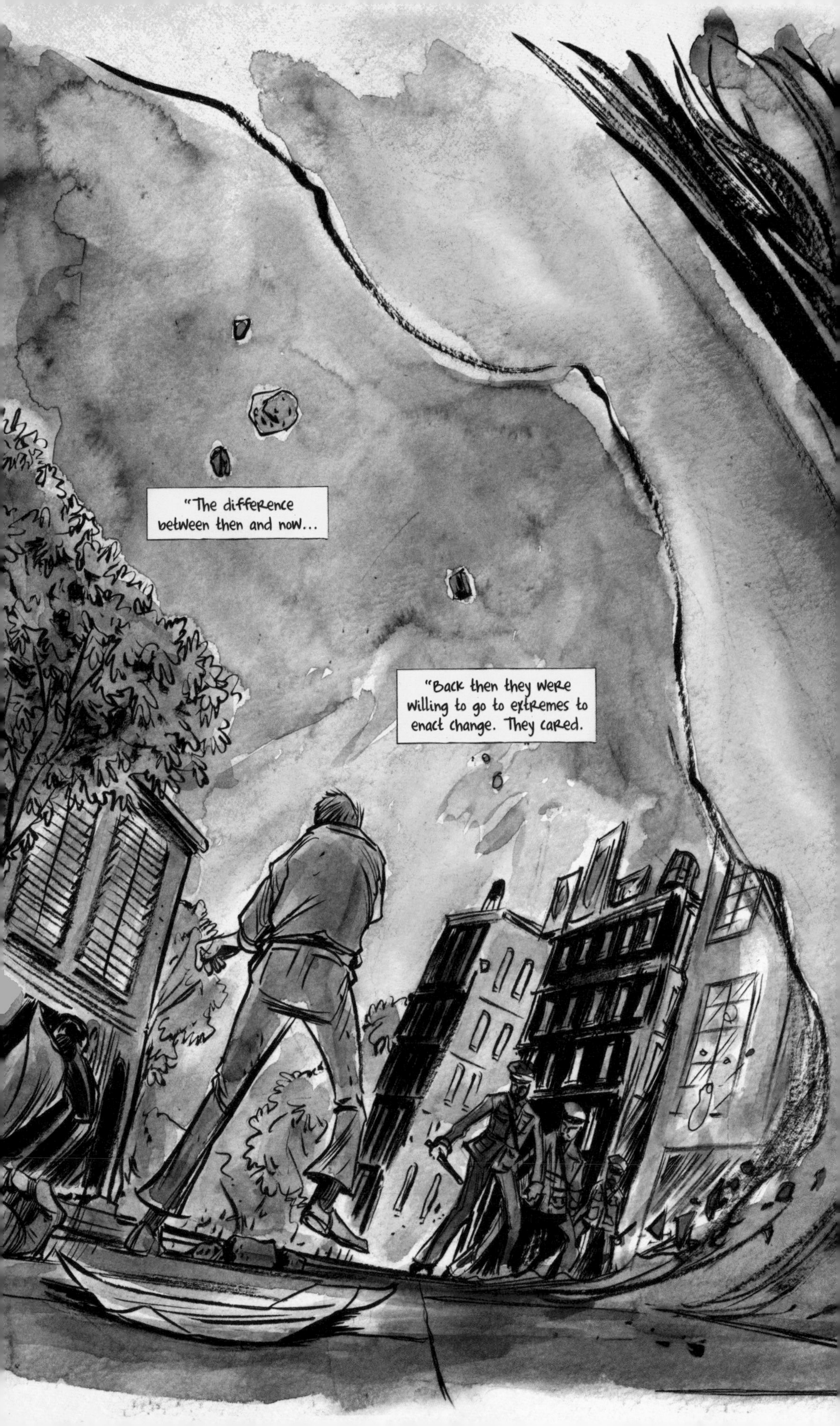
"The difference between then and now...
"Back then they were willing to go to extremes to enact change. They cared.

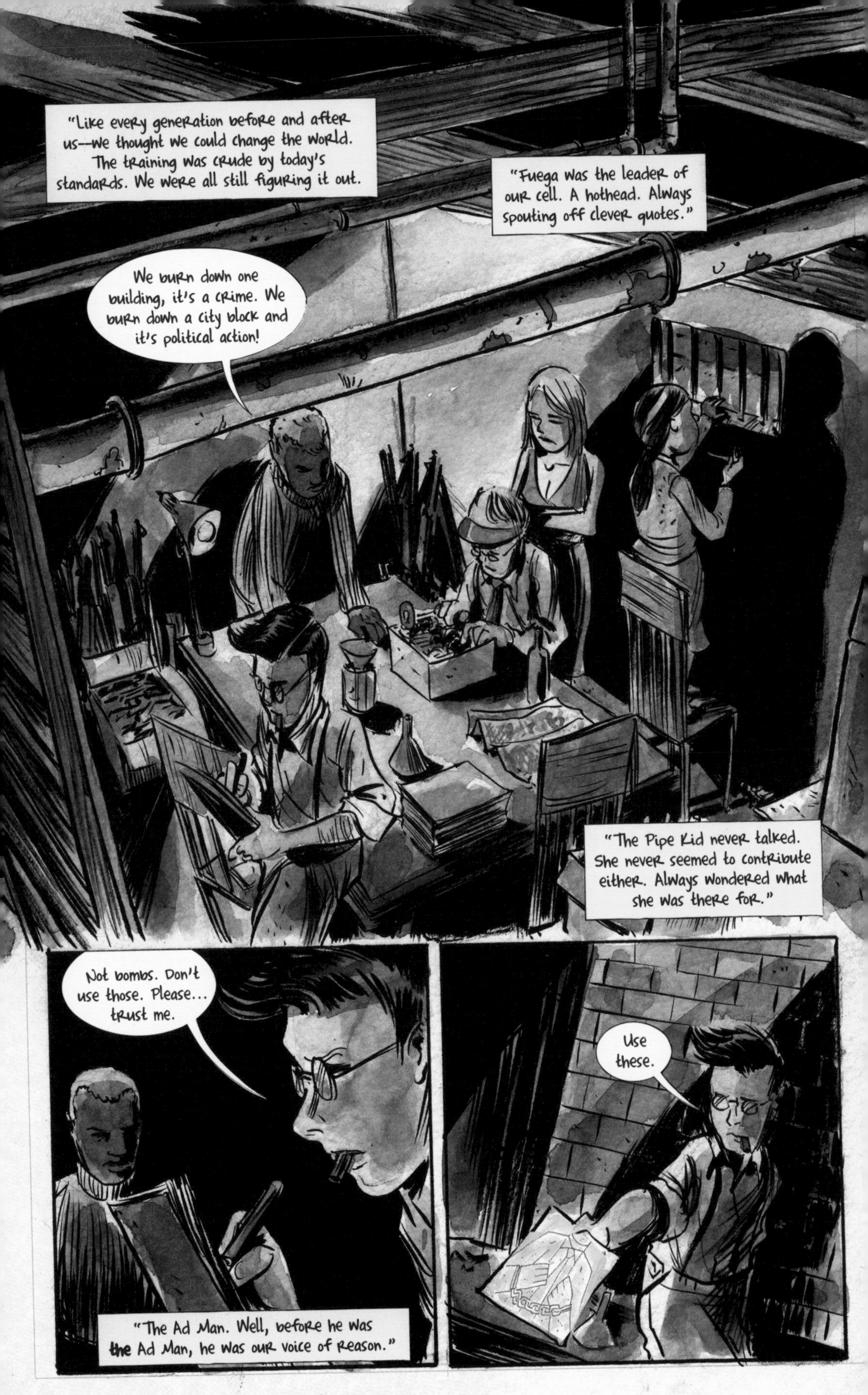
"Like every generation before and after us--we thought we could change the world. The training was crude by today's standards. We were all still figuring it out.
"Fuega was the leader of our cell. A hothead. Always spouting off clever quotes."
We burn down one building, it's a crime. We burn down a city block and it's political action!
"The Pipe Kid never talked. She never seemed to contribute either. Always wondered what she was there for."
Not bombs. Don't use those. Please... trust me.
"The Ad Man. Well, before he was **the** Ad Man, he was our voice of reason."
Use these.

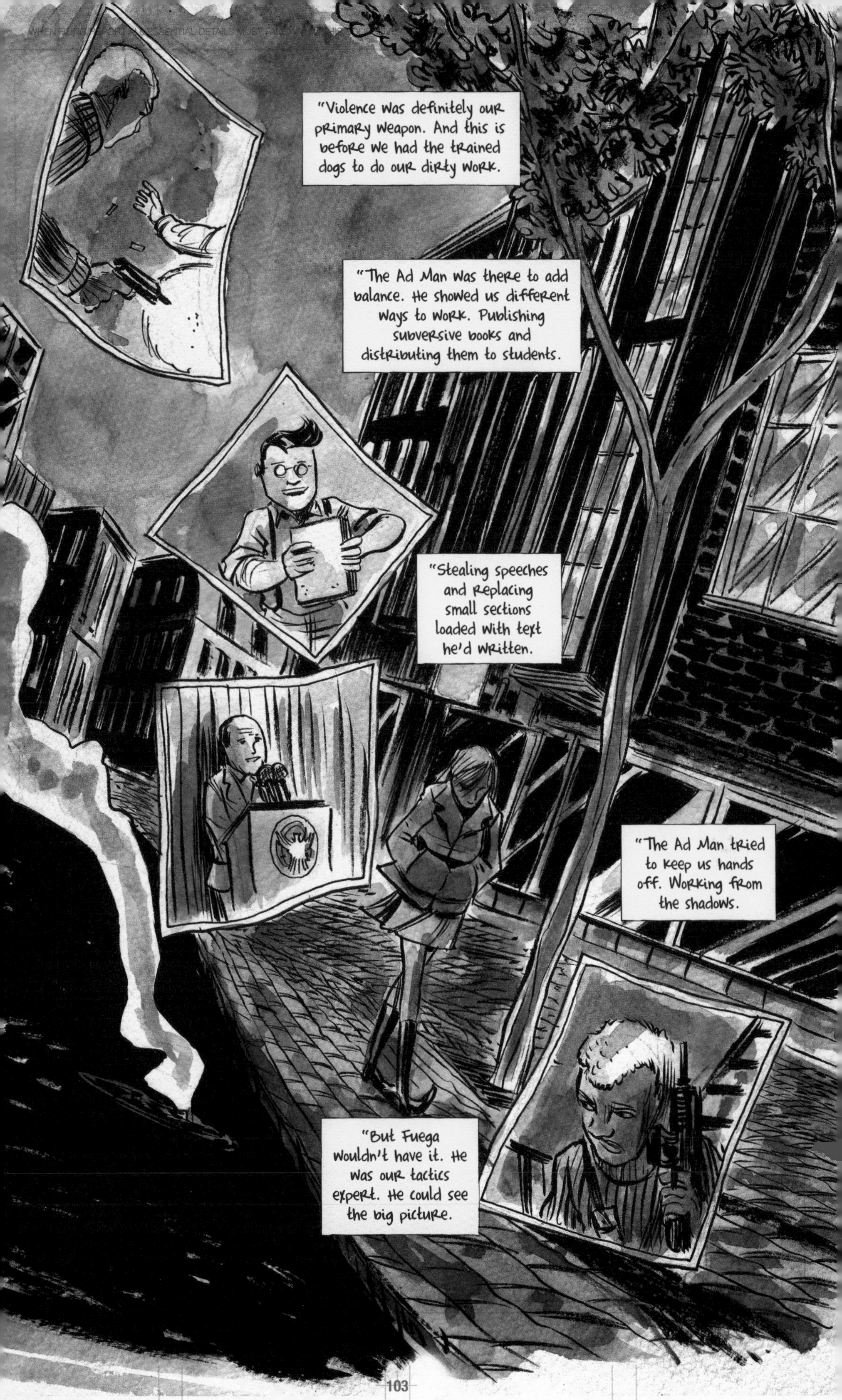
"Violence was definitely our primary weapon. And this is before we had the trained dogs to do our dirty work.
"The Ad Man was there to add balance. He showed us different ways to work. Publishing subversive books and distributing them to students.
"Stealing speeches and replacing small sections loaded with text he'd written.
"The Ad Man tried to keep us hands off. Working from the shadows.
"But Fuega wouldn't have it. He was our tactics expert. He could see the big picture.

The following pages are not intended to make the young reader either a cheat or a trickster.

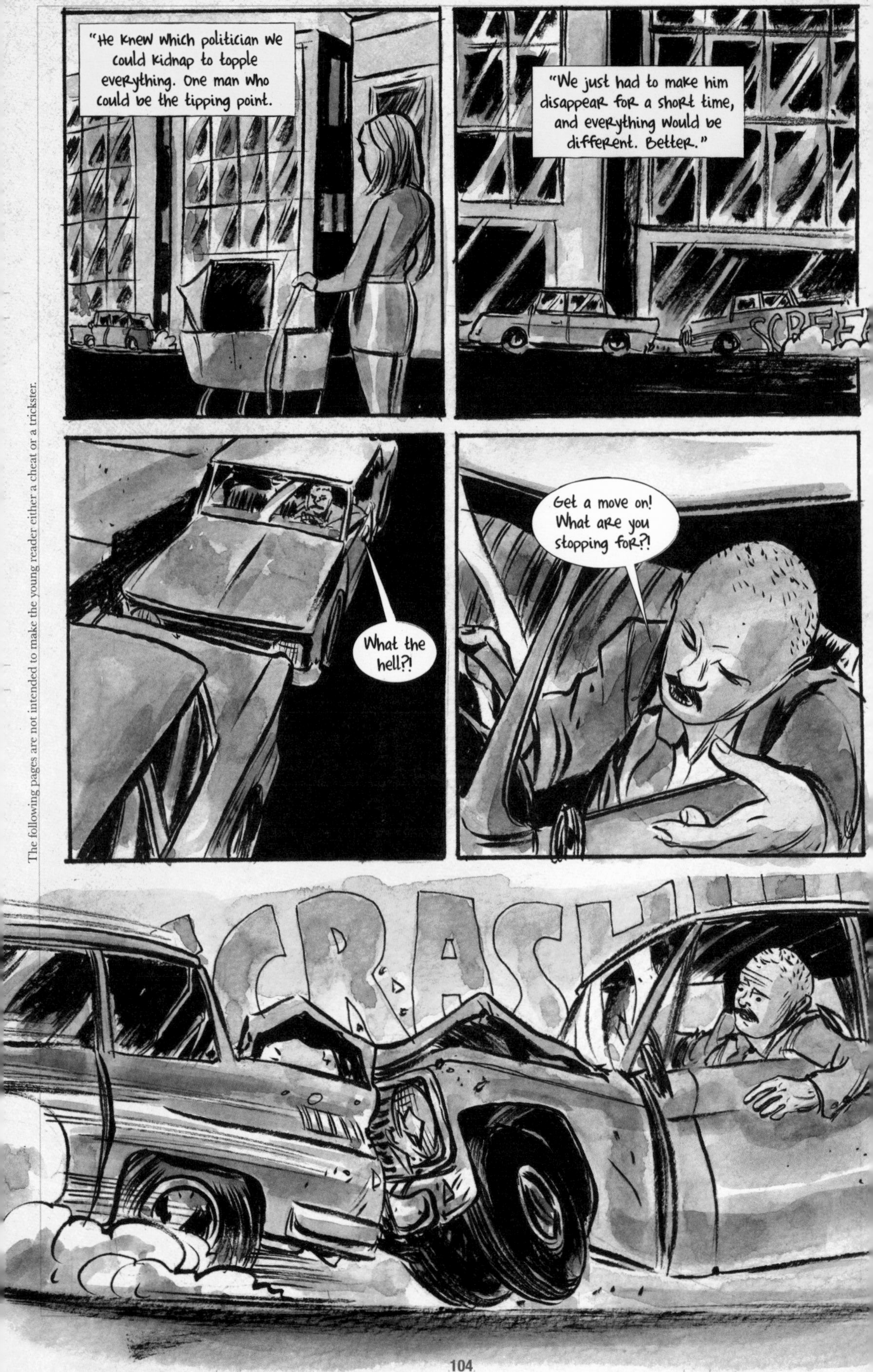
"He knew which politician we could kidnap to topple everything. One man who could be the tipping point.
"We just had to make him disappear for a short time, and everything would be different. Better."
SCREE
What the hell?!
Get a move on! What are you stopping for?!
CRASH

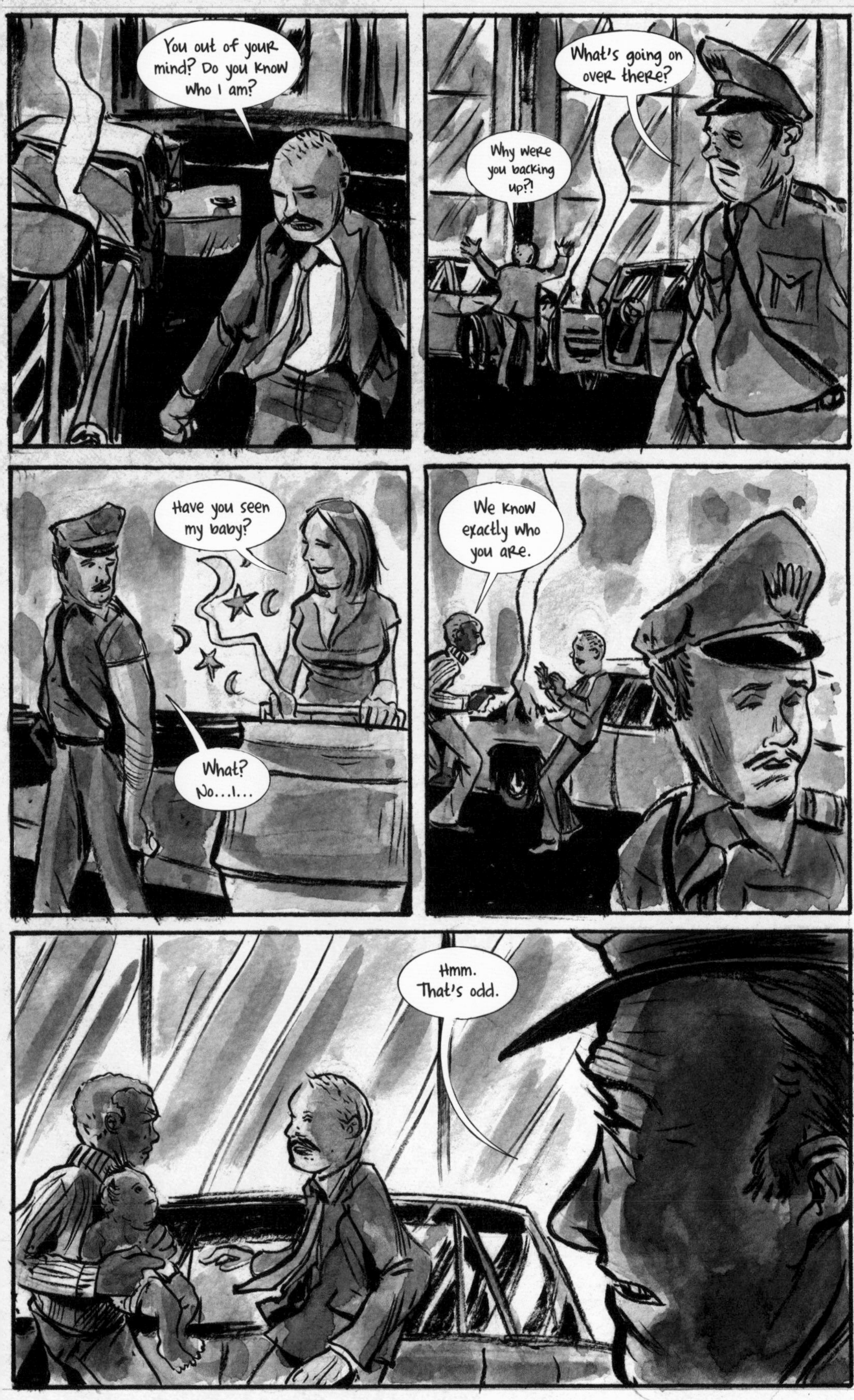
You out of your mind? Do you know who I am?
What's going on over there?
Why were you backing up?!
Have you seen my baby?
What? No...I...
We know exactly who you are.
Hmm. That's odd.

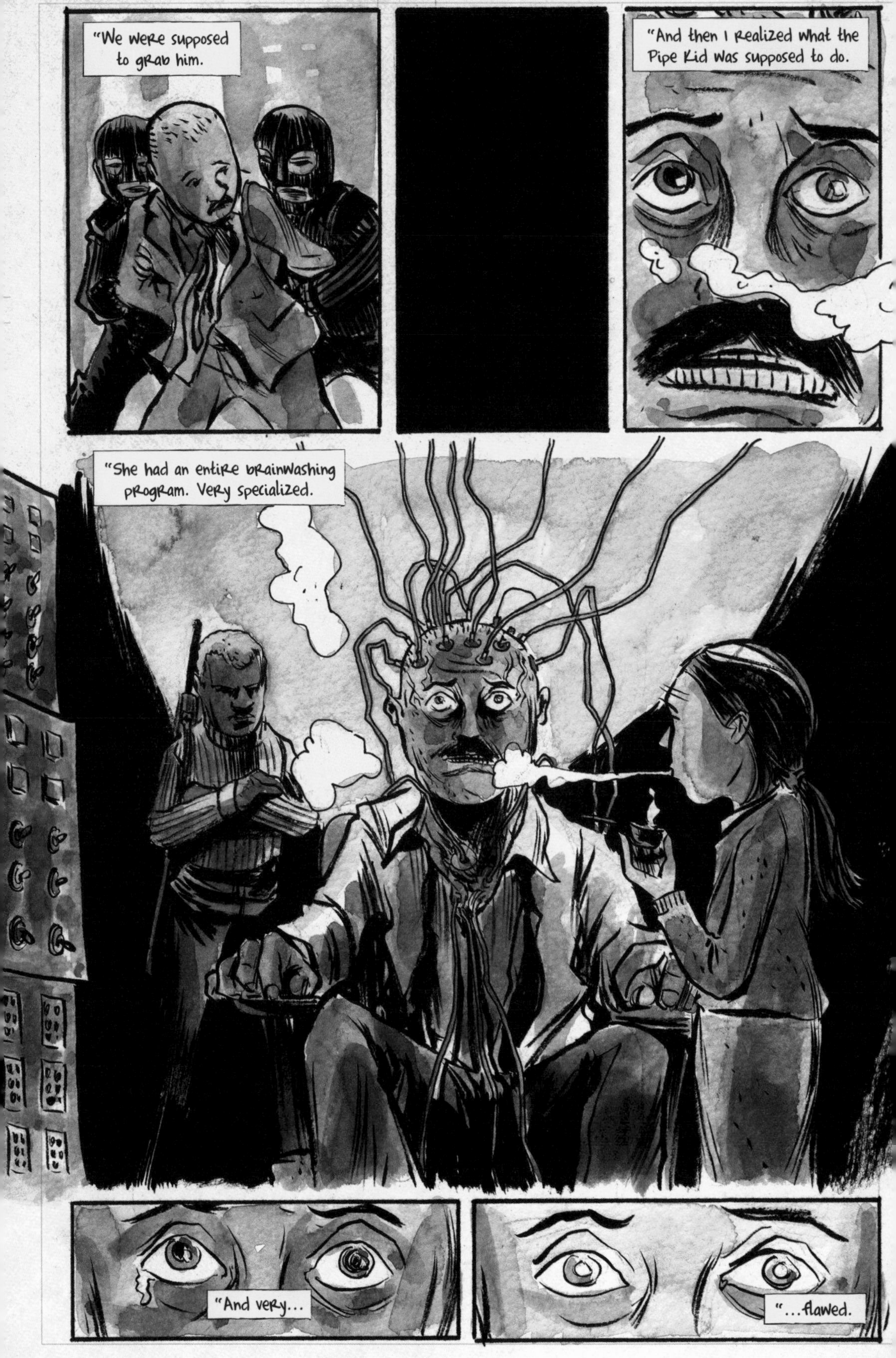
"We were supposed to grab him.
"And then I realized what the Pipe Kid was supposed to do.
"She had an entire brainwashing program. Very specialized.
"And very...
"...flawed.

PROMINENT POLITICIAN KLEIN KIDNAPPED, MURDERED

WANTED FOR KIDNAPPING AND MURDER

"That was the end of us. OR so I thought.

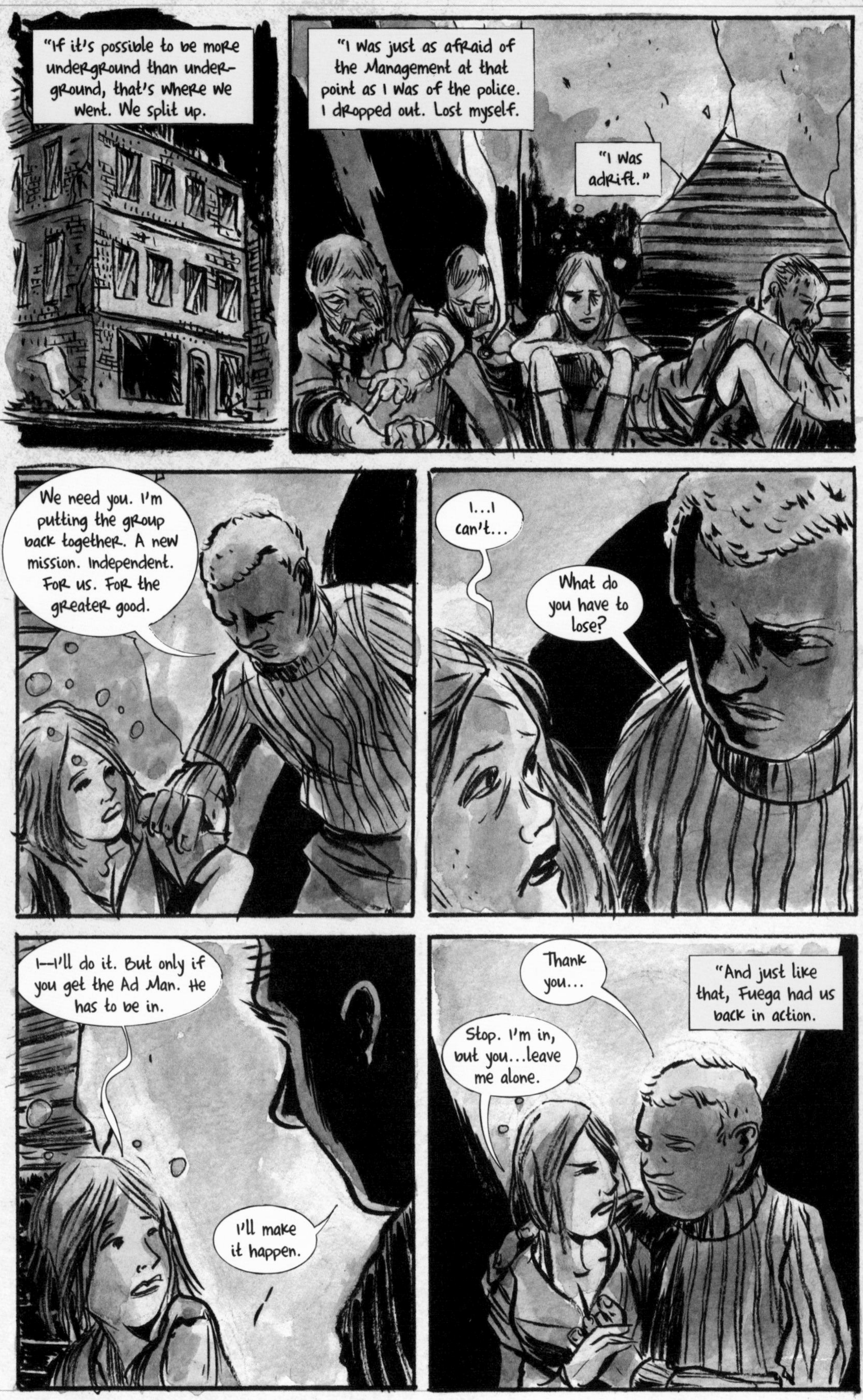
"If it's possible to be more underground than underground, that's where we went. We split up.
"I was just as afraid of the Management at that point as I was of the police. I dropped out. Lost myself.
"I was adrift."
We need you. I'm putting the group back together. A new mission. Independent. For us. For the greater good.
I...I can't...
What do you have to lose?
I--I'll do it. But only if you get the Ad Man. He has to be in.
I'll make it happen.
Thank you...
"And just like that, Fuega had us back in action.
Stop. I'm in, but you...leave me alone.

Deception is allowable in such feats of amusement, because it is in fact not deception at all, when one expects to be puzzled, and is only left to find out the mystery the best way she can.

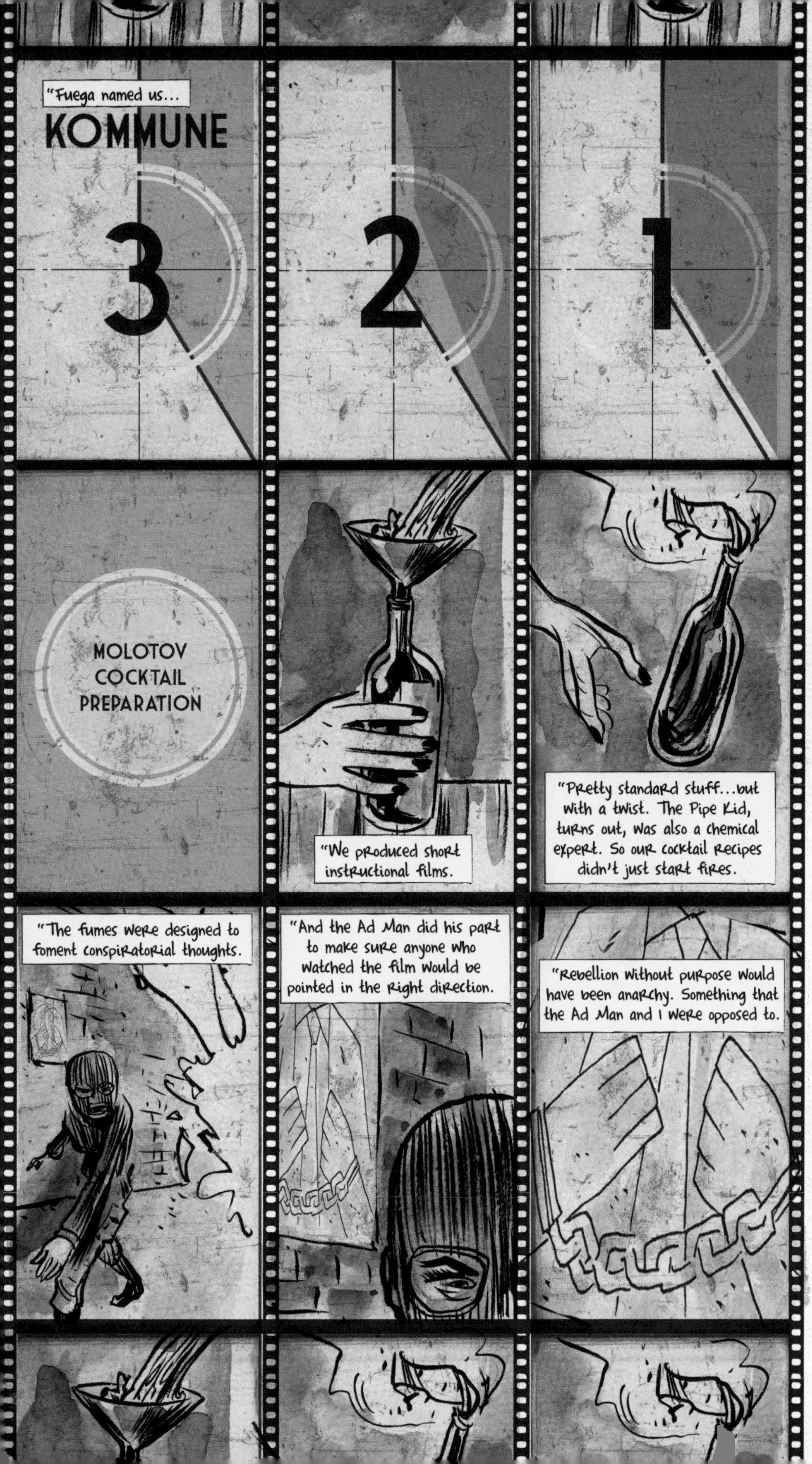
"Fuega named us...
KOMMUNE
3
2
1
MOLOTOV COCKTAIL PREPARATION
"We produced short instructional films.
"Pretty standard stuff...but with a twist. The Pipe Kid, turns out, was also a chemical expert. So our cocktail recipes didn't just start fires.
"The fumes were designed to foment conspiratorial thoughts.
"And the Ad Man did his part to make sure anyone who watched the film would be pointed in the right direction.
"Rebellion without purpose would have been anarchy. Something that the Ad Man and I were opposed to.

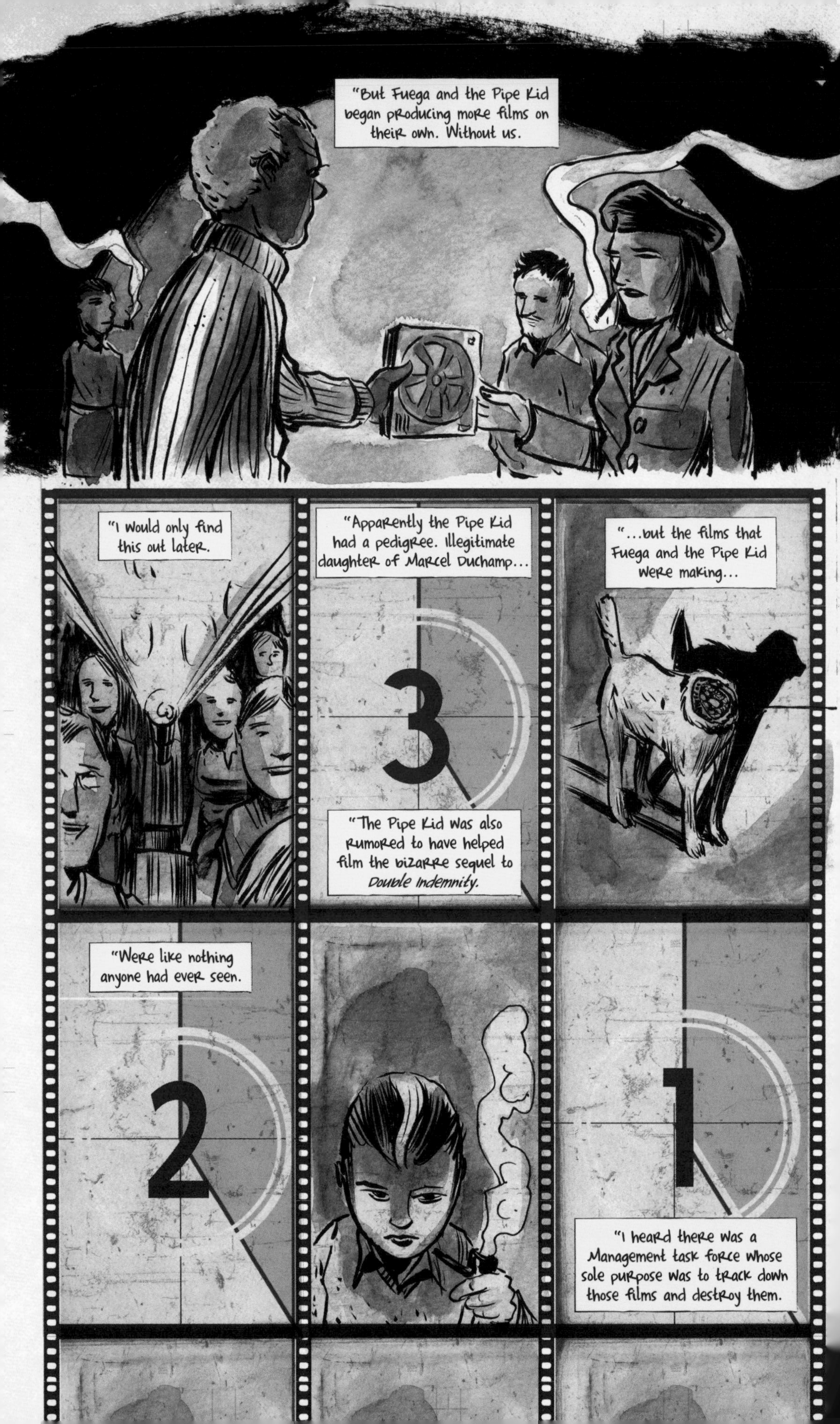
"But Fuega and the Pipe Kid began producing more films on their own. Without us.
"I would only find this out later.
"Apparently the Pipe Kid had a pedigree. Illegitimate daughter of Marcel Duchamp...
3
"The Pipe Kid was also rumored to have helped film the bizarre sequel to *Double Indemnity*.
"...but the films that Fuega and the Pipe Kid were making...
"Were like nothing anyone had ever seen.
2
1
"I heard there was a Management task force whose sole purpose was to track down those films and destroy them.

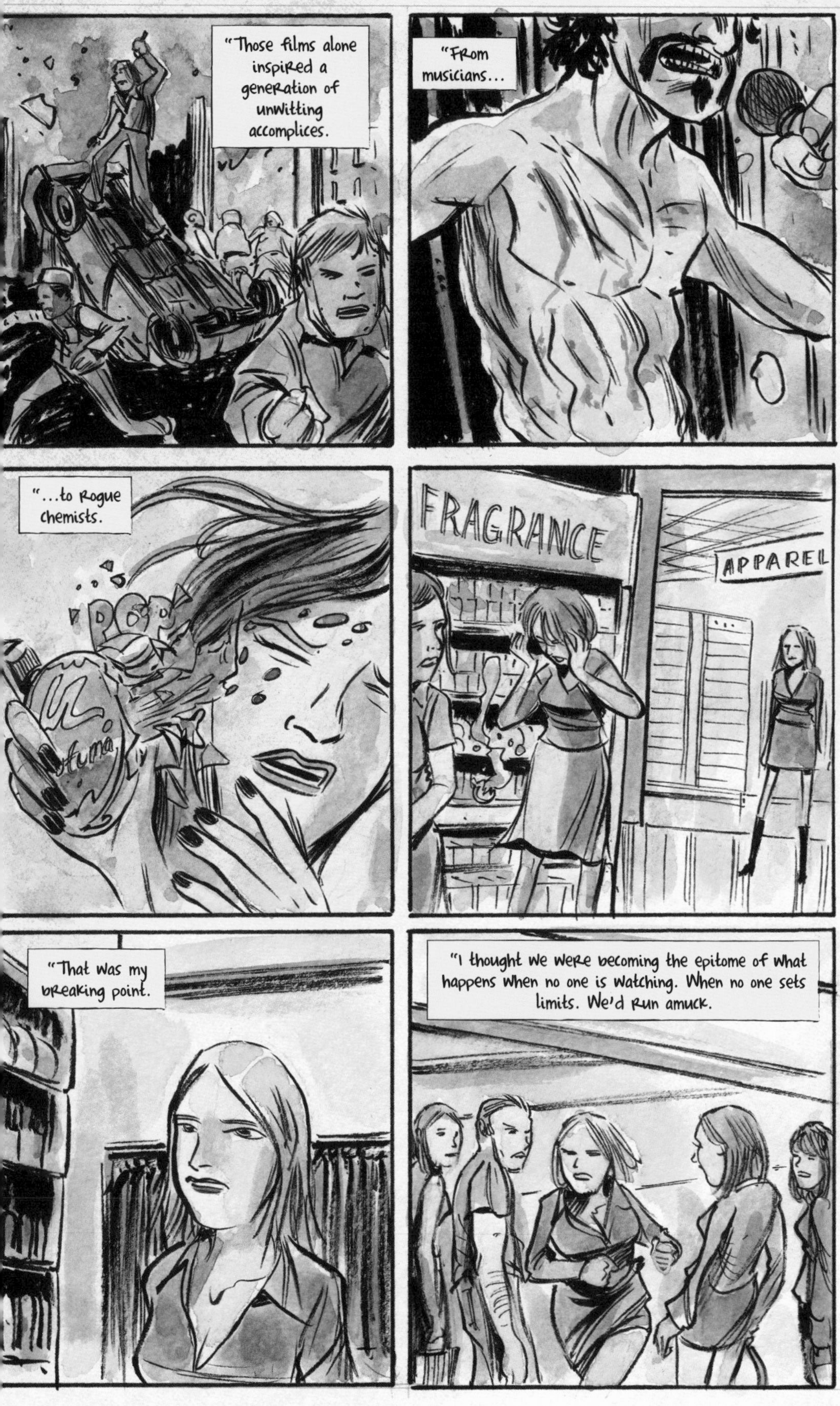
"Those films alone inspired a generation of unwitting accomplices.
"From musicians...
"...to rogue chemists.
POP
FRAGRANCE
APPAREL
"That was my breaking point.
"I thought we were becoming the epitome of what happens when no one is watching. When no one sets limits. We'd run amuck.

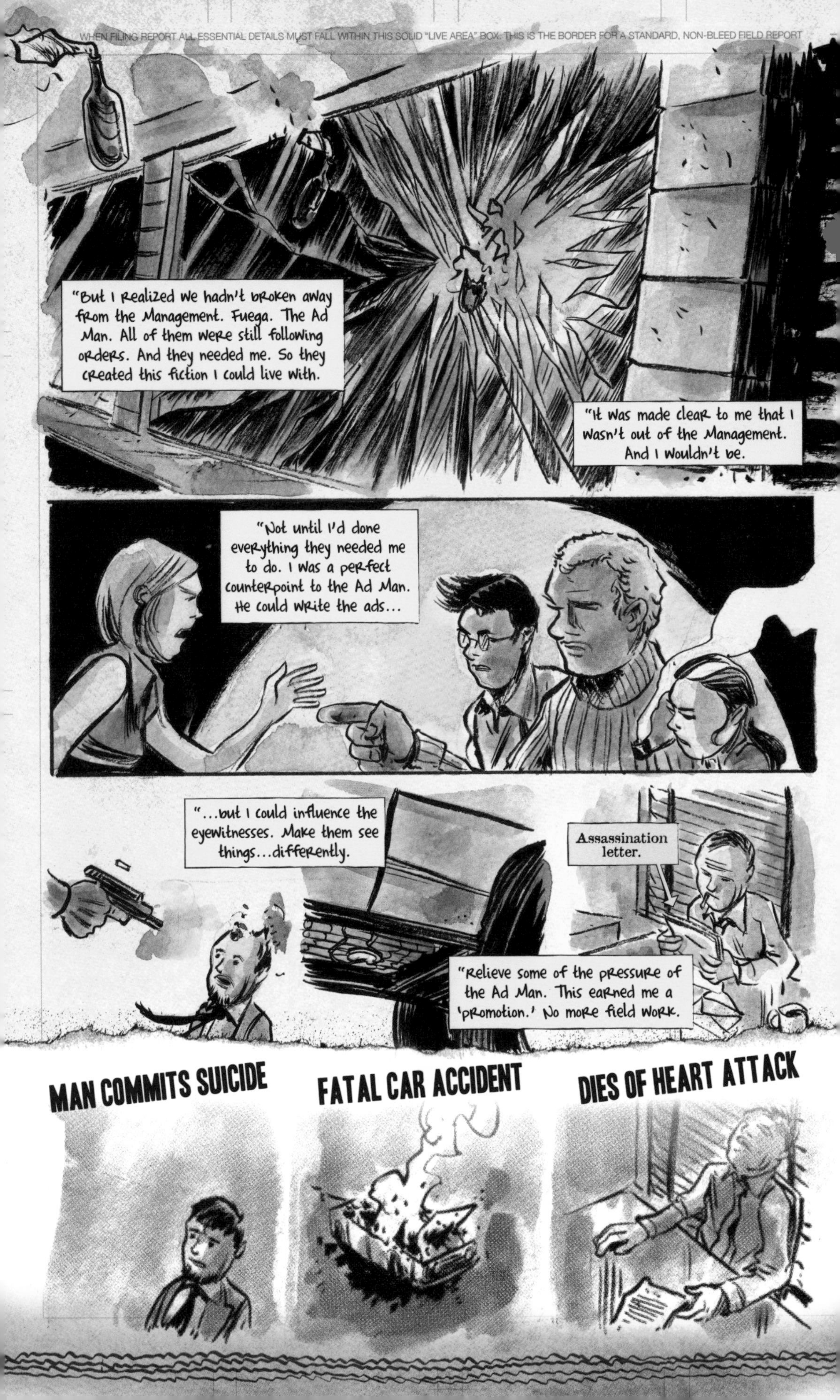
WHEN FILING REPORT ALL ESSENTIAL DETAILS MUST FALL WITHIN THIS SOLID "LIVE AREA" BOX. THIS IS THE BORDER FOR A STANDARD, NON-BLEED FIELD REPORT
"But I realized we hadn't broken away from the Management. Fuega. The Ad Man. All of them were still following orders. And they needed me. So they created this fiction I could live with.
"It was made clear to me that I wasn't out of the Management. And I wouldn't be.
"Not until I'd done everything they needed me to do. I was a perfect counterpoint to the Ad Man. He could write the ads...
"...but I could influence the eyewitnesses. Make them see things...differently.
Assassination letter.
"Relieve some of the pressure of the Ad Man. This earned me a 'promotion.' No more field work.
MAN COMMITS SUICIDE
FATAL CAR ACCIDENT
DIES OF HEART ATTACK

WHEN FILING REPORT ALL ESSENTIAL DETAILS MUST FALL WITHIN THIS SOLID "LIVE AREA" BOX. THIS IS THE BORDER FOR A STANDARD, NON-BLEED FIELD REPORT

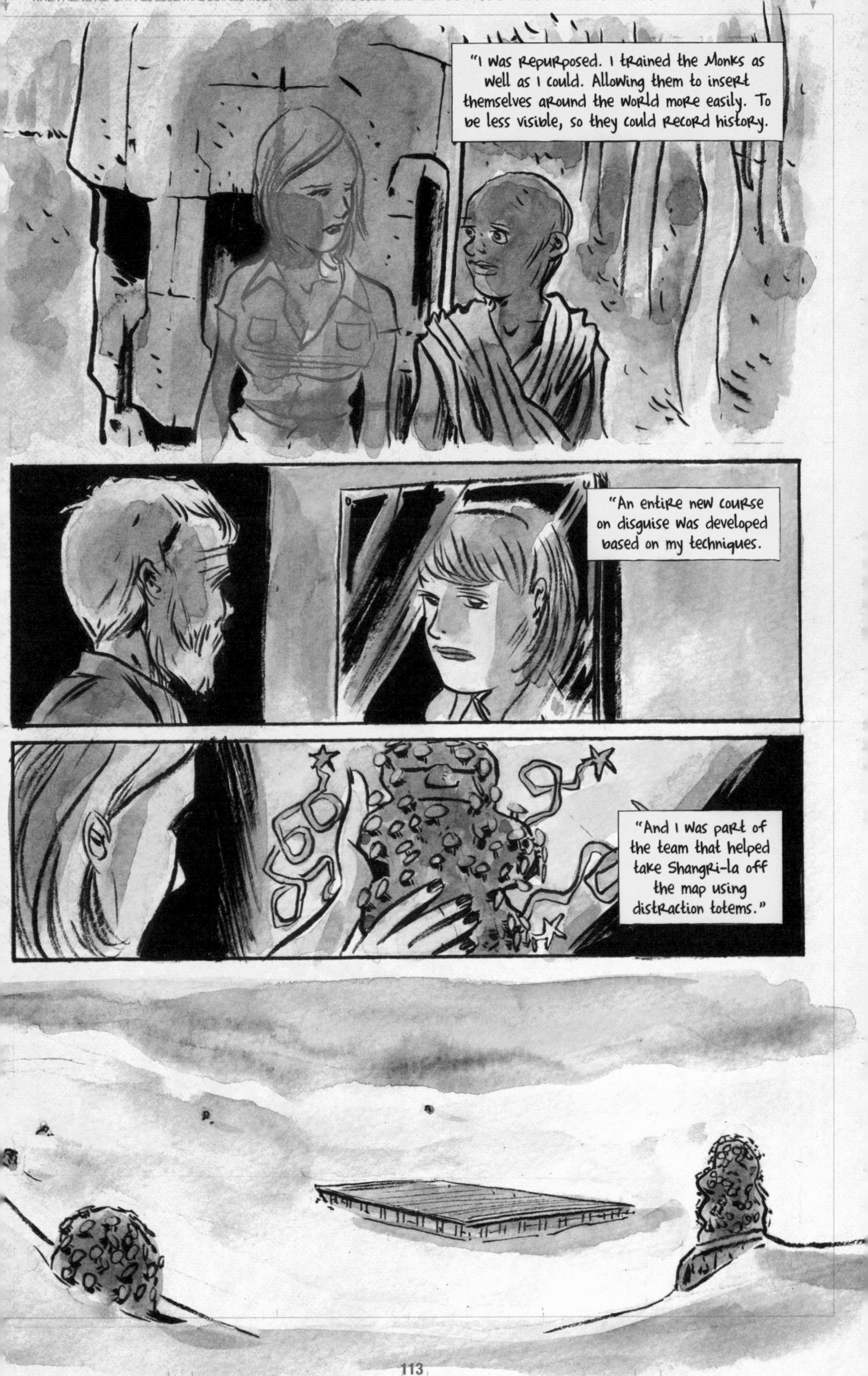
"I was repurposed. I trained the Monks as well as I could. Allowing them to insert themselves around the world more easily. To be less visible, so they could record history.
"An entire new course on disguise was developed based on my techniques.
"And I was part of the team that helped take Shangri-la off the map using distraction totems."

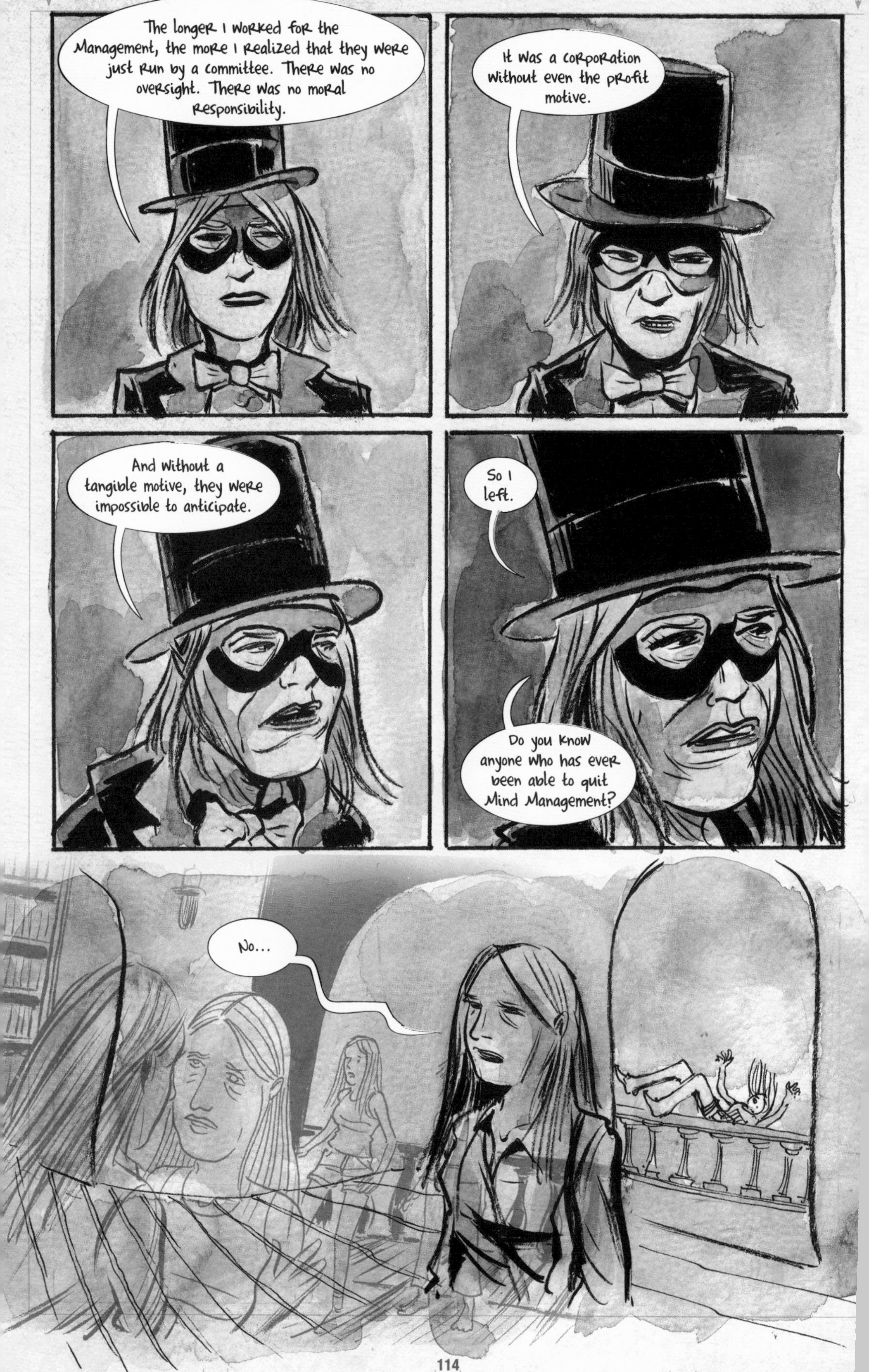
The longer I worked for the Management, the more I realized that they were just run by a committee. There was no oversight. There was no moral responsibility.
It was a corporation without even the profit motive.
And without a tangible motive, they were impossible to anticipate.
So I left.
Do you know anyone who has ever been able to quit Mind Management?
No...

WHEN FILING REPORT ALL ESSENTIAL DETAILS MUST FALL WITHIN THIS SOLID "LIVE AREA" BOX. THIS IS THE BORDER FOR A STANDARD, NON-BLEED FIELD REPORT

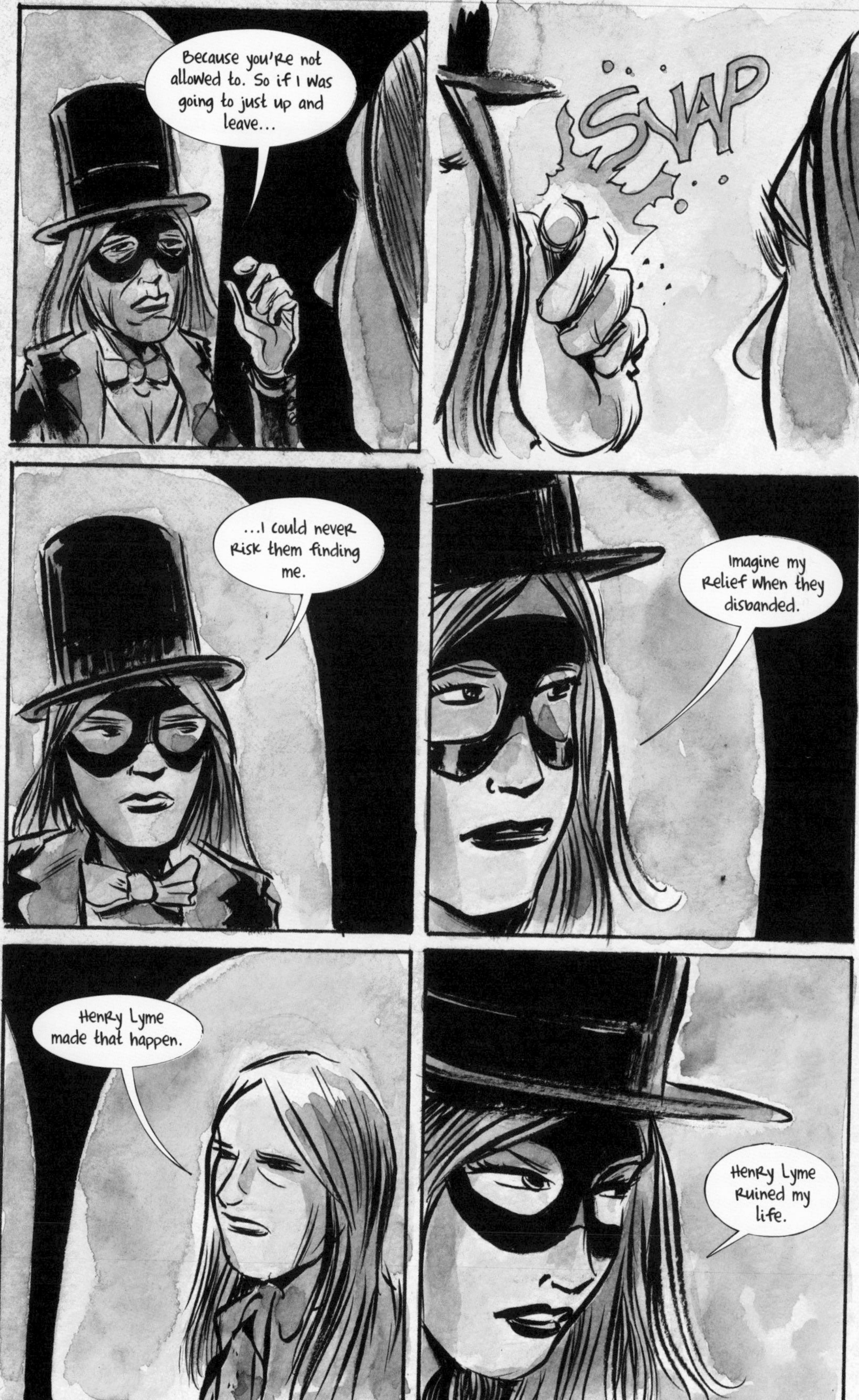

Because you're not allowed to. So if I was going to just up and leave...
SNAP
...I could never risk them finding me.
Imagine my relief when they disbanded.
Henry Lyme made that happen.
Henry Lyme ruined my life.

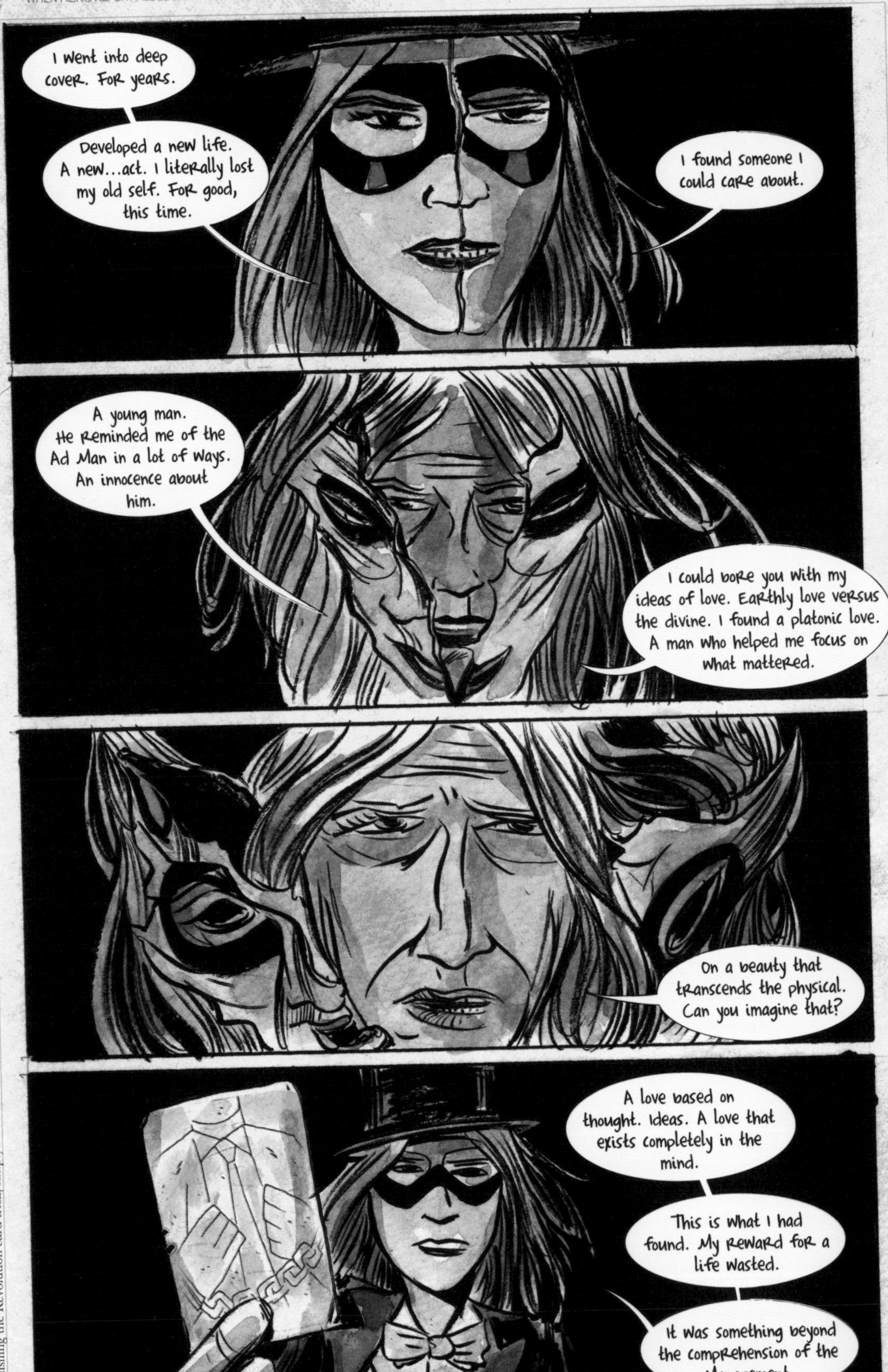
I went into deep cover. For years.
Developed a new life. A new...act. I literally lost my old self. For good, this time.
I found someone I could care about.
A young man. He reminded me of the Ad Man in a lot of ways. An innocence about him.
I could bore you with my ideas of love. Earthly love versus the divine. I found a platonic love. A man who helped me focus on what mattered.
On a beauty that transcends the physical. Can you imagine that?
A love based on thought. Ideas. A love that exists completely in the mind.
This is what I had found. My reward for a life wasted.
It was something beyond the comprehension of the Management.

When finishing the Revolution card trick, simply reveal the card to the audience and let the remaining cards fall to the floor in a flourish.

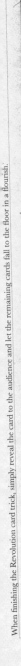

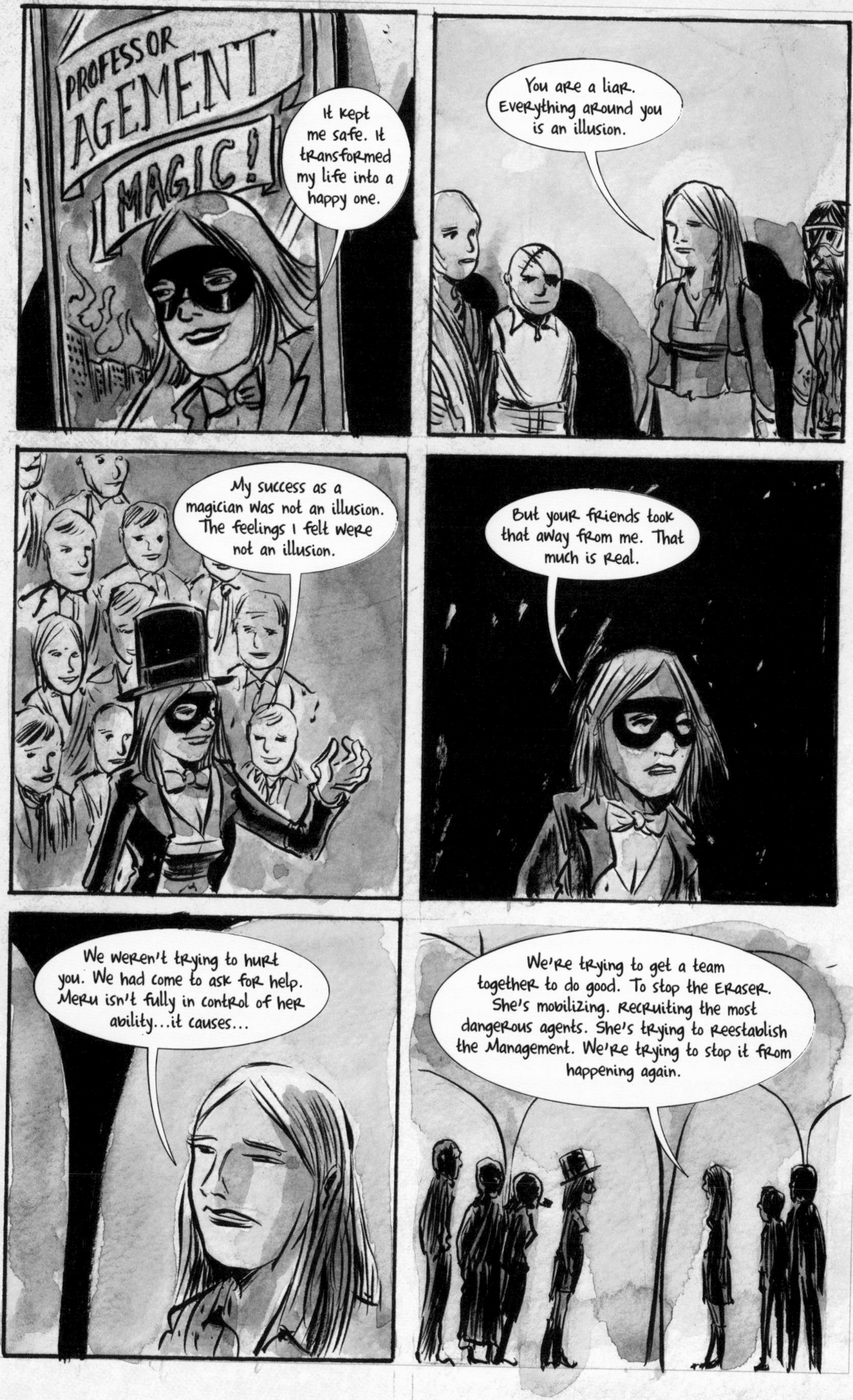
PROFESSOR AGEMENT MAGIC!
It kept me safe. It transformed my life into a happy one.
You are a liar. Everything around you is an illusion.
My success as a magician was not an illusion. The feelings I felt were not an illusion.
But your friends took that away from me. That much is real.
We weren't trying to hurt you. We had come to ask for help. Meru isn't fully in control of her ability...it causes...
We're trying to get a team together to do good. To stop the Eraser. She's mobilizing. Recruiting the most dangerous agents. She's trying to reestablish the Management. We're trying to stop it from happening again.

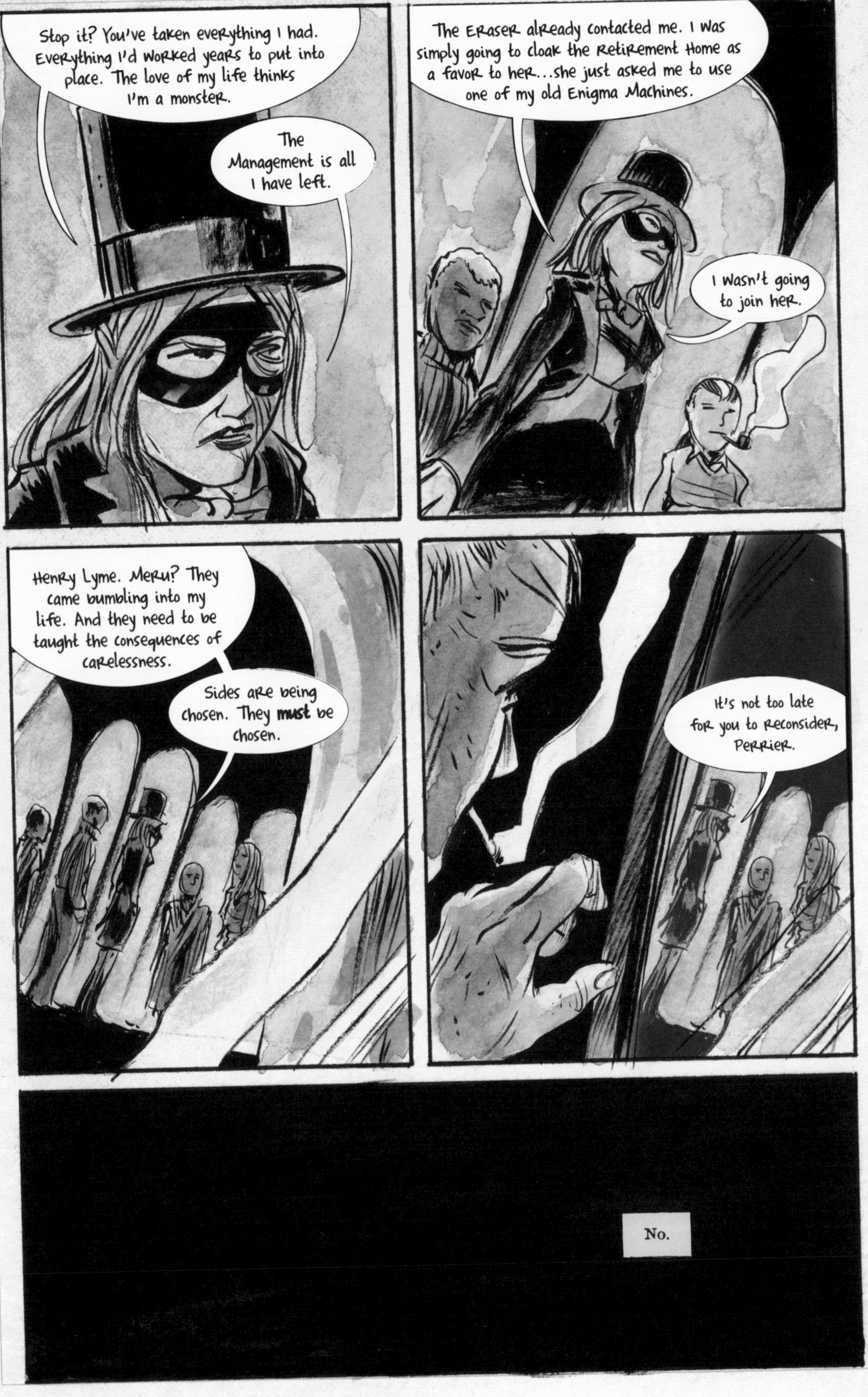
Stop it? You've taken everything I had. Everything I'd worked years to put into place. The love of my life thinks I'm a monster.
The Management is all I have left.
The Eraser already contacted me. I was simply going to cloak the Retirement Home as a favor to her...she just asked me to use one of my old Enigma Machines.
I wasn't going to join her.
Henry Lyme. Meru? They came bumbling into my life. And they need to be taught the consequences of carelessness.
Sides are being chosen. They **must** be chosen.
It's not too late for you to reconsider, Perrier.
No.

The Nailed Card finale: the nail should be put through the face of the card so when the others fall to the floor, the remaining card

WHEN FILING REPORT ALL ESSENTIAL DETAILS MUST FALL WITHIN THIS SOLID "LIVE AREA" BOX. THIS IS THE BORDER FOR A STANDARD, NON-BLEED FIELD REPORT

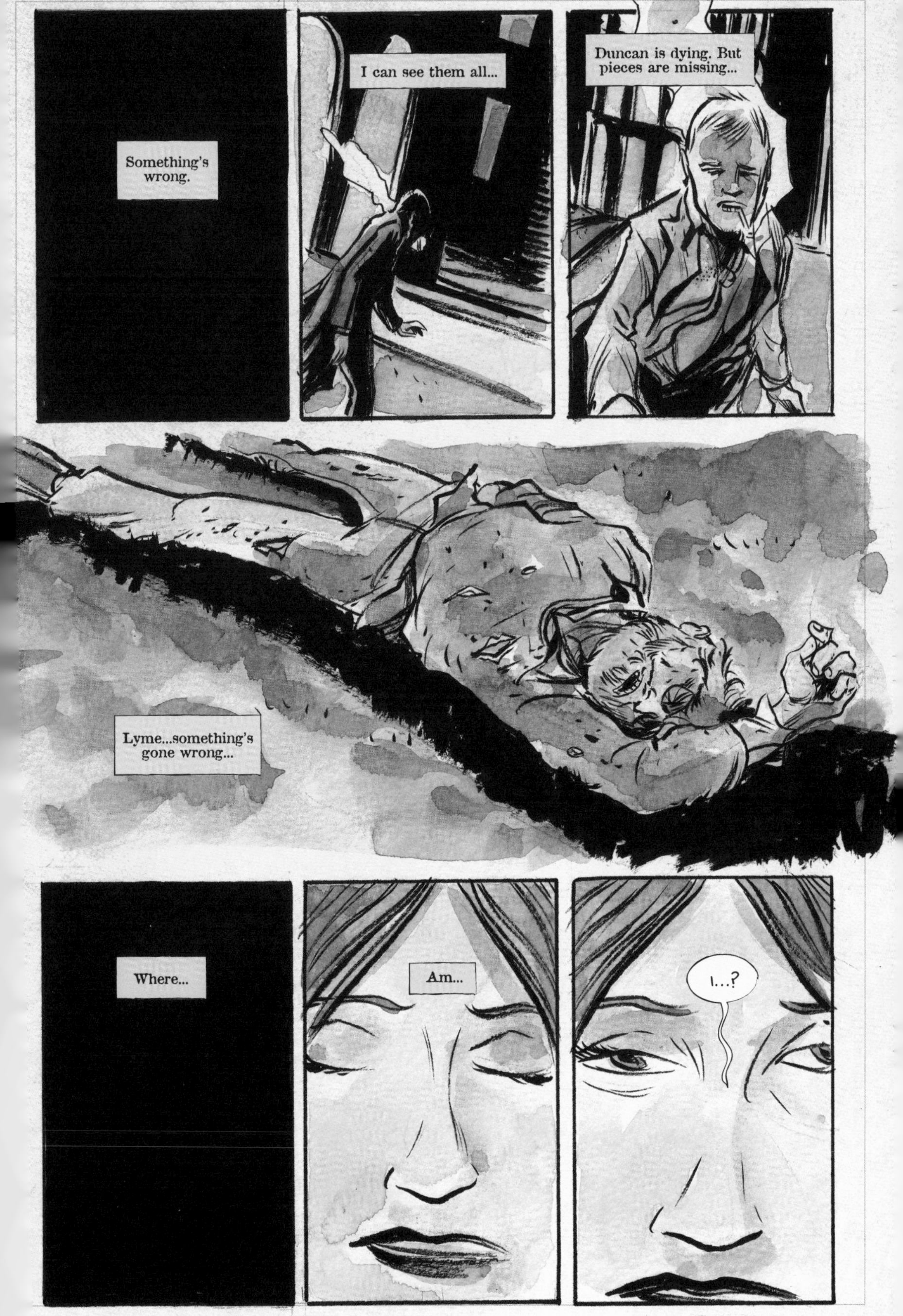

Something's wrong.
I can see them all...
Duncan is dying. But pieces are missing...
Lyme...something's gone wrong...
Where...
Am...
I...?

WHEN FILING REPORT ALL ESSENTIAL DETAILS MUST FALL WITHIN THIS SOLID "LIVE AREA" BOX. THIS IS THE BORDER FOR A STANDARD, NON-BLEED FIELD REPORT

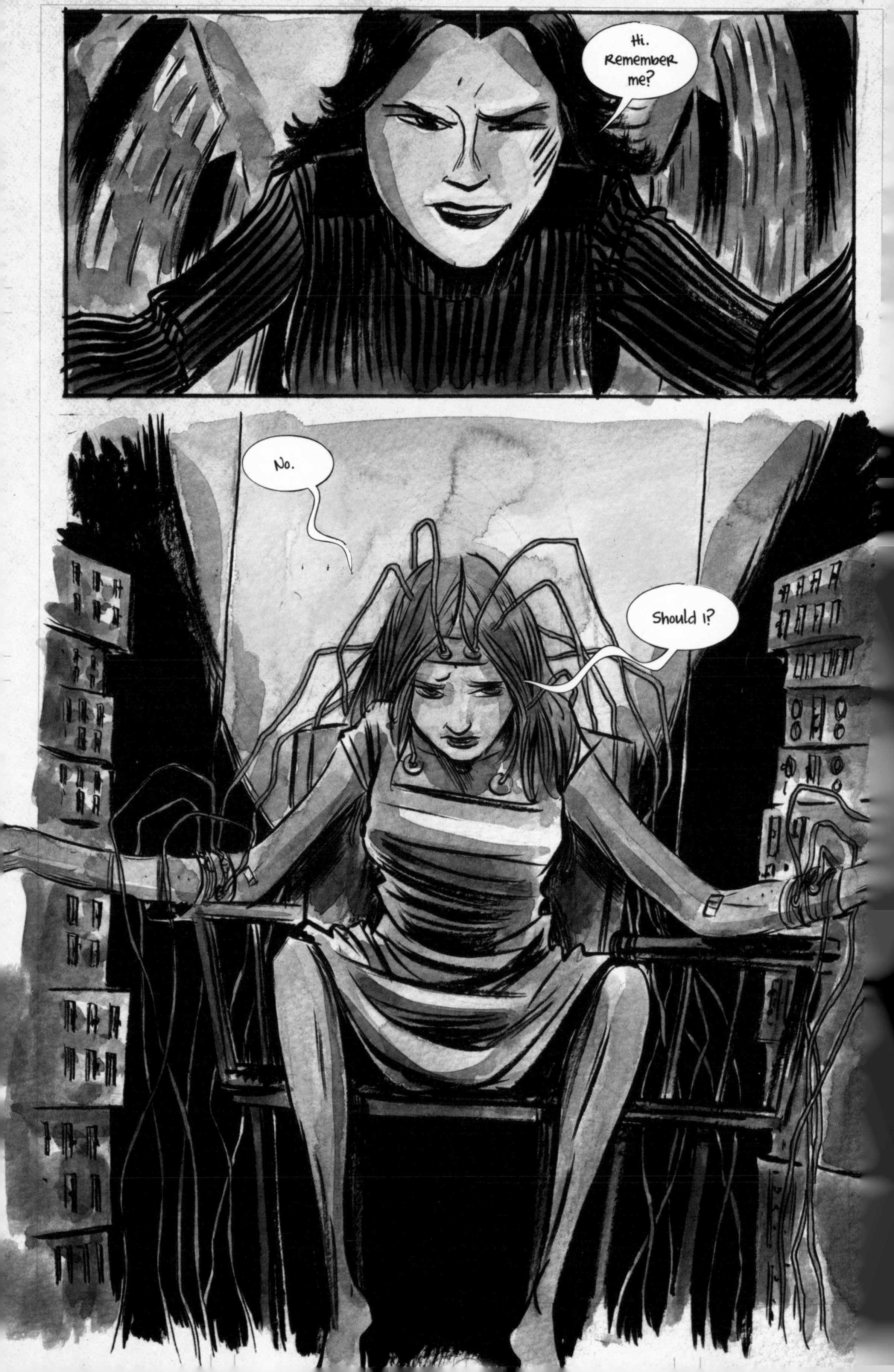
Hi. Remember me?
No.
Should I?

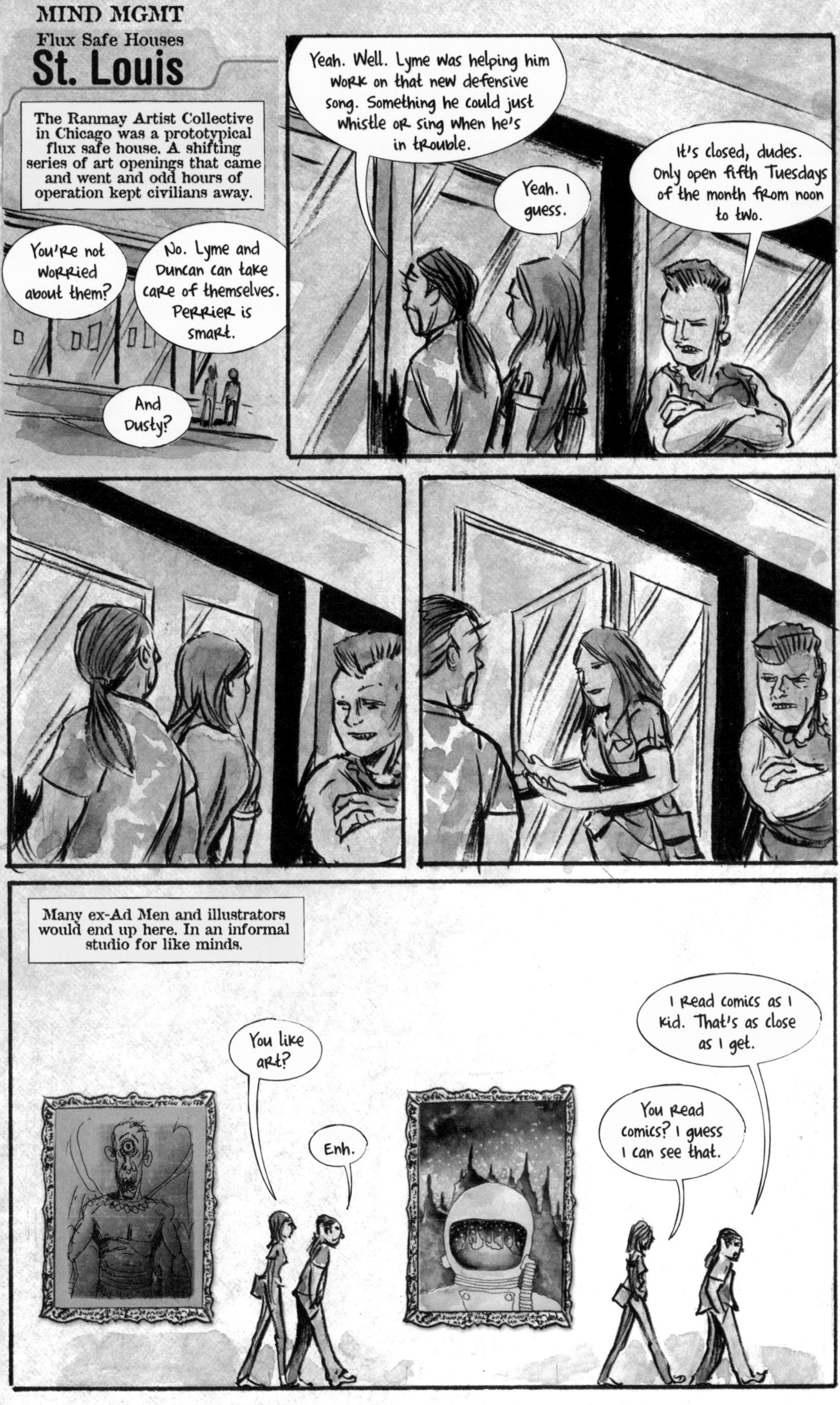
MIND MGMT
Flux Safe Houses
St. Louis
The Ranmay Artist Collective in Chicago was a prototypical flux safe house. A shifting series of art openings that came and went and odd hours of operation kept civilians away.
You're not worried about them?
No. Lyme and Duncan can take care of themselves. Perrier is smart.
And Dusty?
Yeah. Well. Lyme was helping him work on that new defensive song. Something he could just whistle or sing when he's in trouble.
Yeah. I guess.
It's closed, dudes. Only open fifth Tuesdays of the month from noon to two.
Many ex-Ad Men and illustrators would end up here. In an informal studio for like minds.
You like art?
Enh.
I read comics as I kid. That's as close as I get.
You read comics? I guess I can see that.

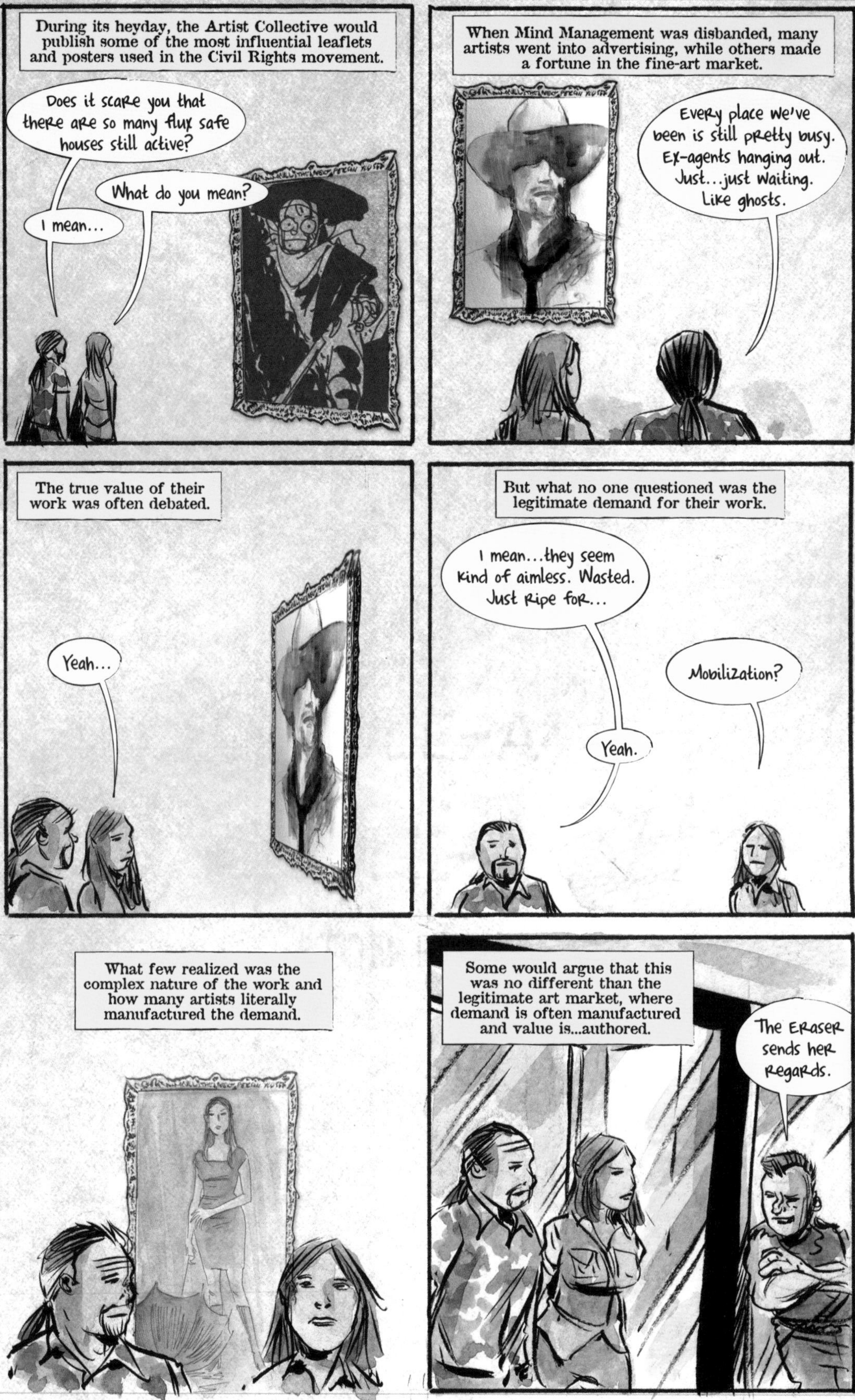
During its heyday, the Artist Collective would publish some of the most influential leaflets and posters used in the Civil Rights movement.
Does it scare you that there are so many flux safe houses still active?
What do you mean?
I mean...
When Mind Management was disbanded, many artists went into advertising, while others made a fortune in the fine-art market.
Every place we've been is still pretty busy. Ex-agents hanging out. Just...just waiting. Like ghosts.
The true value of their work was often debated.
Yeah...
But what no one questioned was the legitimate demand for their work.
I mean...they seem kind of aimless. Wasted. Just ripe for...
Mobilization?
Yeah.
What few realized was the complex nature of the work and how many artists literally manufactured the demand.
Some would argue that this was no different than the legitimate art market, where demand is often manufactured and value is...authored.
The Eraser sends her regards.

End Mind Memo

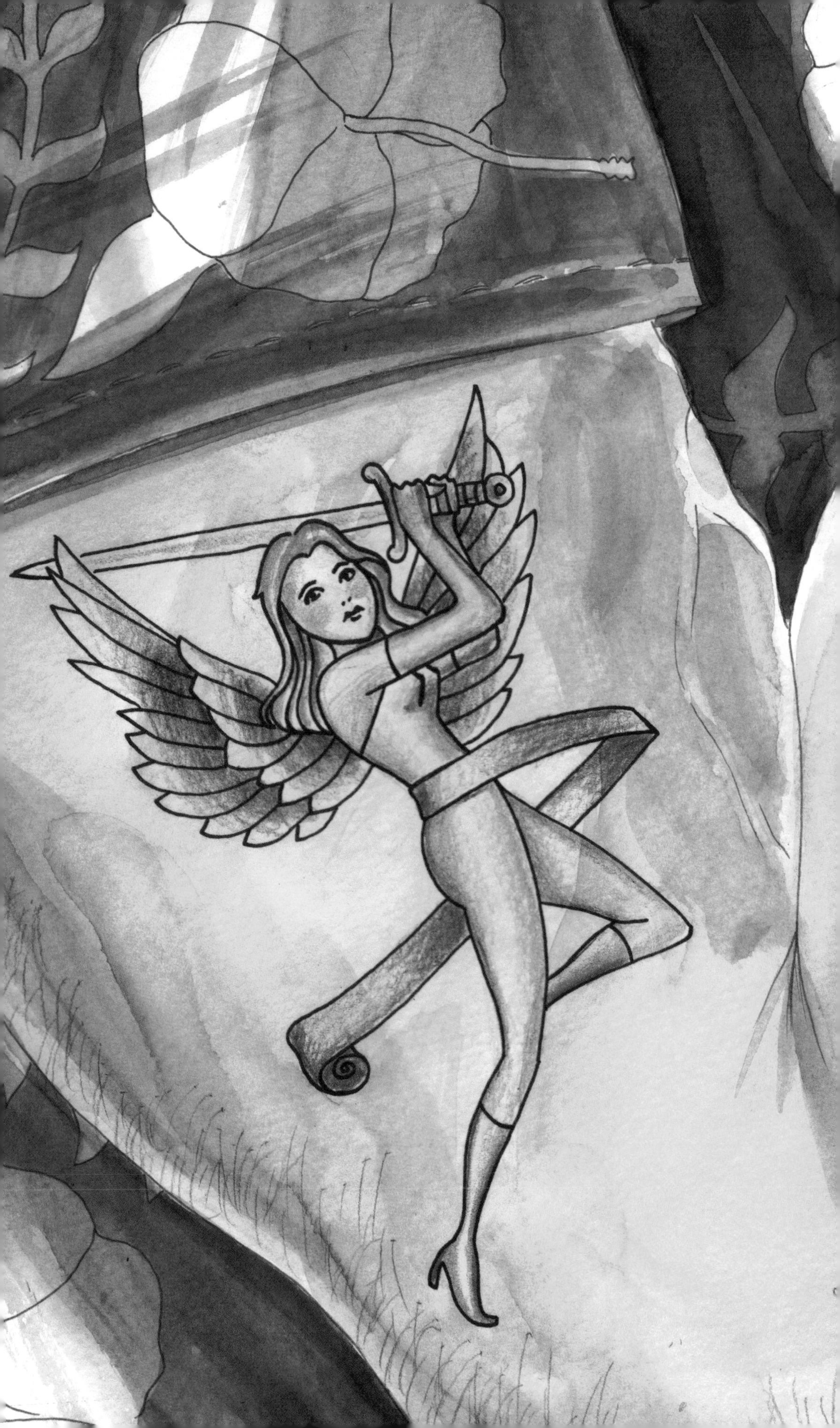

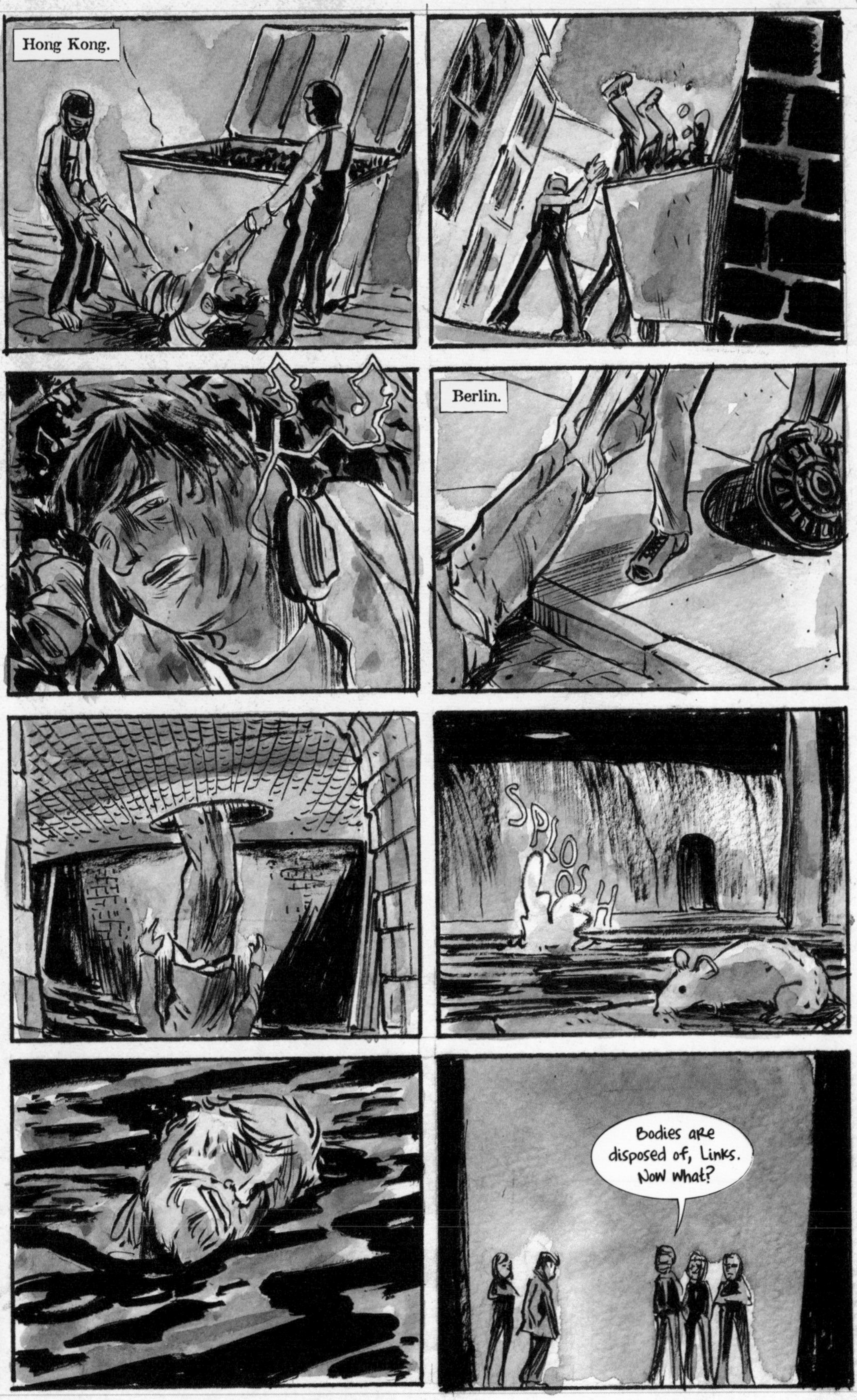
Hong Kong.
Berlin.
SPLOSH
Bodies are disposed of, Links. Now what?

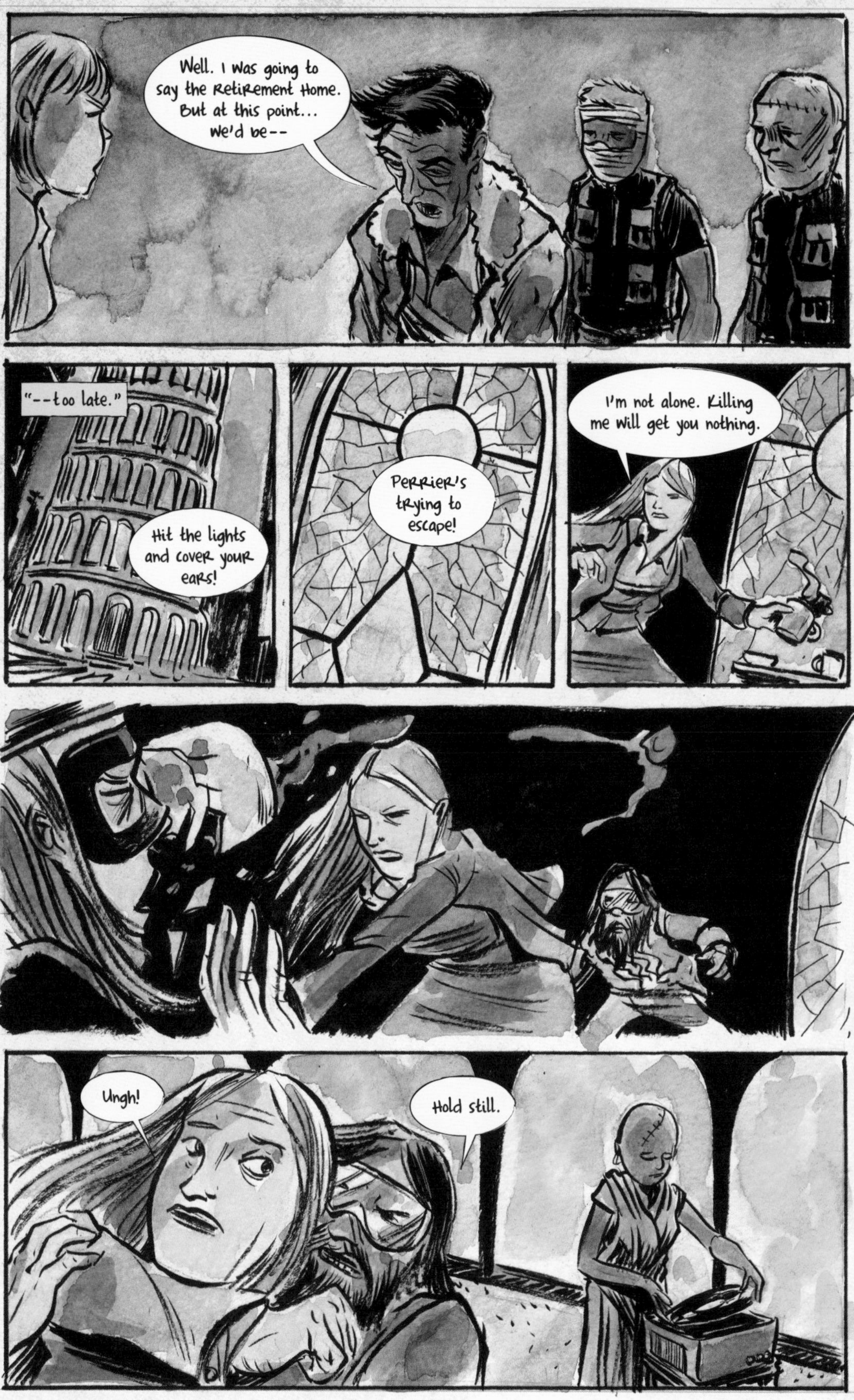
Well. I was going to say the Retirement Home. But at this point... we'd be--
"--too late."
Hit the lights and cover your ears!
Perrier's trying to escape!
I'm not alone. Killing me will get you nothing.
Ungh!
Hold still.

D: I was on the streets. Begging for a cup of coffee and then using the empty cup to get change from people. **RS:** Were you performing on the streets then? **D:** Oh yeah. All the time.

WHEN FILING REPORT ALL ESSENTIAL DETAILS MUST FALL WITHIN THIS SOLID "LIVE AREA" BOX. THIS IS THE BORDER FOR A STANDARD, NON-BLEED FIELD REPORT

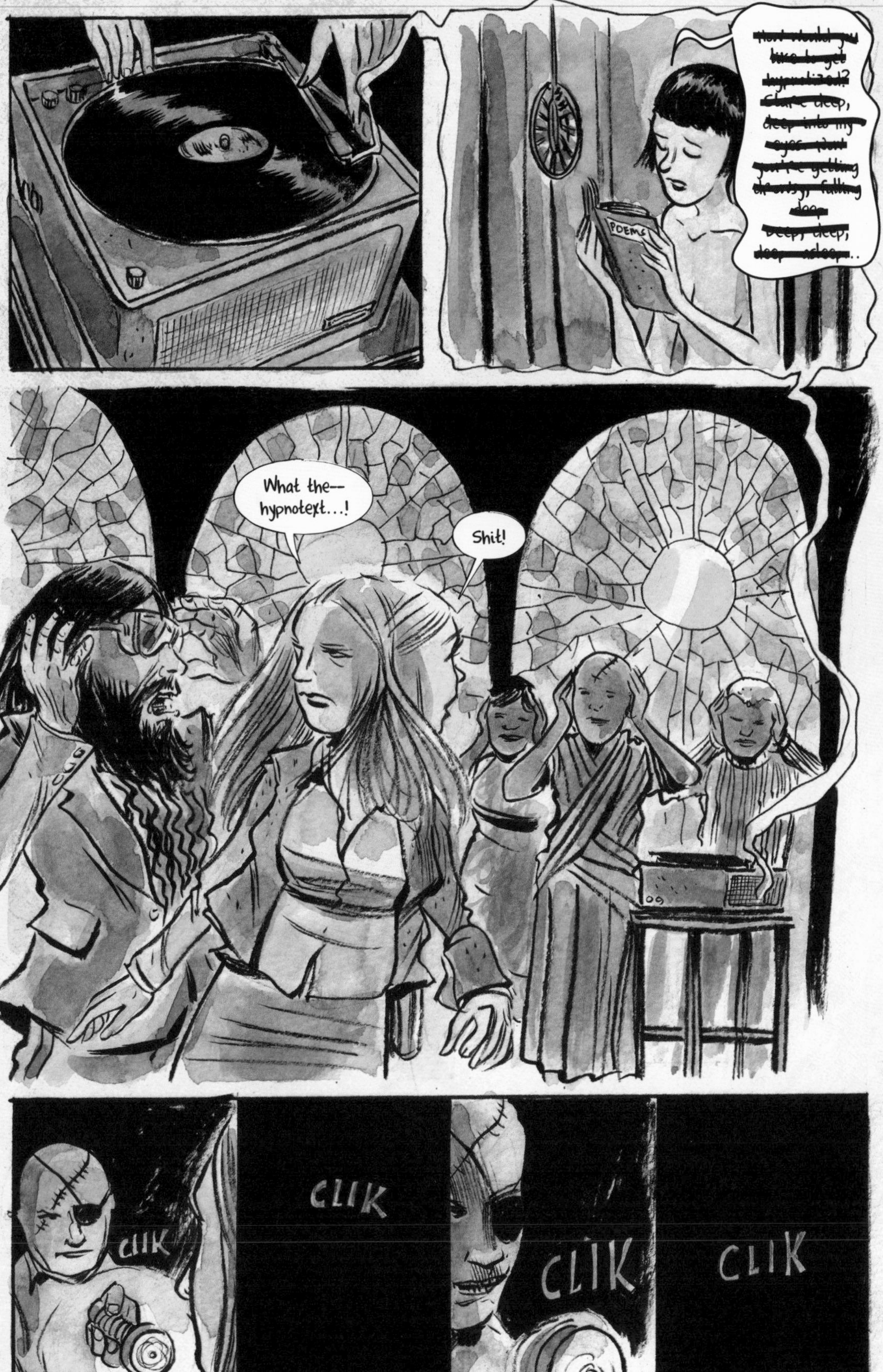

WHAM
CRASH
Stay with me.
And don't trust anything you see.

D: I got up and ran after the car. I thought I was dreaming. Apparently my agent had been looking for me for a month after I dropped off the map.

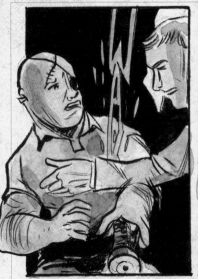

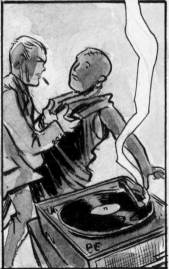

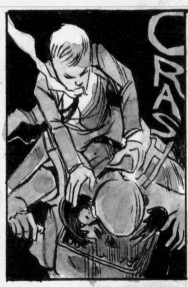

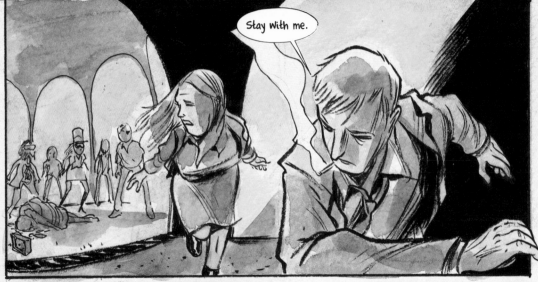

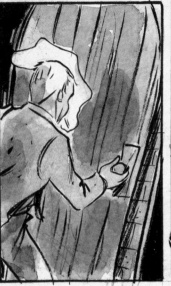

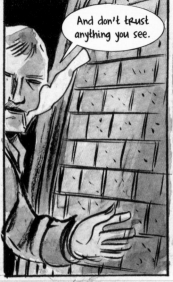

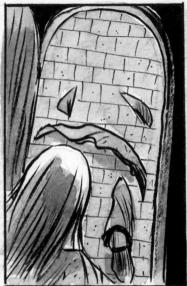

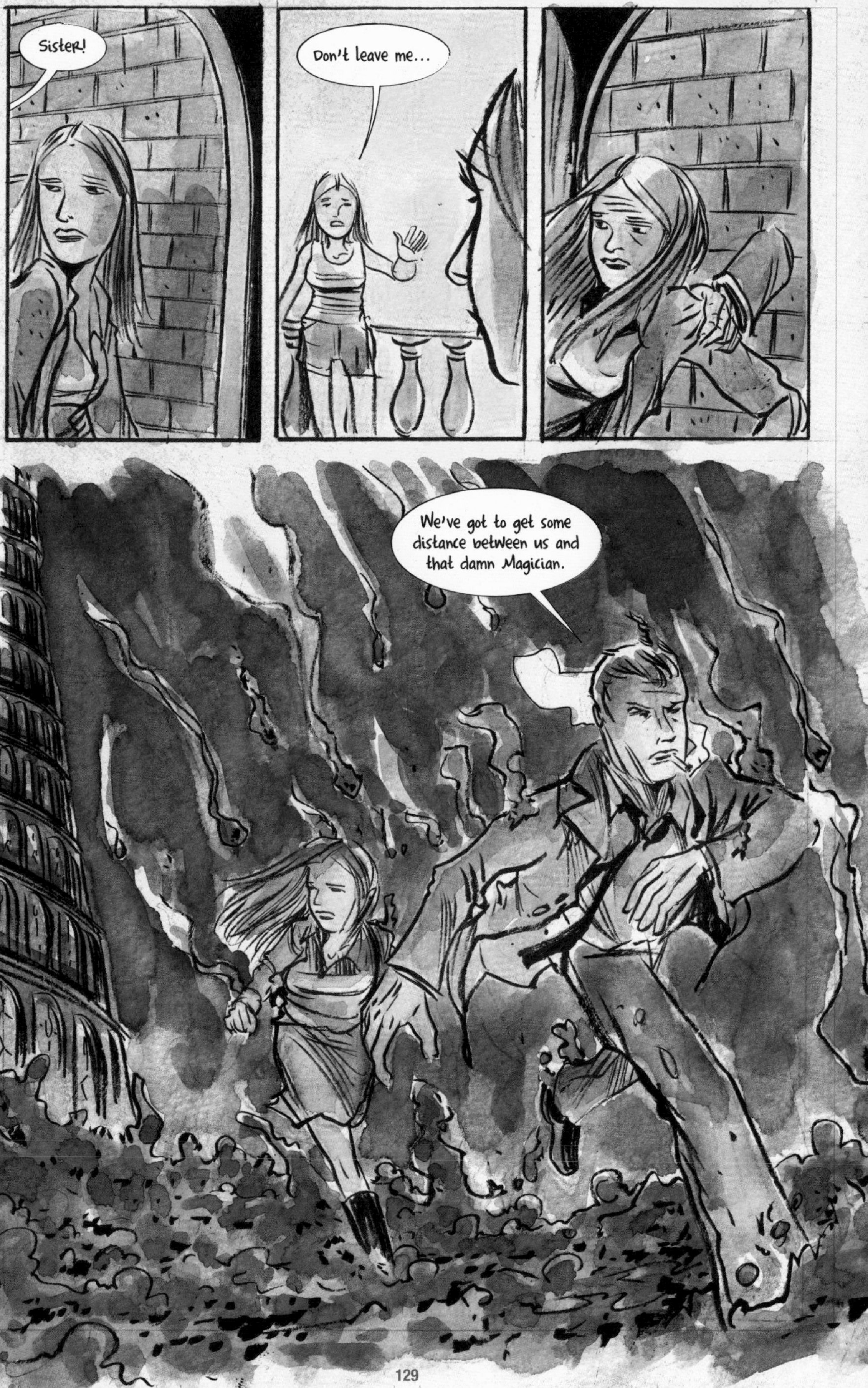
Sister!
Don't leave me...
We've got to get some distance between us and that damn Magician.

WHEN FILING REPORT ALL ESSENTIAL DETAILS MUST FALL WITHIN THIS SOLID "LIVE AREA" BOX. THIS IS THE BORDER FOR A STANDARD, NON-BLEED FIELD REPORT

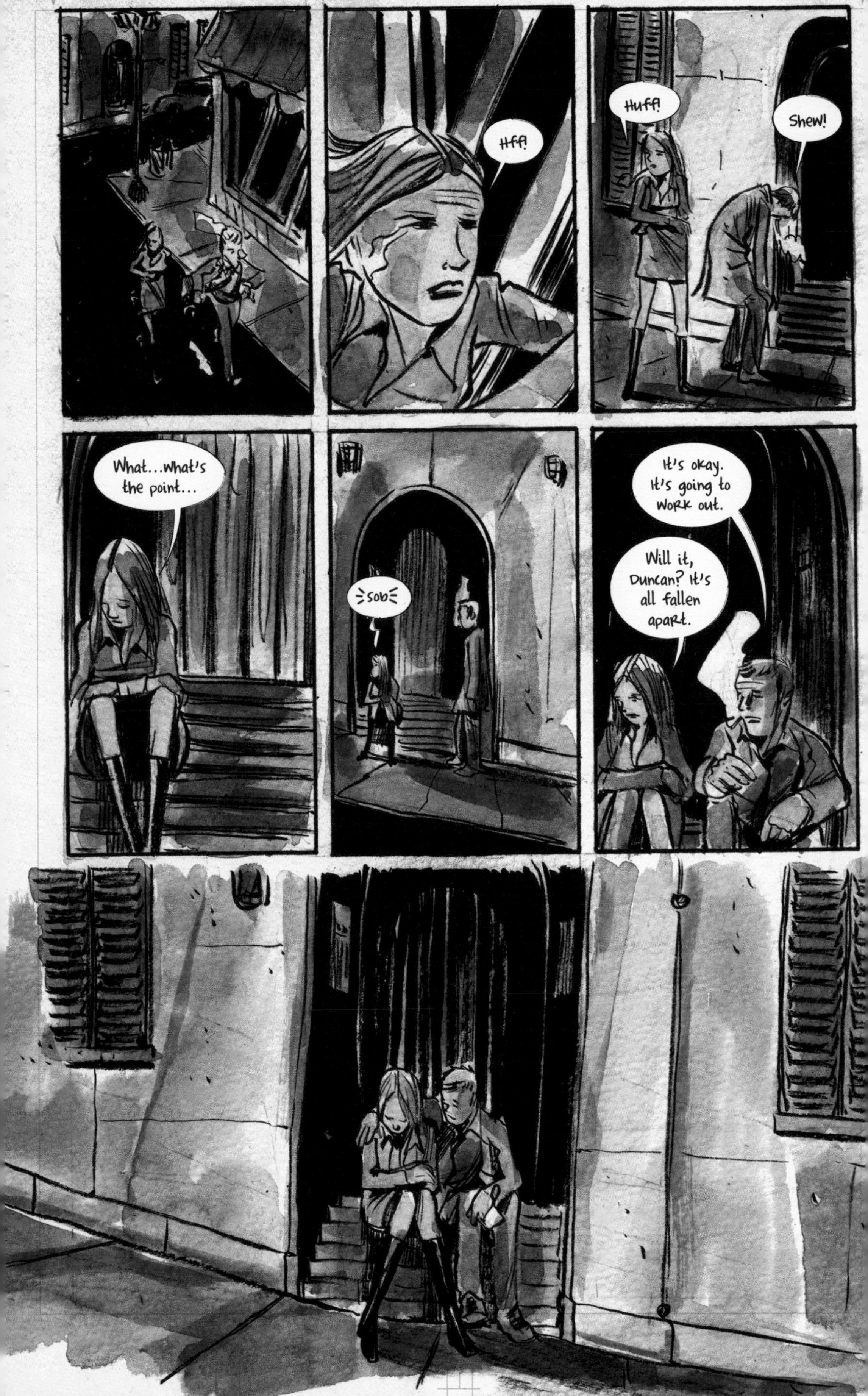

Hff!
Huff!
Shew!
What...what's the point...
Sob
It's okay. It's going to work out.
Will it, Duncan? It's all fallen apart.

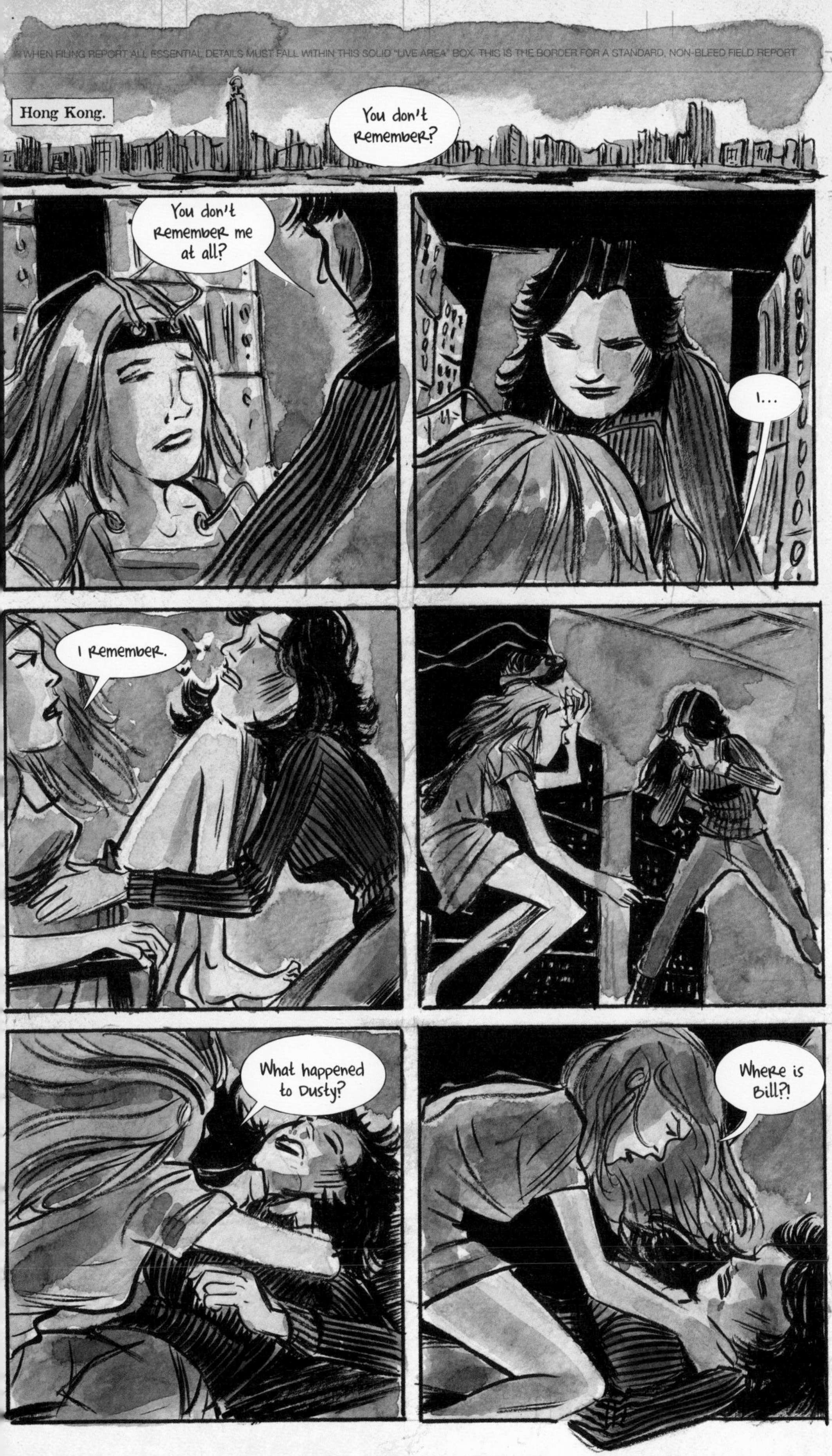
WHEN FILING REPORT ALL ESSENTIAL DETAILS MUST FALL WITHIN THIS SOLID "LIVE AREA" BOX. THIS IS THE BORDER FOR A STANDARD, NON-BLEED FIELD REPORT
Hong Kong.
You don't remember?
You don't remember me at all?
I...
I remember.
What happened to Dusty?
Where is Bill?!

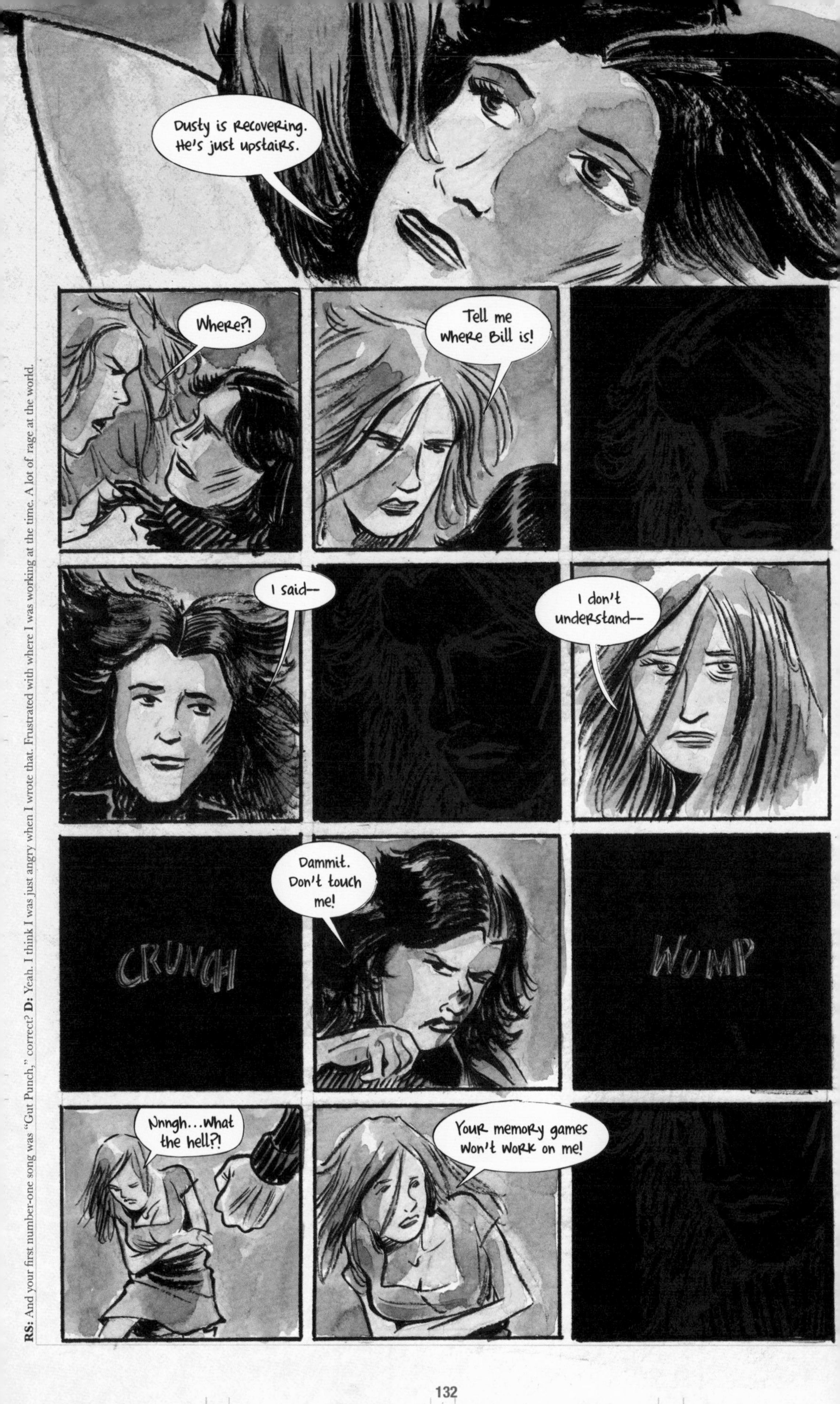
Dusty is recovering. He's just upstairs.
Where?!
Tell me where Bill is!
I said--
I don't understand--
CRUNCH
Dammit. Don't touch me!
WUMP
Nnngh...What the hell?!
Your memory games won't work on me!

RS: And your first number-one song was "Gut Punch," correct? **D:** Yeah. I think I was just angry when I wrote that. Frustrated with where I was working at the time. A lot of rage at the world.

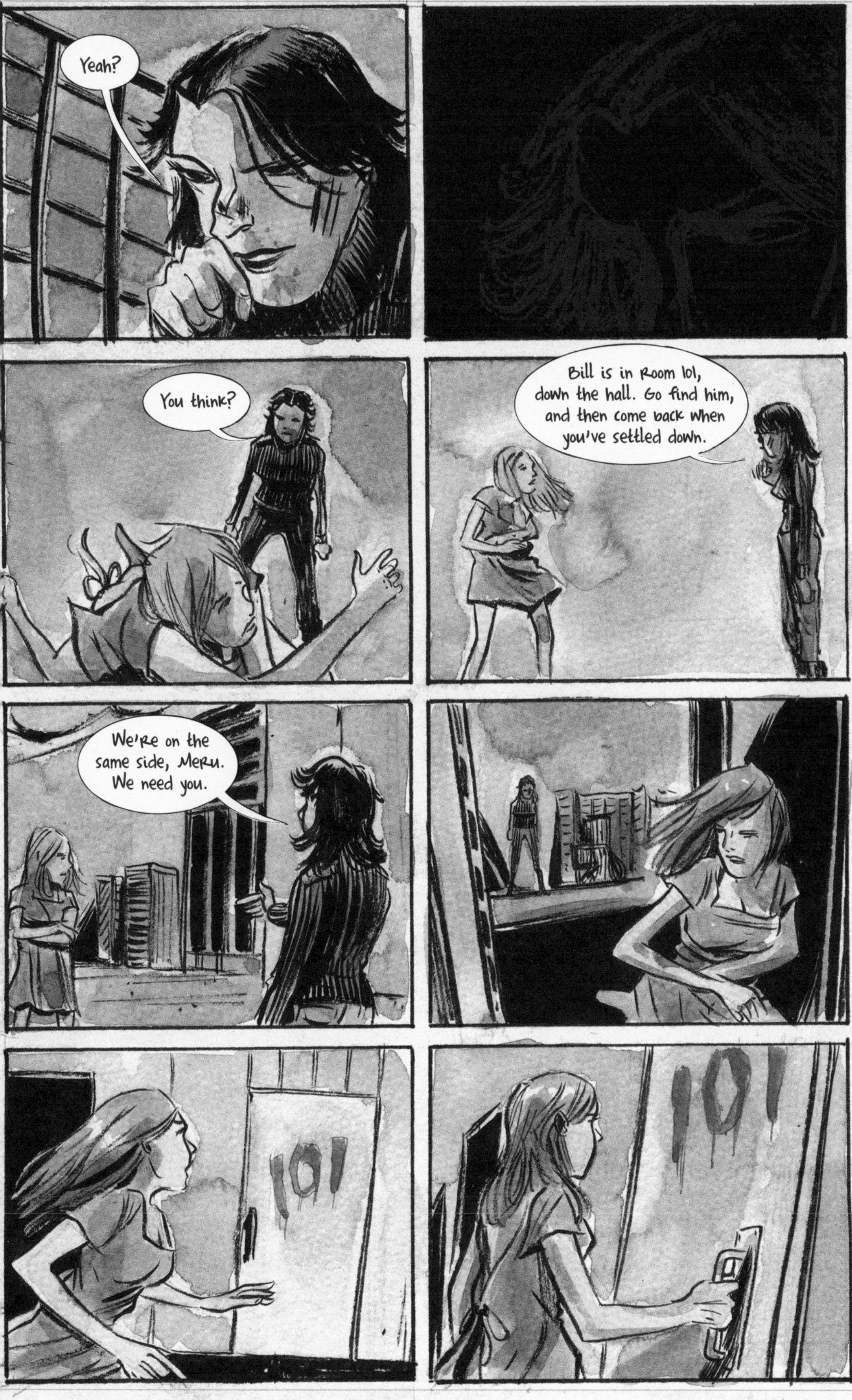
Yeah?
You think?
Bill is in Room 101, down the hall. Go find him, and then come back when you've settled down.
We're on the same side, Meru. We need you.
101
101

WHEN FILING REPORT ALL ESSENTIAL DETAILS MUST FALL WITHIN THIS SOLID "LIVE AREA" BOX. THIS IS THE BORDER FOR A STANDARD, NON-BLEED FIELD REPORT

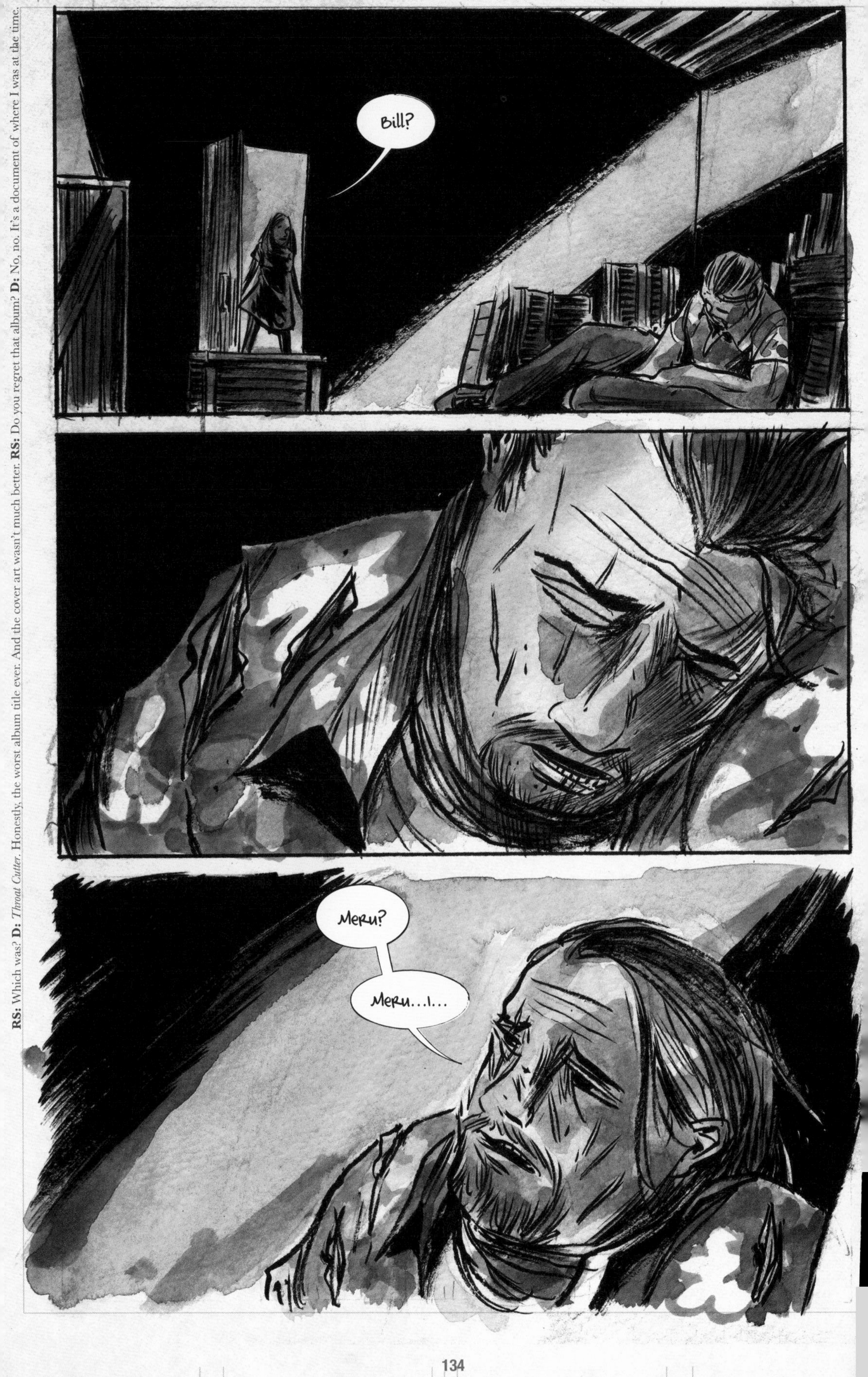
Bill?
Meru?
Meru...I...

RS: Which was? **D:** *Throat Cutter*. Honestly, the worst album title ever. And the cover art wasn't much better. **RS:** Do you regret that album? **D:** No, no. It's a document of where I was at the time.

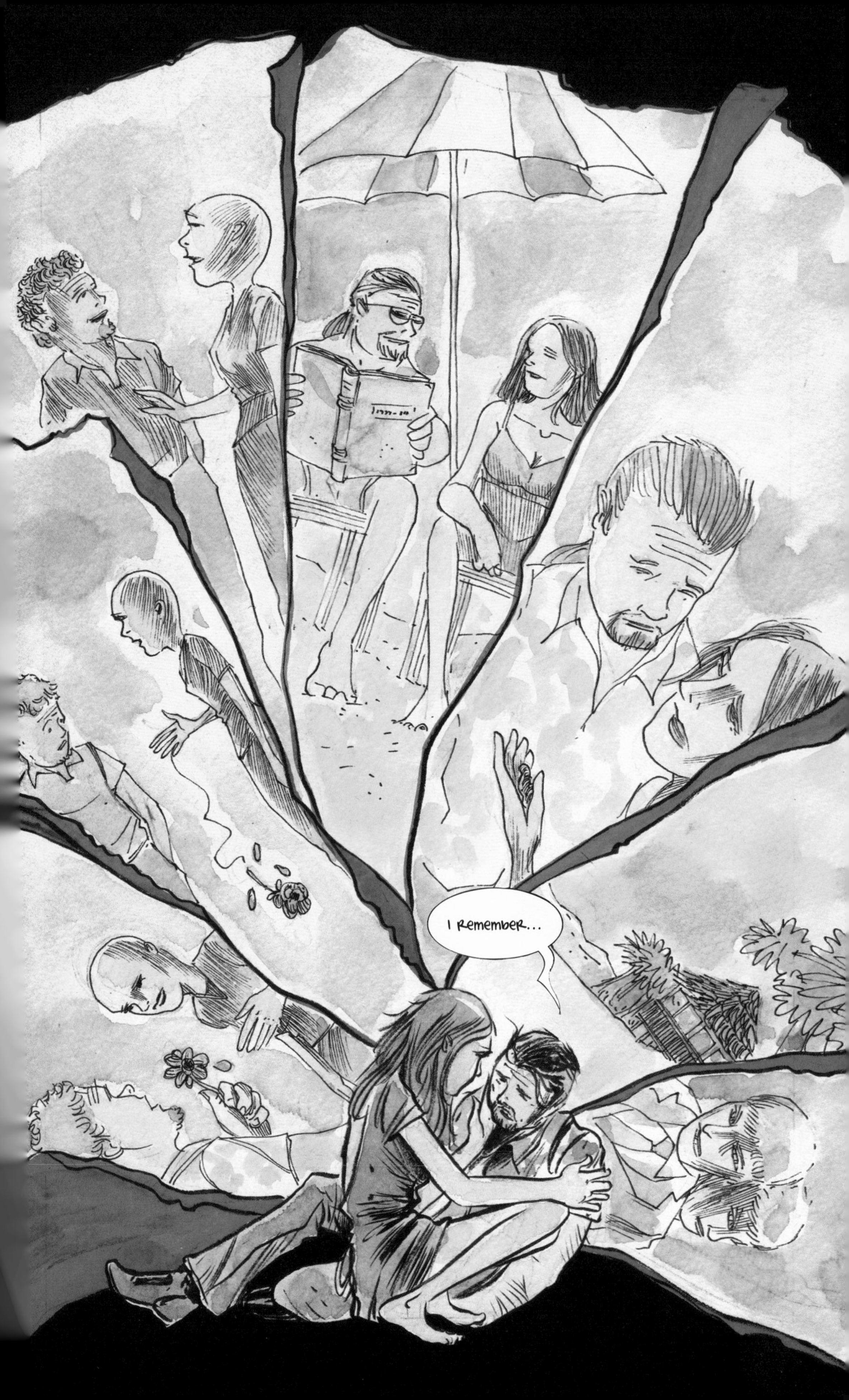
I remember...

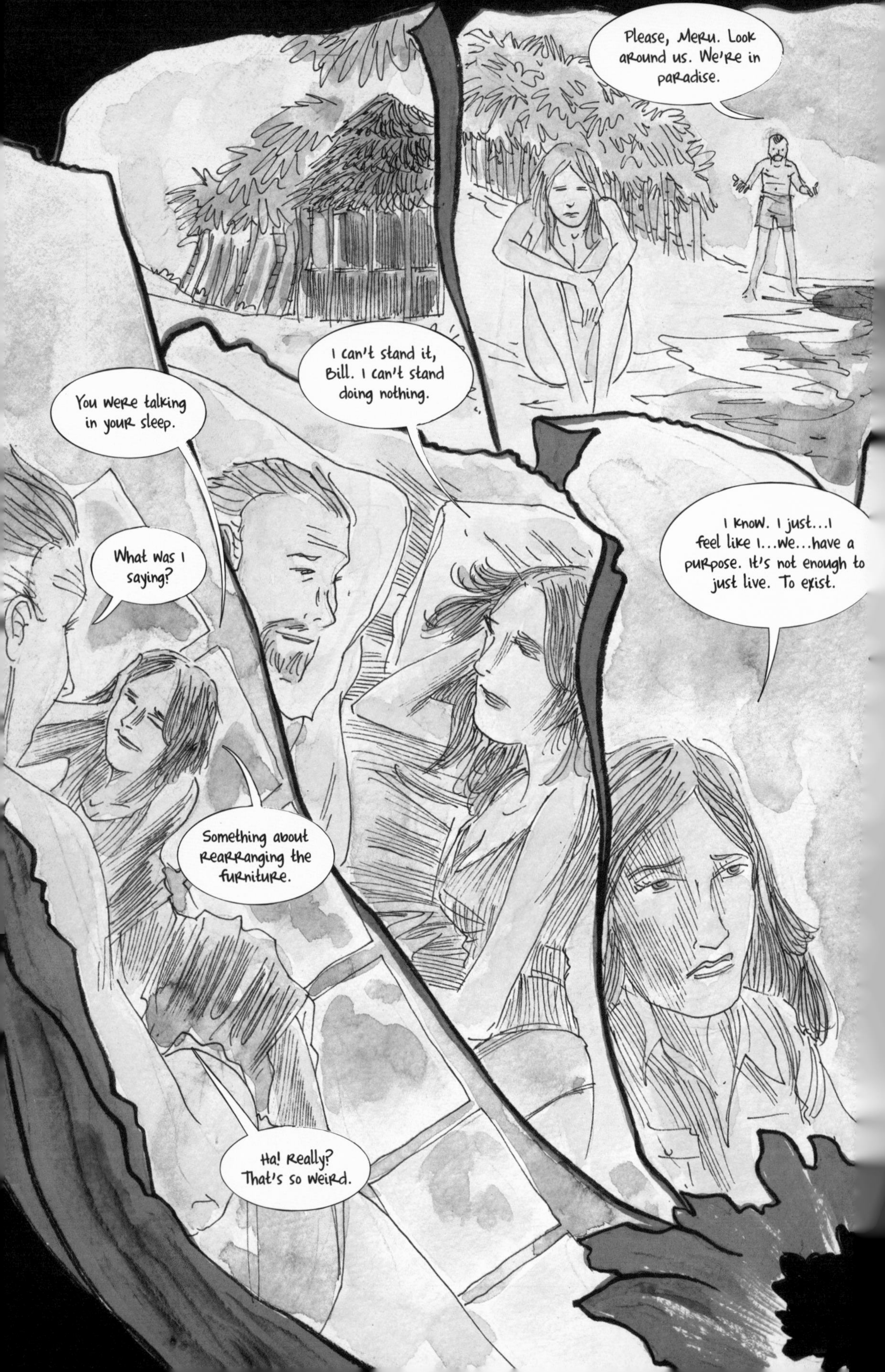
Please, Meru. Look around us. We're in paradise.
I can't stand it, Bill. I can't stand doing nothing.
I know. I just...I feel like I...we...have a purpose. It's not enough to just live. To exist.
You were talking in your sleep.
What was I saying?
Something about rearranging the furniture.
Ha! Really? That's so weird.

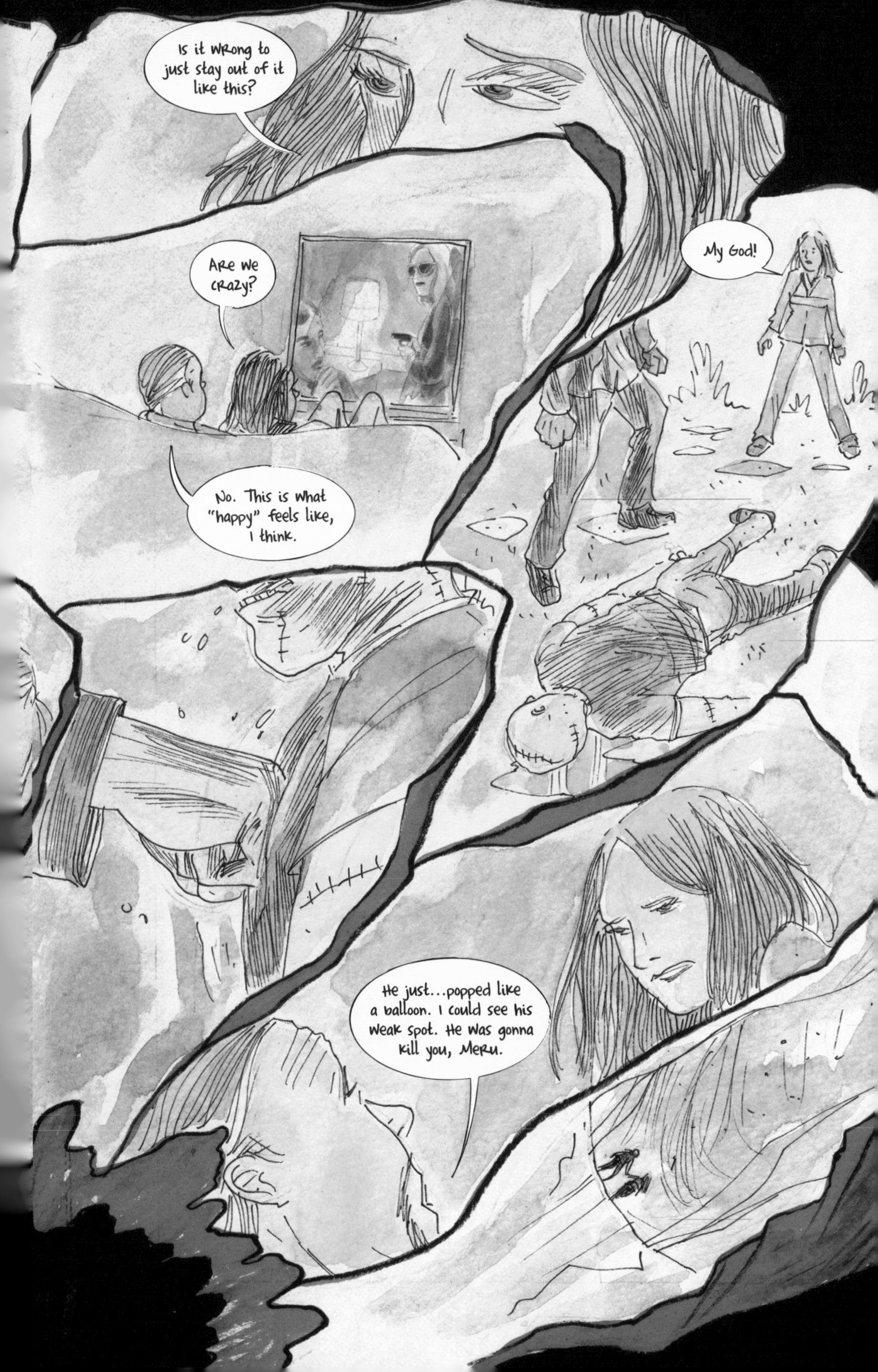
Is it wrong to just stay out of it like this?
Are we crazy?
No. This is what "happy" feels like, I think.
My God!
He just...popped like a balloon. I could see his weak spot. He was gonna kill you, Meru.

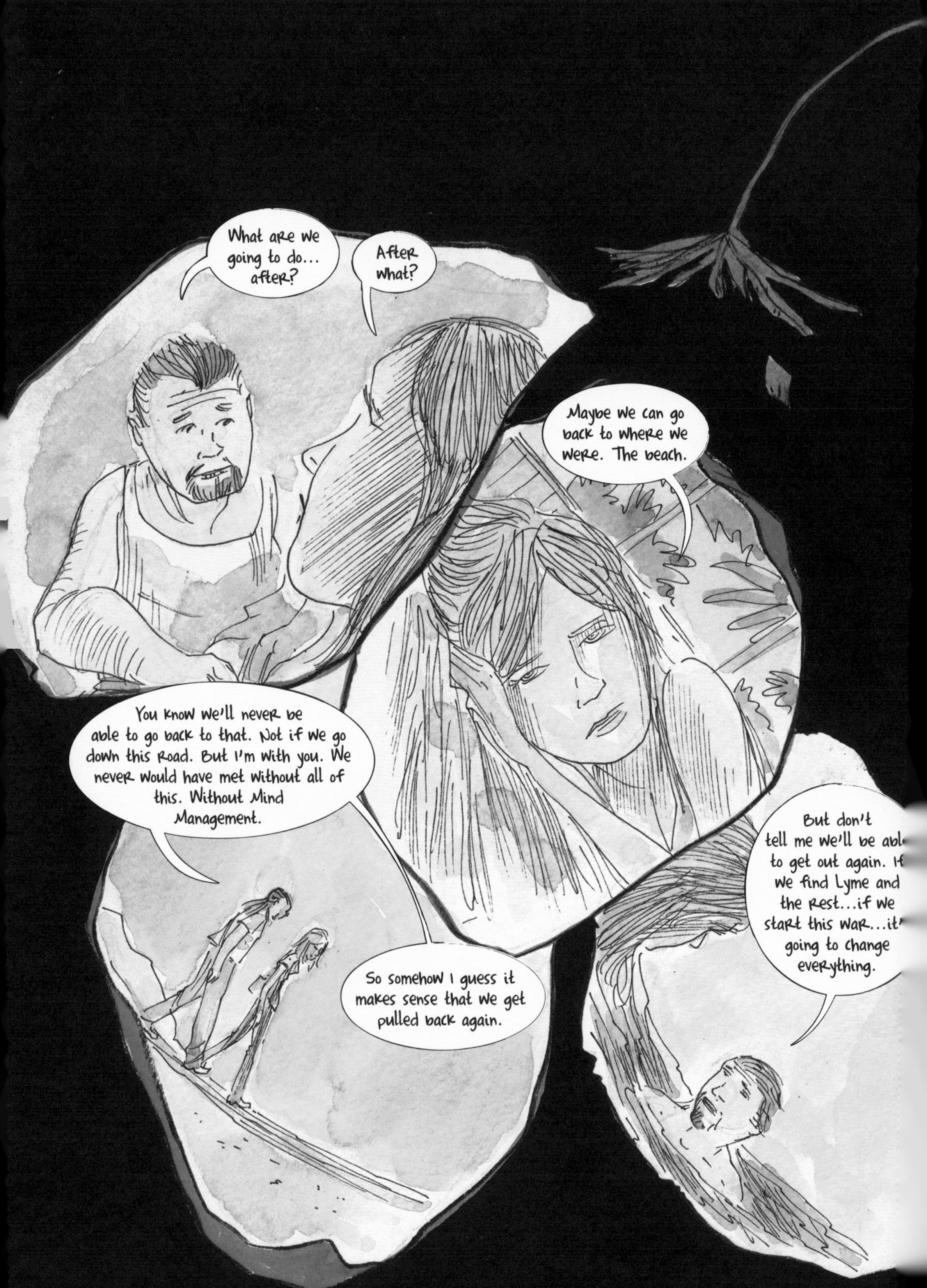
What are we going to do... after?
After what?
Maybe we can go back to where we were. The beach.
You know we'll never be able to go back to that. Not if we go down this road. But I'm with you. We never would have met without all of this. Without Mind Management.
So somehow I guess it makes sense that we get pulled back again.
But don't tell me we'll be abl to get out again. If we find Lyme and the rest...if we start this war...it going to change everything.

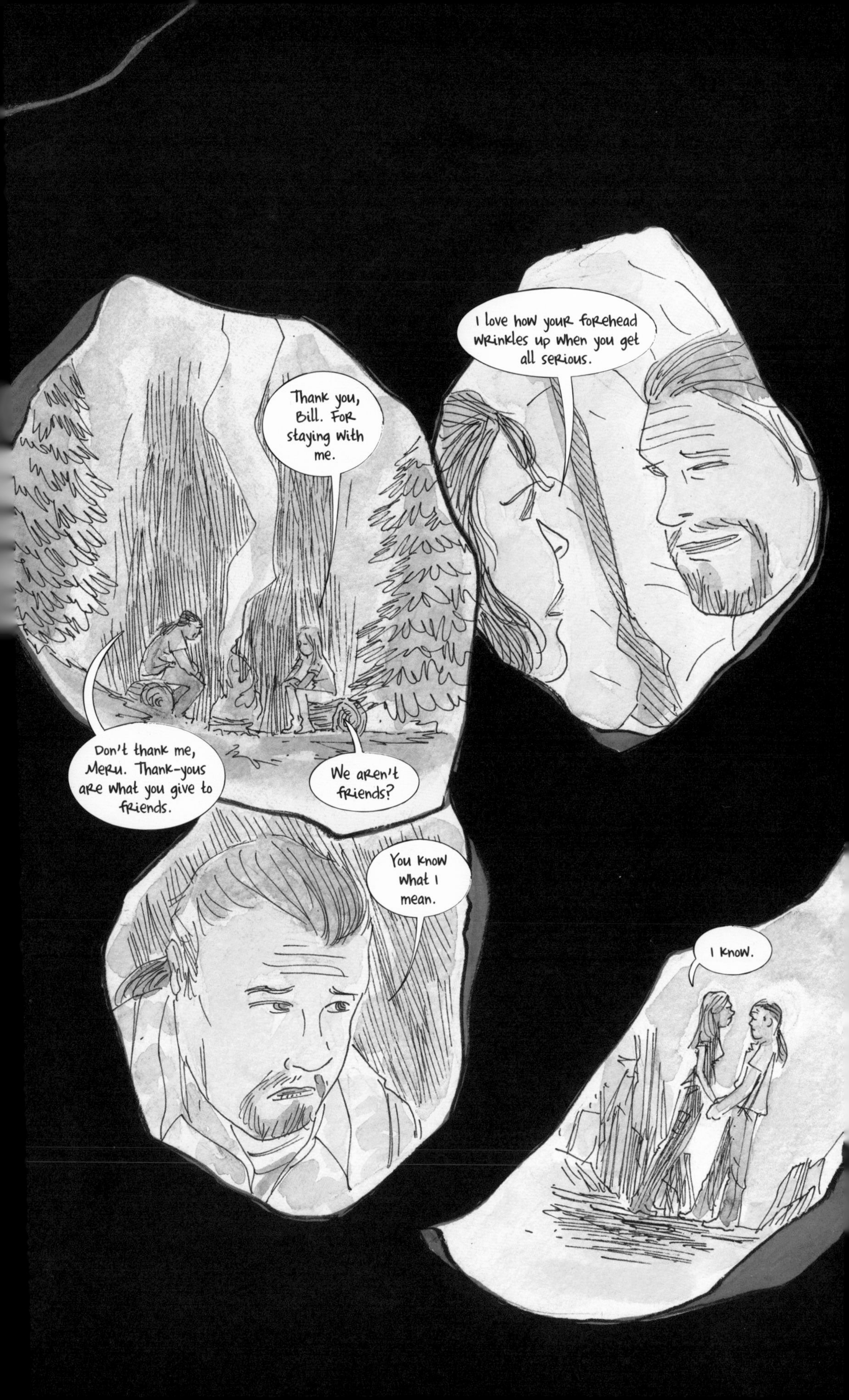
Thank you, Bill. For staying with me.
Don't thank me, Meru. Thank-yous are what you give to friends.
We aren't friends?
I love how your forehead wrinkles up when you get all serious.
You know what I mean.
I know.

WHEN FILING REPORT ALL ESSENTIAL DETAILS MUST FALL WITHIN THIS SOLID "LIVE AREA" BOX. THIS IS THE BORDER FOR A STANDARD, NON-BLEED FIELD REPORT

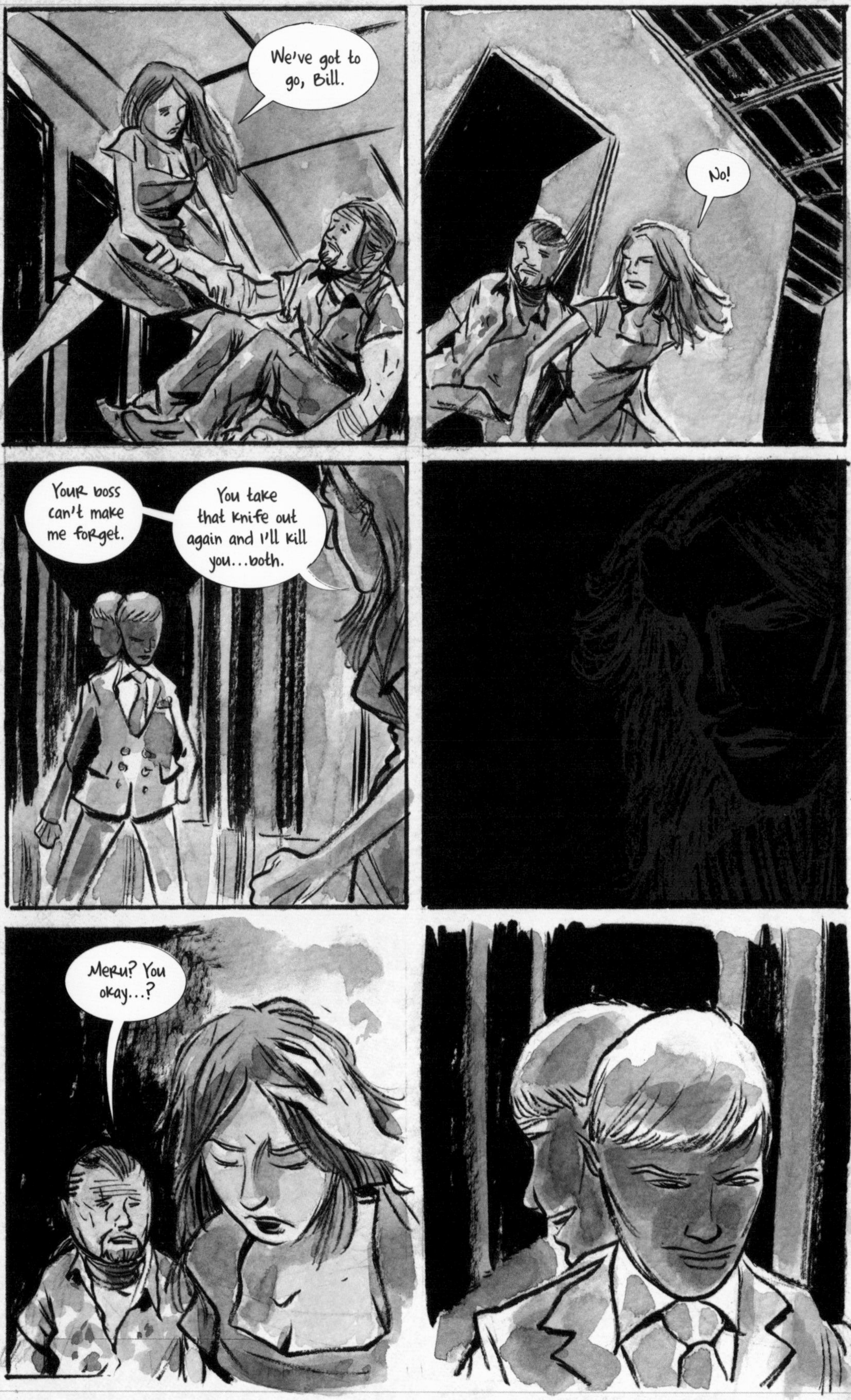

We've got to go, Bill.
No!
Your boss can't make me forget.
You take that knife out again and I'll kill you...both.
Meru? You okay...?

RS: After the failure of your second album, where did you go? **D:** I kind of went into hiding. I found some work back in Palestine and all over the Middle East. Singing in small clubs. Just lying low. Felt kind of like being a spy.

WHEN FILING REPORT ALL ESSENTIAL DETAILS MUST FALL WITHIN THIS SOLID "LIVE AREA" BOX. THIS IS THE BORDER FOR A STANDARD, NON-BLEED FIELD REPORT

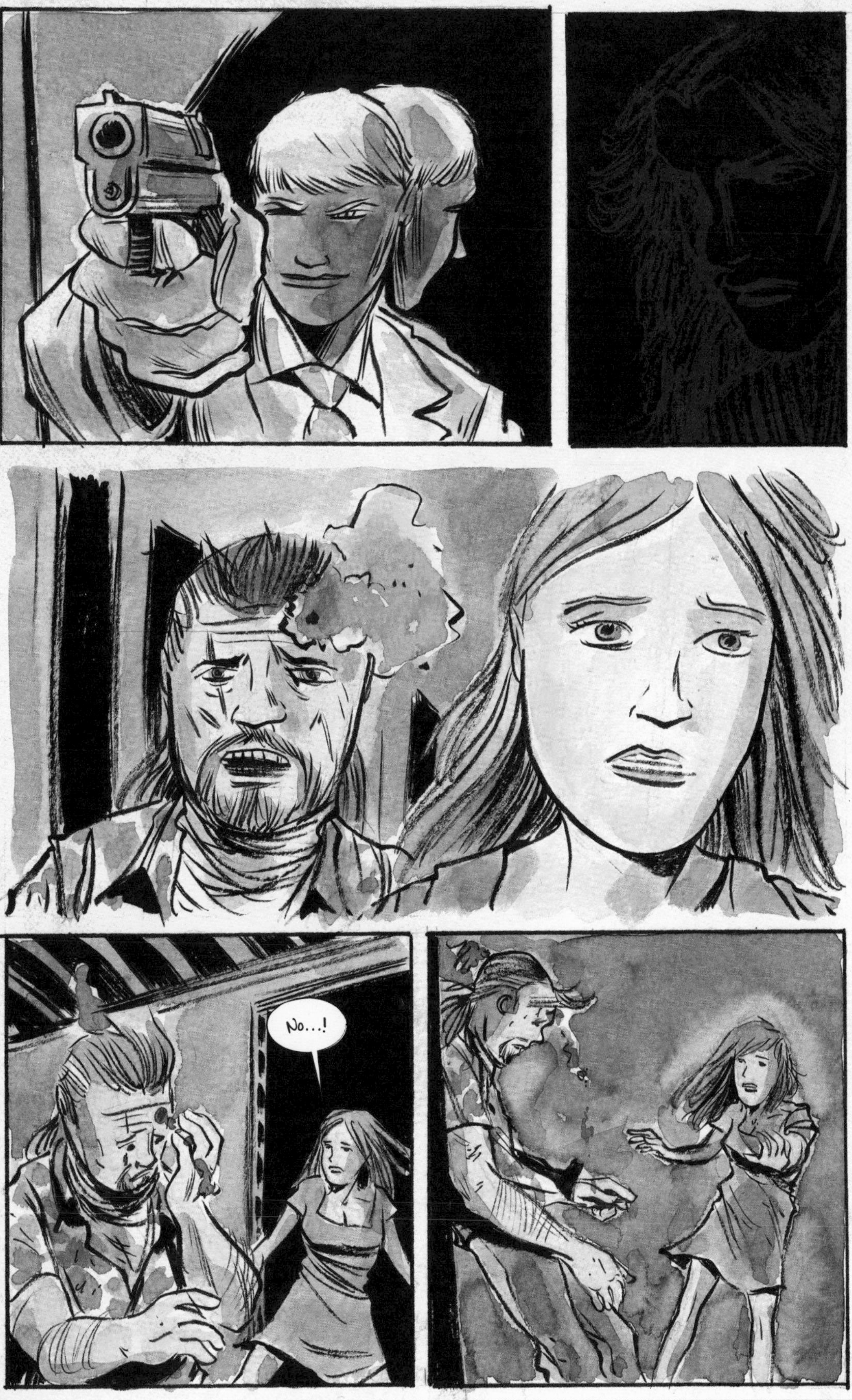

No...!

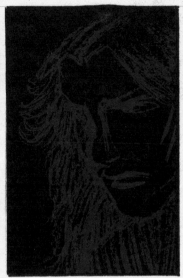

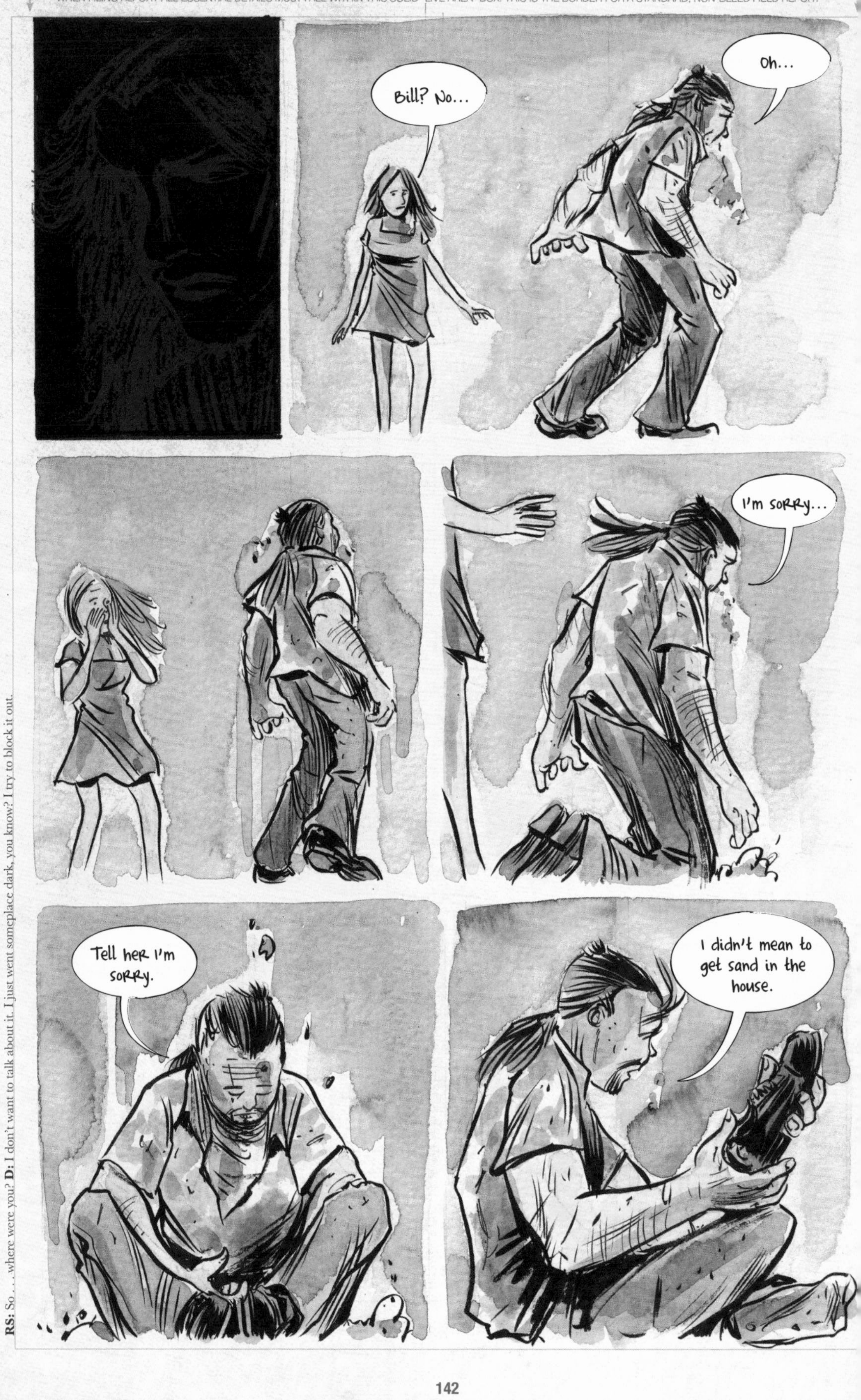
Bill? No...
Oh...
I'm sorry...
Tell her I'm sorry.
I didn't mean to get sand in the house.

RS: So . . . where were you? **D:** I don't want to talk about it. I just went someplace dark, you know? I try to block it out.

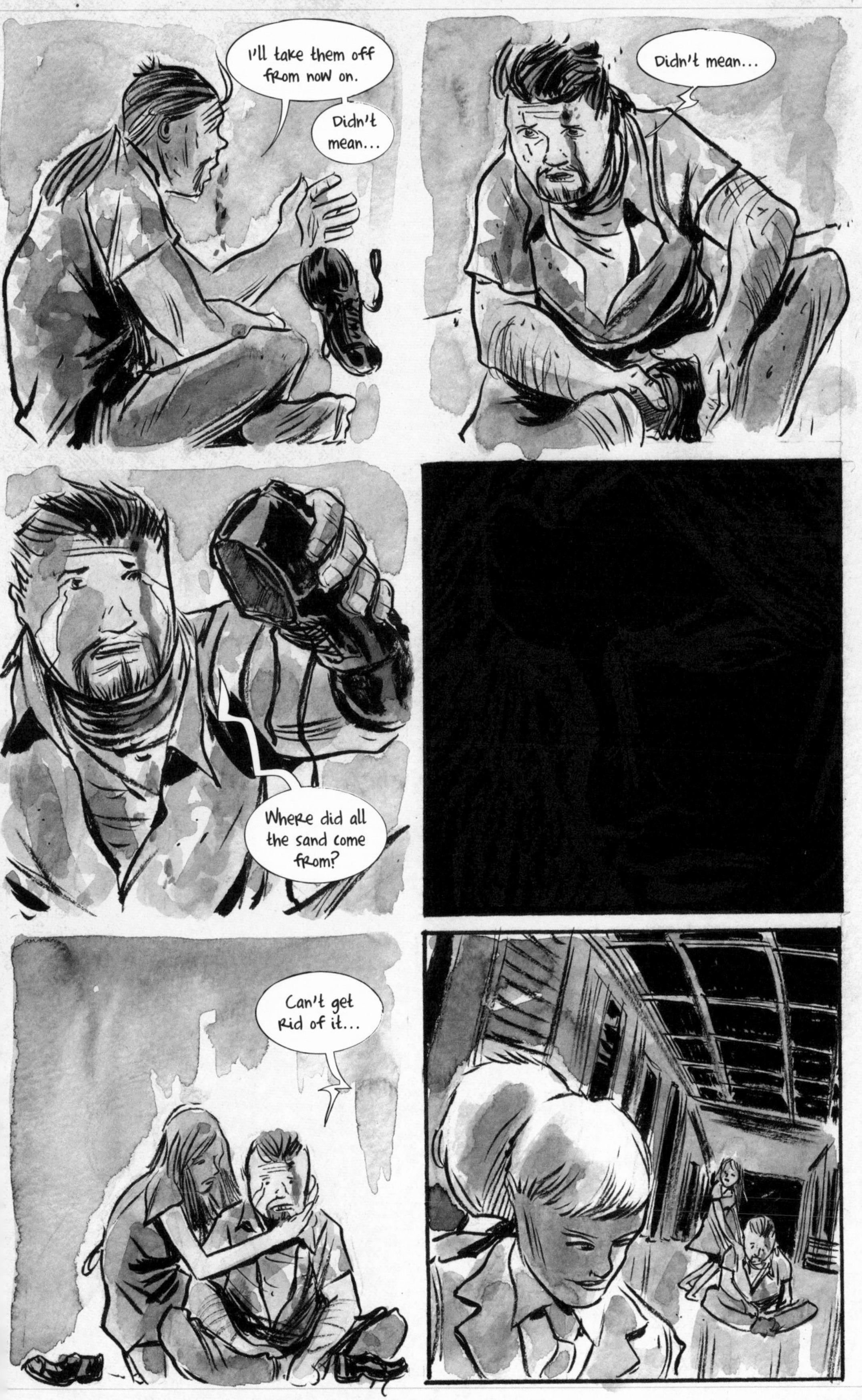
I'll take them off from now on.
Didn't mean...
Didn't mean...
Where did all the sand come from?
Can't get rid of it...

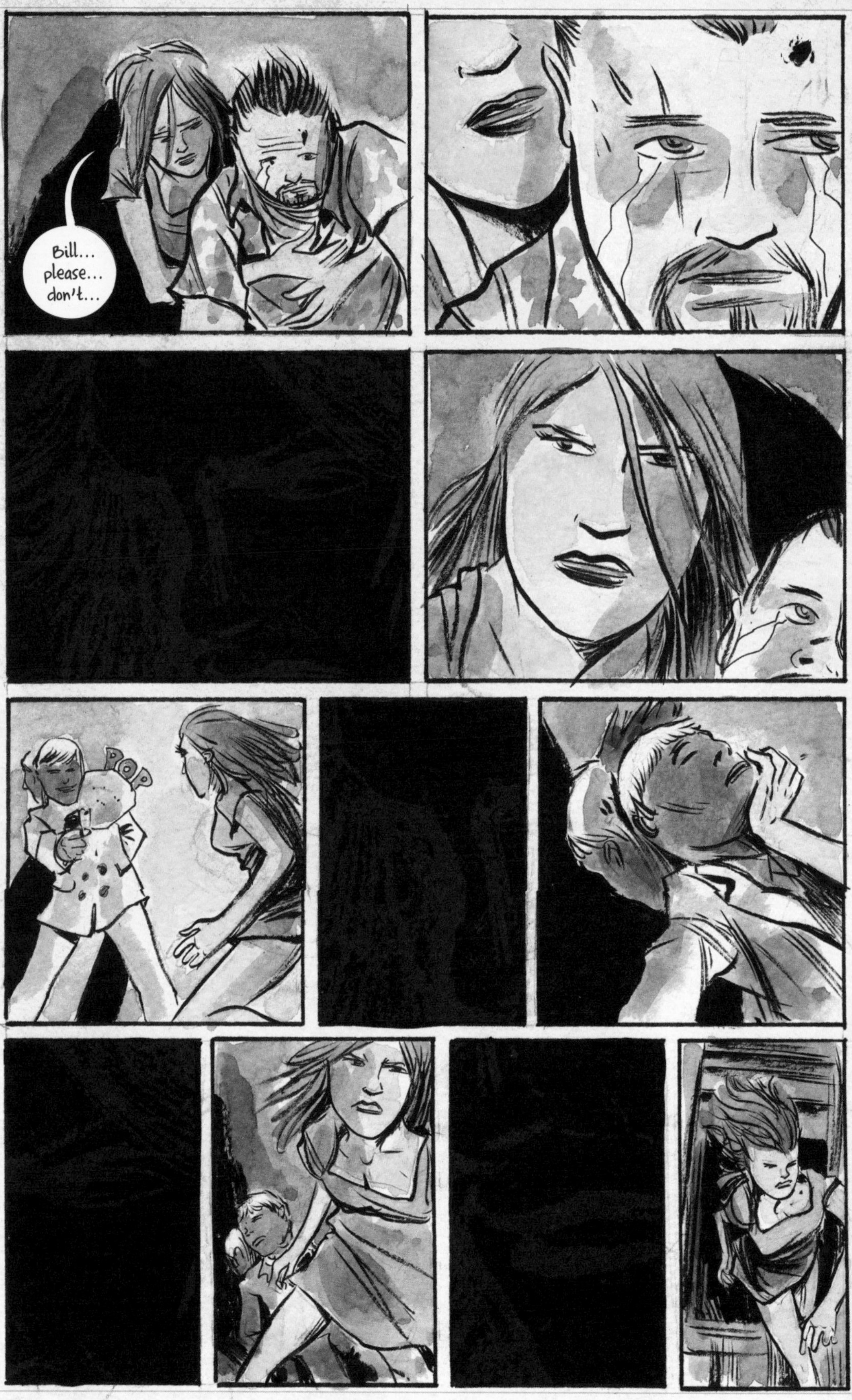
Bill... please... don't...
POP

RS: You built a mansion in Egypt. Not a bad way to get over your problems. **D:** I was tired of conflict. Just tired of it all. I wanted to make music and get it out there. But I was tired of the press taking shots at me.

WHEN FILING REPORT ALL ESSENTIAL DETAILS MUST FALL WITHIN THIS SOLID "LIVE AREA" BOX. THIS IS THE BORDER FOR A STANDARD, NON-BLEED FIELD REPORT

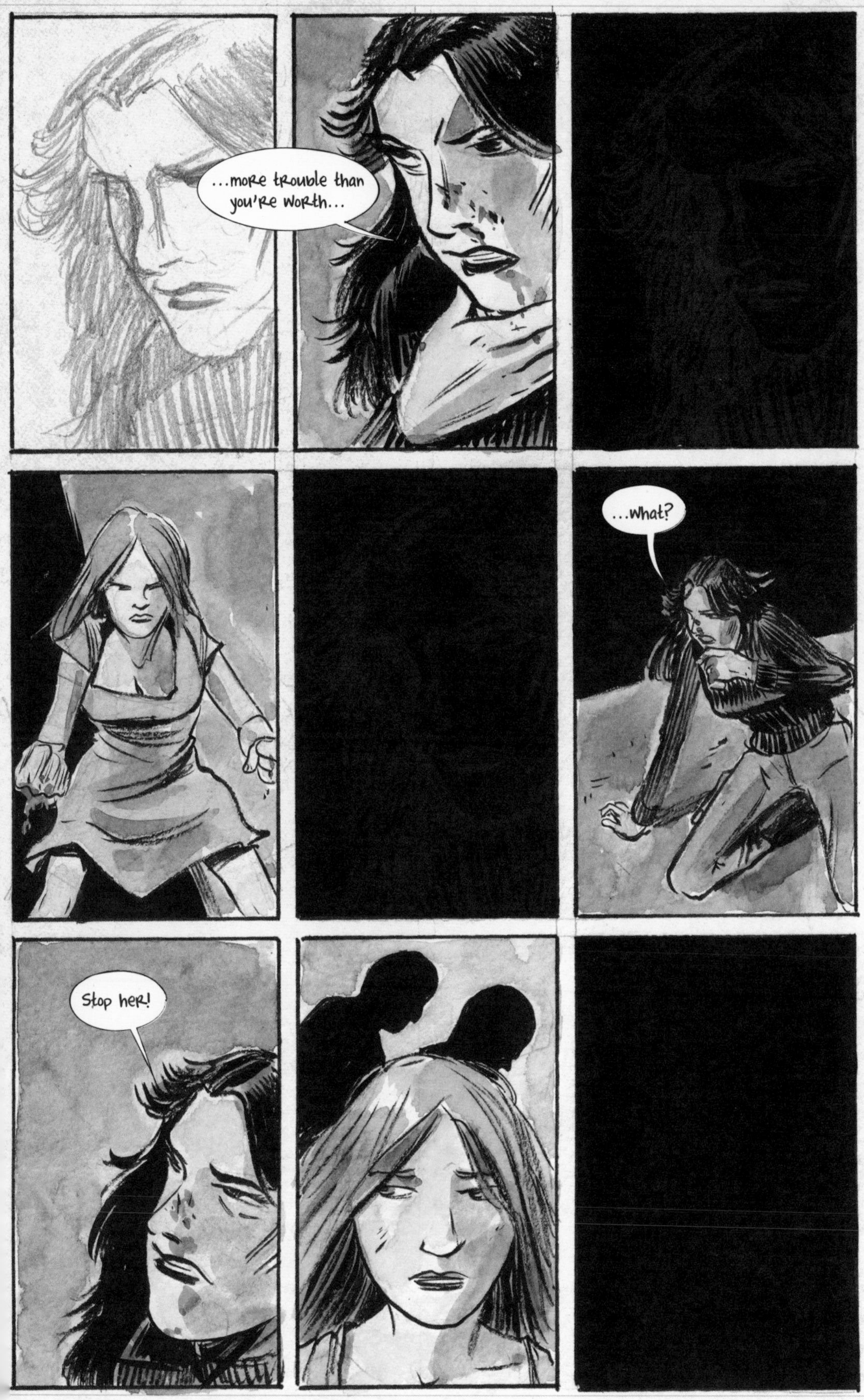
...more trouble than you're worth...
...what?
Stop her!

RS: So out of those new recordings, do you think you'll ever release something from those sessions? **D:** Eventually I will. Everything I'm recording now is part of something bigger. I have a completed album ready to go.

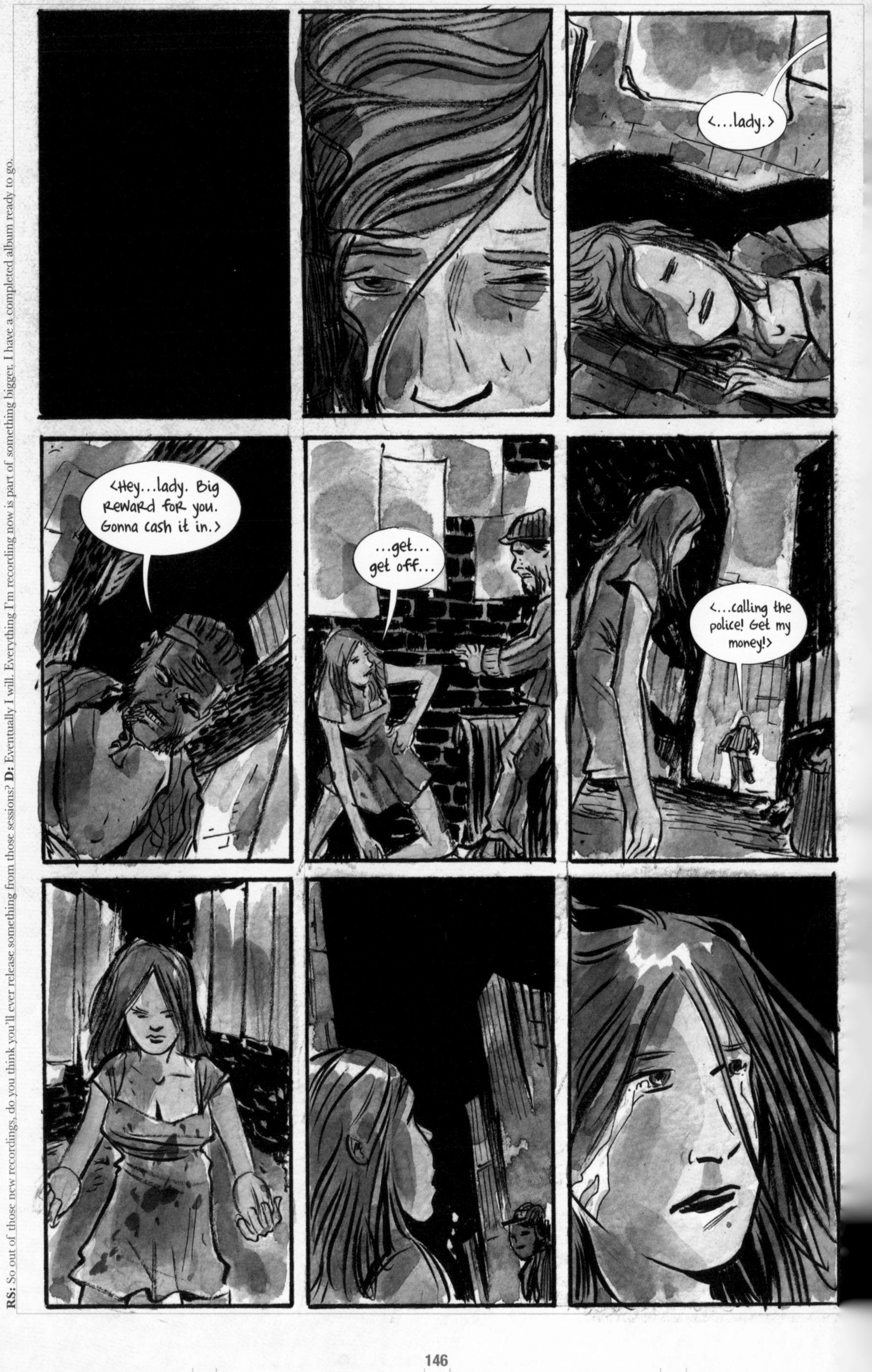
<...lady.>
<Hey...lady. Big reward for you. Gonna cash it in.>
...get... get off...
<...calling the police! Get my money!>

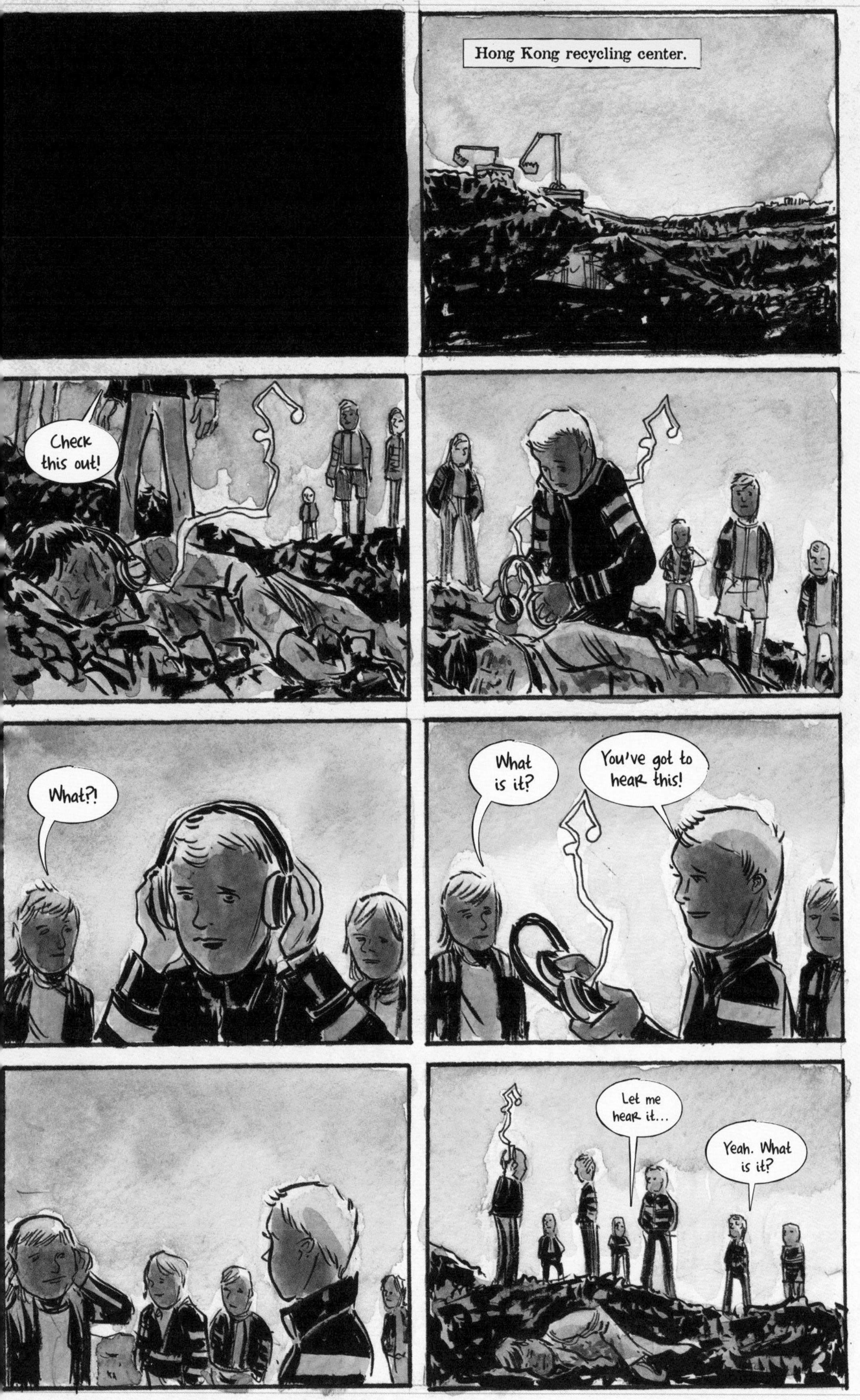
Hong Kong recycling center.
Check this out!
What?!
What is it?
You've got to hear this!
Let me hear it...
Yeah. What is it?

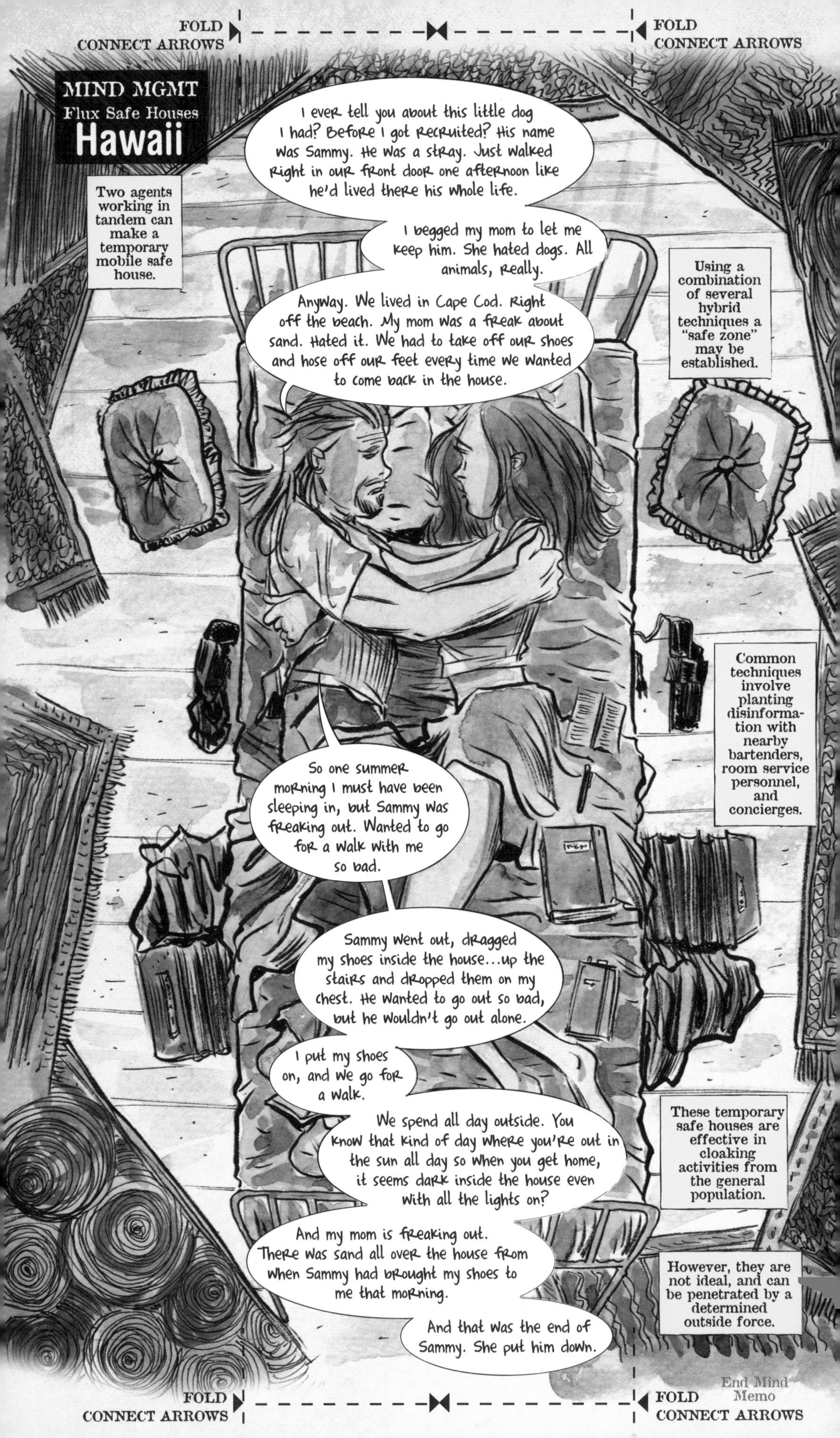

FOLD
CONNECT ARROWS
FOLD
CONNECT ARROWS
MIND MGMT
Flux Safe Houses
Hawaii
Two agents working in tandem can make a temporary mobile safe house.
I ever tell you about this little dog I had? Before I got recruited? His name was Sammy. He was a stray. Just walked right in our front door one afternoon like he'd lived there his whole life.
I begged my mom to let me keep him. She hated dogs. All animals, really.
Anyway. We lived in Cape Cod. Right off the beach. My mom was a freak about sand. Hated it. We had to take off our shoes and hose off our feet every time we wanted to come back in the house.
Using a combination of several hybrid techniques a "safe zone" may be established.
Common techniques involve planting disinformation with nearby bartenders, room service personnel, and concierges.
So one summer morning I must have been sleeping in, but Sammy was freaking out. Wanted to go for a walk with me so bad.
Sammy went out, dragged my shoes inside the house...up the stairs and dropped them on my chest. He wanted to go out so bad, but he wouldn't go out alone.
I put my shoes on, and we go for a walk.
We spend all day outside. You know that kind of day where you're out in the sun all day so when you get home, it seems dark inside the house even with all the lights on?
These temporary safe houses are effective in cloaking activities from the general population.
And my mom is freaking out. There was sand all over the house from when Sammy had brought my shoes to me that morning.
However, they are not ideal, and can be penetrated by a determined outside force.
And that was the end of Sammy. She put him down.
End Mind Memo
FOLD
CONNECT ARROWS
FOLD
CONNECT ARROWS

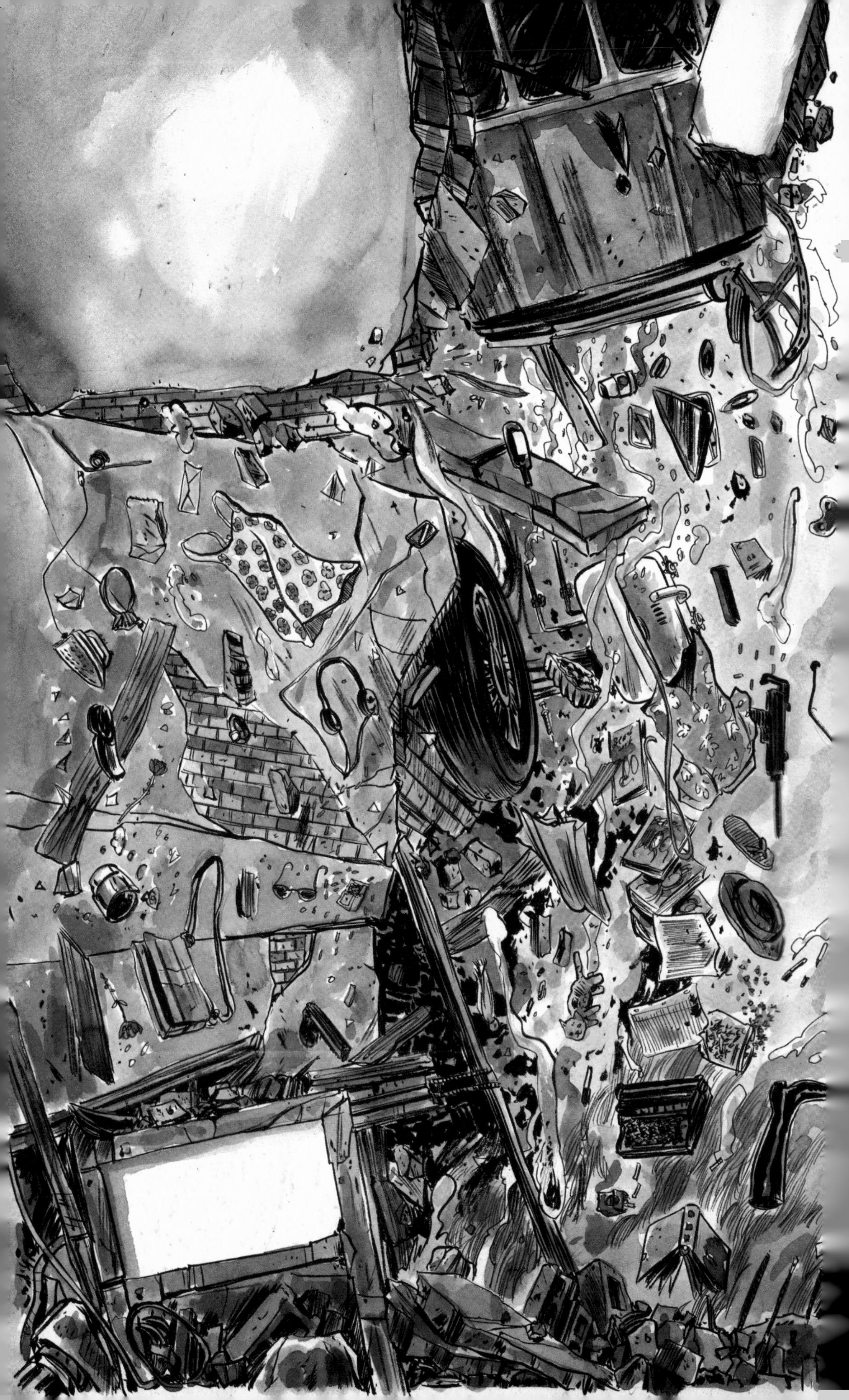

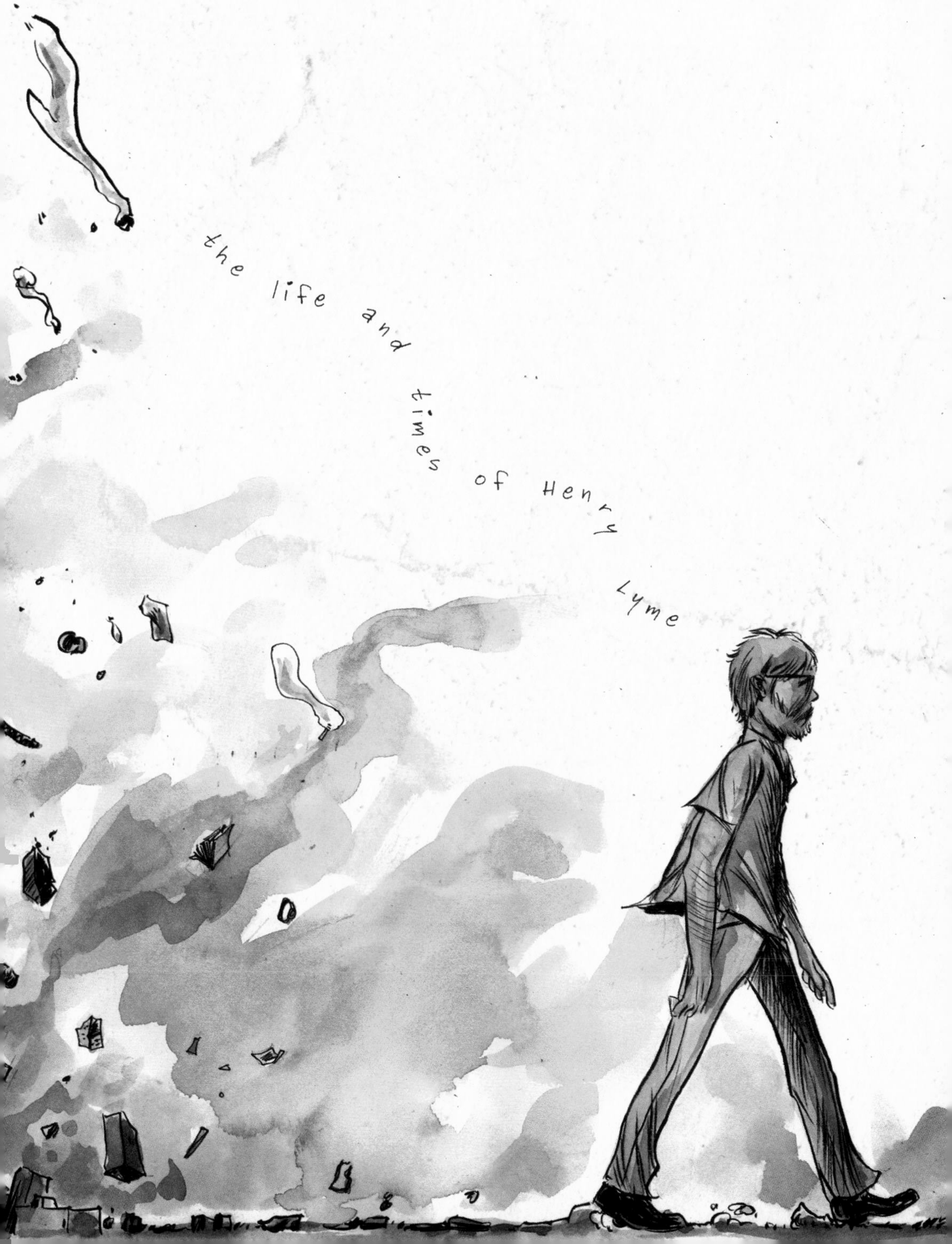
the life and times of Henry Lyme

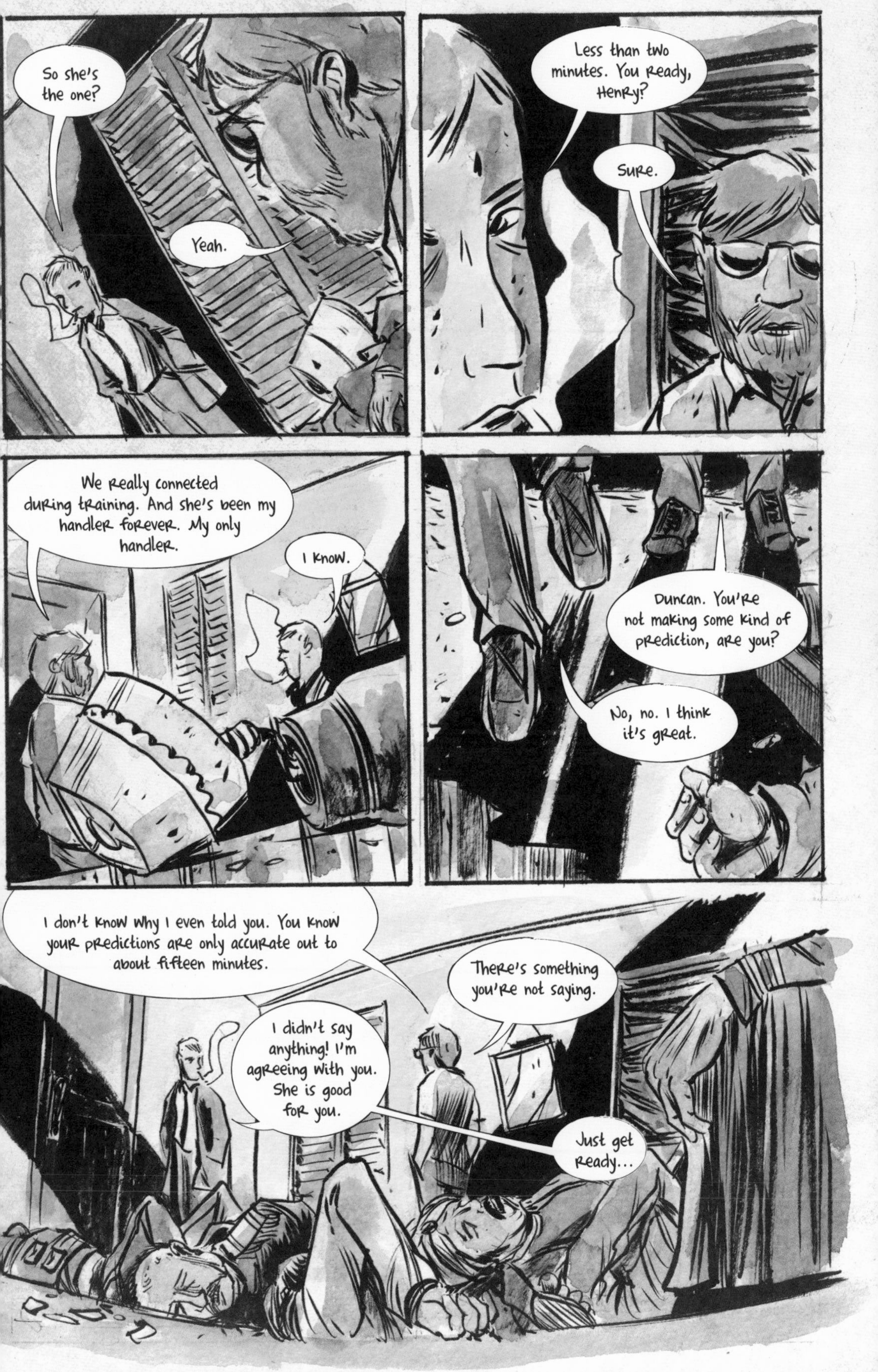
So she's the one?
Yeah.
Less than two minutes. You ready, Henry?
Sure.
We really connected during training. And she's been my handler forever. My only handler.
I know.
Duncan. You're not making some kind of prediction, are you?
No, no. I think it's great.
I don't know why I even told you. You know your predictions are only accurate out to about fifteen minutes.
There's something you're not saying.
I didn't say anything! I'm agreeing with you. She is good for you.
Just get ready...

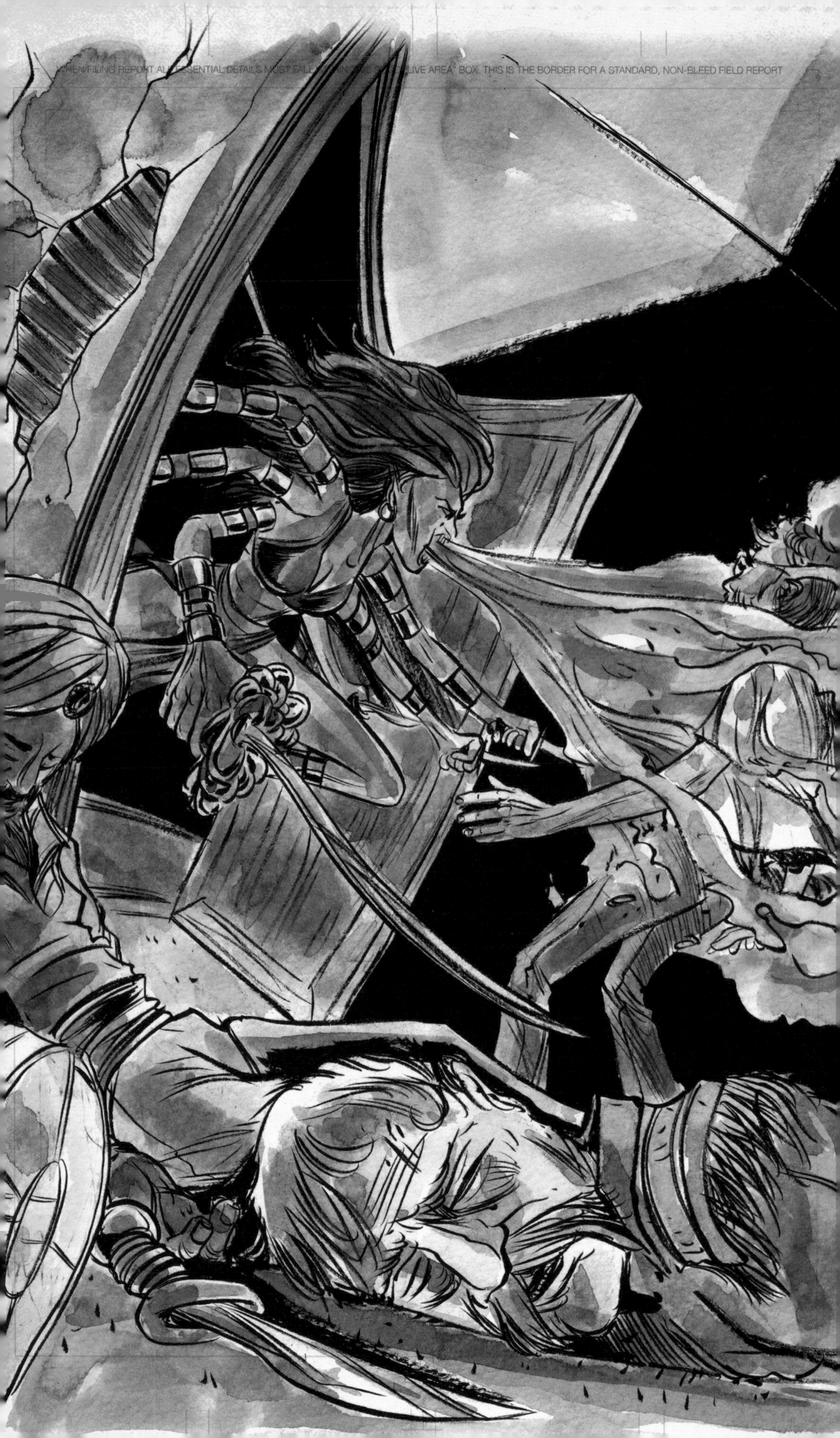
LIVE AREA" BOX. THIS IS THE BORDER FOR A STANDARD, NON-BLEED FIELD REPORT

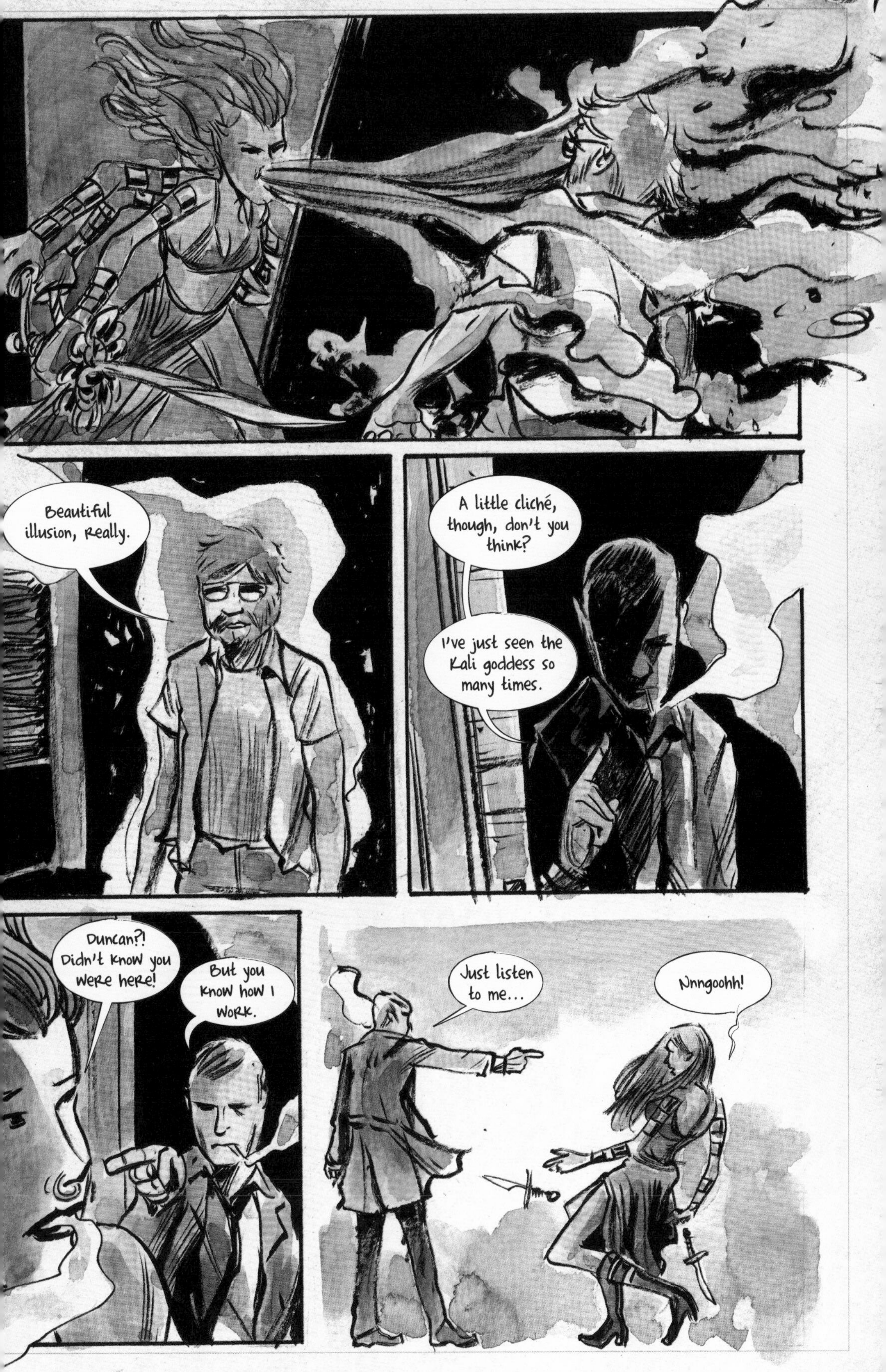
Beautiful illusion, really.
A little cliché, though, don't you think?
I've just seen the Kali goddess so many times.
Duncan?! Didn't know you were here!
But you know how I work.
Just listen to me...
Nnngoohh!

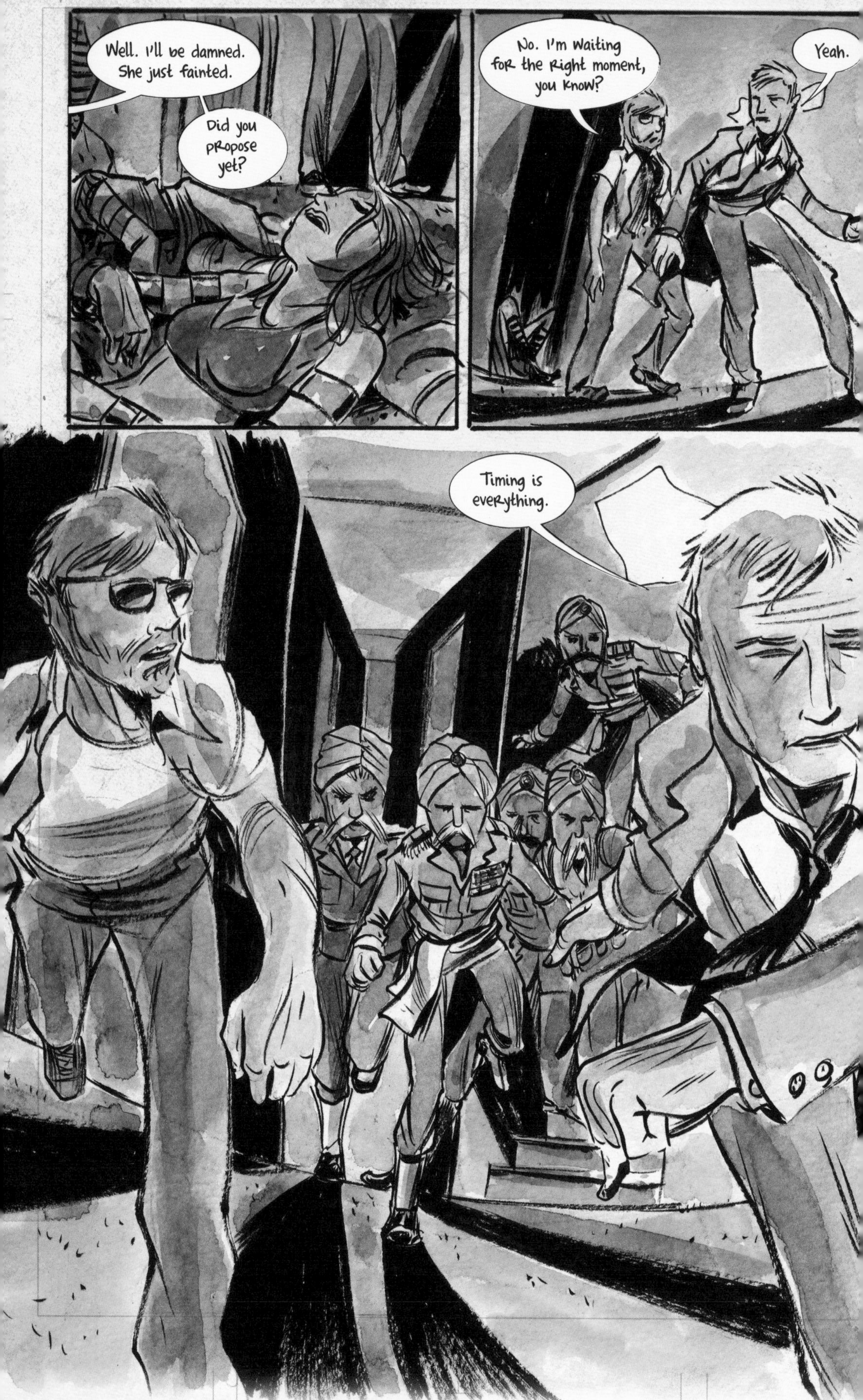
Well. I'll be damned. She just fainted.
Did you propose yet?
No. I'm waiting for the right moment, you know?
Yeah.
Timing is everything.

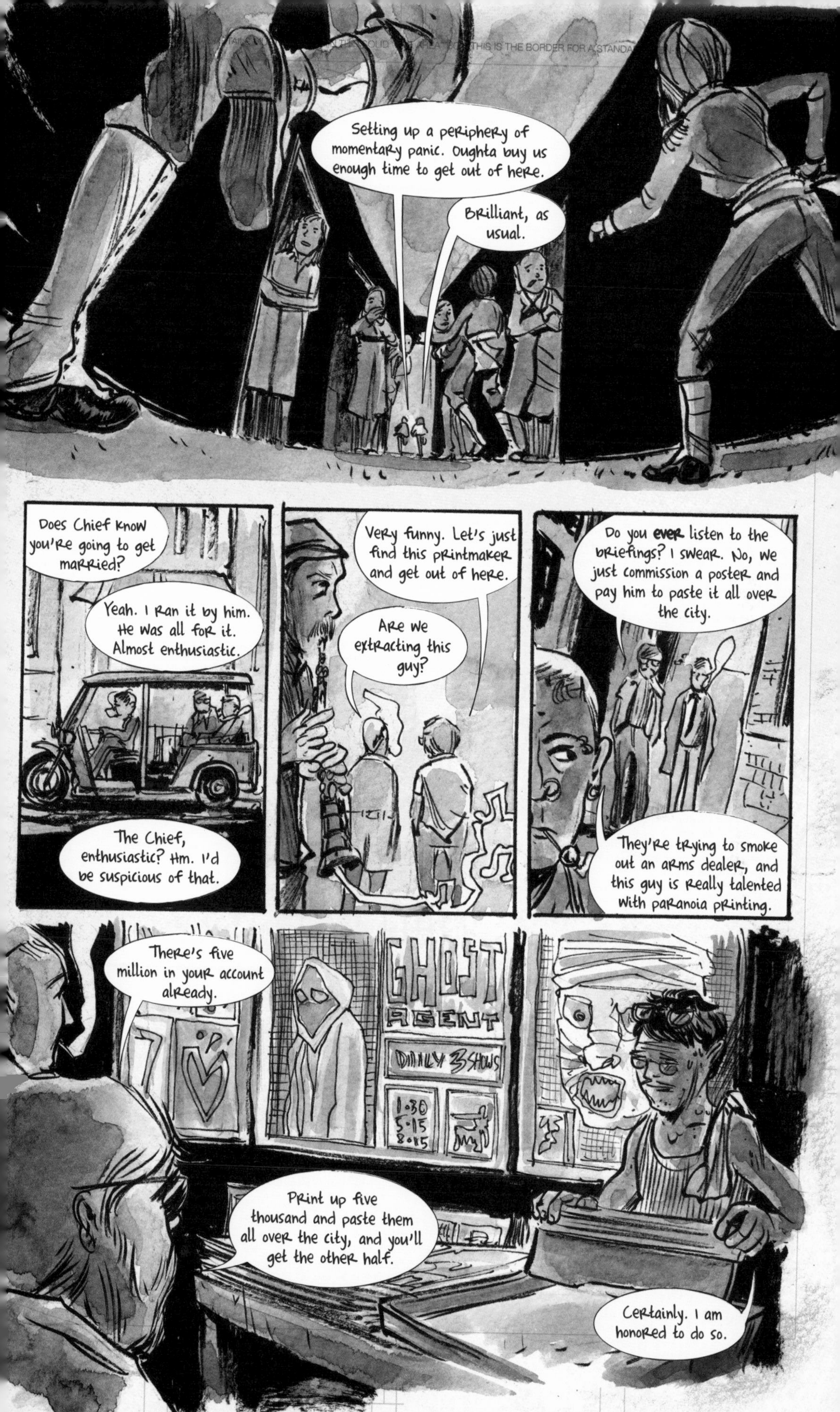
Setting up a periphery of momentary panic. Oughta buy us enough time to get out of here.
Brilliant, as usual.
Does Chief know you're going to get married?
Yeah. I ran it by him. He was all for it. Almost enthusiastic.
The Chief, enthusiastic? Hm. I'd be suspicious of that.
Very funny. Let's just find this printmaker and get out of here.
Are we extracting this guy?
Do you ever listen to the briefings? I swear. No, we just commission a poster and pay him to paste it all over the city.
They're trying to smoke out an arms dealer, and this guy is really talented with paranoia printing.
There's five million in your account already.
GHOST AGENT
DAILY 3 SHOWS
1.30
5.15
8.15
Print up five thousand and paste them all over the city, and you'll get the other half.
Certainly. I am honored to do so.

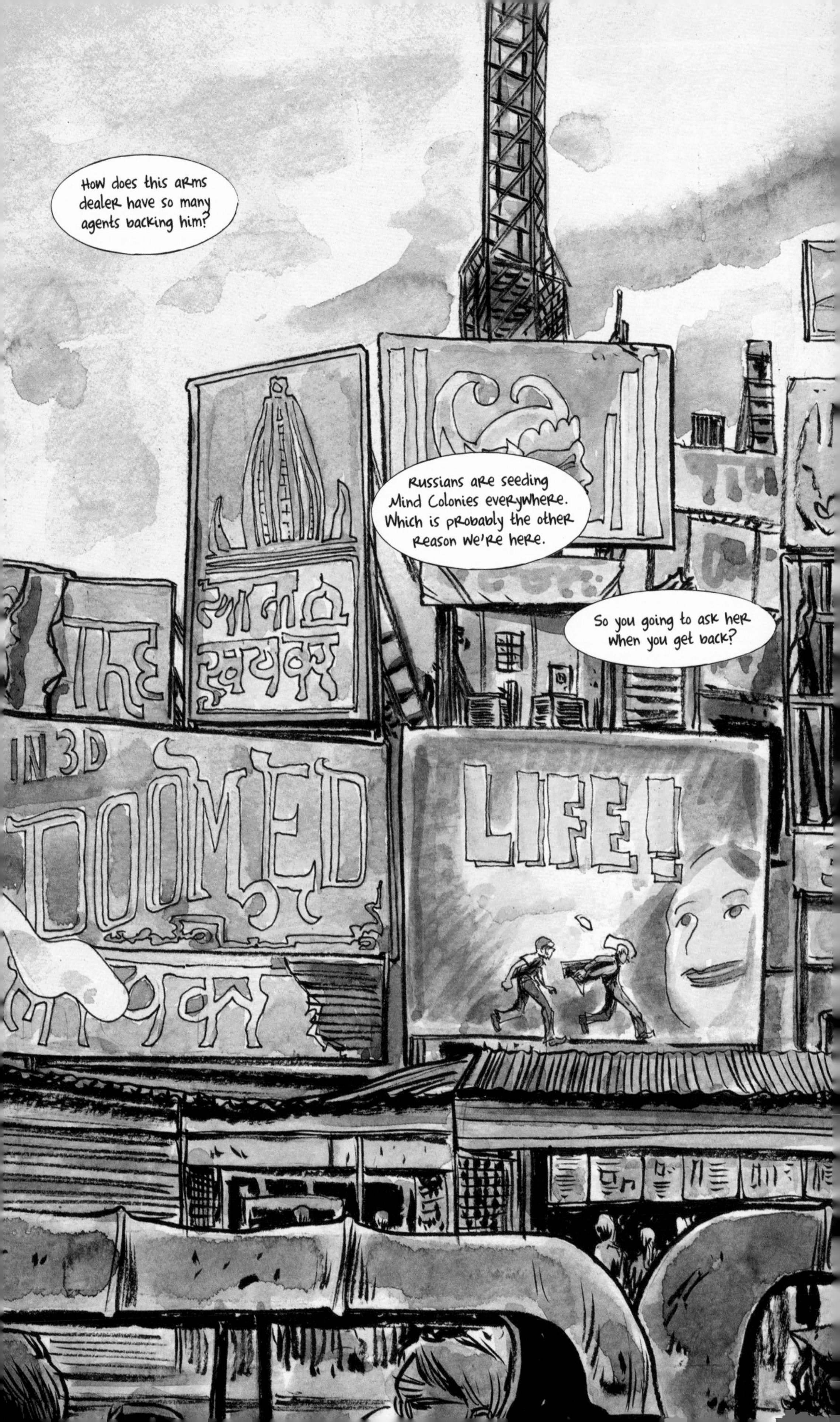
How does this arms dealer have so many agents backing him?
Russians are seeding Mind Colonies everywhere. Which is probably the other reason we're here.
So you going to ask her when you get back?
THE
IN 3D
DOOMED
LIFE!

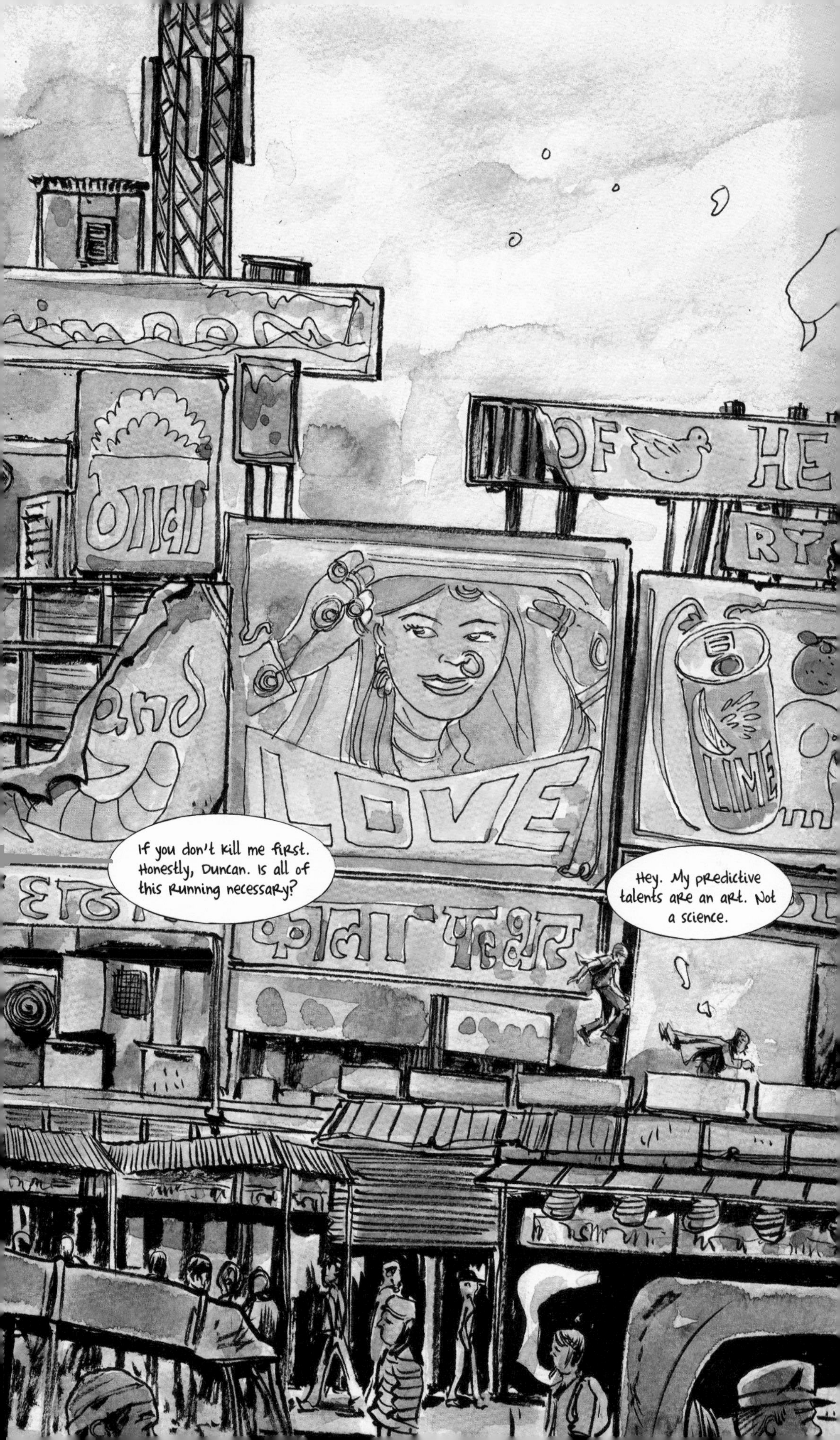
OF HE
RY
and
LOVE
LIME
If you don't kill me first. Honestly, Duncan. Is all of this running necessary?
Hey. My predictive talents are an art. Not a science.

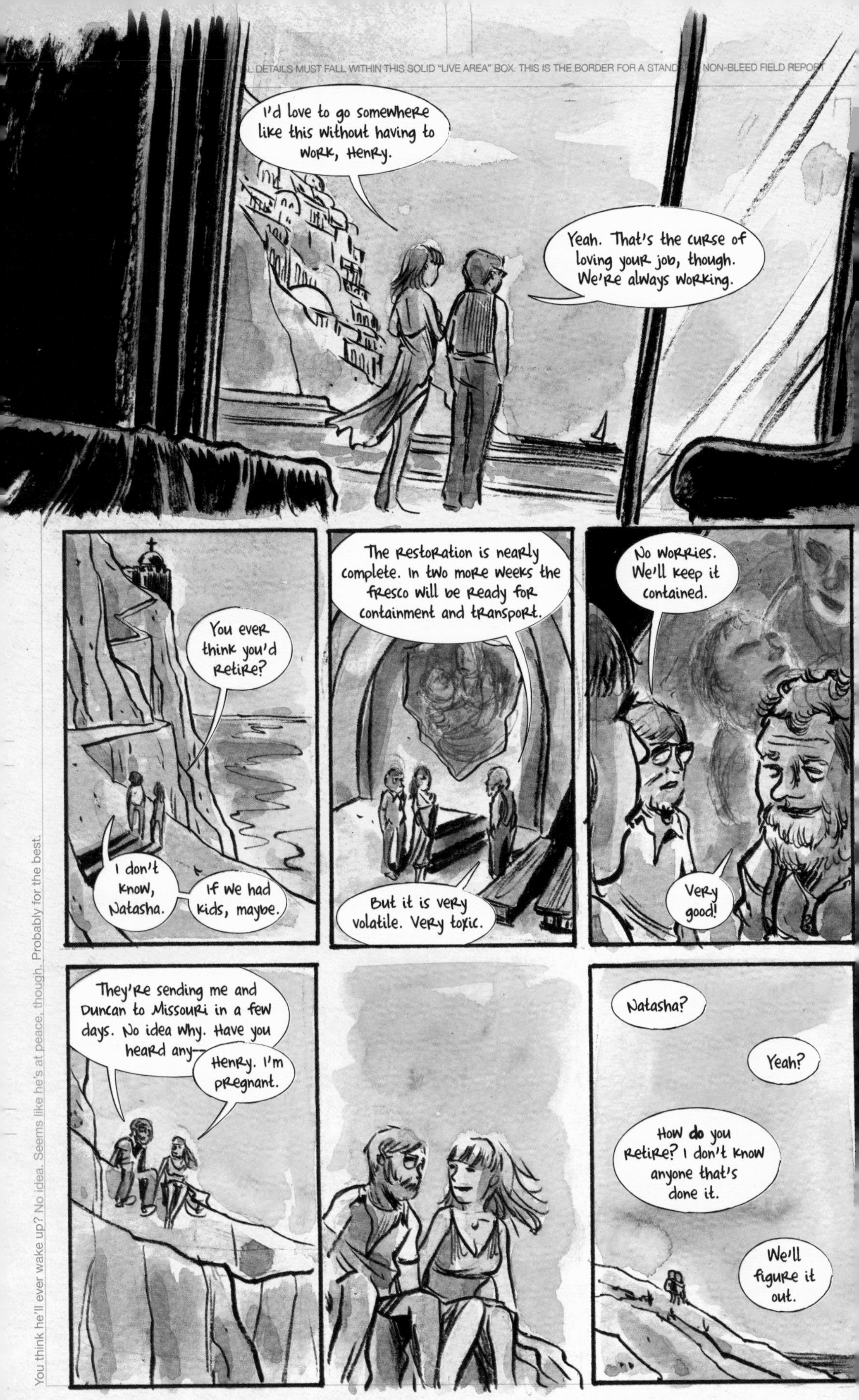
I'd love to go somewhere like this without having to work, Henry.
Yeah. That's the curse of loving your job, though. We're always working.
You ever think you'd retire?
I don't know, Natasha.
If we had kids, maybe.
The restoration is nearly complete. In two more weeks the fresco will be ready for containment and transport.
But it is very volatile. Very toxic.
No worries. We'll keep it contained.
Very good!
They're sending me and Duncan to Missouri in a few days. No idea why. Have you heard any—
Henry. I'm pregnant.
Natasha?
Yeah?
How do you retire? I don't know anyone that's done it.
We'll figure it out.

You think he'll ever wake up? No idea. Seems like he's at peace, though. Probably for the best.

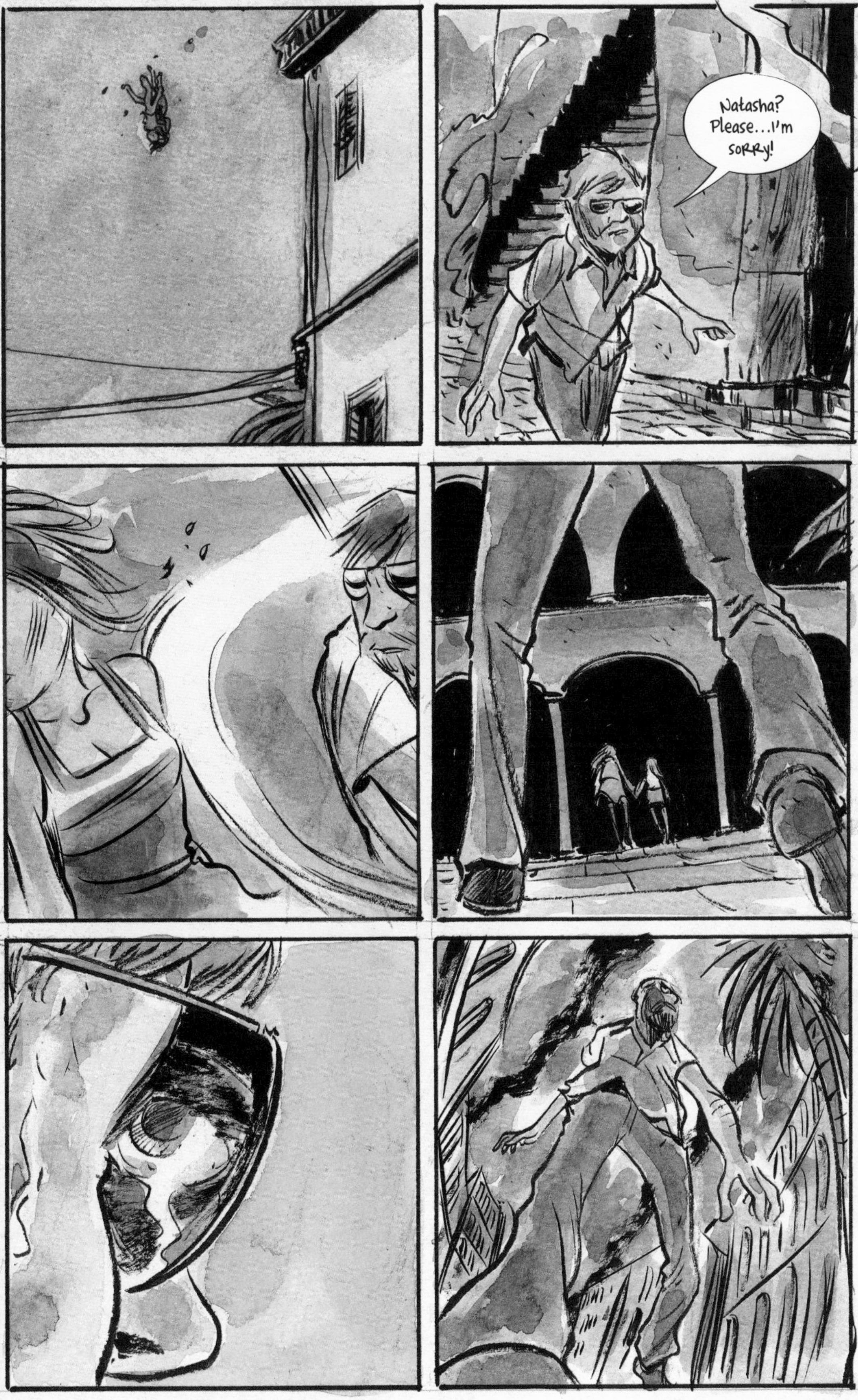
Natasha? Please...I'm sorry!

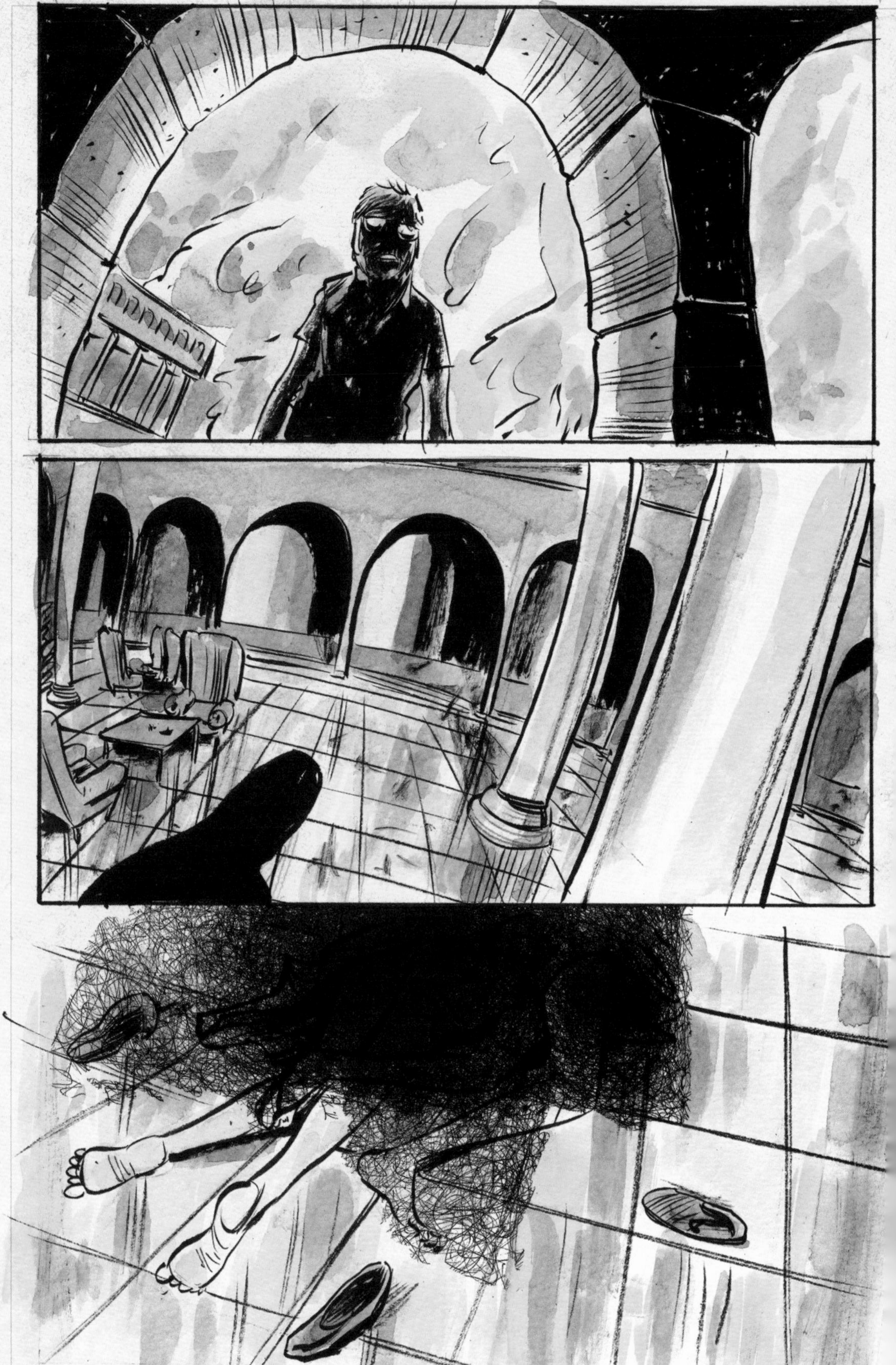

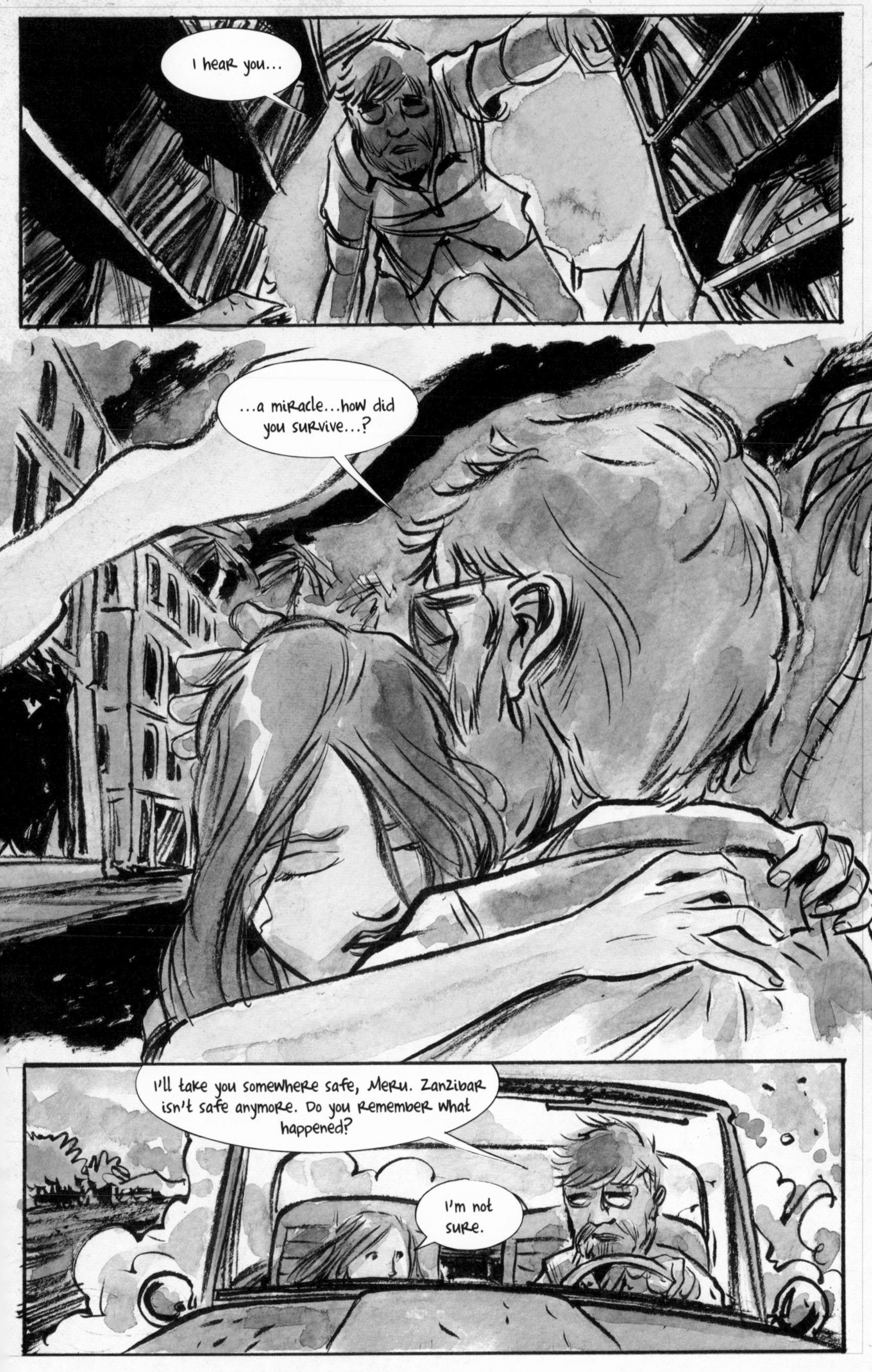
I hear you...
...a miracle...how did you survive...?
I'll take you somewhere safe, Meru. Zanzibar isn't safe anymore. Do you remember what happened?
I'm not sure.

WHEN FILING REPORT ALL ESSENTIAL DETAILS MUST FALL WITHIN THIS SOLID "LIVE AREA" BOX. THIS IS THE BORDER FOR A STANDARD, NON-BLEED FIELD REPORT

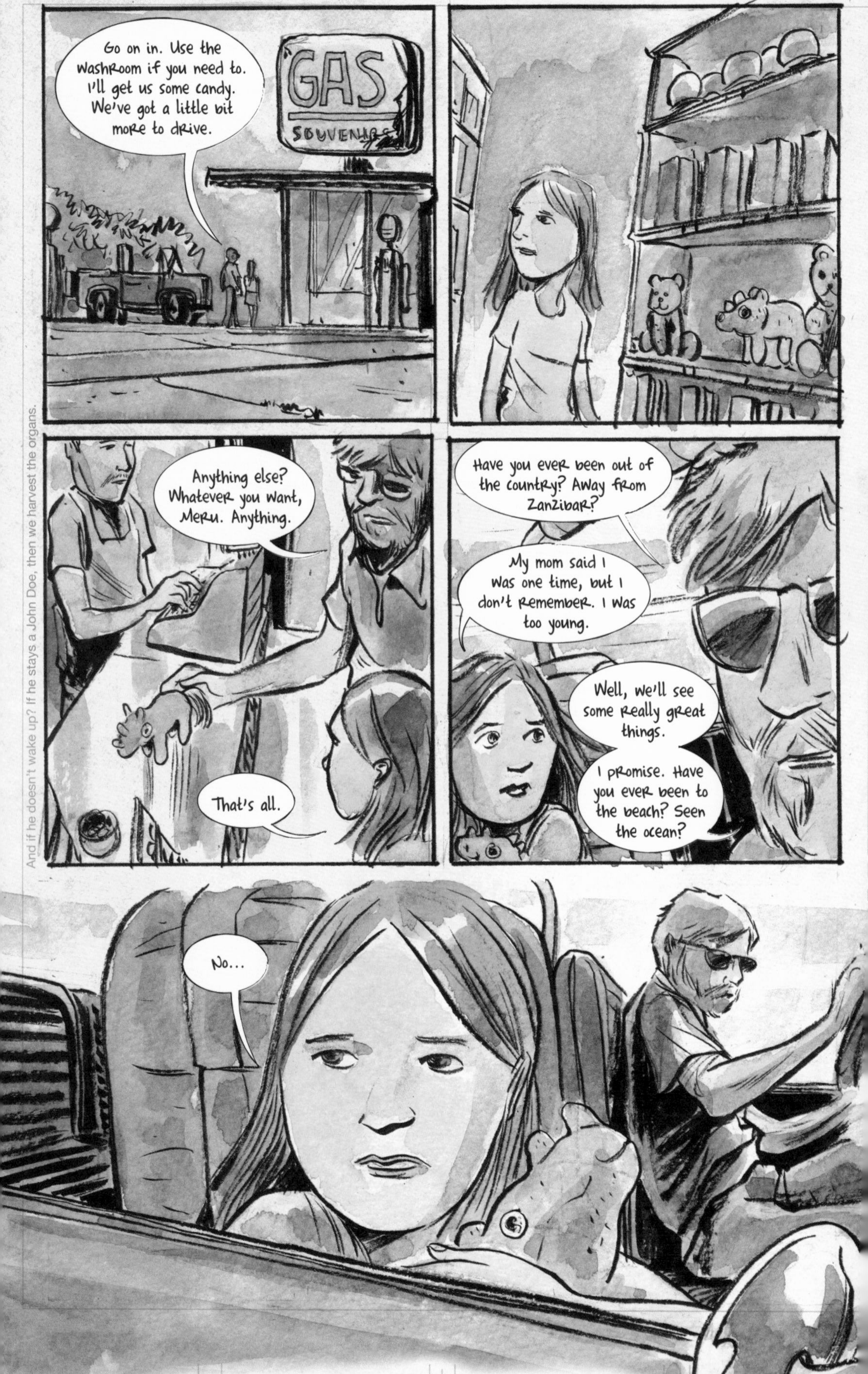

Go on in. Use the washroom if you need to. I'll get us some candy. We've got a little bit more to drive.
GAS
SOUVENIRS
Anything else? Whatever you want, Meru. Anything.
That's all.
Have you ever been out of the country? Away from Zanzibar?
My mom said I was one time, but I don't remember. I was too young.
Well, we'll see some really great things.
I promise. Have you ever been to the beach? Seen the ocean?
No...

And if he doesn't wake up? If he stays a John Doe, then we harvest the organs.

WHEN FILING REPORT ALL ESSENTIAL DETAILS MUST FALL WITHIN THIS SOLID "LIVE AREA" BOX. THIS IS THE BORDER FOR A STANDARD, NON-BLEED FIELD REPORT

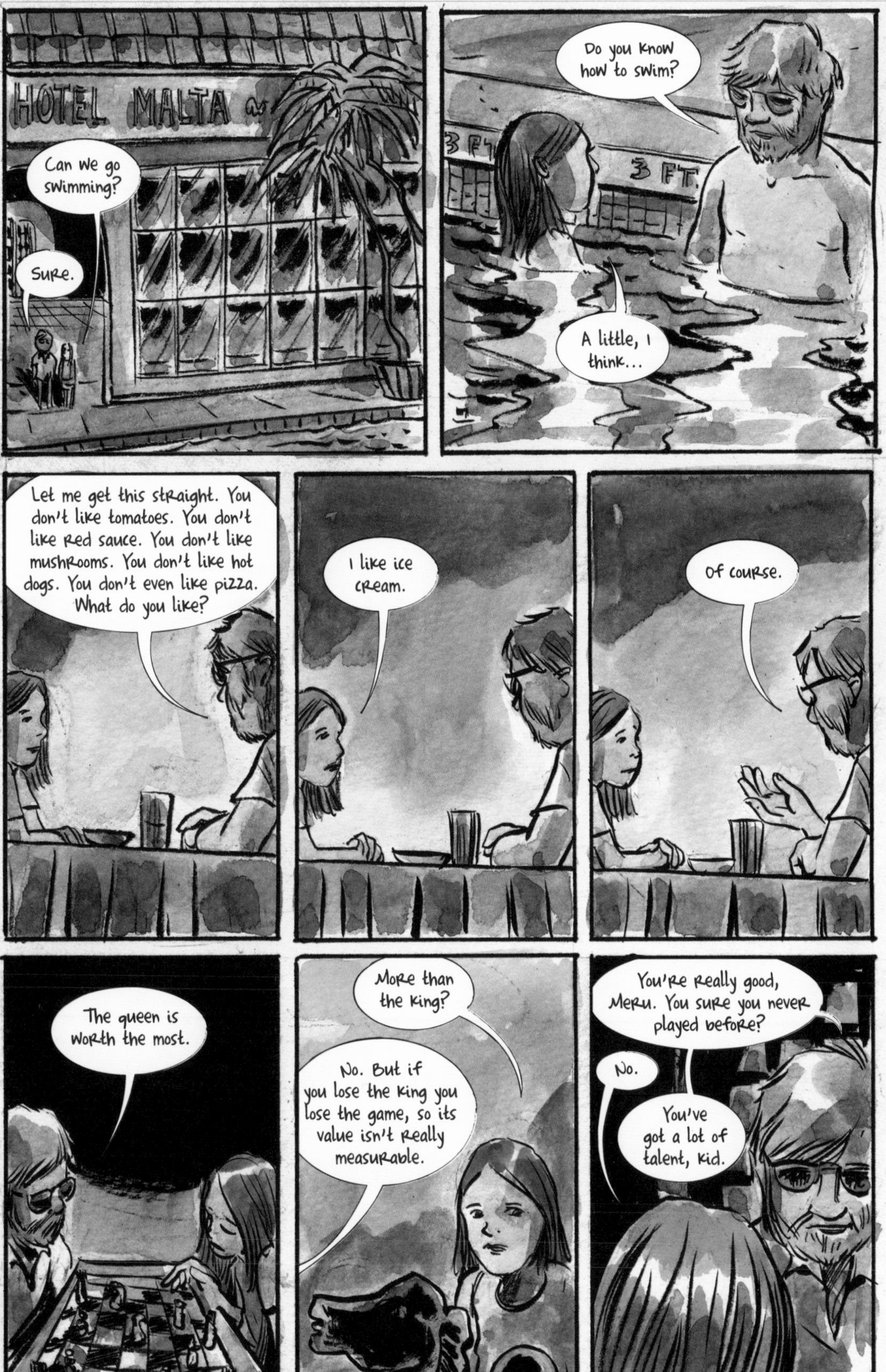
HOTEL MALTA
Can we go swimming?
Sure.
Do you know how to swim?
3 FT
3 FT.
A little, I think...
Let me get this straight. You don't like tomatoes. You don't like red sauce. You don't like mushrooms. You don't like hot dogs. You don't even like pizza. What do you like?
I like ice cream.
Of course.
The queen is worth the most.
More than the king?
No. But if you lose the king you lose the game, so its value isn't really measurable.
You're really good, Meru. You sure you never played before?
No.
You've got a lot of talent, kid.

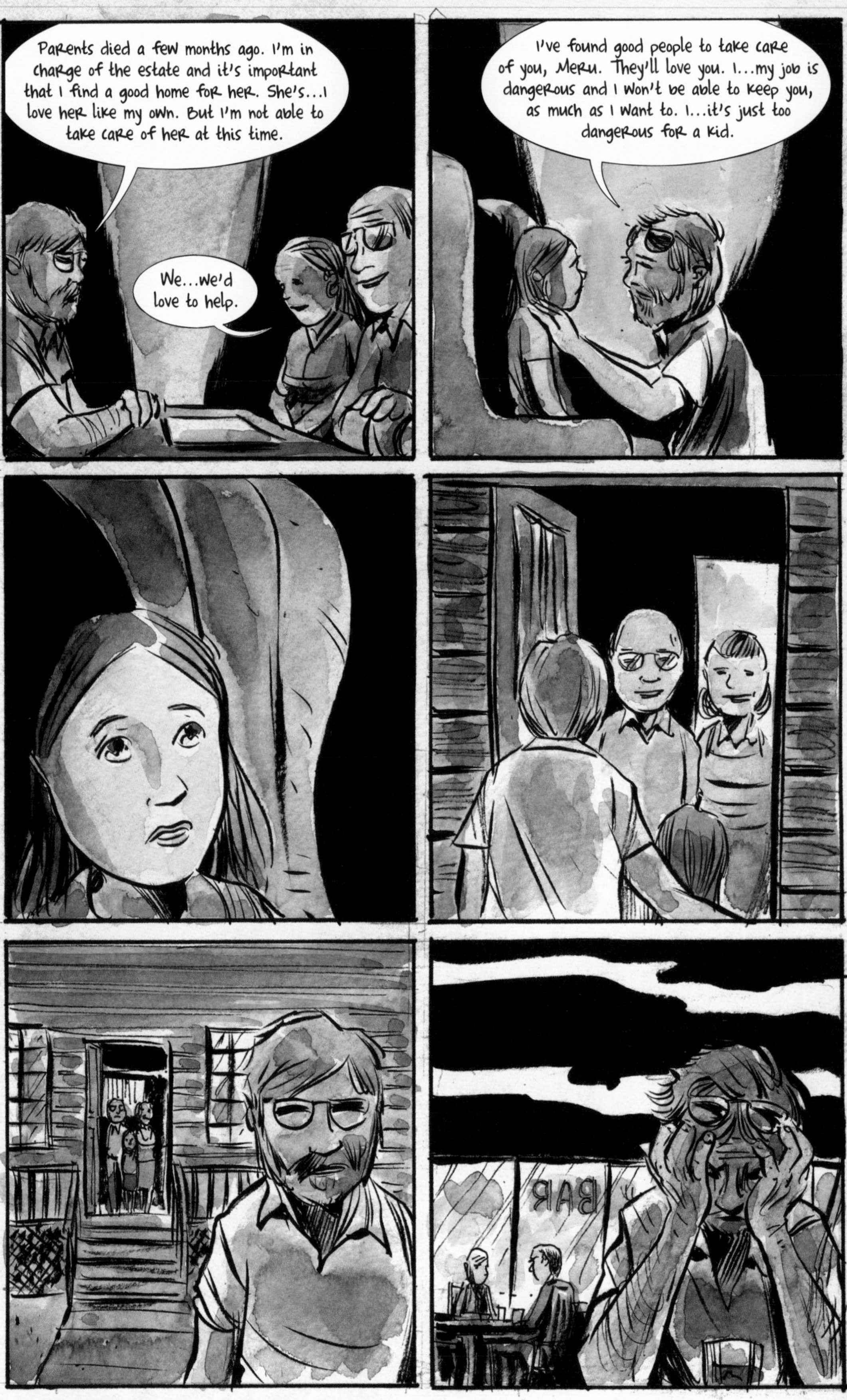
Parents died a few months ago. I'm in charge of the estate and it's important that I find a good home for her. She's...I love her like my own. But I'm not able to take care of her at this time.
We...we'd love to help.
I've found good people to take care of you, Meru. They'll love you. I...my job is dangerous and I won't be able to keep you, as much as I want to. I...it's just too dangerous for a kid.
BAR

What do you think happened to his eyes? No idea, but he wasn't born that way. That damage was inflicted **on** him...with violence.

WHEN FILING REPORT ALL ESSENTIAL DETAILS MUST FALL WITHIN THIS SOLID "LIVE AREA" BOX. THIS IS THE BORDER FOR A STANDARD, NON-BLEED FIELD REPORT

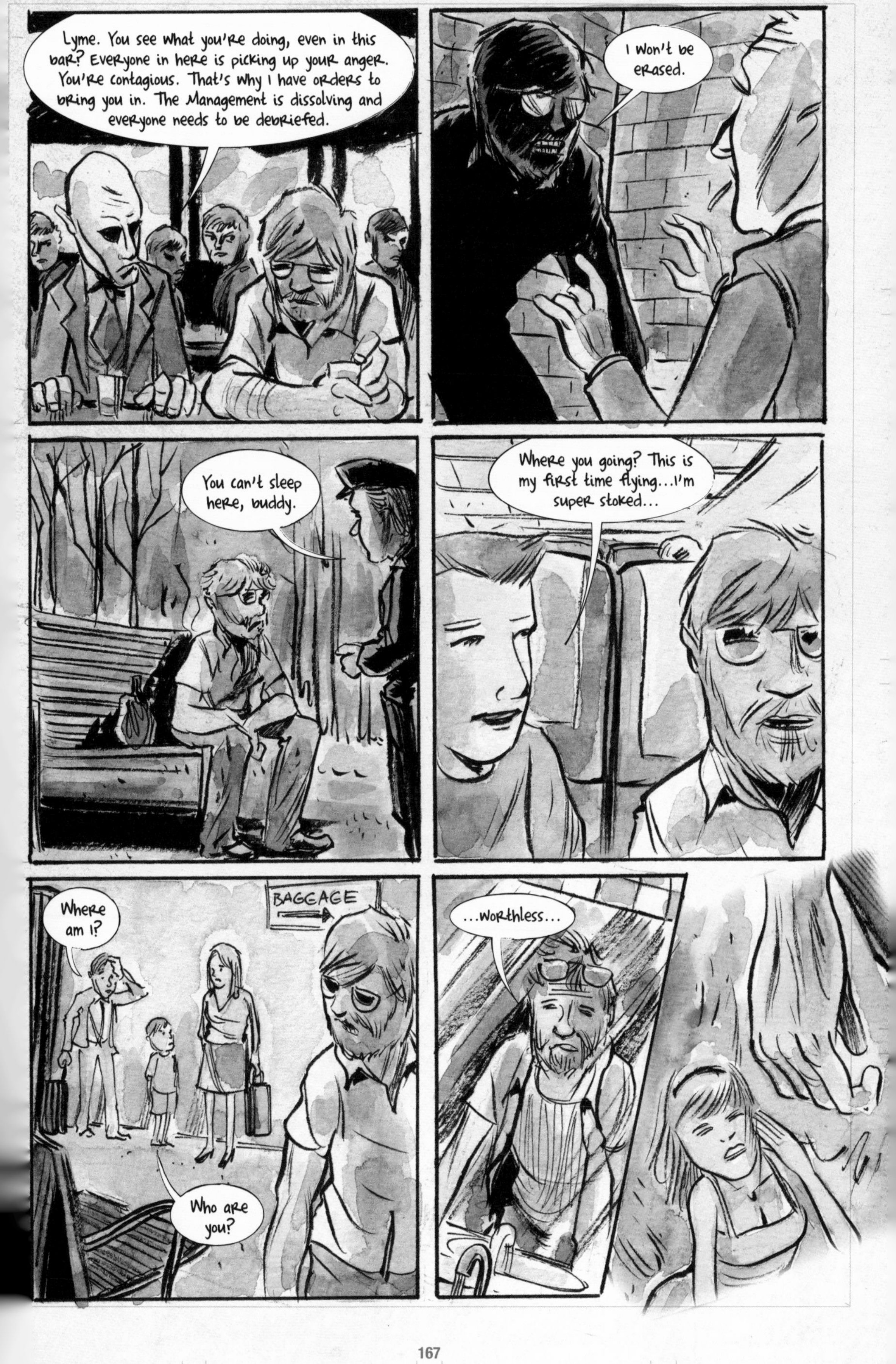

Lyme. You see what you're doing, even in this bar? Everyone in here is picking up your anger. You're contagious. That's why I have orders to bring you in. The Management is dissolving and everyone needs to be debriefed.
I won't be erased.
You can't sleep here, buddy.
Where you going? This is my first time flying... I'm super stoked...
Where am I?
BAGGAGE
Who are you?
...worthless...

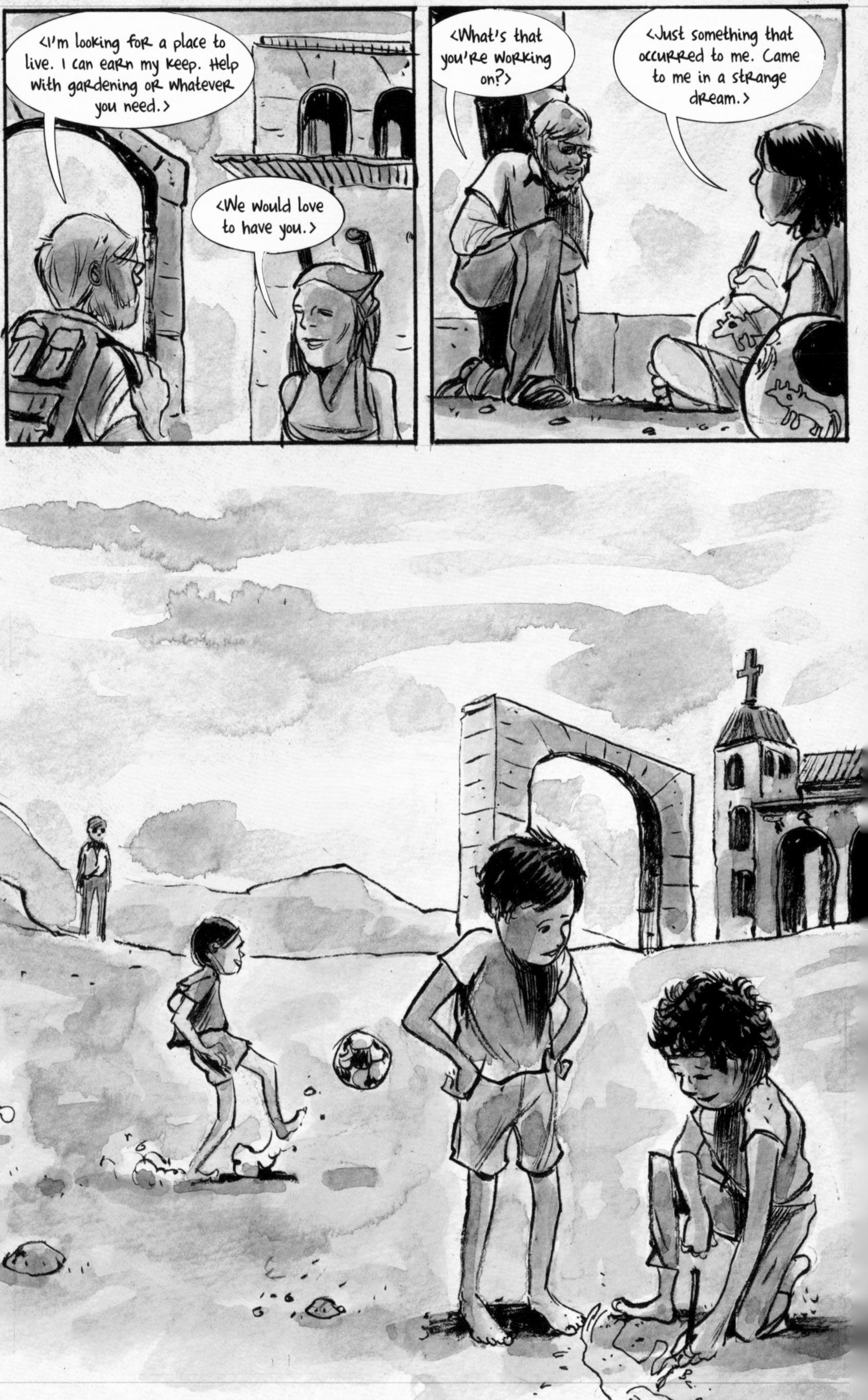
<I'm looking for a place to live. I can earn my keep. Help with gardening or whatever you need.>
<We would love to have you.>
<What's that you're working on?>
<Just something that occurred to me. Came to me in a strange dream.>

WHEN FILING REPORT ALL ESSENTIAL DETAILS MUST FALL WITHIN THIS SOLID "LIVE AREA" BOX. THIS IS THE BORDER FOR A STANDARD, NON-BLEED FIELD REPORT

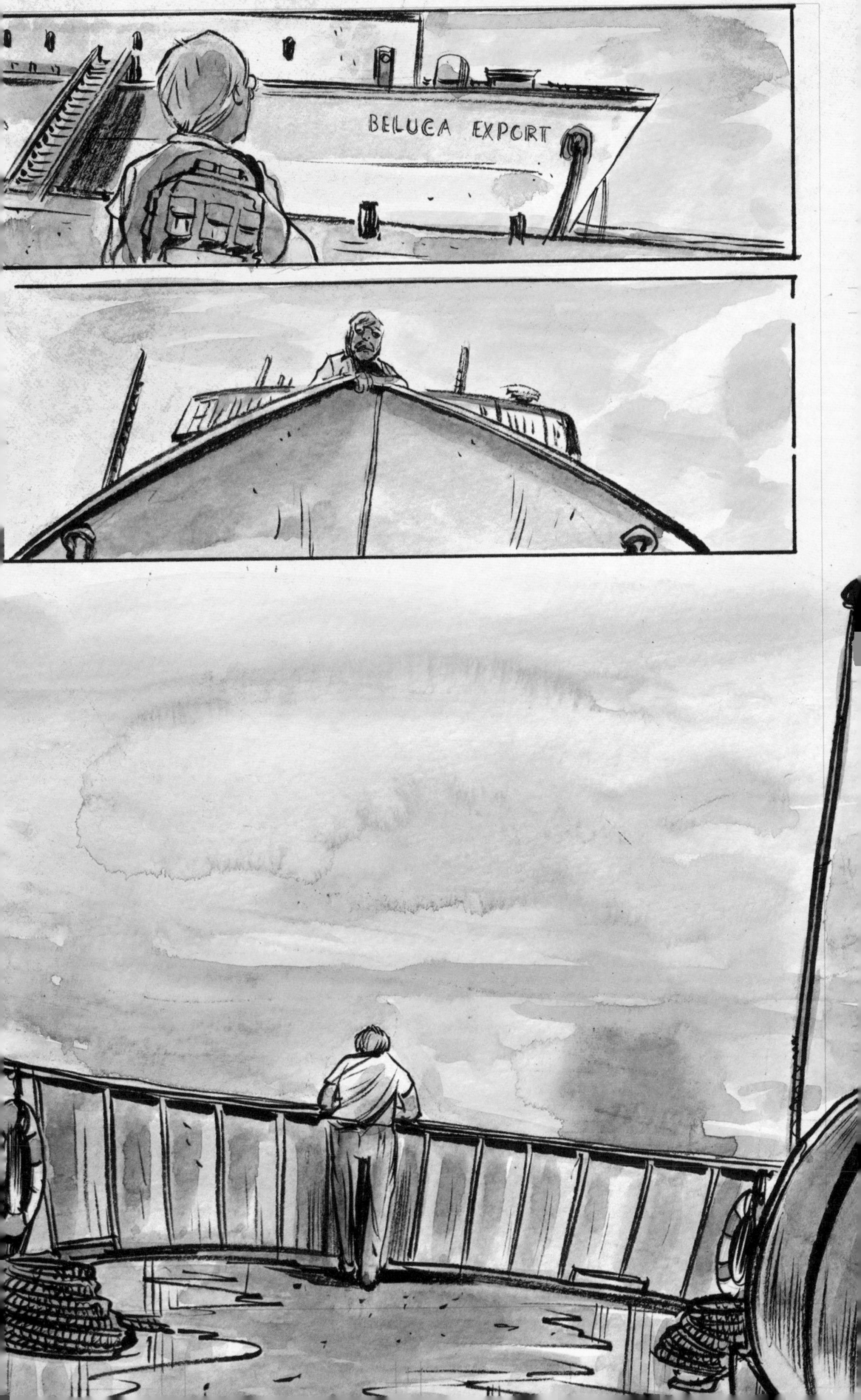
BELUCA EXPORT

Did you hear he got a phone call yesterday? No, really? Someone's claiming him?

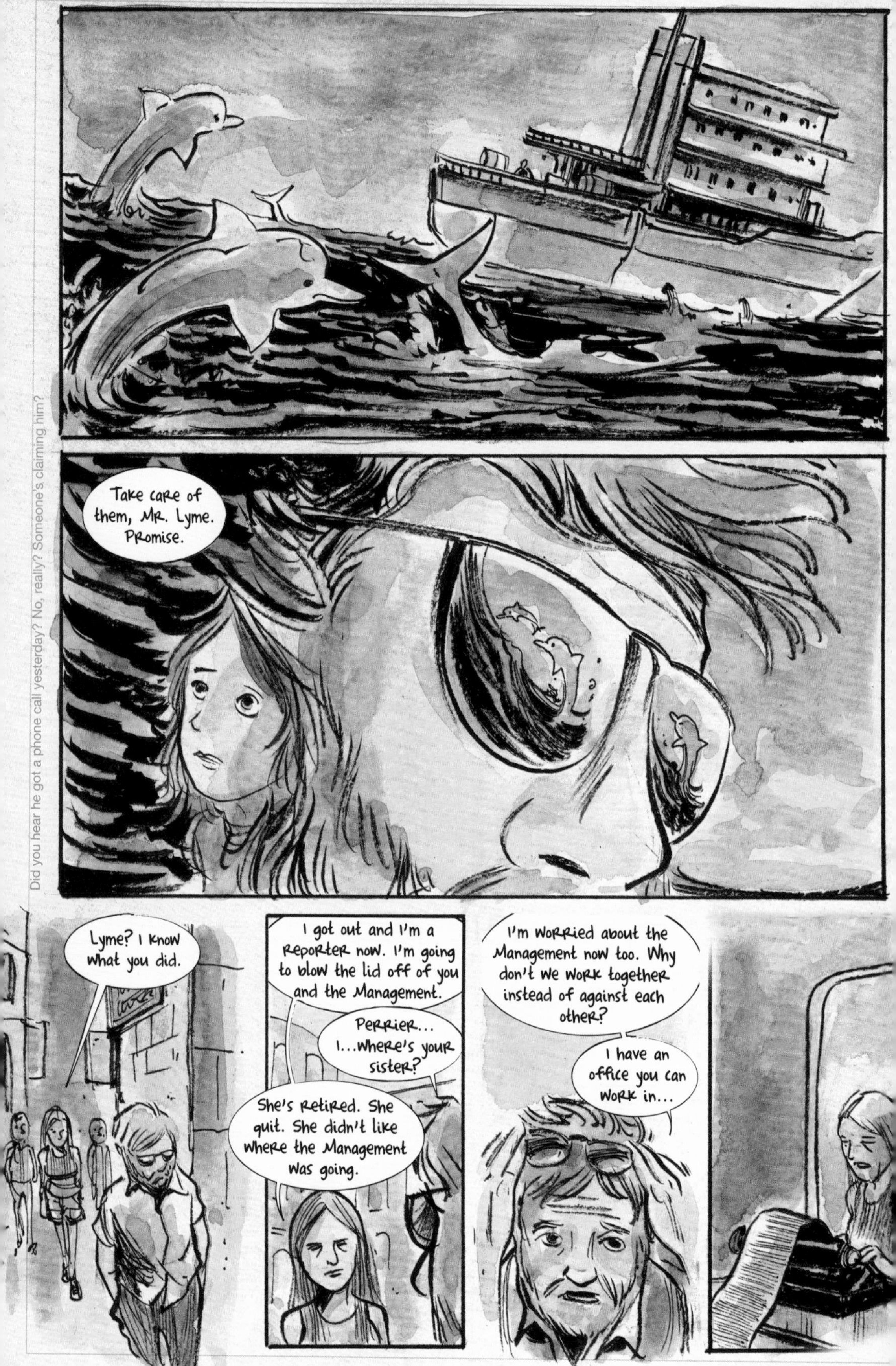
Take care of them, Mr. Lyme. Promise.
Lyme? I know what you did.
I got out and I'm a reporter now. I'm going to blow the lid off of you and the Management.
Perrier... I...where's your sister?
She's retired. She quit. She didn't like where the Management was going.
I'm worried about the Management now too. Why don't we work together instead of against each other?
I have an office you can work in...

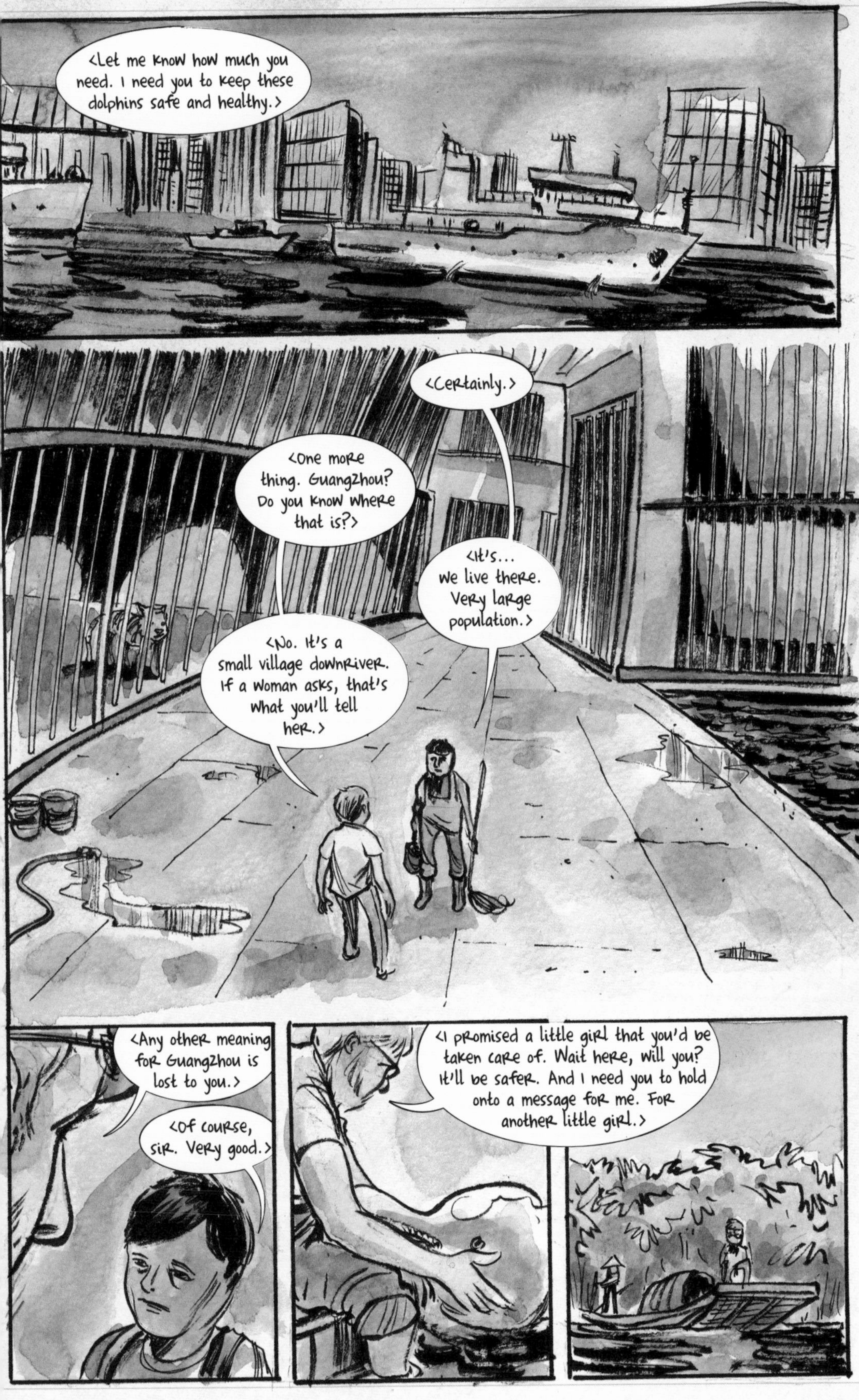
<Let me know how much you need. I need you to keep these dolphins safe and healthy.>
<Certainly.>
<One more thing. Guangzhou? Do you know where that is?>
<It's... we live there. Very large population.>
<No. It's a small village downriver. If a woman asks, that's what you'll tell her.>
<Any other meaning for Guangzhou is lost to you.>
<Of course, sir. Very good.>
<I promised a little girl that you'd be taken care of. Wait here, will you? It'll be safer. And I need you to hold onto a message for me. For another little girl.>

WHEN FILING REPORT ALL ESSENTIAL DETAILS MUST FALL WITHIN THIS SOLID "LIVE AREA" BOX. THIS IS THE BORDER FOR A STANDARD, NON-BLEED FIELD REPORT

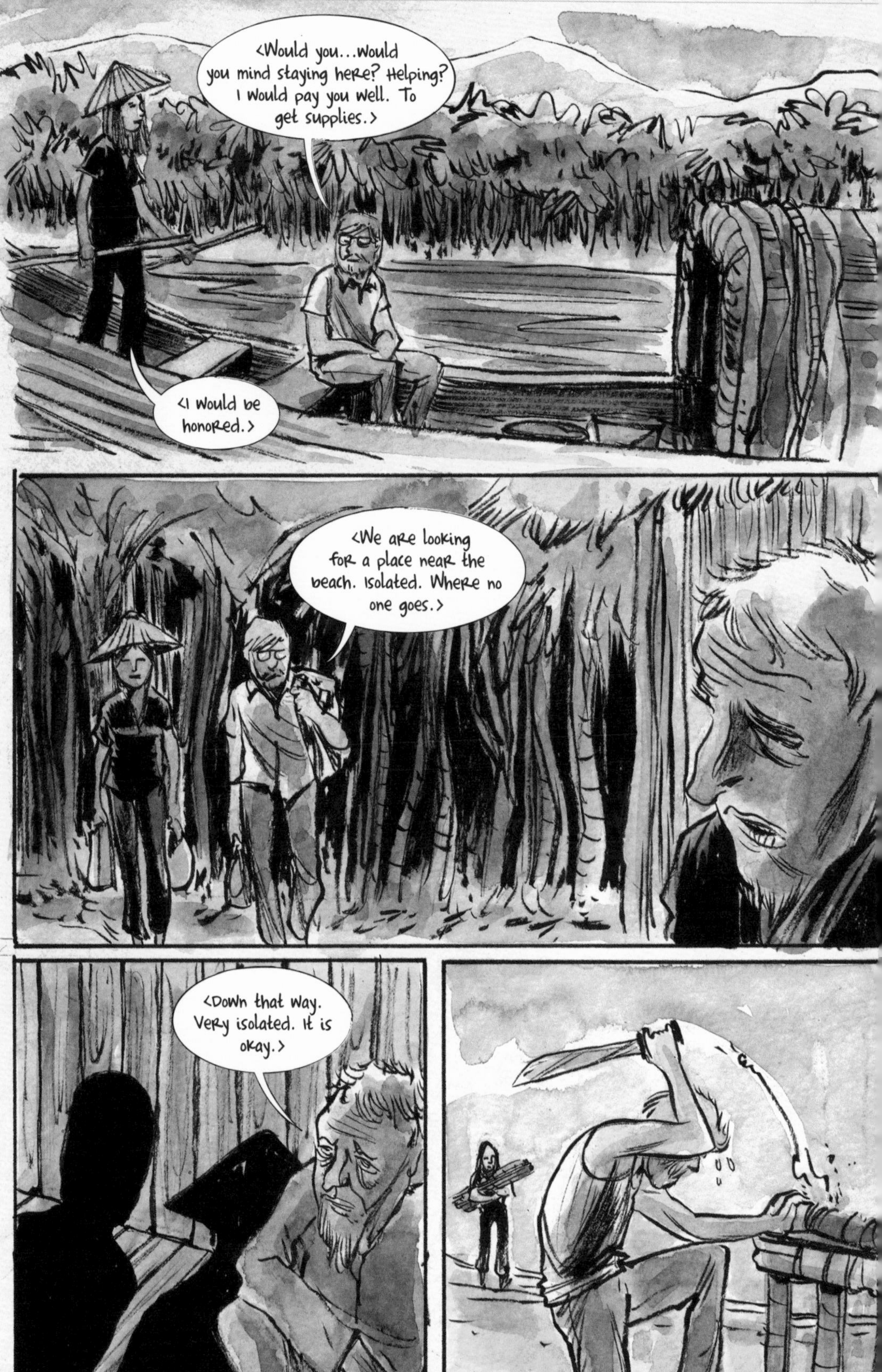

<Would you...would you mind staying here? Helping? I would pay you well. To get supplies.>
<I would be honored.>
<We are looking for a place near the beach. Isolated. Where no one goes.>
<Down that way. Very isolated. It is okay.>

Well, good for him. This guy certainly could use a friend. If he ever wakes up, he's going to need a good one.

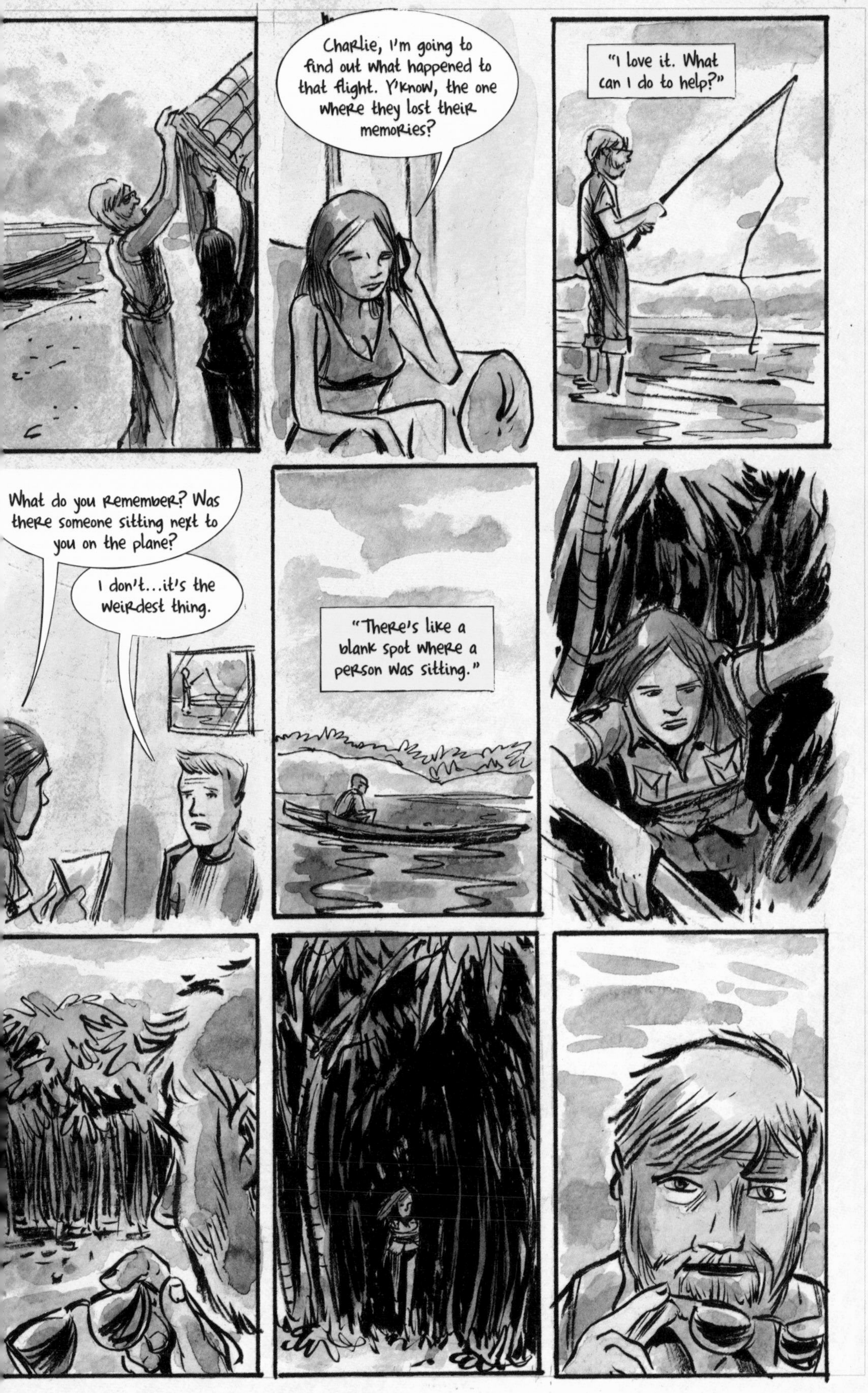
Charlie, I'm going to find out what happened to that flight. Y'know, the one where they lost their memories?
"I love it. What can I do to help?"
What do you remember? Was there someone sitting next to you on the plane?
I don't...it's the weirdest thing.
"There's like a blank spot where a person was sitting."

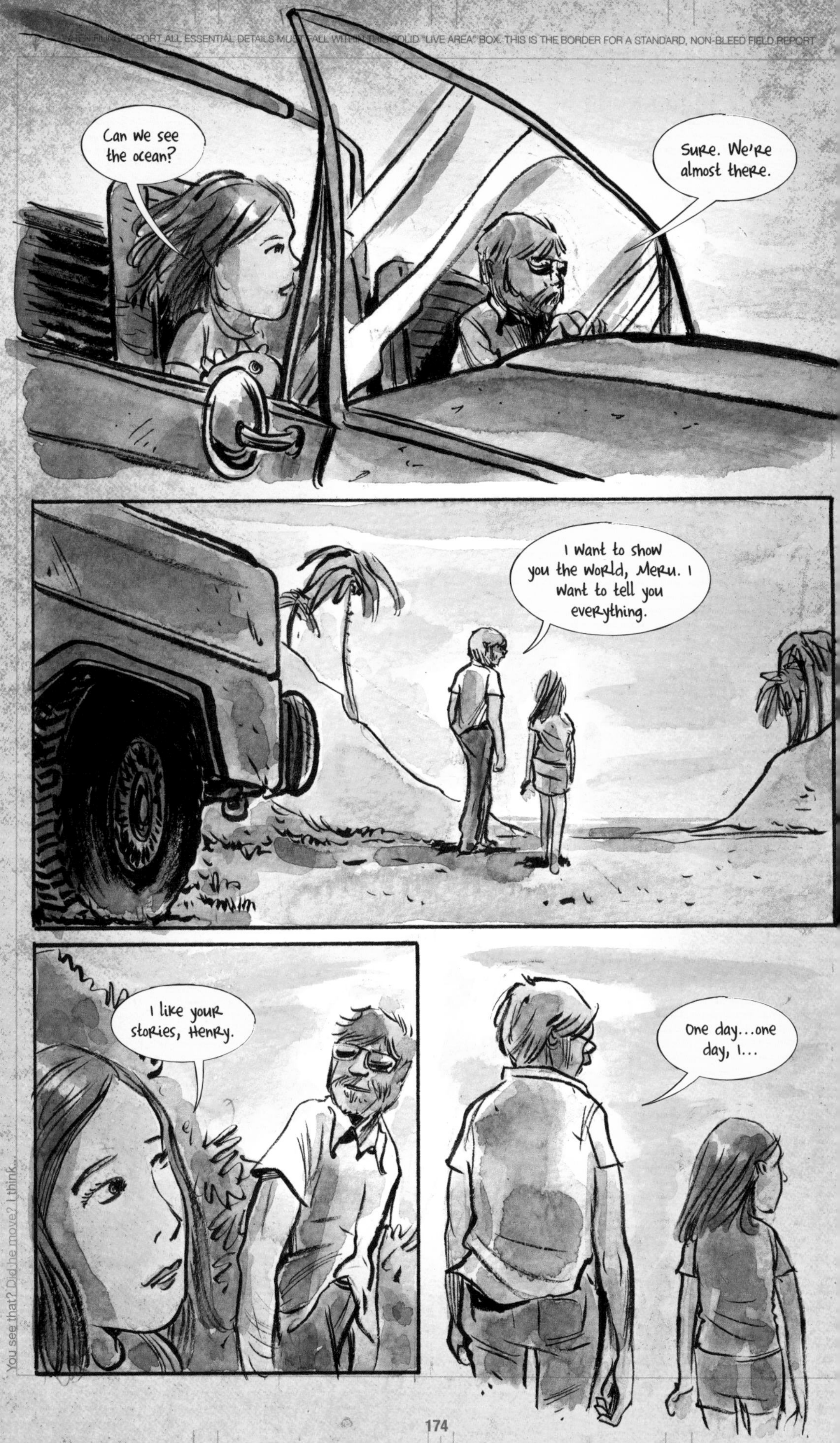
PORT ALL ESSENTIAL DETAILS MUST FALL WITHIN THE SOLID "LIVE AREA" BOX. THIS IS THE BORDER FOR A STANDARD, NON-BLEED FIELD REPORT
Can we see the ocean?
Sure. We're almost there.
I want to show you the world, Meru. I want to tell you everything.
I like your stories, Henry.
One day…one day, I…
You see that? Did he move? I think...

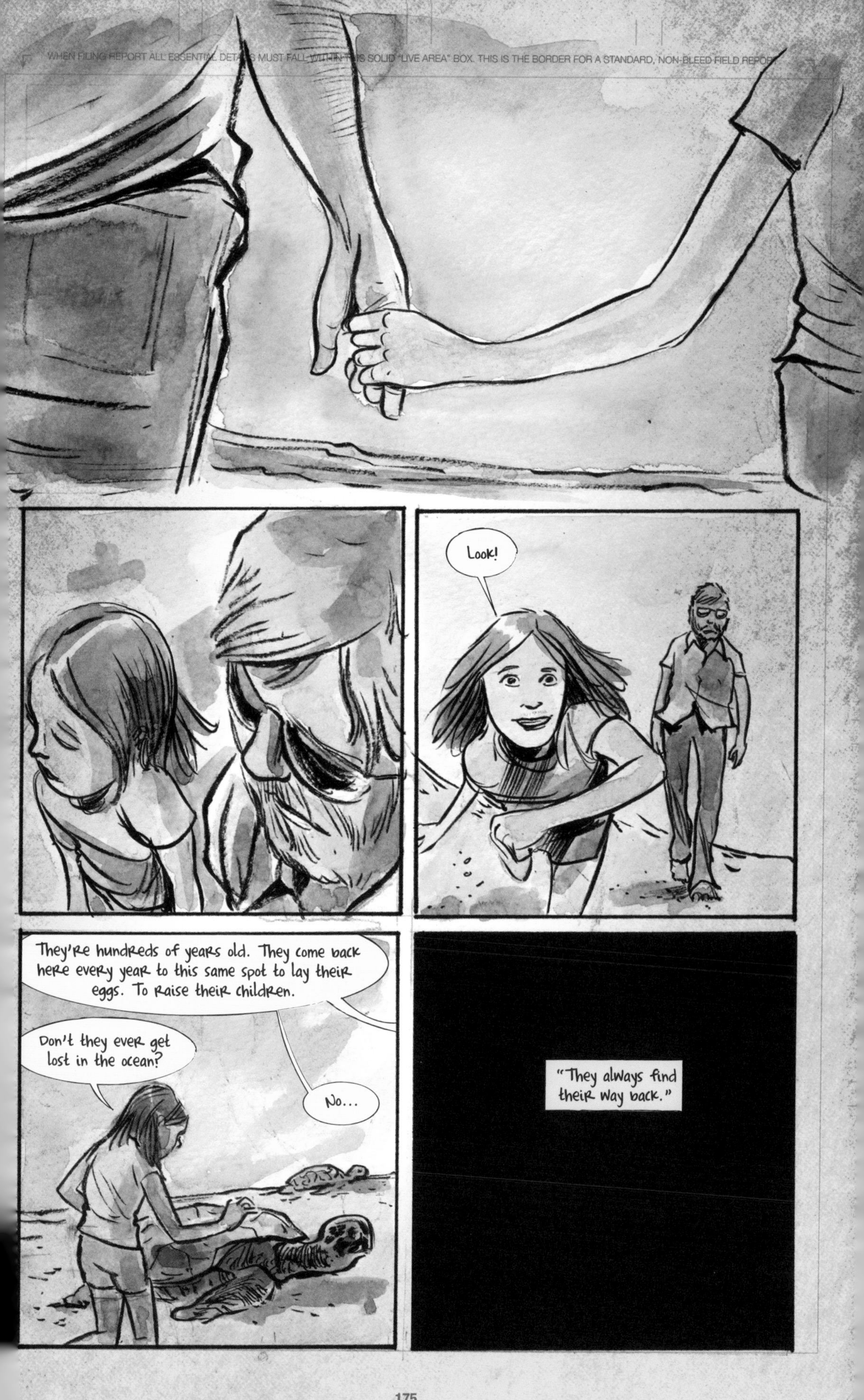
WHEN FILING REPORT ALL ESSENTIAL DETAILS MUST FALL WITHIN THIS SOLID "LIVE AREA" BOX. THIS IS THE BORDER FOR A STANDARD, NON-BLEED FIELD REPORT
Look!
They're hundreds of years old. They come back here every year to this same spot to lay their eggs. To raise their children.
Don't they ever get lost in the ocean?
No...
"They always find their way back."

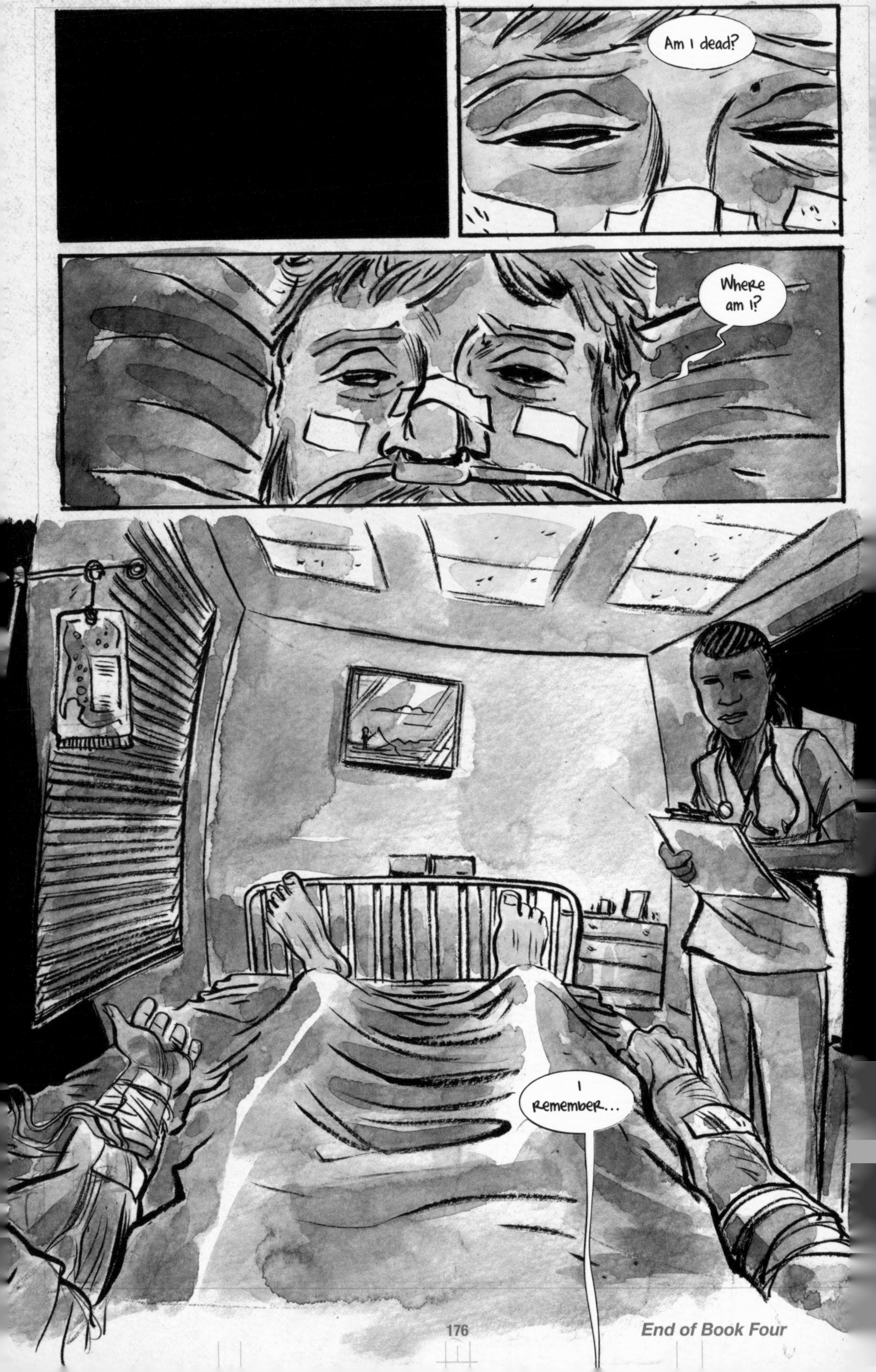
Am I dead?
Where am I?
I remember...

End of Book Four

MIND MGMT
UNDERCOVER

Opposite page: The back covers of issues #19–#23 and #25 featured six separate poster images, which when laid out together combined into a single, larger poster revealing the subliminal control Mind Management exerts through Kommune and other programs disguised as entertainment.

Following pages: Raw scans for the covers of *MIND MGMT* #19 and #21, showing what Matt's original art looks like before he applies his digital trickery to it.

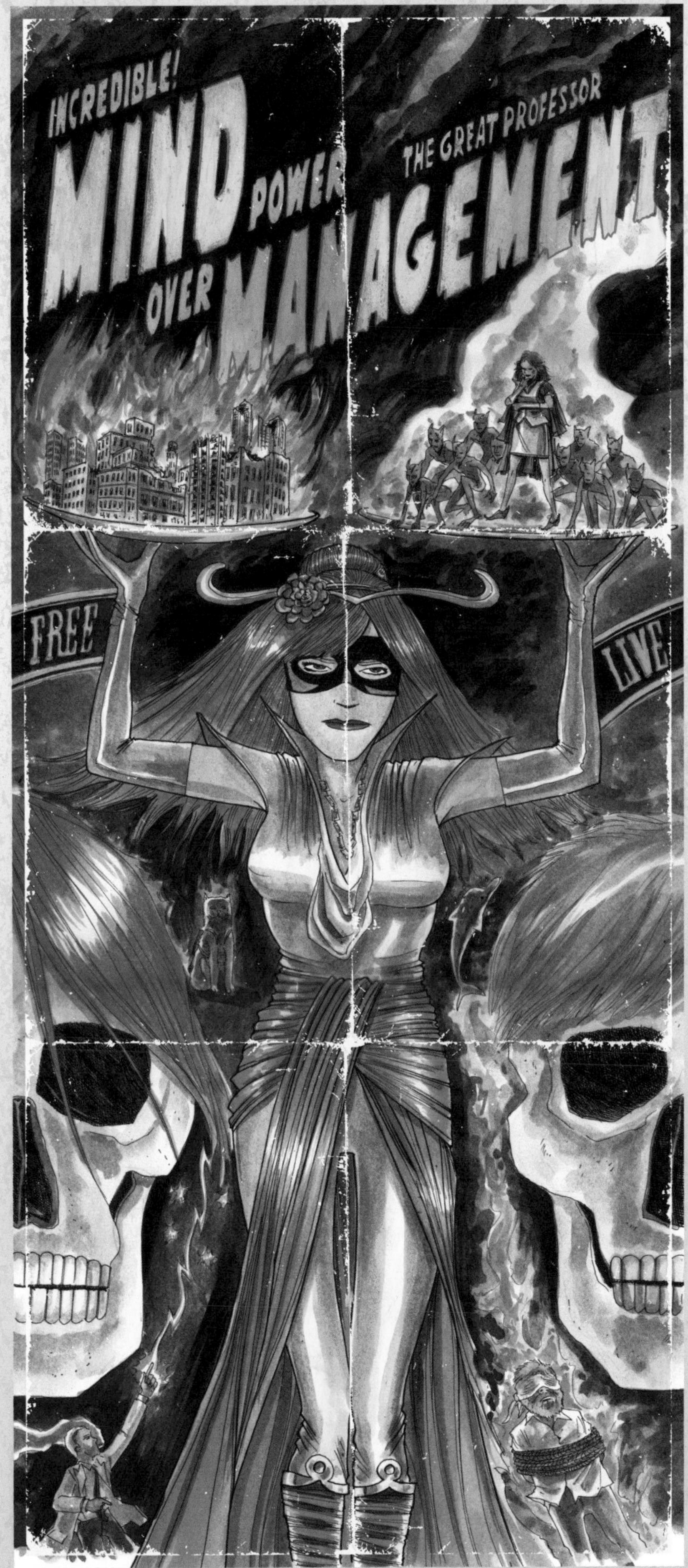
INCREDIBLE!
MIND POWER
OVER MANAGEMENT
THE GREAT PROFESSOR
FREE
LIVE

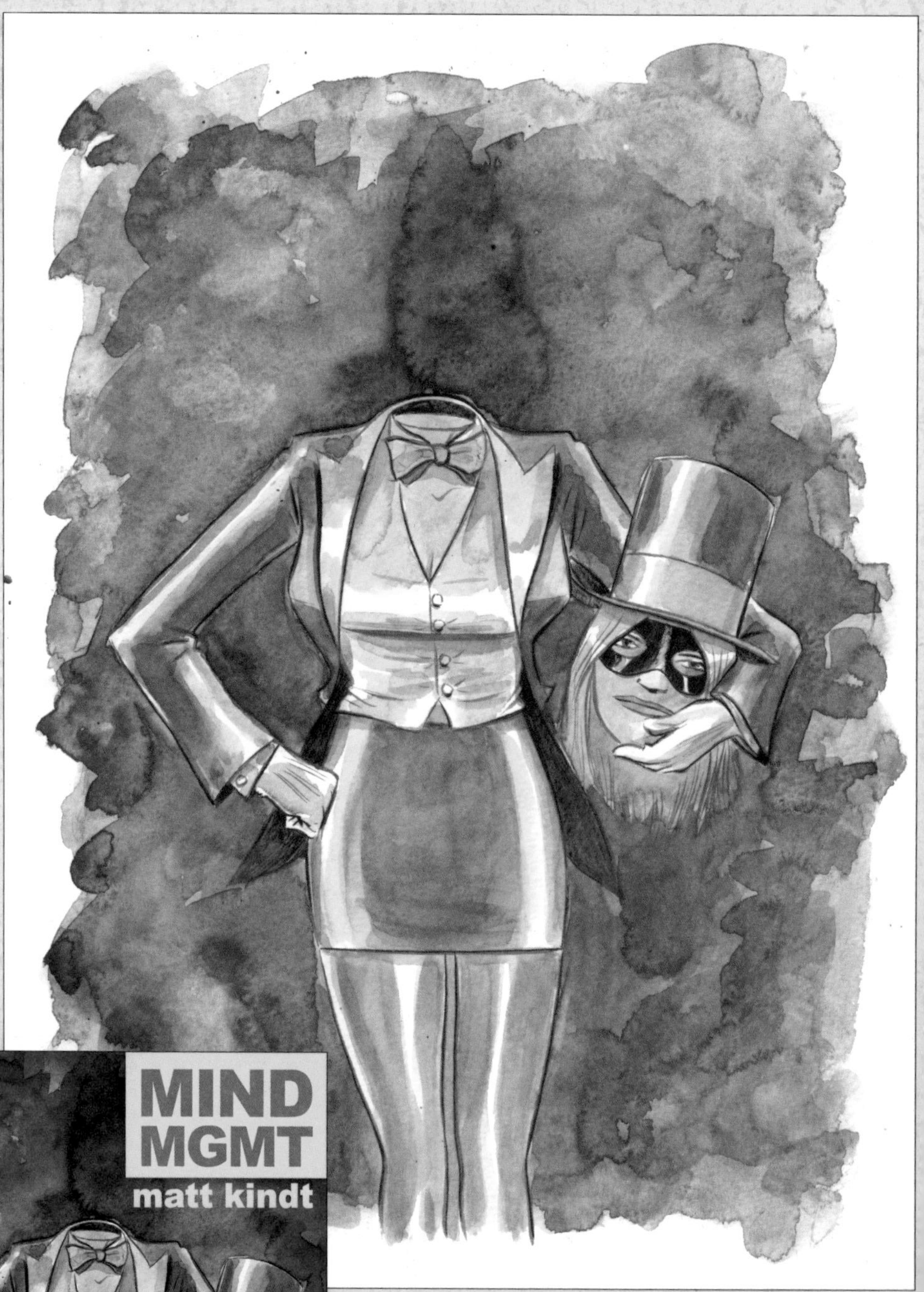

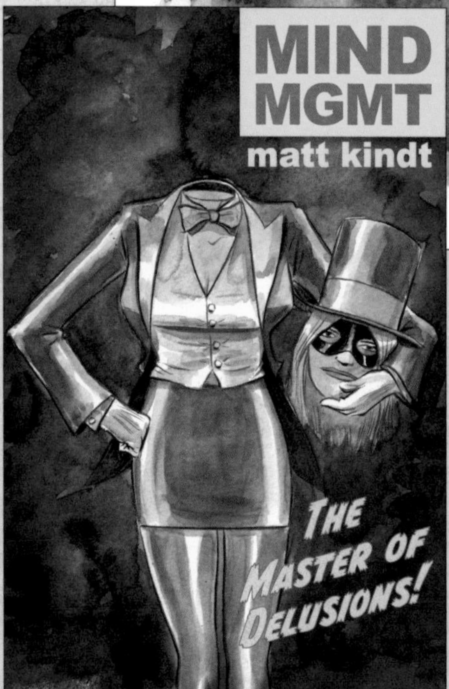

MIND
MGMT
matt kindt
THE
MASTER OF
DELUSIONS!

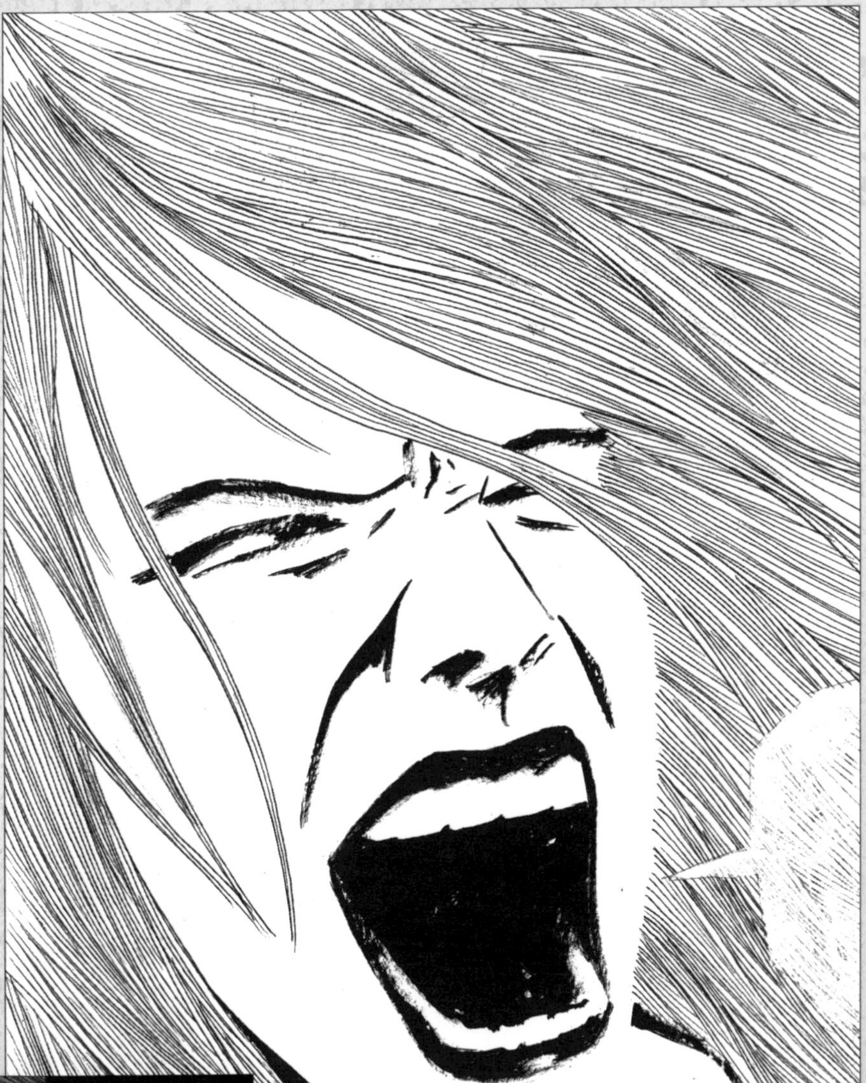

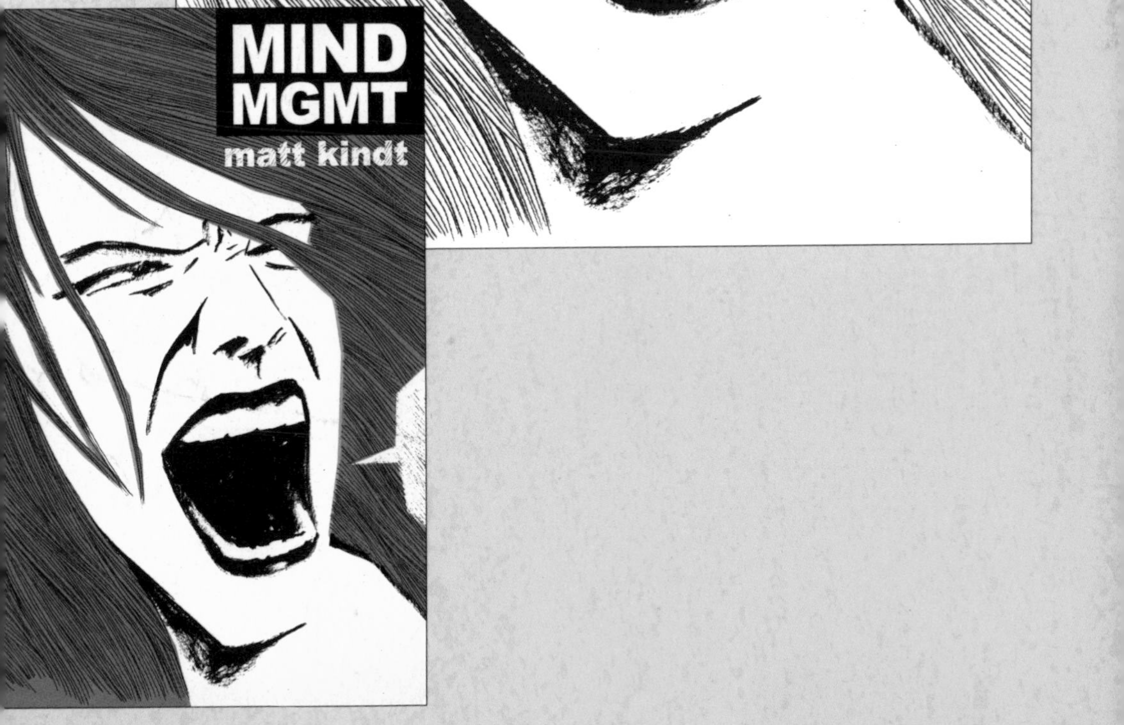
MIND
MGMT
matt kindt

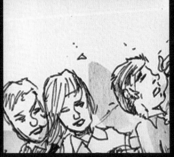

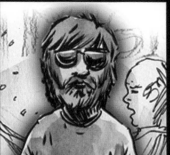

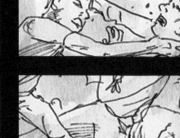

THIS IS NOT AN ADVERTISEMENT
This is not happening.
He is not killing you with his finger.
She is not a mole with mind control.
It is not magic.
He is not immortal.
This is not Matt Kindt's
MIND MGMT™
NOT ON SALE MONTHLY.

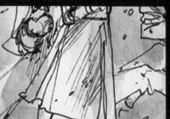

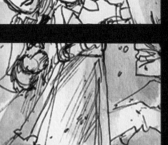

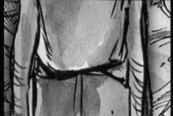

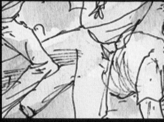

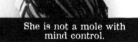

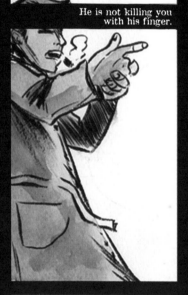

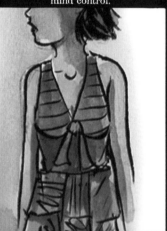

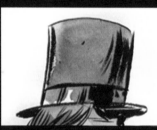

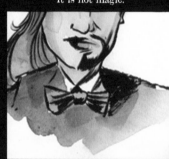

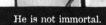

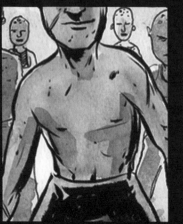

ALSO BY MATT KINDT

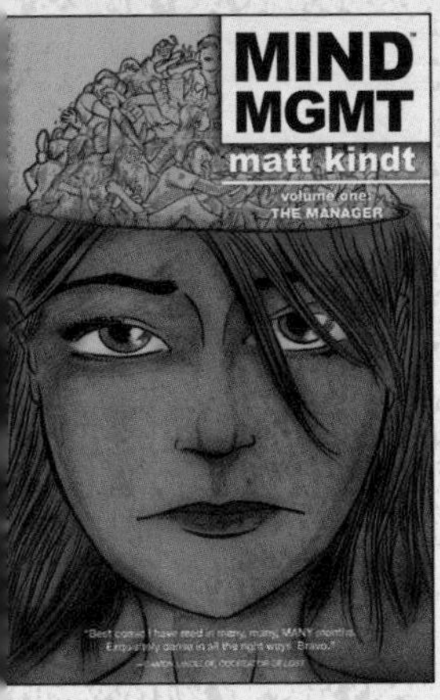
MIND MGMT
matt kindt
volume one: THE MANAGER

MIND MGMT VOLUME 1: THE MANAGER
978-1-59582-797-5
$19.99

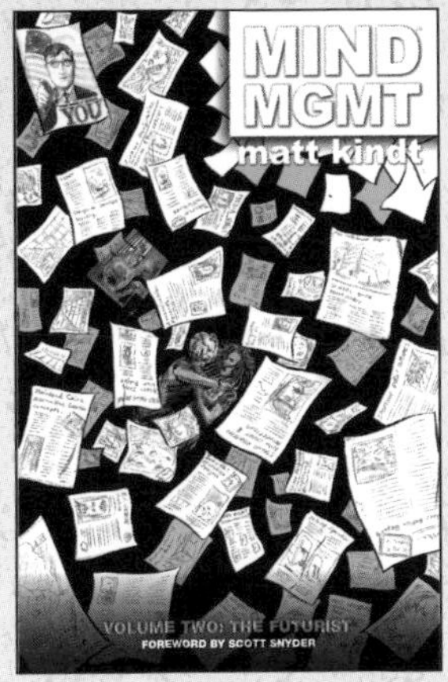
MIND MGMT
matt kindt
VOLUME TWO: THE FUTURIST
FOREWORD BY SCOTT SNYDER

MIND MGMT VOLUME 2: THE FUTURIST
978-1-61655-198-8
$19.99

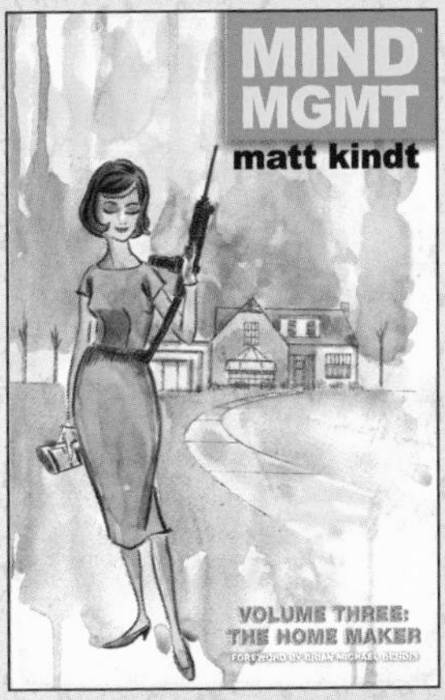
MIND MGMT
matt kindt
VOLUME THREE: THE HOME MAKER

MIND MGMT VOLUME 3: THE HOME MAKER
978-1-61655-390-6
$19.99

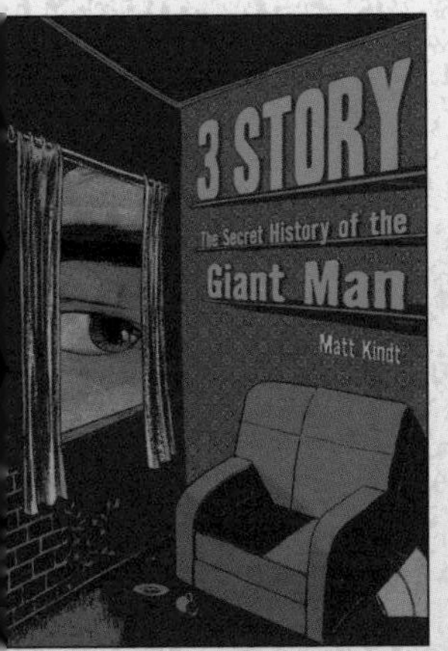
3 STORY
The Secret History of the Giant Man
Matt Kindt

3 STORY: THE SECRET STORY OF THE GIANT MAN
978-1-59582-356-4
$19.99

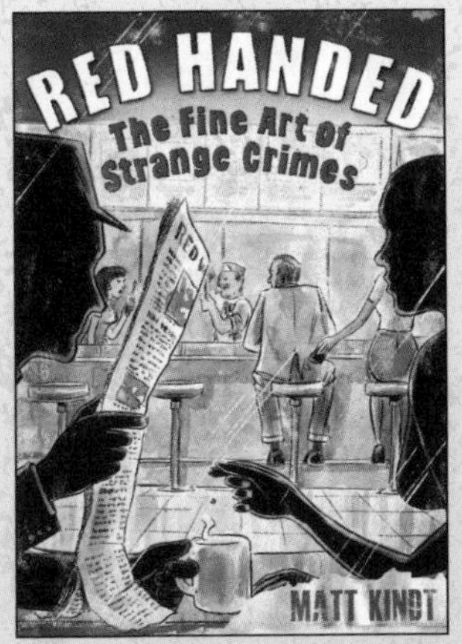
RED HANDED
The Fine Art of Strange Crimes
MATT KINDT

RED HANDED: THE FINE ART OF STRANGE CRIMES
978-1-59643-662-6
$26.99

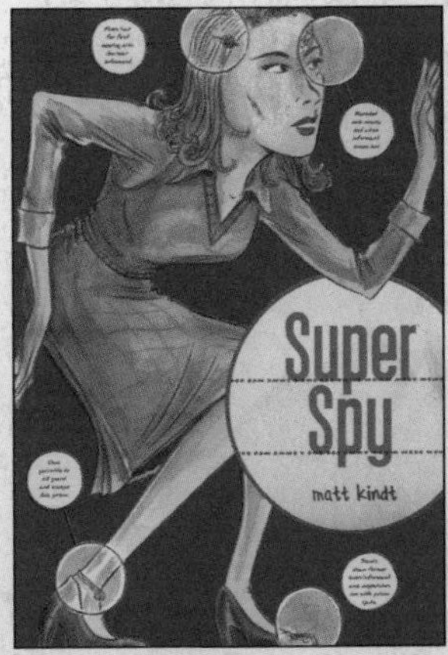
Super Spy
matt kindt

SUPER SPY
978-1-89183-096-9
$19.95

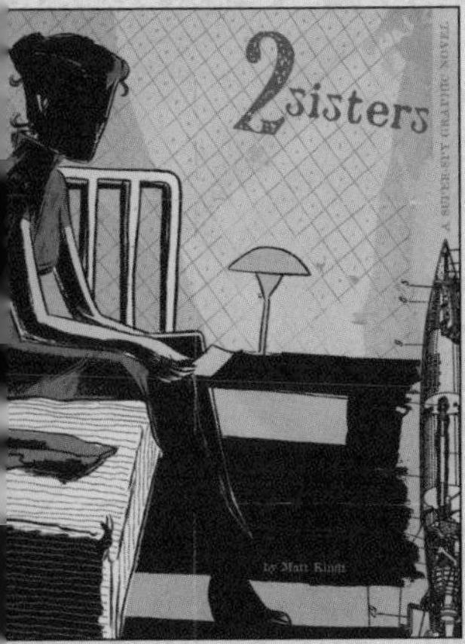
2 sisters
by Matt Kindt

2 SISTERS: A SUPER SPY GRAPHIC NOVEL
978-1-89183-058-7
$19.95

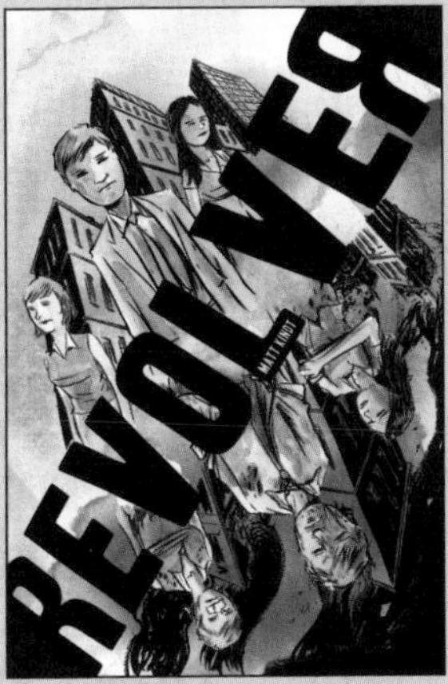
REVOLVER
MATT KINDT

REVOLVER
978-1-40122-242-0
$19.99

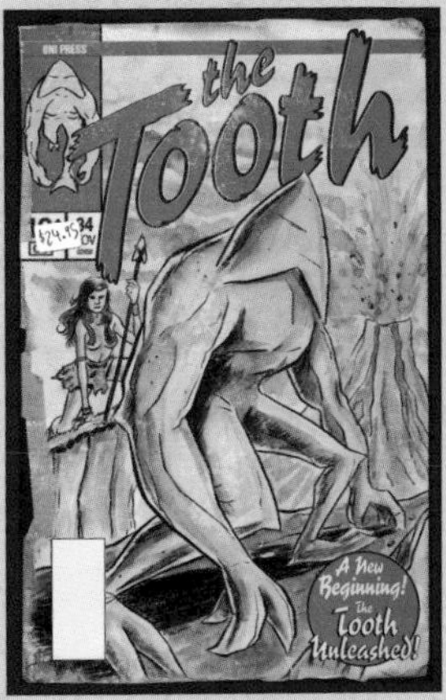
the Tooth
A New Beginning! The Tooth Unleashed!

THE TOOTH
(with Cullen Bunn and Shawn Lee)
978-1-93496-452-1
$24.99

PHOTO BY SHARLENE KINDT

4-09

ABOUT THE AUTHOR

Matt Kindt is the Harvey Award–winning author of the graphic novels *3 Story*, *Red Handed*, *Revolver*, *Super Spy*, and *2 Sisters*, and the artist and cocreator of the *Pistolwhip* series of graphic novels. He has been nominated for four Eisner Awards and three Harveys. Matt lives and works in St. Louis, Missouri, with his wife and daughter. For more information, visit MattKindt.com.